The Standard ML Basis Library

This book provides a description of the Standard ML (SML) Basis Library, the standard library for the SML language. For programmers using SML, it provides a complete description of the modules, types, and functions comprising the library, which is supported by all conforming implementations of the language. The book serves as a programmer's reference, providing manual pages with concise descriptions. In addition, it presents the principles and rationales used in designing the library and relates these to idioms and examples for using the library. A particular emphasis of the library is to encourage the use of SML in serious system programming. Major features of the library include I/O, a large collection of primitive types, support for internationalization, and a portable operating system interface.

This manual will be an indispensable reference for students, professional programmers, and language designers.

Emden R. Gansner is a Principal Technical Staff Member at AT&T Laboratories. Having taught at several prestigious universities, he is currently an adjunct Professor of Computer Science at Stevens Institute of Technology. He has published articles in numerous journals, such as the *Journal of Combinatorial Theory*, *Discrete Mathematics*, and *SIAM Journal of Algorithms and Discrete Methods*. He also jointly received a patent on a technique for drawing directed graphs.

John H. Reppy is an Associate Professor of Computer Science at the University of Chicago. He recently served as Associate Editor of *ACM TOPLAS* and is the author of *Concurrent Programming in ML*, also published by Cambridge University Press.

The Standard ML Basis Library

Edited by

Emden R. Gansner
AT&T Laboratories

John H. Reppy
University of Chicago

CAMBRIDGE
UNIVERSITY PRESS

PUBLISHED BY THE PRESS SYNDICATE OF THE UNIVERSITY OF CAMBRIDGE
The Pitt Building, Trumpington Street, Cambridge, United Kingdom

CAMBRIDGE UNIVERSITY PRESS
The Edinburgh Building, Cambridge CB2 2RU, UK
40 West 20th Street, New York, NY 10011-4211, USA
477 Williamstown Road, Port Melbourne, VIC 3207, Australia
Ruiz de Alarcón 13, 28014 Madrid, Spain
Dock House, The Waterfront, Cape Town 8001, South Africa

http://www.cambridge.org

First published 2004

Printed in the United States of America

Typeface Times 10/13 pt.   *System* LaTeX 2_ε [AU]

A catalog record for this book is available from the British Library.

Library of Congress Cataloging in Publication Data

The Standard ML basis library / edited by Emden R. Gansner, John H. Reppy.
p.   cm.
Includes bibliographical references and index.
ISBN 0-521-79142-1 – ISBN 0-521-79478-1 (pbk.)
1. ML (Computer program language)   I. Gansner, Emden R., 1950–   II. Reppy, John H.
QA76.73.M6S72   2003
005.13′3–dc22   2003058667

ISBN 0 521 79142 1 hardback
ISBN 0 521 79478 1 paperback

Contents

Foreword

Of all modern programming languages, Standard ML has ascribed perhaps the highest priority to rigorous semantic definition. It is therefore the preferred language for many applications where rigour is important; this is notably true of the tools for formal program analysis. It has also gained users who value its high degree of portability, a direct consequence of the unambiguity of its definition.

Now Emden Gansner and John Reppy have equipped SML with another essential ingredient: a library of signatures, structures and functors that will greatly ease the programmer's task. The SML Basis Library has been long in gestation, but this has ensured that it contains the right things. Only by close cooperation with users, over a considerable period of time, can one be sure of consistency and balance in defining a library. We can therefore be confident that the Basis Library will bring SML into still wider use, and we owe warm thanks to its creators for undertaking an arduous task with skill, care and dedication.

Robin Milner

Preface

One essential for the success of a general-purpose language is an accompanying standard library that is rich enough and efficient enough to support the basic, day-to-day tasks common to all programming. Libraries provide the vocabulary with which a language can be used to say something about something. Without a broad common vocabulary, a language community cannot prosper as it might.

This book presents the SML Basis Library. It is a basis library in the sense that it concerns itself with the fundamentals: primitive types such as integers and floating-point numbers, operations requiring runtime system or compiler support, such as I/O and arrays; and ubiquitous utility types such as booleans and lists. The SML Basis Library purposefully does not cover higher-level types, such as collection types, or application-oriented APIs, such as regular expression matching. The primary reason for limiting the scope in this way is that the design space for these interfaces is large (e.g., choosing between functors and polymorphism as a parameterization mechanism), and, unlike the case with lists and arrays, we do not have many years of common practice to guide the design. It is also the case that the SML Basis Library specification is a substantial document and expanding its scope would make it unwieldy.

The primary purpose of this book is to serve as a reference manual for the SML Basis Library, describing as clearly and completely as possible the types, values, and modules making up the Library. This specification is designed to serve both implementors of the SML Basis Library and users. While the specification is not formal, we have tried to make it precise and complete enough to guarantee a high degree of portability between implementations.

It is sometimes difficult to program from a reference manual; all the pieces are there, but it is not clear how they fit together. For the working programmer who wants to use the Library, the book also discusses how the functions were meant to be used alone and together. Although not a tutorial, the book should assist the programmer in understanding and using the Library, clarifying when and how various structures should be used and making the apparent arcana accessible.

There are certain roles the book does not attempt. As we noted above, it is not a textbook, for either the Library or SML. There are already many fine books and papers teaching the joys of writing in SML, some of which address this Library as well. When dealing with the Library's interface to external software such as Unix or Microsoft Windows, it assumes the reader already knows how to use them or has access to sources providing that information.

The Library is certainly not complete; there are some glaring omissions, such as modules for building graphical interfaces or guidelines for internationalization. It is assumed that, as needs are identified and consensus in reached on the design of a structure, new modules will be added to the Library or be standardized as a separate library. The evolution of the Library will be reflected in the online version of this document, the latest version of which can be found at

```
http://standardml.org/Basis
```

Overview of the book

The book is organized in three main parts: an overview of the SML Basis Library, its structure and conventions; a tour of the main areas covered by the Library, providing programming tips, idioms, and examples aimed at library users; and a set of manual pages defining the signatures and structures comprising the Library.

The first three chapters form the first part. Chapter 1 presents the philosophy, principles, and rules underlying the design of the Library. It also notes the conventions used in documenting the Library. The second chapter lists all of the signatures, structures, and functors in the Library, noting their connections and whether they are optional. Chapter 3 considers those parts of the Library that are available at the top level, outside of any structure.

The following chapters describe some of the component areas, such as I/O and text handling, in more depth. These chapters discuss the common themes connecting the modules of a component and note related assumptions and restrictions. The Library includes some elegant solutions to certain programming tasks, but these are not necessarily obvious from a bare presentation of the signatures. Thus, many of these chapters include short tutorial sections that discuss how various types and functions were intended to be used, including examples of idiomatic use.

Chapter 11 is the meat of the book, containing manual pages describing the signatures, structures, and functors specified by the Library, and their semantics. The modules are presented in alphabetical order. Generic modules, those with multiple possible implementations, are gathered under their defining signature. Thus, the `Char` structure is discussed in the `CHAR` section. Each non-generic module, those with a one-to-one correspondence between implementation and interface, such as the `Timer` structure, heads its own section shared with its signature. Significant substructures, for example, `Posix.IO`, also rate their own sections.

In addition to the standard index of topics, the book provides a separate index of the identifiers used in the Library and another index of the Library's exceptions. The identifier index is sorted by name, with sub-entries for the signatures, structures, and functors that contain the identifier. When an identifier is contained in a generic signature (i.e., a signature like `WORD` that has multiple implementations), it will have a sub-entry for the signature, but not the structures instantiating the signature. The page number of an identifier's specification is displayed in *italics* and the page number of its description is displayed in **bold**. The exception index has an entry for each exception defined in the Library, with sub-entries for each function that can raise the given exception.

Contributors

The main architects of the SML Basis Library are Andrew Appel, Dave Berry, Emden Gansner, John Reppy, and Peter Sestoft. In addition, the following people contributed to the design discussions and writing: Nick Barnes, Lal George, Lorenz Huelsbergen, David MacQueen, Dave Matthews, Carsten Müller, Larry Paulson, Riccardo Pucella, Jon Thackray, and Stephen Weeks. This document is edited and maintained by Emden Gansner and John Reppy.

Acknowledgments

As usual in a work like this, many people have been involved in the process. We had helpful comments on the SML Basis Library or this document from Peter Michael Bertelsen, Matthias Blume, Jeremy Dawson, Matthew Fluet, Elsa Gunter, Ken Larsen, Peter Lee, Neophytos Michael, Kevin Mitchell, Brian Monahan, Stefan Monnier, Chris Okasaki, Andreas Rossberg, Olin Shivers, Mads Tofte, and Dan Wang. David Gay and Serban Jora helped with insights and pointers concerning IEEE floating-point numbers and the Microsoft Windows operating system, respectively. We would especially like to thank our editor at Cambridge University Press, Lauren Cowles, whose patience has been unbounded, and our copy editor Elise Oranges.

This document was written using the *ML-Doc* toolkit, which is an SGML-based system for documenting SML interfaces. More information about ML-Doc can be found at

http://www.cs.uchicago.edu/~jhr/tools/ml-doc.html

1
Introduction

This document describes the Standard ML Basis Library. The Library provides an extensive collection of basic types and functions for the Standard ML (SML) language, as described by the Definition of Standard ML (Revised) [MTHM97]. The goals of the Basis library are to:

- serve as the basic toolkit for the SML programmer, whether novice or professional;

- focus attention on the attractiveness of SML as a language for programming in a wide variety of domains, e.g., systems programming;

- replace the many incompatible general-purpose libraries currently available.

The original definition of the Standard ML language [MTH90] was published in 1990, for which reason we refer to it as SML'90. The Definition specified an *initial basis*, i.e., a set of primitive types such as `int` and `string` along with some related operations, which was used to define various derived forms and special constants. Though adequate for the purpose of language specification, it was too limited for programming applications. In response, most implementations of the language extended the basis with large collections of generic libraries. With the libraries coming from different sources, they tended to be incompatible, even when implementing the same abstract types and functions. The result was that, despite the standardization of the language, any significant SML program could be compiled on multiple implementations only if the programmer were willing to provide portable libraries that relied only on the initial basis.

The SML Basis Library is a rich collection of general-purpose modules, which can serve as the foundation for applications programming or for more domain-specific libraries. It provides most of the basic types and operations expected by a working programmer and specifies that anyone using SML can expect to find them in any implementation.

Some goals in designing the Library worked toward its expansion. One, suggested above, was the desire for the Library to be "complete enough." If using a type provided by the Library, the programmer should be able to look in the defining structure and find the right function or, at least, the functions needed to build the desired function easily. In addition, the Library attempts to provide similar functions in similar contexts. Thus, the traditional `app` function for lists, which applies a function to each member of a list, has also been provided for arrays and vectors.

An opposite design force has been the desire to keep the Basis library small. In general, a function has been included only if it has clear or proven utility, with additional emphasis on those that are complicated to implement, require compiler or runtime system support, or are more concise or efficient than an equivalent combination of other functions. Some exceptions were made for historical reasons or for perceived user convenience.

The SML language has the rare property of being a practical, general-purpose programming language possessing a well-defined, indeed formal, semantics. Following in this spirit, some SML-based libraries, e.g., CML [Rep99], build on this precision by supplying their own formal semantics. Although we viewed this goal as beyond what we could provide for the Basis library, we still felt very strongly that the functions included here should be defined as precisely and clearly as possible. In some cases, we have defined the meaning of basis functions via reference implementations. We want SML programs to be *deterministic* (aside from their interaction with the external world), and so we specify the traversal order for higher-level functions such as `List.map`. The description of a function provides the dynamic constraints on the arguments, such as that an integer index into an array must be less than the length of the array, and relates what happens when a function invocation violates these constraints, typically the raising of a particular exception. We have tried to stipulate completely the format of return values, so that, when a type's representation is visible, the programmer will know what to expect concretely, not just abstractly. We have avoided unspecified or implementation-dependent results whenever possible. Some functions were excluded from the Library because we could not provide a clean specification for the function's behavior.

1.1   Design rules and conventions

In designing the Library, we have tried to follow a set of stylistic rules to make library usage consistent and predictable, and to preclude certain errors. These rules are not meant to be prescriptive for the programmer using or extending the Library. On the other hand, although the Library itself flouts the conventions on occasion, we feel the rules are reasonable and helpful and would encourage their use.

1.1.1 Orthographic conventions

We use the following set of spelling and capitalization conventions. Some of these conventions, e.g., the capitalization of value constructors, seem to be widely accepted in the user community. Other decisions were based less on a dominant style or a compelling reason than on compromise and the need for consistency and some sense of good taste.

The conventions we use are

- Alphanumeric value identifiers are in mixed-case, with a leading lowercase letter; e.g., `map` and `openIn`.

- Type identifiers are all lowercase, with words separated by underscores; e.g., `word` and `file_desc`.

- Signature identifiers are in all capitals, with words separated by underscores; e.g., `PACK_WORD` and `OS_PATH`. We refer to this convention as the *signature* convention.

- Structure and functor identifiers are in mixed-case, with initial letters of words capitalized; e.g., `General` and `WideChar`. We refer to this convention as the *structure* convention.

- Alphanumeric datatype constructors follow the signature convention; e.g., `SOME`, `A_READ`, and `FOLLOW_ALL`. In certain cases, where external usage or aesthetics dictates otherwise, the structure convention can be used. Within the Basis library, the only use of the latter convention occurs with the months and weekdays in `Date`, e.g., `Jan` and `Mon`. The only exceptions to these rules are the identifiers `nil`, `true`, and `false`, where we bow to tradition.

- Exception identifiers follow the structure convention; e.g., `Domain` and `SysErr`.

These conventions concerning variable and constructor names, if followed consistently, can be used by a compiler to aid in detecting the subtle error in which a constructor is misspelled in a pattern-match and is thus treated as a variable binding. Some implementations may provide the option of enforcing these conventions by generating warning messages.

1.1.2 Naming

Similar values should have similar names, with similar type shapes, following the conventions outlined above. For example, the function `Array.app` has the type:

```
val app : ('a -> unit) -> 'a array -> unit
```

which has the same shape as `List.app`. Names should be meaningful but concise. We have broken this rule, however, in certain instances where previous usage seemed compelling. For example, we have kept the name `app` rather than adopt `apply`. More dramatically, we have purposely kept most of the traditional Unix names in the optional `Posix` modules, to capitalize on the familiarity of these names and the available documentation.

1.1.3 Comparisons

If a type `ty`, such as `int` or `string`, has a standard or obvious linear order, the defining structure should define the expected relational operators `>`, `>=`, `<`, and `<=`, plus a comparison function

$$\textbf{val}\ \text{compare}\ :\ \textit{ty}\ *\ \textit{ty}\ \text{->}\ \text{order}$$

(where `order` is defined in the `General` structure and has the constructors `LESS`, `EQUAL`, `GREATER`). In all cases, the expected relationships should hold between these functions. For example, we have $x > y$ = `true` if and only if `compare`(x, y) = `GREATER`. If, in addition, `ty` is an equality type, we assume that the operators `=` and `<>` satisfy the usual relationships with `compare` and the relational operators. For example, if `x` = `y`, then `compare(x,y)` = `EQUAL`. Note that these assumptions are not quite true for `real` values; see the `REAL` signature for more details.

For reasons of style and simplicity, we have in general attempted to avoid equality types except where tradition or convenience dictated otherwise. Most of the equality types are abstractions of integral values. We prefer to keep equality evaluation explicit, usually by an associated `compare` function.

Certain abstract types, e.g., `OS.FileSys.file_id`, provide a `compare` function even though elements of the type do not possess an inherent linear order. These functions are useful in maintaining and searching sets of these elements in, for example, ordered binary trees.

1.1.4 Conversions

Most structures defining a type provide conversion functions to and from other types. When unambiguous, we use the naming convention `to`T and `from`T, where T is some version of the name of the other type. For example, in `WORD`, we have

$$\textbf{val}\ \text{fromInt}\ :\ \text{Int.int}\ \text{->}\ \text{word}$$
$$\textbf{val}\ \text{toInt}\ :\ \text{word}\ \text{->}\ \text{Int.int}$$

If this naming is ambiguous (e.g., a structure defines multiple types that have conversions from integers), we use the convention T`From`TT and T`To`TT. For example, in `POSIX_PROC_ENV`, we have

```
val uidToWord : uid -> SysWord.word
val gidToWord : gid -> SysWord.word
```

There should be conversions to and from strings for most types. Following the convention above, these functions are typically called `toString` and `fromString`. Usually, modules provide additional string conversion functions that allow more control over format and operate on an abstract character stream. These functions are called `fmt` and `scan`. The input accepted by `fromString` and `scan` consists of printable ASCII characters. The output generated by `toString` and `fmt` consists of printable ASCII characters. Additional discussion of string scanning and formatting can be found in Chapter 5.

We adopt the convention that conversions from strings should be forgiving, allowing initial whitespace and multiple formats and ignoring additional terminating characters. In addition, for basic types, scanning functions should accept legal SML literals. On the other hand, we have tried to specify conversions to strings precisely. Formatting functions should, whenever possible, produce strings that are compatible with SML literal syntax, but without certain annotations. For example, `String.toString` produces a valid SML string constant, but without the enclosing quotes, and `Word.toString` produces a word constant without the `"0wx"` prefix.

1.1.5 Characters and strings

The revised SML definition [MTHM97] introduces a `char` type and syntax for character literals. The SML Basis Library provides support for both `string` and `char` types, where the `string` type is a *vector* of characters. In addition, we define the optional types `WideString.string` and `WideChar.char`, in which the former is again a vector of the latter, for handling character sets more extensive than Latin-1.

The SML'90 Basis Library did not provide a character type. To manipulate characters, programmers used integers corresponding to the character's code. This situation was unsatisfactory for several reasons: there were no symbolic names for single characters in patterns, character to string conversions required unnecessary range checks, and there was no provision for the extended character sets necessary for international use. Alternatively, programmers could use strings of length one to represent characters, which was less efficient and could not be enforced by the type system.

1.1.6 Operating system interfaces

The Library design probably has the least freedom concerning access to an implementation's operating system (OS). To allow code written using the Library to be as portable as possible, we have adopted standard interfaces, either *de jure* or *de facto*. We have layered the structures dealing with the OS. The facilities encapsulated in the `OS` structure and the I/O modules represent models common to most current operating systems;

code restricted to these should be generally portable. Structures such as `Unix` are more OS-specific but still general enough to be available on a variety of systems. Structures such as the `Posix` structure provide an interface to a particular OS in detail; it would be unlikely that an implementation would provide this structure unless the underlying OS were a version of POSIX. Finally, an implementation may choose to provide additional structures containing bindings for all of the types and functions supported by a given OS.

When two structures both define a type that has the same meaning, e.g., both the `OS` and `Posix.Error` structures define a `syserror` type, then these types should be equivalent or there should be an effective way to map between the types. Implementations should preserve lower-level information. For example, on a POSIX system, if a program calls `OS.Process.exit(st)`, where `Posix.Process.from-Status(st)` evaluates to `Posix.Process.W_EXITSTATUS(v)`, then the program should exit using the call `Posix.Process.exit(v)`.

Most OS interfaces involve certain specified values, such as the platform IDs specified in `Windows.Config` or the error values given in `Posix.Error`. Any static list is bound to be incomplete, either due to changes over time or from variations among implementations. To allow for differences and extensibility, the Library typically does not use a datatype for these types; it allows implementations to generate values not specified in the signature; and, when possible, it will allow the programmer access to the primitive representation of such values. Conforming implementations of the SML Basis Library can not extend the signatures given by the Library.

1.1.7 Miscellany

Functional arguments that are evaluated solely for their side effects should have a return type of `unit`. For example, the list application function has the type:

$$\textbf{val} \; \text{app} \; : \; (\text{'a} \; \text{->} \; \text{unit}) \; \text{->} \; \text{'a list} \; \text{->} \; \text{unit}$$

It is also recommended that implementations generate a warning message when an expression on the left-hand side of a semicolon in a sequence expression (i.e., e_1 in $(e_1; e_2)$) does not have `unit` type.

The use and need for exceptions should be limited. If possible, the type of an argument should prevent an exceptional condition from arising. Thus, rather than have `Posix.FileSys.openf` return an `int` value, as its analogue does in C, the Library uses the `Posix.FileSys.file_desc` type. In cases where multiple function arguments have the same type, opening the possibility that the programmer may switch them, the Library employs SML records, as with `OS.FileSys.rename`. The avoidance of exceptions is particularly apparent in functions that parse character input to create a value, which uniformly return a value of NONE to indicate incorrect input rather than raising exceptions.

If a curried function can raise an exception, the exception should be raised as soon as sufficient arguments are available to determine that the exception should be raised. Thus, given a function

```
val gen : int -> string -> string
```

that raises an exception if the first argument is negative, the evaluation of gen ~1 should trigger the exception.

SML is a value-oriented language which discourages the gratuitous use of state. Thus, the Library tries to minimize the use of state. In particular, we note that, although the Library allows imperative-style input, it provides stream-based input with unbounded lookahead and many of the routines for converting characters to values work most naturally in this style.

The language does allow functions to have side effects. To take this fact into account, the Library requires that the implementations of higher-order functions over aggregates invoke their function-valued arguments at most once per element.

Whenever possible, structures specified as signature instances are matched opaquely, so that all types are abstract unless explicitly specified in the signature or any associated **where type** clauses.

1.2   Documentation conventions

This section describes the conventions used in this document. These include the layout of the manual pages, notational conventions, and liberties that we have taken with the SML syntax and semantics to make the specification clearer.

When applicable in multiple contexts, some information is repeated. We felt it was better to accept some redundancy rather than to force the reader to glean information scattered all over the document.

1.2.1   Organization of the manual pages

The bulk of the SML Basis Library specification consists of *manual pages* specifying the signature and semantics of the Basis modules. These pages are organized in alphabetical order. Each manual page typically describes a single signature and the structure or structures that implement it.

A manual page, which is typically comprised of several physical pages, is organized into at most five sections. The first of these is the "Synopsis," which lists the signature, structure, and functor names covered by the manual page. With the exception of manual pages that cover functors, which can have both argument and result signatures, the synopsis consists of a signature name and the names of the structures matching the signature. The second section is the "Interface," which gives the SML specifications that form the body of the signature. Functor specifications can have multiple interface sections, since there are both argument and result signatures involved. Following the interface part is the "Description," which consists of detailed descriptions of each of the SML specifications listed in the interface. Some manual pages follow the description section with a "Discussion" section that covers broader aspects of the interface. Finally, there is the "See also" section, which gives cross references to related manual pages.

1.2.2   Terminology and notation

For functions that convert from strings to primitive types, we often use a standard regular expression syntax to describe the accepted input language.

Regular Expression	Meaning
$re^?$	An optional instance of re.
re^*	A sequence of zero or more instances of re.
re^+	A sequence of one or more instances of re.
$re_1 re_2$	An instance of re_1 followed by an instance of re_2.
$re_1 \mid re_2$	An instance of either re_1 or re_2.

In a regular expression, a character in teletype font represents itself. As a shorthand, we write [abc] for a | b | c. A choice of consecutive characters (in the ASCII ordering) can be specified using a range notation, e.g., [a−c].

When specifying the meaning of certain operations, we will sometimes use various standard mathematical notations in the SML Basis Library specification, implicitly mapping SML values to values in the domain of natural numbers, integers, or real numbers. The intended meaning should be clear from the context. The greatest integer less than or equal to a real-valued expression r (i.e., the *floor* of r) is written $\lfloor r \rfloor$ and, likewise, the least integer greater than or equal to a real-valued expression r (i.e., the *ceiling* of r) is written $\lceil r \rceil$. For integers i and m, the notation $i \pmod{m}$ is the remainder $i - m\lfloor \frac{i}{m} \rfloor$. The notation $[a, b]$ denotes the range of values x where $a \le x \le b$ in some corresponding domain. The sign function, $sgn(x)$, returns -1, 1, or 0, depending on whether x is negative, positive, or equal to zero, respectively.

For sequence types (i.e., lists, vectors, and arrays), we use the terminology *left-to-right* to mean the order of increasing index and *right-to-left* to mean the order of decreasing index. Sequences are indexed from zero. If seq is a value of a sequence type, then $|seq|$ means the number of elements, or length, of seq and $seq[i..j]$ is the subsequence of seq consisting of the items whose indices are in the range $[i, j]$, where $0 \le i \le j < |seq|$.

For the numeric types, we define generic signatures that are implemented at multiple precisions. For example, an implementation might provide `Int32` for 32-bit integers and `Int64` for 64-bit integers. Rather than list a sample of possible structures, we use the notation `Int`*N* to specify the *family* of structures that implement the `INTEGER` signature, where *N* specifies the number of bits in the representation.

Syntactic and semantic liberties

We have taken a few liberties with the syntax and semantics of SML in the SML Basis Library specification. In a couple of cases, we define interfaces that include a signature, which overlaps with other specifications in the interface. For example, the `TEXT_IO` signature has a `StreamIO` substructure and also includes the `IMPERATIVE_IO` signature, which itself specifies a `StreamIO` substructure. The intention is clear: the two `StreamIO` substructures are intended to be identified while matching the more detailed signature, in this case `TEXT_STREAM_IO`. While these violate the rules for well-formed signatures in SML, they avoid useless redundancy in the documentation.

Another place where we depart from strict SML semantics is in **where type** specifications. These specifications imply a dependency from the module with the specification to the module that defines the type. We want to allow implementations freedom in how they organize the Basis library modules, so when there is not a clear ordering of the modules we attach symmetric **where type** specifications to both modules. For example, the `String.string` and `CharVector.vector` types are equal, so we attach **where type** specifications to both the `String` and `CharVector` modules. Implementations are free to define one of these types in terms of the other or to define both in terms of some third type.

The "Description" section of the manual pages sometimes provides a prototypical use of a function when describing the function. When part of the argument of a function is a record type, the prototype does not use the correct record construction syntax, but rather the pattern-matching syntax as might be used in the definition of the function. For example, the description of the `Posix.IO.dup2` function has the prototype usage `dup2 {old,new}` rather than the syntactically correct `dup2 {old=old,new=new}`.

Finally, for functions returning an `option` type, in the cases when it actually returns a value as `SOME(v)`, the description will usually just say that the function returns v, with the `SOME` wrapper being understood.

2

Library modules

The Basis Library is organized using the SML module system. Almost every type, exception constructor, and value belongs to some structure. Although some identifiers are also bound in the initial top-level environment, we have attempted to keep the number of top-level identifiers small. Infix declarations and overloading are specified for the top-level environment.

We view the signature and structure names used below as being reserved. For an implementation to be conforming, any module it provides that is named in the SML Basis Library must exactly match the description specified in the Library. For example, the `Int` structure provided by an implementation should not match a superset of the `INTEGER` signature. Furthermore, an implementation may not introduce any new non-module identifiers into the top-level environment. If an implementation provides any types, values, or exceptions not described in the SML Basis Library, they must be encapsulated in structures whose names are not used by the SML Basis Library.

Some structures have signatures that refer to types that will belong to another structure. Rather than include the other structure as a substructure, we have chosen to rebind just the necessary types. It was felt that this policy makes the code easier to reorganize in large systems. Explicit connections between structures are specified by sharing constraints in the language, or by descriptions in the text.

2.1 Required modules

We have divided the modules into *required* and *optional* categories. Any conforming implementation of SML Basis Library must provide implementations of all of the required modules.

Many of the structures are variations on some generic module (e.g., single and double-precision floating-point numbers). Table 2.1 gives a list of the required generic signatures. A system will typically provide multiple implementations of some of these signatures; it is assumed that multiple implementations are allowed for all of them. Generic

Table 2.1: Required generic signatures

Signature	Description
CHAR	Generic character interface
INTEGER	Generic integer interface
IMPERATIVE_IO	Imperative I/O interface
MATH	Generic math library interface
MONO_ARRAY	Mutable monomorphic arrays
MONO_ARRAY_SLICE	Mutable monomorphic subarrays
MONO_VECTOR	Immutable monomorphic vectors
MONO_VECTOR_SLICE	Immutable monomorphic subvectors
PRIM_IO	System-call operations for I/O
REAL	Generic floating-point number interface
STREAM_IO	Stream I/O interface
STRING	Generic string interface
SUBSTRING	Generic substring interface
TEXT	Package for related text structures
TEXT_IO	Text I/O interface
TEXT_STREAM_IO	Text stream I/O interface
WORD	Generic word (i.e., unsigned integer) interface

signatures are meant to be instantiated by several structures; the required ones are all matched by at least one required structure. We list these structures next (Table 2.2). Although the signatures IMPERATIVE_IO, STREAM_IO and TEXT_STREAM_IO do not appear explicitly in this table, we note that the first is matched by TextIO and the last two are matched by TextIO.StreamIO.

Non-generic signatures typically define the interface of a unique structure. Table 2.3 lists the required non-generic signatures and their corresponding required structures.

2.2 Optional modules

The Library specifies a large collection of signatures and structures that are considered optional in a conforming implementation. They provide features that, although useful, are not considered fundamental to a workable SML implementation. These modules include additional representations of integers, words, characters, and reals; more efficient array and vector representations; and a subsystem providing POSIX compatibility.

Although an implementation may or may not provide one of these modules, if it provides one, the module must exactly match the specification given in this document. The names specified here for optional signatures and structures must be used at top-level only to denote implementations of the specified Library module. On the other hand, if

Table 2.2: Required structures implementing generic signatures

Structure	Signature	Description
BinPrimIO	PRIM_IO	Low-level binary I/O
Char	CHAR	Default character type and operations
CharArray	MONO_ARRAY	Mutable arrays of characters
CharArraySlice	MONO_ARRAY_SLICE	Mutable subarrays of characters
CharVector	MONO_VECTOR	Immutable arrays of characters
CharVectorSlice	MONO_VECTOR_SLICE	Immutable subarrays of characters
Int	INTEGER	Default integer type and operations
LargeInt	INTEGER	Largest integer representation
LargeReal	REAL	Largest floating-point representation
LargeWord	WORD	Largest word representation
Math	MATH	Default math structure
Position	INTEGER	File system positions
Real	REAL	Default floating-point type
String	STRING	Default strings
Substring	SUBSTRING	Substrings
Text	TEXT	Collects together default text structures.
TextIO	TEXT_IO	Text input/output types and operations
TextPrimIO	PRIM_IO	Low-level text I/O
Word	WORD	Default word type
Word8	WORD	8-bit words
Word8Array	MONO_ARRAY	Arrays of 8-bit words
Word8ArraySlice	MONO_ARRAY_SLICE	Subarrays of 8-bit words
Word8Vector	MONO_VECTOR	Immutable arrays of 8-bit words
Word8VectorSlice	MONO_VECTOR_SLICE	Immutable subarrays of 8-bit words

an implementation offers features related to an optional module, it should also provide the optional module.

As with the required signatures, we have both generic and non-generic optional signatures. The optional generic signatures are listed in Table 2.4.

The next four tables list the optional structures matching generic signatures as follows: Table 2.5 lists the various structures that implement the non-sequence generic signatures, Table 2.6 lists optional monomorphic array and vector structures, Table 2.7 lists optional monomorphic array-slice structures, and Table 2.8 lists optional monomorphic vector-slice structures. Note that some of the structures match required signatures.

Table 2.9 lists the optional non-generic signatures and their corresponding optional structures.

Table 2.3: Required non-generic signatures and structures

Structure	Signature	Description
Array	ARRAY	Mutable polymorphic arrays
ArraySlice	ARRAY_SLICE	Mutable polymorphic subarrays
BinIO	BIN_IO	Binary input/output types and operations
Bool	BOOL	Boolean type and values
Byte	BYTE	Conversions between Word8 and Char values
CommandLine	COMMAND_LINE	Program name and arguments
Date	DATE	Calendar operations
General	GENERAL	General-purpose types, exceptions, and values
IEEEReal	IEEE_REAL	Floating-point classes and hardware control
IO	IO	Basic I/O types and exceptions
List	LIST	Utility functions for computing with lists of pairs and pairs of lists.
ListPair	LIST_PAIR	List of pairs utility functions
Option	OPTION	Optional values and partial functions
OS	OS	Basic operating system (OS) services
OS.FileSys	OS_FILE_SYS	File status and directory operations
OS.IO	OS_IO	Support for polling I/O devices
OS.Path	OS_PATH	File-system pathname operations
OS.Process	OS_PROCESS	Simple process operations
StringCvt	STRING_CVT	Support for conversions between strings and various types
Time	TIME	Representation of time values
Timer	TIMER	Timing operations
Vector	VECTOR	Immutable polymorphic arrays
VectorSlice	VECTOR_SLICE	Subarrays of immutable polymorphic arrays

Finally, there are three optional functors for creating a new I/O layer from a more primitive layer. These functors are listed in Table 2.10.

Table 2.4: Optional generic signatures

Signature	Description
BIT_FLAGS	Support for set operations on system flags
MONO_ARRAY2	Mutable monomorphic two-dimensional arrays
PACK_REAL	Support for packing floats into vectors of 8-bit words
PACK_WORD	Support for packing words into vectors of 8-bit words

Table 2.5: Optional structures implementing generic signatures

Structure	Signature	Description
FixedInt	INTEGER	Largest fixed precision integers
Int$N$	INTEGER	N-bit, fixed precision integers
PackRealBig	PACK_REAL	Big-endian packing for default floats
PackRealLittle	PACK_REAL	Little-endian packing for default floats
PackWord$N$Big	PACK_WORD	Big-endian packing for N-bit words
PackWord$N$Little	PACK_WORD	Little-endian packing for N-bit words
Real$N$	REAL	N-bit floating-point numbers
SysWord	WORD	Words sufficient for OS operations
WideChar	CHAR	Wide characters
WideString	STRING	Wide strings
WideSubstring	SUBSTRING	Wide substrings
WideText	TEXT	Text package for wide characters
WideTextPrimIO	PRIM_IO	Low-level wide char I/O
WideTextIO	TEXT_IO	Text I/O on wide characters
Word$N$	WORD	N-bit words

Table 2.6: Optional monomorphic array and vector structures

Structure	Signature	Description
BoolArray	MONO_ARRAY	Mutable arrays of booleans
BoolArray2	MONO_ARRAY2	Two-dimensional arrays of booleans
BoolVector	MONO_VECTOR	Immutable arrays of booleans
CharArray2	MONO_ARRAY2	Two-dimensional arrays of characters
IntArray	MONO_ARRAY	Mutable arrays of default integers
IntArray2	MONO_ARRAY2	Two-dimensional arrays of default integers
Int$N$Array	MONO_ARRAY	Mutable arrays of N-bit integers
Int$N$Array2	MONO_ARRAY2	Two-dimensional arrays of N-bit integers
Int$N$Vector	MONO_VECTOR	Immutable arrays of N-bit integers
IntVector	MONO_VECTOR	Immutable arrays of default integers
LargeIntArray	MONO_ARRAY	Mutable arrays of large integers
LargeIntArray2	MONO_ARRAY2	Two-dimensional arrays of large integers
LargeIntVector	MONO_VECTOR	Immutable arrays of large integers
LargeRealArray	MONO_ARRAY	Mutable arrays of large floats
LargeRealArray2	MONO_ARRAY2	Two-dimensional arrays of large floats
LargeRealVector	MONO_VECTOR	Immutable arrays of large floats
LargeWordArray	MONO_ARRAY	Mutable arrays of large words
LargeWordArray2	MONO_ARRAY2	Two-dimensional arrays of large words
LargeWordVector	MONO_VECTOR	Immutable arrays of large words
PackReal$N$Big	PACK_REAL	Big-endian packing for N-bit floats
PackReal$N$Little	PACK_REAL	Little-endian packing for N-bit floats
RealArray	MONO_ARRAY	Mutable arrays for default floats
RealArray2	MONO_ARRAY2	Two-dimensional arrays of default floats
Real$N$Array	MONO_ARRAY	Mutable arrays of N-bit floats
Real$N$Array2	MONO_ARRAY2	Two-dimensional arrays of N-bit floats
Real$N$Vector	MONO_VECTOR	Immutable arrays of N-bit floats
RealVector	MONO_VECTOR	Immutable arrays for default floats
WideCharArray	MONO_ARRAY	Mutable arrays of wide characters
WideCharArray2	MONO_ARRAY2	Two-dimensional arrays of wide characters
WideCharVector	MONO_VECTOR	Immutable arrays of wide characters
WordArray	MONO_ARRAY	Mutable arrays of default words
WordArray2	MONO_ARRAY2	Two-dimensional arrays of default words
WordVector	MONO_VECTOR	Immutable arrays of default words
Word8Array2	MONO_ARRAY2	Two-dimensional arrays of 8-bit words
Word$N$Array	MONO_ARRAY	Mutable arrays of N-bit words
Word$N$Array2	MONO_ARRAY2	Two-dimensional arrays of N-bit words
Word$N$Vector	MONO_VECTOR	Immutable arrays of N-bit words

Table 2.7: Optional instances of MONO_ARRAY_SLICE

Structure	Description
BoolArraySlice	Mutable subarrays of booleans
IntArraySlice	Mutable subarrays of default integers
Int$N$ArraySlice	Mutable subarrays of N-bit integers
LargeIntArraySlice	Mutable subarrays of large integers
LargeRealArraySlice	Mutable subarrays of large floats
LargeWordArraySlice	Mutable subarrays of large words
RealArraySlice	Mutable subarrays for default floats
Real$N$ArraySlice	Mutable subarrays of N-bit floats
WideCharArraySlice	Mutable subarrays of wide characters
WordArraySlice	Mutable subarrays of default words
Word$N$ArraySlice	Immutable subarrays of N-bit words

Table 2.8: Optional instances of MONO_VECTOR_SLICE

Structure	Description
BoolVectorSlice	Immutable subarrays of booleans
IntVectorSlice	Immutable subarrays of default integers
Int$N$VectorSlice	Immutable subarrays of N-bit integers
LargeIntVectorSlice	Immutable subarrays of large integers
LargeRealVectorSlice	Immutable subarrays of large floats
LargeWordVectorSlice	Immutable subarrays of large words
RealVectorSlice	Immutable subarrays for default floats
Real$N$VectorSlice	Immutable subarrays of N-bit floats
WideCharVectorSlice	Immutable subarrays of wide characters
WordVectorSlice	Immutable subarrays of default words
Word$N$VectorSlice	Vectors of N-bit words

Table 2.9: Optional non-generic signatures and structures

Structure	Signature	Description
Array2	ARRAY2	Mutable polymorphic two-dimensional arrays
GenericSock	GENERIC_SOCK	Extended socket addresses and types
INetSock	INET_SOCK	Support for Internet-domain sockets
IntInf	INT_INF	Arbitrary-precision integers
NetHostDB	NET_HOST_DB	Access to the network host database
NetProtDB	NET_PROT_DB	Access to the network protocol database
NetServDB	NET_SERV_DB	Access to the network services database
Posix	POSIX	Root POSIX structure
Posix.Error	POSIX_ERROR	POSIX error values
Posix.FileSys	POSIX_FILE_SYS	POSIX file system operations
Posix.IO	POSIX_IO	POSIX I/O operations
Posix.ProcEnv	POSIX_PROC_ENV	POSIX process environment operations
Posix.Process	POSIX_PROCESS	POSIX process operations
Posix.Signal	POSIX_SIGNAL	POSIX signal types and values
Posix.SysDB	POSIX_SYS_DB	POSIX system database types and values
Posix.TTY	POSIX_TTY	Control of POSIX TTY drivers
Socket	SOCKET	General socket types and operations
Unix	UNIX	Unix-like process invocation
UnixSock	UNIX_SOCK	Support for sockets in the Unix address family
Windows	WINDOWS	Various high-level, Microsoft Windows-specific operations

Table 2.10: Optional I/O functors

Functor	Result Signature	Description
ImperativeIO	IMPERATIVE_IO	Functor to convert stream I/O into imperative I/O
PrimIO	PRIM_IO	Functor to build a PRIM_IO structure
StreamIO	STREAM_IO	Functor to convert primitive I/O into stream I/O

3

Top-level environment

This chapter describes the standard initial top-level environment, that is, those identifiers available unqualified before the user introduces additional top-level bindings. As special aspects of this environment, infix identifiers and overloading are also discussed.

There are two reasons for including (non-module) identifiers in the top-level environment. The first is convenience. Certain types and values are used so frequently that it would be perverse to force the programmer to always open the containing structures or to use the qualified names, especially for interactive usage, where notational simplicity and fewer keystrokes are desirable. The second reason is to allow operator overloading.

3.1 Modules in the top-level environment

There are no default requirements on which modules will be initially available at top-level for either interactive or batch-oriented sessions. Each implementation may provide its own mechanism for making its various modules available to the user's code. Even the presence of a top-level identifier that is logically defined in a structure (e.g., the type `int` is defined in the `Int` structure) is no guarantee that the structure name is in the environment.

3.2 Top-level type, exception, and value identifiers

Various types, exceptions, and values are available in the top-level environment without qualification. In particular, everything in the `General` structure is available.

We note that the special identifiers `=` and `<>`, corresponding to polymorphic equality and inequality, are available in the top-level environment but are not bound in any module.

Table 3.1 presents the top-level types and their defining structures, if any.

Although the types `bool` and `list` are considered primitive and defined in the top-

Table 3.1: Top-level types

Type	Defined in
eqtype unit	General
eqtype int	Int
eqtype word	Word
type real	Real
eqtype char	Char
eqtype string	String
type substring	Substring
type exn	General
eqtype 'a array	Array
eqtype 'a vector	Vector
eqtype 'a ref	*primitive*
datatype bool = false | true	*primitive*
datatype 'a option = NONE | SOME **of** 'a	Option
datatype order = LESS | EQUAL | GREATER	General
datatype 'a list = nil | :: **of** ('a * 'a list)	*primitive*

level environment, for consistency they are also bound in the structures Bool and List, respectively.

The next table presents the exception constructors available at top-level. All of these are defined in the General structure, except for Option, which is defined in the Option structure, and Empty, which is defined in the List structure.

exception Bind
exception Chr
exception Div
exception Domain
exception Empty
exception Fail **of** string
exception Match
exception Option
exception Overflow
exception Size
exception Span
exception Subscript

Table 3.2 presents the non-overloaded functions available at top-level, plus the structure value to which each is bound. Note that the use function is special. Although it is not defined precisely, its intended purpose is to take the pathname of a file and treat the contents of the file as SML source code typed in by the user. It can be used as a simple build mechanism, especially for interactive sessions. Most implementations will provide a more sophisticated build mechanism for larger collections of source files. Implementations are not required to supply a use function.

Table 3.2: Top-level functions

`val ! :   'a ref -> 'a`	`General.!`
`val := :   'a ref * 'a -> unit`	`General.:=`
`val @ :   ('a list * 'a list) -> 'a list`	`List.@`
`val ^ :   string * string -> string`	`String.^`
`val app :   ('a -> unit) -> 'a list -> unit`	`List.app`
`val before :   'a * unit -> 'a`	`General.before`
`val ceil :   real -> int`	`Real.ceil`
`val chr :   int -> char`	`Char.chr`
`val concat :   string list -> string`	`String.concat`
`val exnMessage :   exn -> string`	`General.exnMessage`
`val exnName :   exn -> string`	`General.exnName`
`val explode :   string -> char list`	`String.explode`
`val floor :   real -> int`	`Real.floor`
`val foldl :   ('a*'b->'b)-> 'b`	`List.foldl`
`            -> 'a list -> 'b`	
`val foldr :   ('a*'b->'b)-> 'b`	`List.foldr`
`            -> 'a list -> 'b`	
`val getOpt :   ('a option * 'a) -> 'a`	`Option.getOpt`
`val hd :   'a list -> 'a`	`List.hd`
`val ignore :   'a -> unit`	`General.ignore`
`val implode :   char list -> string`	`String.implode`
`val isSome :   'a option -> bool`	`Option.isSome`
`val length :   'a list -> int`	`List.length`
`val map :   ('a -> 'b) -> 'a list`	`List.map`
`            -> 'b list`	
`val not :   bool -> bool`	`Bool.not`
`val null :   'a list -> bool`	`List.null`
`val o :   ('a->'b) * ('c->'a) -> 'c->'b`	`General.o`
`val ord :   char -> int`	`Char.ord`
`val print :   string -> unit`	`TextIO.print`
`val real :   int -> real`	`Real.fromInt`
`val ref :   'a -> 'a ref`	*primitive*
`val rev :   'a list -> 'a list`	`List.rev`
`val round :   real -> int`	`Real.round`
`val size :   string -> int`	`String.size`
`val str :   char -> string`	`String.str`
`val substring :   string * int * int`	`String.substring`
`            -> string`	
`val tl :   'a list -> 'a list`	`List.tl`
`val trunc :   real -> int`	`Real.trunc`
`val use :   string -> unit`	*implementation dependent*
`val valOf :   'a option -> 'a`	`Option.valOf`
`val vector :   'a list -> 'a vector`	`Vector.fromList`

3.3 Overloaded identifiers

The SML Standard Basis includes a fixed set of overloaded identifiers; programmers may not define new overloadings. These identifiers, with their type schemas and default bindings are as follows:

val + :	*num* ***** *num* **->** *num*			Int.+
val - :	*num* ***** *num* **->** *num*			Int.-
val * :	*num* ***** *num* **->** *num*			Int.*
val div :	*fixnum* ***** *fixnum* **->** *fixnum*			Int.div
val mod :	*fixnum* ***** *fixnum* **->** *fixnum*			Int.mod
val / :	*real* ***** *real* **->** *real*			Real./
val ~ :	*num* **->** *num*			Int.~
val abs :	*realint* **->** *realint*			Int.abs
val < :	*numtext* ***** *numtext* **->** bool			Int.<
val > :	*numtext* ***** *numtext* **->** bool			Int.>
val <= :	*numtext* ***** *numtext* **->** bool			Int.<=
val >= :	*numtext* ***** *numtext* **->** bool			Int.>=

where

$$int \;=\; \{I.\texttt{int} \mid \text{where } I \text{ is a basis module matching the } \texttt{INTEGER} \text{ signature}\}$$

$$word \;=\; \{W.\texttt{word} \mid \text{where } W \text{ is a basis module matching the } \texttt{WORD} \text{ signature}\}$$

$$real \;=\; \{R.\texttt{real} \mid \text{where } R \text{ is a basis module matching the } \texttt{REAL} \text{ signature}\}$$

$$text \;=\; \{\texttt{String.string}, \texttt{Char.char}, \texttt{WideString.string}, \texttt{WideChar.char}\}$$

$$fixnum \;=\; word \cup int$$

$$realint \;=\; real \cup int$$

$$num \;=\; fixnum \cup real$$

$$numtext \;=\; num \cup text$$

The same type must be chosen throughout the entire type schema of an overloaded operator. For example, the function abs cannot have type int **->** real, but only a type like int **->** int. In addition, we note that Int*N*.int, IntInf.int, Word*N*.-word, Real*N*.real, WideString.string, and WideChar.char are optional types.

The function identifiers have a default binding that is adopted in lieu of any type information supplied by the surrounding context. All overloaded value identifiers default to the corresponding operation from the `Int` structure, except for the operator `/`, whose default binding is `Real./`. Thus, the following code would typecheck:

```
fun f(x,y) = x <= y

val x = (1 : LargeInt.int)
val y = x + 1

fun g x = x + x before ignore (x + 0w0)
```

with `f`, `y`, and `g` having the following types:

```
val f : int * int -> bool
val y : LargeInt.int
val g : word -> word
```

3.4 Infix identifiers

The top-level environment has the following infix identifiers:

```
infix   7   * / div mod
infix   6   + - ^
infixr  5   :: @
infix   4   = <> > >= < <=
infix   3   := o
infix   0   before
```

The digit in each row gives the precedence (binding power) of each identifier, so that `+` and `-` bind equally tightly, and both bind more tightly than `::` and `@`. All these identifiers are left-associative (bind more tightly to the left) except `::` and `@`, which are right-associative.

3.5 The process environment

The Basis Library specifies very little about the process or operating system environment in which SML programs are executed, which gives implementations the widest possible freedom. Programs may be executed as part of an interactive session, as stand-alone executables, or as server processes.

There are a few points, however, where the surrounding environment does impinge on the Basis Library. We summarize these points here.

The `CommandLine` structure defines functions that return the name and arguments with which a program was invoked. The method for setting these values is entirely up to the implementation. We would expect that if a stand-alone executable is run from a command line, then these values would be determined from the name and arguments specified on that command line.

Implementations may provide a mechanism for taking a function and producing a stand-alone executable. If such a mechanism is provided, the type of the function being exported must be

```
(string * string list) -> OS.Process.status
```

When the stand-alone executable is invoked, the function should be called with a first argument equal to `CommandLine.name ()` and a second argument equal to `CommandLine.arguments ()`.

The `OS.Process.getEnv` function assumes that the environment associates a set of *name-value* pairs with the invocation of a program, where both *name* and *value* are strings. This function returns the value associated with the given name. It is essentially a mechanism for providing global variables, by which the user can provide values that can be used deep within a program. The method for specifying this set is OS-dependent. The set may be empty.

The `OS.Process.exit` and `OS.Process.terminate` functions return a status value to the environment. The type of this value, and how the environment interprets it, is OS-dependent.

The `OS.Process.atExit` function adds an argument function to the actions that are executed when the program reaches a normal termination. A normal termination is a call to `OS.Process.exit`, or as defined by the implementation. If a stand-alone executable is created from a function as above, then normal termination occurs when that function returns. We would expect other methods for creating stand-alone executables to behave similarly.

Abnormal terminations include calls to `OS.Process.terminate`, or when a stand-alone executable does not handle a raised exception. The functions registered by `OS.Process.atExit` are not evaluated in the event of an abnormal program termination.

Some actions are implicitly registered with `OS.Process.atExit`, so that they always occur on a normal program termination. These must include the flushing and closing of all open output streams created by the open functions in `BinIO` and `TextIO` and the flushing (but not closing) of `TextIO.stdOut` and `TextIO.stdErr`. Although this exit protocol covers most usual cases, for maximum portability and robustness, code should flush streams explicitly.

4

General usages

In SML programming, there are certain library features that are used over and over, in many different contexts, whether in text manipulation, numerical computations, or systems programming. At times, they can seem like part of the core language, especially when specified as an infix operator. Most of these features are gathered into the General module. This chapter will discuss some of these types and values, and give examples of how they are typically used.

We start with a brief mention of the bool type and its two values true and false, which are defined as part of the initial static basis for the language and redeclared in the Bool structure. This type provides the values used by predicates and logical expressions. The library module Bool defines boolean negation not, while the core language defines boolean conjunction AND and disjunction OR as **andalso** and **orelse**, respectively. These binary operators provide conditional evaluation, in that if the value of the expression can be deduced from evaluating just one subexpression, the other is left unevaluated. In practice, these operators are more useful than their strict logical counterparts AND and OR. In addition to avoiding unnecessary calculation, they capture nicely the condition where the evaluation of one expression only makes sense in certain conditions. A typical instance would be the function

```
fun skipLine (l : substring) = let
    val l' = Substring.dropl (Char.isSpace) l
    in
      Substring.isEmpty l'
      orelse Substring.sub (l,0) = #"#"
    end
```

which could be used to skip empty lines or those whose first non-space character is #"#". The initial check for an empty substring is necessary to avoid an exception by calling sub on an empty substring. In the rare cases where the strict semantics of AND and OR are required, the programmer need only wrap the built-in operators in a function

```
fun && (b1 : bool, b2 : bool) = b1 andalso b2
fun || (b1 : bool, b2 : bool) = b1 orelse b2
infix && ||
```

to guarantee the evaluation of both expressions.

4.1   Linear ordering

By extending the two-valued range of true and false, equal and not equal, to the three-valued range of less than, equal to, and greater than, we obtain a basis for a wide assortment of basic and efficient searching and sorting data structures such as red-black trees and splay trees and algorithms such as quicksort. To provide a uniform encoding of the three relations, the General structure defines the datatype order with its three constructors LESS, EQUAL, and GREATER. Functors and structures implementing sorting and searching will typically take a function returning order values as a parameter. Sometimes an algorithm requires a more limited comparison function such as a greater than operator. Given an order-valued function compare, the code

```
fun a > b = Int.compare (a,b) = GREATER
```

provides the necessary operator. On the other hand, if the various relational operators <, <=, >, and >= are available, it is a simple matter to construct a compare function.

When defining a new abstract type ty, the programmer should consider whether it makes sense to provide a comparison function

```
val compare : ty * ty -> order
```

on the type. The answer will depend on whether the type has a natural linear ordering and on how useful having an ordering might be. As usual, answering the latter question can be difficult, requiring an educated guess as to how the type will be used; but if an abstract type does not have a compare function, it can prove nearly impossible to implement sets of such objects efficiently. It is for this reason that the Library defines a compare function for most primitive types.

Often there are straightforward techniques for deriving a linear ordering. If the concrete representation of the type has a field that is a key for values of the type, and the type of that field has a linear ordering, the type can inherit the ordering of the key. More generally, some types, such as string, can be viewed as a sequence of values of a base type, such as char, with an ordering. In this case, an ordering can be defined as the lexicographic ordering derived from the ordering of the base type. This approach can be further extended to the case where some collection of fields, of possibly differing types, each with an ordering, serves as a key. An ordering of the type can then be defined as a lexicographic ordering of the key fields. When considering the order of the key fields, it is useful compare the fields that provide the most discrimination first. This technique can speed up the computation in cases of inequality.

When defined, it is recommended that the usual relations hold amongst the relational operators, the equality operators and the `compare` function. Thus, if `compare(a, b)` = `GREATER`, the expression $a > b$ should be true.

When calculating the ordering of integral values A and B, one should be careful if the calculation relies on the sign of A - B. If the values are integers, the subtraction might cause the `Overflow` exception to be raised; and if the values have `word` type, the difference will always be non-negative.

4.2 Option

Values of `option` type can play many different roles in an SML program, all related to the occurrence of missing values. Formally, a function whose return type is `ty option` can be viewed as a partial function, being undefined for those values in its domain for which it returns NONE. A typical example of this view is provided by the `OS.Process.getEnv` function, which returns the string value associated with a name in the process environment. If a name is undefined, the function returns NONE. Pragmatically, a NONE value can be considered as a type-safe version of the convention in the C language in which a NULL pointer is used to indicate no value.

A common situation in which a function value is undefined is the case of errors. In particular, the Library has adopted the convention that all functions used to create a value from a string representation should have `option` type, with NONE denoting that conversion was not possible. Thus, `Int.fromString " B2"` returns NONE. Such occurrences were deemed not that exceptional but to be expected, to be handled directly, not via an exception.

When dealing with strings and lists, the programmer has alternative ways to indicate a missing value, using an empty string `" "` or an empty list `[]`. In certain contexts, though, these empty objects are valid and meaningful values. In these cases, the programmer must rely on NONE to indicate the actual absence of a legal value.

Another use of the `option` type occurs when we wish to denote a default or unspecified value. For example, we specify subsequences using a starting index and the number of elements to be included. When the latter value is NONE, the subsequence extends to the end of the base sequence. This convention is a convenient shorthand, as the corresponding value involving the length of the sequence and the starting index is cumbersome to express.

When the default is not determined by convention, the programmer can use `getOpt` to supply the value. For example, the function

```
fun getInt (dflt : int) (s : string) =
    getOpt (Int.fromString s, dflt)
```

returns an integer scanned from s or, if this conversion fails, the default value dflt.

In addition to getOpt, the Option structure contains other functions for manipulating option values. The most frequently used are valOf and its predicate form isSome, both of which, along with getOpt, are available unqualified in the top-level environment. The valOf function strips away the SOME from an option value, raising an exception if the value is NONE. It is often used when the code guarantees an option value is not NONE, as illustrated in the following code:

```
fun checkLine ins = (case TextIO.inputLine ins
        of "" => NONE
         | s => (case valOf (Substring.getc (Substring.full s))
               of (#"#", rest) => SOME(true, rest)
                | (_, rest) => SOME(false, rest)
             (* end case *))
       (* end case *))
```

This function evaluates a line as to whether or not it begins with a #"#" character. As the code has already checked that the line is non-empty, it is safe to apply valOf to the result of Substring.getc.

Values of option type can be thought of as list of zero or one elements. The Option structure includes analogues of some of the standard sequence functions (see Chapter 7) such as app, map, mapPartial, and a variation of filter. The function

```
      fun find (p : 'a -> bool) (x : 'a option) =
            mapPartial (filter p) x
```

works as a find function. In general, these operations allow one to work functionally with option values, without having to check the case or wrap and unwrap values explicitly. For example, the data structure for a parse tree might represent a case statement as

```
            CASE of {
                arg : exp,
                cases : (int * stmt) list,
                default : stmt option
            }
```

Code to apply a function to a case element might use Option.app f default and rewriting the tree might employ Option.map f default. Recalling that getEnv returns an option type, one might convert an optional, string-valued environment variable "SSH_AGENT_PID" into an optional integer parameter by

```
        fun getAgentPid () =
            Option.mapPartial
              Int.fromString
                (OS.Process.getEnv "SSH_AGENT_PID")
```

For the interested reader, we note that it is possible to describe the option type in a totally different framework. One technique for emulating impure features, such as mutable arrays, in pure functional languages, such as Haskell [Jon03], is to employ monads, an algebraic construct from category theory. A monad is a type constructor M together with three functions:

```
val unit : 'a -> 'a M
val map : ('a -> 'b) -> ('a M -> 'b M)
val join : 'a M M -> 'a M
```

satisfying a certain handful of axioms. Wadler [Wad90] has observed out that `option` is a monad using the `Option.map` and `Option.join` functions and letting `unit = SOME`.

4.3 Exception handling

As we noted in the introductory chapter, we feel the programmer should give special attention to the use of exceptions and attempt to avoid them when possible. Although crucial for handling errors at the right place, exceptions, by their nature, make code harder to analyze and understand. Another difficulty with exceptions is deciding what exception to use. At one extreme, a programmer could employ the standard exception `General.Fail` everywhere, letting it carry a string describing the particular failure. Usually, this approach is not fine enough for effective error handling, so exception handlers need to do string matching on the string carried by `Fail`. For example, one technique is to have a function `sampleFn` in a structure `Sample` raise the exception `Fail "Sample.sampleFn"`. If a function can raise multiple exceptions, the string can be extended in an obvious fashion. These string-based approaches quickly become cumbersome and error-prone, essentially replacing typed values with untyped strings. At the other extreme, the code could provide a unique exception for every place and type of error possible. Although this approach provides the finest detail, it can become a cognitive nightmare, making it difficult for the programmer to understand and use appropriate exceptions. There is the related problem in object-oriented programming, where the temptation to define new types can lead to an overly complex type hierarchy.

The derived types available in an object-oriented language can be used to impose some structure on the definition and use of exceptions. Although the SML programmer does not have this option, she can employ the type system to obtain some classification of exceptions. The `IO.Io` exception illustrates an example of this approach, where the value carried by the exception contains an exception.

The `General` structure provides a collection of general-purpose exceptions that the programmer can use to limit the generation of new exceptions. Thus, there are many instances that might justify the use of the `Domain` or `Size` exceptions. For miscellaneous cases, or in prototype code, the all-purpose `Fail` exception is available.

As for catching and handling exceptions, the `General` structure supplies the two functions `exnName` and `exnMessage`, which are applicable to any exception. In the ideal case, a programmer is aware of all the possible exceptions that might arise at a particular place and can therefore provide an exhaustive exception handler. This is not always the case in practice, so it is usually a good bit of defensive programming to provide some information concerning an unexpected error. The following code exhibits an example of this technique applied to a function ready to be exported as a stand-alone program.

```
fun main (name : string, arguments : string list) = let
      fun errMsg msg = TextIO.output (TextIO.stdErr, msg^"\n")
      fun error (Fail msg) = errMsg msg
        | error e = errMsg (exnMessage e)
      val ret = (action (name, arguments); OS.Process.success)
              handle e => (error e; OS.Process.failure)
    in
      ret
    end
```

4.4 Miscellaneous functions

One class of mistakes which can occur with a language like SML involves failing to use the value of a function call. The availability of higher-order functions admits a particularly subtle form of this bug in which a curried function is only partially evaluated. For example, say the programmer has a function

`val put : string -> string -> unit`

which is then used in a sequence expression

`...; put "abc"; ...`

It looks correct to the eye, as the programmer knows the function is meant to return `unit` and therefore the return value can be ignored. This type of mistake can be difficult to find. For this reason, the Library insists that functions evaluated for side effects only have a result type of `unit` and suggests that implementations warn the programmer when a function value is not used.

There are times, though, when the programmer really wants to ignore the results of a function that returns non-trivial values. In these cases, the programmer can use the `ignore` function to discard the results. For example, assume the `put` function has both a side effect and produces a result. Then, applying it to a list `l` can be done as follows:

`List.app (ignore o put) l`

This example also involves another useful library function: the function composition operator `o`. The composition operator and the `before` operator are simple to define, but are useful enough to be included in the Library. The `before` operator also touches on the issue of side effects. It is typically used after computing a value to perform some side-effecting operation, followed by returning the value. For example,

```
fun readAndClose (f : TextIO.instream) =
      (TextIO.inputAll f) before (TextIO.closeIn f)
```

creates a string from the input of a file, closes the input stream, and returns the string. When compared with the equivalent version:

```
fun readAndClose (f : TextIO.instream) = let
      val s = TextIO.inputAll f
    in
      TextIO.closeIn f;
      s
    end
```

the advantages may seem minimal, but the operator provides a pleasing elegance.

5

Text

The SML Basis Library provides a number of features aimed at enabling easy manipulation of textual data. There are three basic text types: characters (represented by the type `char`), strings (represented by the type `string`), and substrings (represented by the type `substring`). The default text types and modules are implemented using 8-bit ASCII characters.

There is a "home" module for each of the basic text types: `Char` for characters, `String` for strings, and `Substring` for substrings. Strings and substrings are special instances of the more general vector and vector slice types, so the Basis Library equates the type `string` with `CharVector.vector` and the type `substring` with `CharVectorSlice.slice`. These equivalences can be useful as they allow additional vector and vector slice operations to be used on strings and substrings. The `String-Cvt` module provides common definitions for string conversions (e.g., the `reader` type) and the `Byte` structure provides support for casting characters and strings to bytes (`Word8.word` values) and sequences of bytes.

In addition to being available at top-level, the default text modules are also substructures of the `Text` module. An implementation may also provide text modules encapsulated in the optional `WideText` structure, where the `WideChar.char` type represents a larger (e.g., Unicode [Uni03]) character set. Since the operations and semantics are essentially equivalent between 8-bit and wide text, we only consider the 8-bit representation here.

5.1 Characters

Characters are the basic element from which all text is comprised. As noted above, the `Char.char` type represents the traditional 8-bit character set and serves as the default character type (`char`) for SML. The `Char` structure provides a collection of predicate functions for classifying characters. For example, the function `isUpper` returns true if its argument is an uppercase letter. It is also possible to create a custom character classifier using the `contains` and `notContains` functions. These functions have the type

```
val contains    : string -> char -> bool
val notContains : string -> char -> bool
```

Their first argument is a string that represents a set of characters and their second argument is a character to be tested for membership in the set. The `contains` function returns true if the character is in the set, while `notContains` returns true if the character is not in the set. For example, we can test for octal digits using the following predicate:

```
val isOctDigit = Char.contains "01234567"
```

As will be seen below, character classification functions are useful as predicate arguments to the higher-order operations on strings and substrings.

5.2   Strings and substrings

The SML Basis Library provides two types for the compact representation of character sequences: `string` and `substring`. The `string` type is an immutable vector of characters. Unlike in C, the size of a string is part of its representation, and a string may contain any valid character, including the NULL character `"\000"`. The `substring` type represents a subsequence (or slice) of some underlying string value. Substrings provide a way to work with parts of a string without copying. They are also useful for scanning over a string.

5.3   Conversions to and from text

The SML Basis Library provides functions to convert between most primitive types (e.g., `int` and `real`) and their string representations.

5.3.1   The `StringCvt` structure

A number of types and functions related to conversions to and from printable representations are collected in the `StringCvt` structure. These include datatypes for specifying the format of integer, word, and real conversions (the `radix` and `realfmt` types). There are also utility functions for scanning and formatting strings.

The `padLeft` and `padRight` functions provide a way to extend strings to a specific width. For example, to convert a `word` value to an eight-digit hexadecimal representation, we can use the following function:

```
fun w2s w = StringCvt.padLeft #"0" 8 (Word.toString w)
```

while to left-justify a string in a field of width ten, we can use the following:

```
fun left s = StringCvt.padRight #" " 10 s
```

Note that if the size of s is greater than ten, then no padding will be added. If we wanted to guarantee at least one space to the right of the string, we could use the following implementation:

```
fun left s = StringCvt.padRight #" " (Int.max(9, size s)+1) s
```

The StringCvt structure is also home to the reader type constructor, which is defined as follows:

```
type ('item, 'strm) reader = 'strm -> ('item * 'strm) option
```

where the type variable 'item represents the type of items being scanned and the type variable 'strm represents the input stream of items. Of particular interest are character readers (i.e., readers where the item type is char). The StringCvt structure defines a few utility functions on character readers. The skipWS function advances the reader over any initial whitespace characters. The splitl function takes a character predicate and scans the longest prefix from the reader that satisfies the predicate. For example, the following function skips any initial whitespace and then scans a word (i.e., a non-empty sequence of letters) from the given reader:

```
fun scanWord rdr strm = let
      val strm = StringCvt.skipWS rdr strm
      in
        case StringCvt.splitl Char.isAlpha rdr strm
         of ("", _) => NONE
          | (w, strm) => SOME(w, strm)
        (* end case *)
      end
```

Notice that this function is a mapping from a character reader to a string reader, where the strings will be words. Lastly, the scanString function can be used to convert a general scan function into a toString function. More discussion of the use of readers can be found below in Section 5.4.2.

5.3.2 Converting to text

For most primitive types, the SML Basis Library provides two functions for converting a value of the type to a string representation. For a given type *ty* defined in a structure *M*, the *M*.fmt function is a customizable conversion function with the specification

$$\textbf{val } fmt \, : \, \textit{info} \to \textit{ty} \to string$$

where *info* specifies properties of the string representation, such as radix and precision. The `M.toString` function is a default conversion function, with the specification

val `toString` : *ty* -> `string`

which is suitable for most uses. In some cases, no `fmt` function is provided since there is only one way to format the type.

The conversion functions are designed for presenting a readable format while allowing maximum user flexibility in the final output. Thus they do not always produce a valid SML literal of the given type. For example, the expression

`Word.fmt StringCvt.HEX 0wx19`

produces the string `"19"` instead of the SML literal `"0wx19"`. To produce a valid SML literal, we would write

`"0wx" ^ Word.fmt StringCvt.HEX 0wx19`

while to produce a valid C literal we would write

`"0x" ^ Word.fmt StringCvt.HEX 0wx19`

Two forms of `toString` functions are provided for converting character and string values to printable format. The `Char.toString` and `String.toString` functions use SML escape sequences to represent non-printable characters, while `Char.-toCString` and the `String.toCString` functions use C escape sequences. Note that these functions do not add the surrounding quotes to their results; to produce a valid SML string literal one needs code like the following:

```
fun toLiteral s = String.concat["\"", String.toString s, "\""]
```

5.3.3 Converting from text

The SML Basis Library also provides two functions for parsing a string representation of values for most primitive types. For a given type *ty* defined in a structure *M*, the `M.scan` function is a general-purpose conversion function with the following specification:

val `scan` : *info*
    -> `(char, 'a) StringCvt.reader`
        -> `(`*ty*`, 'a) StringCvt.reader`

where *info* specifies properties of the string representation, such as radix and precision. The `StringCvt.reader` type is a higher-order representation of a stream and is discussed in detail in Section 5.4.2. For some types (e.g., `bool`), there is no *info* argument and the specification is simply

```
val scan : (char, 'a) StringCvt.reader
       -> (ty, 'a) StringCvt.reader
```

The `fromString` function provides a simple mechanism for converting from strings to a primitive type. It has the following specification:

```
val fromString : string -> ty option
```

Like the `scan` function, `fromString` ignores initial whitespace, but, unlike `scan`, it does not return any residual text that was not consumed in the parse. The `fromString` function is most useful when combined with another scanning or parsing mechanism. For example, `Int.fromString` might be used to convert the text matched by the regular expression $[0-9]^+$ in a generated lexer.

As with converting characters and strings to printable representations, the SML Basis Library provides both `fromString` and `fromCString` functions in the `Char` and `String` structures. Note that since the space character is a valid character in a character or string literal, these functions do not skip initial whitespace prior to scanning.

5.3.4 The `Byte` structure

In languages without strong type systems, such as C, it is possible to view strings as byte sequences. The SML Basis Library uses distinct abstract types (`string` and `Word8Vector.vector`) for these views, but it is sometimes useful to be able to directly convert between the two. The operations provided by the `Byte` structure provide three levels of conversions between the character and the byte-oriented view of text. Unlike the `fromString` and `toString` functions described above, these operations do not change the byte-level representation of the data (i.e., there are no escape sequences).

The `byteToChar` and `charToByte` functions convert between the `char` and `Word8.word` types. For example, `Byte.charToByte(#"x")` returns `0wx78`, which is the ASCII code for lowercase "x."

Constant-time coercions between the `string` and `Word8Vector.vector` types are supported by the `bytesToString` and `stringToBytes` functions. These functions can be useful for text I/O on top of a binary stream. For example, the *Portable Pixmap* (PPM) file format [Pos03] has an ASCII header and binary data. Listing 5.1 defines a function for writing a 24-bit per pixel image as a PPM file. The header consists of a special identifier (the `"P6"` string), the image width and height, and the maximum value per color component. Following the textual header comes the binary data (note that the use of `output1` for output is not the most efficient technique; see Section 8.2.6 for more discussion). Another example can be found in Section 10.6.2, where these operations from the `Byte` structure are used to build text I/O on a binary network connection.

```sml
type rgb = {r : Word8.word, g : Word8.word, b : Word8.word}
type ppm = {wid : int, ht : int, data : rgb array}

fun writePPM (fname, ppm : ppm) = let
      val outS = BinIO.openOut fname
      fun pr s = BinIO.output(outS, Byte.stringToBytes s)
      fun putByte b = BinIO.output1(outS, b)
      fun putRGB {r, g, b} = (putByte r; putByte g; putByte b)
    in
      pr "P6\n";
      pr (concat[
          Int.toString(#wid ppm), " ",
          Int.toString(#ht ppm), "\n"
        ]);
      pr "255\n";
      Array.app putRGB (#data ppm);
      BinIO.closeOut outS
    end
```

Listing 5.1: Writing a PPM file

Lastly, the `Byte` structure provides functions for working with byte array or vector slices. The `unpackString` function extracts a slice of a byte array and returns it as a string (the `unpackStringVec` is similar and works on byte vectors). The `packString` function packs a substring into a byte array. These functions are useful for data marshalling and unmarshalling of strings.

5.4   Taking strings apart

The SML Basis Library provides a collection of functions for parsing and decomposing strings. When efficiency is not an issue, one can work directly with `string` values; the `substring` type allows one to decompose strings in situ, while the `reader` type supports incremental scanning of character sequences.

5.4.1   Tokenizing

One common operation on strings is scanning a string to decompose it into a sequence of *tokens*. (This process is sometimes called *tokenization*.) In its most general form, one uses a regular-expression library or scanner-generator tool for this problem, but in many cases the input language is simple enough that a direct implementation is feasible. The SML Basis Library provides several mechanisms to support tokenization.

In the simplest case, one is interested in a sequence of tokens separated by some specific character or characters. For example, say we have an input string that contains a list of numbers separated by commas or whitespace. The following function will convert this input string into a list of integers:

```
fun numbers s = let
        fun isSep #"," = true
          | isSep c = Char.isSpace c
        in
          List.map (valOf o Int.fromString)
            (String.tokens isSep s)
        end
```

Note that the mechanism for tokenization does not do any syntax checking; it treats any non-empty sequence of commas and whitespace characters as a separator and any sequence of non-separator characters as a token.

If we are tokenizing large input strings, we may want to avoid creating the intermediate list of strings. Instead, we can tokenize to a list of substrings and then convert the substrings to integers.

```
fun numbers s = let
      fun isSep #"," = true
        | isSep c = Char.isSpace c
      fun atoi ss =
            #1(valOf(Int.scan StringCvt.DEC Substring.getc ss))
      in
        List.map atoi
          (Substring.tokens isSep (Substring.full s))
      end
```

Of course, this approach still requires building the intermediate list of substrings.

A variation on the `tokens` function is the `fields` function, which treats each separator character as delimiting two fields. For example, the expression

```
String.tokens isSlash "/a//b/c"
```

where the `isSlash` function is

```
fun isSlash #"/" = true | isSlash _ = false
```

evaluates to the list `["a","b","c"]`, whereas

```
String.fields isSlash "/a//b/c"
```

evaluates to the list `["","a","","b","c"]`.

For large strings or for string data coming from other sources (e.g., text files), it is usually more efficient to process the data incrementally as it is parsed. The next section describes techniques for scanning text from arbitrary sources.

If we are only interested in extracting a particular field of a comma-separated record, we can use the `drop1` and `take1` functions to skip and extract fields. For example, the following function takes a string and a field index and returns the selected field:

```
fun nthField (s, i) = let
      fun notComma #"," = false | notComma _ = true
      fun nth (ss, 0) = Substring.takel notComma ss
        | nth (ss, i) = let
              val rest = Substring.triml 1 (Substring.dropl notComma ss)
              in
                nth (rest, i-1)
              end
      in
        if (i < 0) then raise Subscript else ();
        Substring.string (nth (Substring.full s, i))
      end
```

We are using `triml` to remove the separating comma. Since the `dropl`, `takel`, and `triml` functions act as the identity on the empty substring, the `nthField` function will return an empty string if there are fewer fields than the one indexed.

5.4.2   Readers

The type constructor `StringCvt.reader` is used throughout the SML Basis Library to specify the interface to functional streams.

The power of the reader type is that we can define combinators for constructing higher-level scanning and parsing functions. For example, we can define a higher-order function for scanning bracketed, comma-separated lists of items.

```
fun scanList scanItem getc strm = let
        val scanItem = scanItem getc
        fun scan (strm, items) = (case scanItem strm
                of NONE => NONE
                 | SOME(item, strm) => (
                     case getc(StringCvt.skipWS strm)
                      of NONE => NONE
                       | SOME(#"]", strm) =>
                           SOME(rev(item::items), strm)
                       | SOME(#",", strm) =>
                           scan(strm, item::items)
                     (* end case *))
                (* end case *))
        in
          case getc(StringCvt.skipWS strm)
           of SOME(#"[", strm) => scan(strm, [])
            | _ => NONE
          (* end case *)
        end
```

This function has the type

```
val scanList :
        ((char, 'strm) reader -> ('item, 'strm) reader)
         (char, 'strm) reader -> ('item list, 'strm) reader
```

In other words, it takes a character reader and an item scanner and returns an item list reader. We can get a scanner for lists of integers by

```
val scanIntList = scanList (Int.scan StringCvt.DEC)
```

We can, in turn, specialize this function to work on substrings by

```
val scanIntListFromSubstring = scanIntList Substring.getc
```

or on functional input streams by

```
val scanIntListFromStream = scanIntList TextIO.StreamIO.input1
```

The `StringCvt` module also provides the `scanString` function for producing a "`fromString`" function from a scanner. For example,

```
val intListFromString = StringCvt.scanString scanIntList
```

has the type

```
val intListFromString : string -> int list option
```

6

Numerics

6.1   Numerical conversions

The SML Basis Library defines a framework for varying sizes (or precisions) of integer, word, and floating-point types. Since the SML Basis Library does not specify which sizes an implementation should provide, we need a flexible mechanism for numeric conversions that is not tied to assumptions about which numeric types are available. This section considers conversions involving integral types. Conversions involving floating-point values will be discussed in Section 6.2.

6.1.1   Integer to integer conversions

Conversions between integers go through the `LargeInt` structure using the `toLarge` and `fromLarge` functions. Thus, to convert from `Int`N`.int` to `Int`M`.int`, the following function is used:

$$\texttt{Int}M\texttt{.fromLarge o Int}N\texttt{.toLarge}$$

`Int`N`.toLarge` converts the `Int`N`.int` type into a `LargeInt.int` type, and the function `Int`M`.fromLarge` brings it down to an `Int`M`.int` value. The conversion is guaranteed to succeed when $N \leq M$. When $M < N$, however, an `Overflow` exception will be raised if bits are lost during the conversion.

6.1.2   Word to word conversions

Conversions between words are similar, except that two different conversion operations are possible between `Word`N`.word` and `Word`M`.word` via the `LargeWord.word` type:

$$\texttt{Word}M\texttt{.fromLarge o Word}N\texttt{.toLarge}$$
$$\texttt{Word}M\texttt{.fromLarge o Word}N\texttt{.toLargeX}$$

Both `WordN.toLarge` and `WordN.toLargeX` copy the `WordN.word` value into the lower-order position of `LargeWord.word`. The difference occurs in how the higher-order bits are filled. With `WordN.toLarge`, the remaining higher-order bits are filled with zeros; with `WordN.toLargeX`, the higher-order bits are a sign extension of the most significant bit. In other words, `toLargeX` assumes that the word value is signed. The function `WordM.fromLarge` truncates the `LargeWord.word` value to the size of `WordM.word`. Note that bits may be lost when $M < N$, and no exception is raised.

6.1.3 Word to integer conversions

Conversion from words to integers are mediated through the `LargeInt.int` type. Again, two forms are possible, depending on how the most significant bit in the word type is to be treated:

$$IntM.fromLarge \ o \ WordNtoLargeInt$$
$$IntM.fromLarge \ o \ WordN.toLargeIntX$$

where `WordN.toLargeIntX` performs sign extension of the most significant bit of the `WordN.word` value. The function `WordN.toLargeInt` treats the word as an N-bit unsigned quantity in the range $[0, 2^N - 1]$, whereas, with `WordN.toLargeInt-X`, the word is considered to be the presentation of an N-bit signed integer in the range $[-2^{N-1}, 2^{N-1} - 1]$. An `Overflow` is generated if the result cannot be represented using `IntM.int`. For example:

SML expression	Value
`(Int32.fromLarge o Word8.toLargeInt) 0w1`	1
`(Int32.fromLarge o Word8.toLargeIntX) 0w1`	1
`(Int32.fromLarge o Word8.toLargeInt) 0wxff`	255
`(Int32.fromLarge o Word8.toLargeIntX) 0wxff`	~1
`(Int8.fromLarge o Word8.toLargeInt) 0wxff`	`Overflow` exception
`(Int8.fromLarge o Word8.toLargeIntX) 0wxff`	~1

6.1.4 Integer to word conversions

Conversions from integers to words are performed using:

$$WordM.fromLargeInt \ o \ IntN.toLarge$$

The `toLarge` function performs sign extension (if necessary), and the `fromLargeInt` takes the resulting lower-order M bits. One rarely treats the value in an `IntN.int` type as unsigned, so there is no equivalent of `toLargeX`. This interpretation, however, can be implemented using the operations already defined.

6.1.5   Default integer-type conversions

Due to the ubiquitous nature of the default integer type, there are functions in the INTEGER and WORD signatures that support conversions directly to and from the default integer type: `fromInt` to convert from the default integer, and `toInt` to convert to the default integer with the usual `toIntX` for word types. In all, we have:

```
IntN.toInt
IntN.fromInt
WordN.toInt
WordN.toIntX
WordN.fromInt
```

6.2   Floating-point numbers

The SML Basis Library provides a broad collection of floating-point functions via the REAL signature and its `Math` substructure, which provide support for numerical computation. The auxiliary structure `IEEEReal` specifies related types and functions that are independent of the particular floating-point implementation.

The Basis library has adopted the IEEE standard for floating-point numbers with non-trapping semantics. The latter means that when the result of a calculation goes outside the range of normal `real` values, it is mapped to a set of special values. Thus, the value of 3.0/0.0 is `posInf` while 0.0/0.0 is a NaN value (e.g., `isNan(0.0/0.0)` is true), denoting an undefined value. Note that there is one negative infinity `negInf` and one positive infinity `posInf`, while there are many NaN values.

This model differs from that of SML'90, in which expressions evaluating to values outside the normal range caused an exception to be raised. The Basis allows implementations to provide a special operating mode in which NaNs and infinities are reported when created. Even if an implementation does not provide such a mode, it is a simple matter to provide exception-raising versions of the real-valued functions. For example, one could use

```
exception SQRT

fun sqrt x = if x < 0.0 then raise SQRT
                 else Math.sqrt x
```

in place of `Math.sqrt`. In addition, the REAL signature provides the `checkFloat` function, which can be used to trap non-finite values. It raises the exception `Div` if its argument is a NaN and `Overflow` if its argument is an infinity; otherwise it acts as the identity function. For example,

```
val asin = Real.checkFloat o Math.asin
```

defines an arc sine function that raises the `Div` exception if its argument is greater than 1.0.

Signed zeros are another feature of the IEEE model. Normally, this feature is transparent, especially as the sign is ignored in all comparisons. For example, the expression `Real.==(~0.0,0.0)` evaluates to true. The difference, however, does exhibit itself in certain calculations. The expression `Real.==(atan2(0.0,~1.0),pi)` evaluates to true, whereas false is returned by `Real.==(atan2(~0.0,~1.0),pi)`.

The use of the `Real.==` function above brings up another aspect of SML floating-point numbers: they are not equality types. The `REAL` signature provides the equality-like operators defined in the IEEE standard. To mimic having equality, one can employ SML's **infix** declaration:

```
val == = Real.==
val != = Real.!=
infix 4 == !=
```

IEEE specifies four rounding modes: round to nearest, round to negative infinity, round to positive infinity, and round to zero. In the Basis, these are defined in the `IEEEReal` structure as the values `TO_NEAREST`, `TO_NEGINF`, `TO_POSINF`, and `TO_ZERO`, respectively, of the datatype `rounding_mode`. All arithmetic functions involve the rounding mode. The standard requires that calculations be performed to arbitrary precision and then be rounded according to the rounding mode to fit the relevant precision. The `IEEEReal` structure gives the programmer control over the hardware's rounding mode using the `setRoundingMode` and `getRoundingMode` functions.

6.2.1 Floating-point conversions

The functions `fromInt` and `fromLargeInt` convert integers to floating-point numbers. Note that neither function raises an exception. Loss of precision is handled by the current rounding mode, and if the argument has a large enough absolute value, the appropriate infinity is returned.

Transforming a floating-point value to an integer is done using the `toInt` and `toLargeInt` functions. These explicitly take a rounding mode as a parameter. Infinities cause the `Overflow` to be raised, while NaNs generate the `Domain` exception. The functions `floor`, `ceil`, `trunc`, and `round` are shorthand for `toInt` curried with the corresponding rounding mode.

A difficulty can arise when converting a large `word` value into a `real` value. This conversion must rely on the `toLargeIntX` function. Although the Basis guarantees that `LargeInt.int` has sufficient precision to preserve the bits of any `word`, if `LargeInt.precision` equals `LargeWord.wordSize`, the resulting integer might be negative. This behavior is no problem if we know that `IntInf` exists, or even if we just have `LargeWord.wordSize` < `LargeInt.precision`. Barring this case, we need a function such as

```
fun w32ToReal (w : Word32.word) = let
    val shift =
        ~2.0 * Real.fromLargeInt(valOf LargeInt.minInt)
    val i = Word32.toLargeIntX w
    in
      if (i < 0)
        then shift + Real.fromLargeInt i
        else Real.fromLargeInt i
    end
```

to do the conversion correctly.

As with integral values, conversion between floating-point representations goes through the `LargeReal` structure using the `toLarge` and `fromLarge` functions. To convert from Real*N*.`real` to Real*M*.`real`, the following function is used:

$$(\text{Real}M.\texttt{fromLarge } mode) \text{ o } \text{Real}N.\texttt{toLarge}$$

where *mode* is the desired rounding mode. Unlike in the integral case, loss of precision does not cause an exception; rather, it is specified by the *mode* parameter.

There are times when it is useful to have a decimal representation of a floating-point number. Because the hardware representation is typically binary, handling the conversion accurately and concisely can be tricky. For this purpose, the Basis provides the functions

```
val toDecimal : real -> decimal_approx
val fromDecimal : decimal_approx -> real option
```

converting between `real` values and values of type

```
type decimal_approx = {
    class : float_class,
    sign : bool,
    digits : int list,
    exp : int
}
```

Note that values of the latter type are concrete and are not required to have canonical form. As with conversions from strings, the Library is forgiving about the argument to `fromDecimal`. The function will produce an appropriate `real` value unless the *digits* field contains a non-digit integer. `decimal_approx` values can be used with the `IEEEReal.toString` and `IEEEReal.scan` functions to produce exact string representations for the given precision. In addition, the composition `IEEEReal.to-String o Real.toDecimal` is equivalent to `Real.fmt IEEEReal.EXACT`.

6.3 Packed data

Communication between processes, especially across networks, is usually handled as blocks or streams of bytes. In the transmission of values of primitive types, strings and characters naturally fit this model (see the `Byte` structure). With numeric values, one can construct string representations and send them, but the conversion to and from strings exacts a significant cost. When efficiency is of concern, one would prefer to transmit numbers in binary form. The Basis library defines two generic signatures, `PACK_REAL` and `PACK_WORD`, to deal with this situation. They specify functions for converting floating-point and integral values into arrays and vectors of `Word8.word` values and back again.

There are both big-endian and little-endian structures that match these signatures. In big-endian structures, the first byte is the most significant, while the little-endian structures treat the first byte as the least significant. These structures have a boolean component `isBigEndian` which can be tested to determine which policy a given structure implements.

Note that this specification is independent of the natural hardware order of the runtime machine. To set up communication, the sending and receiving machines need to agree on the representation used. If both machines have the same endianness, they will typically elect the packing structures that agree with their bias. If the machines do not agree, they will decide on an endianness for communication, with one machine handling the extra work of reversing the byte order.

These structures also have a `bytesPerElem` value, which indicates the number of bytes used to store a number. The indices used in dealing with packed arrays or vectors are not byte offsets, but element offsets, i.e., byte offsets scaled by `bytesPerElem`. For example, the call `PackRealBig.update(`*arr*`, 2, 1.23)` stores the value `1.23` starting at byte `2*bytesPerElem` in the array *arr*.

Because an implementation may provide packed-word structures for sizes without providing the corresponding word size, the packed-word structures use the `Large-Word.word` type to represent arguments. For example, the following functions read and write 16-bit words in big-endian format, where the default word type is used to represent the values being transmitted:

```
fun sendWord16 (outs : BinIO.outstream, w : word) = let
    val arr =
        Word8Array.array(PackWord16Big.bytesPerElem, 0w0)
    in
      PackWord16Big.update (arr, 0, Word.toLargeWord w);
      BinIO.output (outs, Word8Array.vector arr)
    end

fun getWord16 (ins : BinIO.instream) = let
    val v = BinIO.inputN (ins, PackWord16Big.bytesPerElem)
    in
      Word.fromLargeWord (PackWord16Big.subVec (v, 0))
    end
```

Likewise, the packing and unpacking of integers is handled through `LargeInt`.

```
fun sendInt16 (outs : BinIO.outstream, i : int) = let
    val arr =
            Word8Array.array (PackWord16Big.bytesPerElem, 0w0)
    val w = LargeWord.fromLargeInt (Int.toLarge i)
    in
      PackWord16Big.update (arr, 0, w);
      BinIO.output (outs, Word8Array.vector arr)
    end

fun getInt16 (ins : BinIO.instream) = let
    val v = BinIO.input (ins, PackWord16Big.bytesPerElem)
    in
      Int.fromLarge (
        LargeWord.toLargeIntX (
          PackWord16Big.subVecX (v, 0))
    end
```

The use of the conversions `PackWord16Big.subVecX` and `LargeWord.toLarge-IntX` preserve the sign bit, allowing the creation of negative integers from non-negative words (the "X" signifies sign eXtension)..

By convention, the names of the structures implementing these packing operations reflect the endianness and number of bits involved. Big-endian structures will have `"Big"` in their names; structures providing little-endian conversions will have `"Little"` in their names. Thus, the structure for packing 32-bit words in little-endian order will be named `PackWord32Little`.

7

Sequential data

A sequence is a *linearly ordered*, *homogeneous* (all elements of the same type) collection of values. Manipulating finite sequences is an extremely common task in programming, and particularly in functional programming. Our purpose here is to review the techniques provided by the SML Basis Library for manipulating sequences, emphasizing common patterns for building and manipulating sequences that apply to all sequence types.

The SML Basis Library supports programming with sequences through three representations: lists, vectors, and arrays. Lists are inherited from the Lisp tradition and provide sequences which can be built incrementally and are typically processed sequentially. The list type and its operations are packaged in the `List` structure. For "random access" sequences, we have mutable *arrays* from the Algol tradition and their pure variant, *vectors*. They are packaged with their respective suites of polymorphic operations in the `Array` and `Vector` structures.

These general sequence types are polymorphic, being able to contain values of any type. For certain basic types, such as characters and integers, such arrays and vectors may waste a good deal of space. To provide more compact representations for these special cases, there are a number of monomorphic vector and array types packaged in their respective structures, such as `RealVector`, `RealArray`, `Word8Vector`, and `Word8Array`. These specialized structures conform to the generic `MONO_VECTOR` and `MONO_ARRAY` signatures. Also, we remind the reader that the `string` type is identical to `CharVector.vector`, which means that any of the sequence operations applicable to vectors are applicable to strings as well.

7.1   Common patterns

We now turn to the common patterns for working with sequences, regardless of the underlying representation. We imagine the elements of a sequence being written from left to right, starting with the 0th element. Thus, we use the phrase "left to right" to indicate a traversal of increasing index starting at 0. Conversely, "right to left" indicates a traversal of decreasing index starting with the maximum index.

Note that not all three classes of sequences will have all operations. For example, the map function is not necessary for arrays. In other cases, analogous functions may have different names, depending on the type. Another distinction to keep in mind is that arrays and vectors have constant-time access for a given element, whereas lists require linear time. Thus, analogous functions may have very different performances.

Concerning efficiency, the programmer should consider using the array and vector iterators supplied by the Library when possible. In addition to eliminating the messiness of handling indices from the user's code, the library iterators can avoid the overhead of doing an array bounds check for every access.

As each sequence type models a finite linear sequence of values, starting at index 0, each type provides a length function, which returns the number of elements in the sequence, and each has a function providing random access of the nth element of the sequence. For lists, this function is named nth, while for arrays and vectors it is called sub, the difference arising from tradition.

The most commonly used sequence iterators are map, foldl, foldr, and app. The first three, perhaps with different names, have historically been found in SML libraries. They reflect the language's functional nature, using functions to produce functions, which then produce new values from old. The app function, named for "apply," (not "append"), exposes SML's acceptance of side effects; in a pure functional language, it would be meaningless.

The map function is used to transform a sequence of one type into a sequence, with the same length, of another type. The new sequence is derived from the old by applying the function parameter to each element in turn. For example, we can map a vector of strings into a vector of integers representing their lengths as follows:

```
Vector.map size (Vector.fromList ["george","alice","marsha"])
```

which produces a vector equal to

```
Vector.fromList [6,5,6]
```

Another example, is mapping a list of pairs of lists to a list of lists:

```
List.map (op @) [([1,2],[3,4]),([2,1,0],[0,5])]
```

which produces the result

```
[[1,2,3,4],[2,1,0,0,5]]
```

Note the need for **op** in front of @ in order to remove the latter's infix nature.

The app function also applies its function parameter to each sequence element in turn, but no new sequence is created. Instead, `app` is used for the side effects of its first argument. It is frequently used for performing I/O, updating arrays or initializing references. For example, the function

```
fun pr (l : string list) = List.app TextIO.print l
```

writes a list of strings to `TextIO.stdOut`. The apply function requires that its arguments have `unit` type. One can use a non-`unit` valued function with `app` by composing it with `ignore`.

Note that the result of using the expression

```
pr ["dog"," ","bites"," ","man"]
```

relies on the left-to-right nature of `app`. This property is obvious here, but it may be less so in other contexts or when using a side-effecting function with `map` or one of the `fold` functions. If the programmer is not careful, the result of `map f l` may be the expected sequence, but some background calculations may have been done in the wrong order. The Library explicitly specifies the order of evaluation for these functions, so that possible side effects are predictable across implementations.

The most general and powerful of these iterator functions are the `fold` operations. There are two variants: `foldl`, which accumulates from left to right, and `foldr`, which accumulates from right to left. The `fold` operations take a binary function and an initial value and successively combine the elements of the sequence using the function, starting with the initial value. For example, with a list of three elements, we have:

```
foldl f b [x,y,z] = f(z, f(y, f(x, b)))
foldr f b [x,y,z] = f(x, f(y, f(z, b)))
```

More concretely,

```
foldl (op ::) [] [1,2,3] = [3,2,1]
foldr (op ::) [] [1,2,3] = [1,2,3]
```

Note that `foldl` starts by applying `f` to `x`, then `y`, then `z`, i.e., from left to right. `foldr` applies `f` from right to left. This behavior is the rationale for the directional suffixes "l" and "r".

In both cases, the second argument of `f` is an accumulator argument whose initial value is `b`. The value of `b` and the return value of `f` have to agree in type, but they can have a different type from the sequence elements. Both `foldl` and `foldr` have the type

```
('a * 'b -> 'b) -> 'b -> 'a seq -> 'b
```

Typical applications of `fold` might be to accumulate the sum or product of a sequence of numbers:

```
foldl Int.+ 0 [2,3,5] = 10
foldl Int.* 1 [2,3,5] = 30
```

They can also extract a list of elements stored in a sequence value *ag*:

```
foldr (op ::) [] ag
foldl (op ::) [] ag
```

The result of the first expression maintains the element order in *ag*; the second reverses this order.

The power of the `fold` operations is illustrated by the fact that most other sequence functions can be easily (though not necessarily efficiently) defined in terms of `fold`. For instance, we have

```
fun length l = foldl (fn (_,y) => y+1) 0 l

fun app f l = foldl (fn (x,_) => f x) () l

fun map f l = foldl (fn (x,y) => y @ [f x]) nil l

fun find p l =
      foldl (fn (x,NONE) => if p x then SOME x else NONE
              | (x,y as SOME _) => y)
          NONE l
```

for lists.

As illustrated by the `find` example, `fold` operators do not have a short-circuit capability — all elements of the subject sequence have to be processed, even if the final result can be determined by looking at only part of the sequence. If necessary, truncation can be introduced in some cases by having an argument function raise an exception. Note also that the following simpler, more efficient definition of map in terms of `foldr` could be used, but only if f is pure (i.e., has no side effects), since `mapr` applies f to the elements of l in reverse order.

```
fun mapr f l = foldr (fn (x,y) => f x :: y) nil l
```

There is an additional handful of functions shared by the sequence types. The `exists` and `all` functions take a predicate and return true or false depending on whether any elements (respectively, all elements) of the sequence satisfy the predicate. Frequently, one needs to actually find an element in a sequence satisfying a predicate, rather than just knowing one exists. In this case, the `find` function is available, which guarantees it will return the leftmost such element.

Since all of the structure signatures are parameterized by the element type, the signatures do not define a `compare` function and a linear ordering for sequences. All sequence types, however, have a `collate` function. By applying this function to a `compare` function for the element type, one obtains a lexicographic ordering on the sequence.

There are two value constructors shared by the sequence types: `tabulate` and `concat`. When the values of a sequence can be specified as a function of the index, the `tabulate` function provides a convenient way to construct the sequence. For example, the expression

```
Array.tabulate (10,(fn i => i*i))
```

creates an array of the first 10 square integers. To supply the missing `map` function for arrays, one could use

```
fun map f arr = Array.tabulate (Array.length arr,
                        fn i => f (Array.sub (arr,i)))
```

As usual, `tabulate` traverses the indices in increasing order. Although `tabulate` is convenient and useful, the specified order means that the list cannot be created as efficiently as it could using a decreasing order of evaluation.

The `concat` function takes a list of sequences and returns the sequence that is the concatenation of all the sequences in the list. It thus generalizes the `List.@` and `String.^` operators. When joining together more than two sequences, the `concat` function is likely to be more efficient than a chain of the corresponding binary operator. Note also that `concat` is not defined for arrays.

7.1.1 Indexed iterations

For vectors and arrays, any element-wise operation involves selecting elements by their indices, and so it is natural to allow for operations to work not only on the elements themselves but their indices as well. Thus, for these sequence types, the iterator functions `app`, `map` (vectors only), `fold`, and `find` have variants that operate on index-element pairs (i.e., pairs of the form $(i, sub(s, i))$) rather than elements. The index-passing variants have an "i" appended to the function name, e.g., `appi`.

As an example, here `appi` is used to print out a table of the elements of a vector of strings numbered by their indices:

```
fun prVector (v : string vector) = let
    fun f (i, x) = (
            TextIO.print(Int.toString i); TextIO.print " ";
            TextIO.print x; TextIO.print "\n")
    in
      Vector.appi f v
    end
```

The non-index-passing form of an iterator can be derived from the index-passing version by providing functions that ignore the index parameter. For instance, `map f s` is equivalent to `mapi (f o #2) s`. On the other hand, the index-passing versions can be constructed using the basic `foldl` function. Thus, `mapi` can be written as

```
fun mapi f s = let
        fun g (v,(i,l)) = (i+1,(f(i,v))::l)
        in rev (#2 (foldl g (0,[]) s)) end
```

This type of construction has to be used with lists, since indexed iterations are not provided for them.

7.2   Lists

As one of the basic types in functional programming, lists have been extensively used in a wide variety of applications and are the subject of many libraries. The Basis library intentionally provides just a small set of what were deemed the most basic and useful list functions. We have described many of these above, in the context of sequences. Of those that are specific to lists, we here wish to mention just two. For further information on lists, we refer the reader to any book on SML programming.

First is the getItem function, which is the list analogue of the getc and input1 functions for substrings and stream I/O. With it, the programmer can use a char list as a character source, which can be fed to scanning functions to read in values. See Chapter 5 for a complete discussion of this approach. As an example, the function

```
fun scanPair (l : char list) = let
        val scan = Int.scan StringCvt.HEX List.getItem
        val (i1, rest) = valOf (scan l)
        val rest = StringCvt.skipWS List.getItem rest
        val (i2, rest) = valOf (scan rest)
        in
           SOME (i1, i2)
        end handle _ => NONE
```

takes a list of characters and scans in two hexadecimal integers separated by space.

The second function worth mentioning is revAppend. Consider a function that takes a predicate and a list and removes the first item in the list satisfying the predicate. We can implement the function as

```
fun remove pred l = let
        fun f (l', []) = rev l'
          | f (l', x::rest) = if pred x then (rev l')@rest
                                        else f (x::l', rest)
        in
           f ([], l)
        end
```

In the case where an item is found, the expression (rev *l'*)@*rest* involves a lot of unnecessary work, in essence reversing *l'* twice. The same semantics are supplied more efficiently by replacing the expression with revAppend(*l'*,*l*), which recursively moves the head of *l'* to the head of *l*.

Another way to implement remove is

```
fun remove pred l = let
    fun f [] = []
      | f (x::rest) = if pred x then rest
                              else x::(f rest)
    in
      f l
    end
```

thereby avoiding the auxiliary list entirely. Unfortunately, because of overhead, the performance here typically tends to be much worse than using the previous implementation with `revAppend`. In general, this pattern of partially traversing a list and then reinserting the processed items in their original order is most effectively handled using an auxiliary list and the `revAppend` function.

Another use for `revAppend` arises when one wishes to combine two lists but the element order is unimportant. In this case, `revAppend(l,l')` will be less expensive than the normal *l@l'*.

7.3 Array modification

The distinguishing property of arrays, and the reason for their existence in SML, is that they are mutable. To alter an entry, one simply updates the entry in place rather than creating a whole new array, as must be done with vectors. Thus, there is no `map` function for arrays. In its place, we have the `modify` operation and its corresponding index-passing version `modifyi`. Each entry in the array is replaced by its image under the function parameter.

At times, it is useful to copy an entire block of elements from one array into another. For this purpose, the Library provides the two functions `copy` and `copyVec`, the latter for the case when the source is a compatible vector. These operations are akin to the `BitBlt` operation from raster graphics.

7.4 Subsequences and slices

Many common manipulations of sequences are based on operations on subsequences. Hence, the Basis library provides various functions that create or work on subsequences. The treatment of subsequences for lists is quite different from that for vectors and arrays, but there is some overlap in function.

For lists, we have `filter`, `partition`, and `mapPartial`. The `filter` and `partition` operations select elements of a list using a predicate, returning subsequence(s) consisting of selected elements of the original sequence. The former is a specialization of the latter:

```
filter = #1 o partition
```

The `mapPartial` function combines the map iterator with filtering based on whether the function returns `NONE` or `SOME`.

There are also `take` and `drop` operations that return initial and final segments of a list. These can be combined to yield a list analogue of the vector/array slices discussed below.

```
fun slice (l, start, NONE) =
        List.drop (l, start)
  | slice (l, start, SOME len) =
        List.take (List.drop (l, start), n)
```

Note that this definition of `slice` for a list produces a new list from which one cannot recover the original list, a difference from array and vector slices.

For vectors and arrays, the notion of subsequence is captured by a *slice*. Conceptually, a slice denotes a triple

$$\{seq: \text{ 'a array, start: int, len: int}\}$$

and represents the subsequence

$$seq[start..start + len - 1]$$

where `start` must satisfy $0 \leq$ `start` $\leq$ `length(arr)` and `len` must satisfy $0 \leq$ `len` $\leq$ `length(arr)` $-$ `start`. The slice types are abstract in order to guarantee these constraints. The `base` function maps a slice back to its corresponding triple, so it is possible to extract the underlying sequence.

All of the iterators defined for vector and array sequences (both plain and indexed) have analogues defined for the corresponding slice types. Note that, for slices, the iterators providing an index, such as `appi`, use the index of the element in the slice rather than the index of the element in the base array. These functions are packaged in the `ArraySlice` and `VectorSlice` structures. There are also monomorphic slice structures for each of the monomorphic array and vector structures (e.g., `Word8Vector-Slice` for `Word8Vector`).

When a vector of characters is more naturally viewed as a string, structures matching the signature `SUBSTRING` provide `substring` types. The substring and slice types are identical, but the interfaces are different.

7.5   Operating on pairs of lists

It is not uncommon to want to process two lists simultaneously. To support these situations, there is a `ListPair` structure that provides versions of the iterators `app`, `map`, `foldl`, `foldr`, `all`, and `exists`. It also provides the functions `zip` and `unzip` for transforming a pair of lists into a list of pairs, and vice versa.

When simultaneously iterating over two lists, there is a choice of how to handle the situation where the lists do not have the same length. One can either stop whenever the shorter list has been exhausted, or one can fail (raise an exception) when the lists are of different lengths. Since both policies are appropriate in the right circumstances, the `ListPair` provides two versions of each iterator and the `zip` function. For instance, there is an `app` function that accepts lists of different length, and a `appEq` function that requires it's arguments to have the same length.

7.6 Two-dimensional arrays

There are no analogues of `ListPair` for arrays and vectors, but there is support for rectangular two-dimensional arrays in the `Array2` structure and its monomorphic variants (`MONO_ARRAY2`).

The `Array2` structure provides two-dimensional generalizations of the array constructors `array`, `fromList`, and `tabulate`. It also provides two-dimensional versions of the iterators `app` and `fold` and the updating function `modify` (in basic and index-passing forms), as well as the updating function `copy`. The basic iterators traverse the entire array. The index-passing forms, as well as `copy`, provide additional flexibility by accepting a parameter of type `region`. This type is the two-dimensional analogue of the `slice` type. In contrast to the `slice` types, a `region` is a concrete record:

```
{ base : 'a array,
  row : int, col : int,
  nrows : int option, ncols : int option}
```

so there are no special functions for dealing with it. It represents the rectangular subarray of `base` consisting of those elements with position (i, j) where $row \leq i < rmax$ and $col \leq j < cmax$. Here, $rmax$ is `nRows(base)` if `nrows` is NONE and `row + nr` if `nrows` is `SOME(nr)`. An analogous definition holds for $cmax$.

All the iterators (and `tabulate`) are parameterized with a `traversal` argument, which determines whether the traversal of the array region will be in row-major or column-major order. Thus, with iterators, indices are always non-decreasing; the only variation is whether the row index or the column index is in the inner loop.

8

Input/Output

8.1 The I/O model

The I/O subsystem provides standard functions for reading and writing files and devices. In particular, the subsystem provides:

- buffered reading and writing;

- arbitrary lookahead, using an underlying "lazy streams" mechanism;

- dynamic redirection of input or output;

- uniform interface to text and binary data;

- layering of stream translations, through an underlying "reader/writer" interface;

- unbuffered input/output, through the reader/writer interface or even through the buffered stream interface;

- primitives sufficient to construct facilities for random access on a file.

The subsystem allows for efficient implementation, minimizing system calls and memory-memory copying. In addition, the interfaces provided are abstract over both the type of items being handled and the source of the items. Although typically the items will be characters or `Word8.word` values, associated with an operating system file, the specification equally allows reading a stream of integers generated by some algorithm.

The I/O system is a four-layer stack of interfaces. From top to bottom, they are

Imperative I/O Buffered, conventional (side-effecting) input and output with redirection facility.

Stream I/O Buffered "lazy functional stream" input; buffered conventional output.

Primitive I/O A uniform interface for unbuffered reading and writing at the "system call" level, though not necessarily via actual system calls.

System I/O Input and output operating directly on operating system file descriptors or handles using `Posix.IO` or its equivalent for some other operating system. These structures are optional; an implementation may choose not to make I/O at this level directly available to the SML programmer.

Most programmers will want to operate at the stream I/O or imperative I/O layer; only for special purposes should it be necessary to go to a lower layer of the I/O stack.

All conforming implementations must provide two instances of the I/O stacks: `Text-IO`, where the individual elements are characters (`Char.char`), and `BinIO`, where the elements are unsigned bytes (`Word8.word`). The former provides a few additional operations specific to text-oriented I/O. Users can also create new instantiations of the hierarchy using other element types. The Library defines optional functors, `Imperative-IO`, `StreamIO`, and `PrimIO`, to facilitate building new I/O stacks.

Concerning the semantics of I/O, those functions at the lowest level are dependent on a given operating system and, if available, are described in corresponding structures. The model provided by the primitive I/O layer is fairly basic and is described in the `PRIM_IO` manual pages below. Here we concentrate on some of the concepts concerning the top two layers. Further details can be found in the `IMPERATIVE_IO` and `STREAM_IO` manual pages.

The examples we give in this chapter use `TextIO` and characters, but the principles are the same for `BinIO` or any element type. Using `TextIO` also allows us to note some text-specific aspects of I/O.

8.1.1 Imperative I/O

We can quickly dispose of explanations about the imperative I/O level, as the semantics of that level can be given by defining imperative streams as references to the underlying stream I/O types and delegating I/O operations to that level. Input at the imperative I/O level simply rebinds the reference to the new "lazy stream." For example, Listing 8.1 shows what part of a structure matching `IMPERATIVE_IO` might look like. The principal feature of the imperative level, beyond allowing an imperative programming style, is the ability to redirect I/O, so that the source or target of I/O operations can be changed dynamically. This feature is described in Section 8.2.2 and Section 8.2.4.

8.1.2 Stream I/O

An input stream coming from the stream I/O layer provides a way to read data in a functional style. A program reading from an input stream receives the input, as would

```
structure ImperativeIO : IMPERATIVE_IO =
  struct
    structure StreamIO : STREAM_IO = ...
    datatype instream = INS of StreamIO.instream ref
    datatype outstream = OUTS of StreamIO.outstream ref
    fun input (INS(i as ref ins)) = let
          val (v, ins') = StreamIO.input ins
          in
            i := ins';
            v
          end
    fun output (OUTS(ref outs), v) = StreamIO.output (outs, v)
    ...
  end
```

Listing 8.1: Part of an implementation for `ImperativeIO`

occur with traditional imperative I/O, plus a new input stream, which represents the rest
of the stream. To get additional input, the program reads from the new stream; reading
from the original stream will only supply the same input that the program received
originally. Thus, the function

```
fun twoLines (ins : TextIO.StreamIO.instream) = let
      val (line1, ins') = valOf(TextIO.StreamIO.inputLine ins)
      val (line2, _) = valOf(TextIO.StreamIO.inputLine ins')
      in
        (line1, line2)
      end
```

reads and returns two lines of text input (assuming that there are two lines available).
The use of `ins'` rather than `ins` for reading the second line is crucial. Without the
prime, the input operation would simply reread the first line. Using a functional input
stream provides the programmer with a simple mechanism for unbounded lookahead.

Internally, each input stream s can be viewed as a sequence of "available" elements
(the buffer or sequence of buffers) and a mechanism (the `reader`) for obtaining more.
After an input operation, e.g., `val (v, s') = input(s)`, it is guaranteed that v
is a prefix of the available elements of s.

An output stream is simply an abstraction for writing bytes to some operating system
device, such as a disk, a network, or a terminal. It will typically implement a buffering
mechanism to store output, and actually write it, using the underlying `writer`, only
when necessary, in order to reduce the number of relatively expensive operating system
writes. Note that there is really no operational difference between imperative and non-
imperative output streams.

When finished with a stream, the program can close the stream using `closeIn` or `closeOut`. Closing the stream has the effect of closing the underlying `reader` or `writer`, which in turn usually releases operating system resources such as open file descriptors. In addition, when an `outstream` is closed, its buffer is first flushed before its `writer` is closed. Note also that it is perfectly legal to continue to read from a closed input stream, whereas writing to an output stream will cause an exception.

As a convenience, the Basis requires that any streams opened using `TextIO` or `BinIO` will be closed automatically upon exit. In general, it is good programming practice to close streams explicitly.

The `STREAM_IO` interface allows the user direct access to the underlying `reader` or `writer`, but at a cost. The operations `getReader` or `getWriter` return the corresponding component of the I/O stack and, as a side effect, make the stream inactive. When applied to an `instream`, we refer to the stream as *truncated*. The stream appears to still be active, in that reading from the stream will return input as usual, up to a point. Once it has exhausted its buffers, a truncated stream has no mechanism for refilling them. From that point on, input operations always return the empty vector. In the case of an `outstream`, we refer to the stream as *terminated*. It is essentially closed, in that any output operation will cause an exception to be raised.

In essence, the only difference between a closed stream and one that is truncated or terminated is that, in the former case, the underlying `reader` or `writer` is closed.

8.1.3   End-of-stream

In Unix, and perhaps in other operating systems, the notion of *end-of-stream* refers to a condition on the input rather than a value read from the input or a place in the input. By convention, a `read` system call that returns zero bytes is interpreted to mean that the current end-of-stream has been reached. The next read on that stream, however, could return more bytes. This situation might arise if, for example,

- the user enters control-D (`#"^D"`) on an interactive terminal stream and then types more characters;

- input reaches the end of a disk file, but then some other process appends more bytes to the file.

Consequently, the following function is *not* guaranteed to return true:

```
fun atEnd (f : TextIO.StreamIO.instream) = let
    val z = TextIO.StreamIO.endOfStream f
    val (a, f') = TextIO.StreamIO.input f
    val x = TextIO.StreamIO.endOfStream f'
in
    x = z
end
```

whereas the following function will always return true:

```
fun atEnd' (f : TextIO.StreamIO.instream) = let
    val z = TextIO.StreamIO.endOfStream f
    val (a, f') = TextIO.StreamIO.input f
    val x = TextIO.StreamIO.endOfStream f
  in
    x = z
  end
```

The difference is the use of `f` rather than `f'` in the second call to `endOfStream`. For untruncated input streams, when an input operation returns an empty vector (or `endOfStream` returns `true`), we are *currently* at the end of the stream. If further data are appended to the underlying file or stream, the next input operation will deliver new elements. Thus, a file may have more than one end-of-stream. If the end-of-stream condition holds, an input will return the empty vector, but the end-of-stream condition may become false as a result of this input operation. Note that, after all buffered input is read from a truncated input stream, the input stream remains in a permanent end-of-stream condition.

8.1.4 Translation

Text streams (`TextIO`) contain lines of text and control characters. A text line is terminated with a newline (NL) character `#"\n"`, also referred to as a linefeed (LF) character.

In some environments, the external representation of a text file is different from its internal representation. For example, in Microsoft Windows, text files on disk have lines ending with a carriage return (CR) character `#"\r"` as well as the newline, while in memory they contain only `"\n"` at the end of each line. Thus, on input, the `"\r\n"` terminators are translated to a single `#"\n"` character. The inverse translation is done on output. More substantial translation will be done on systems that support, for example, escape-coded Unicode [Uni03] text files.

Binary streams (`BinIO`) match the external files byte for byte.

8.2 Using the I/O subsystem

We next consider how to do I/O using the Library and the facilities in the top three I/O layers: `IMPERATIVE_IO`, `STREAM_IO`, and `PRIM_IO`, and how to move from one layer to another.

8.2.1 Opening files

Given a filename, `TextIO.openIn` and `TextIO.openOut` open a file for input or output, respectively:

```
fun openInAndOut (inname,outname) = let
      val f : TextIO.instream  = TextIO.openIn inname
      val g : TextIO.outstream = TextIO.openOut outname
    in
      (f,g)
    end
```

Of course, something might go wrong: perhaps a file does not exist or (in the case of `openOut`) cannot be created. Then the exception `IO.Io` will be raised, giving information about what operation failed (e.g., `"openIn"`), upon what filename (e.g., `"myfile"`), and the cause of the failure (e.g., `OS.SysErr("No such file or directory",...)`). As usual, a good way of telling the user what went wrong is with `exnMessage`:

```
fun openIt (filename : string) : TextIO.instream option =
      SOME(TextIO.openIn filename)
        handle e => (print(exnMessage e ^ "\n"); NONE)
```

which prints something like

```
Io: openIn failed on "myfile", No such file or directory
```

There are other ways to open streams. One can use `TextIO.openString(s)` to open an input stream whose content is the string s. Opening a file for writing causes output to go at the beginning of the file, erasing the previous content of the file if it already existed. To avoid this truncation, the code can use `TextIO.openAppend`, which preserves the current file content and causes any output to be written at the end of the file.

Operating system interfaces will typically provide a mechanism for converting an open file descriptor into a TYREF STRID=PrimIO/reader/, which can then easily be converted into a functional or imperative stream. For example, the following function uses a POSIX file descriptor to create a functional input stream:

```
fun openIn (fd : Posix.IO.file_desc, name : string) = let
      val rdr = Posix.IO.mkTextReader {
                    fd = fd,
                    name = name,
                    initBlkMode = true
                }
    in
      TextIO.StreamIO.mkInstream(rdr, "")
    end
```

8.2.2 Imperative stream input (`IMPERATIVE_IO`)

The `TextIO` module provides side-effecting operations on input streams. It is a simple task to open a file, read its contents into a string, and close the file:

```
fun getContents (filename: string) = let
      val f : TextIO.instream = TextIO.openIn filename
      val s : string = TextIO.inputAll f
   in
      TextIO.closeIn f; s
   end
```

Or we can read one character at a time, but the program will typically be much less efficient:

```
fun getContents (filename: string) = let
      val f = TextIO.openIn filename
      fun loop (accum: char list) = (case TextIO.input1 f
            of NONE => accum
             | SOME c => loop (c::accum)
            (* end case *))
      val s = String.implode (rev (loop []))
   in
      TextIO.closeIn f; s
   end
```

A good compromise between reading the whole file at once and reading one character at a time is to read one "chunk" at a time, where chunks are defined at the convenience of the SML system and the operating system. The `TextIO.input` function returns a bunch of characters (typically a thousand or two) at once, usually quite efficiently:

```
fun getContents (filename: string) = let
      val f = TextIO.openIn filename
      fun loop(accum: string list) = (case TextIO.input f
            of "" => accum
             | s => loop(s::accum)
            (* end case *))
      val s = String.concat(rev(loop []))
   in
      TextIO.closeIn f; s
   end
```

If the stream is interactive (e.g., receiving characters from a keyboard), the chunks returned by `input` are typically individual lines of text; but this behavior is not guaranteed. To get one line at a time, use `TextIO.inputLine`.

To read exactly n characters from a stream f, use `TextIO.inputN(f, n)`.

One advantage of imperative stream input is the ability to redirect the source. For example, one might be aware of a function g that reads from `TextIO.stdIn`. To use g to read from another source, we can do the following:

```
fun redirectIn (g, fname) = let
      val f = TextIO.openIn fname
      val saveStdIn = TextIO.getInstream TextIO.stdIn
   in
      TextIO.setInstream (TextIO.stdIn, TextIO.getInstream f);
      g ();
      TextIO.setInstream (TextIO.stdIn, saveStdIn)
   end
```

This function opens the file `fname` for reading and saves the stream I/O component un-derlying `stdIn`, replacing it with the stream I/O component associated with the stream open on `fname`. When `g` is called, its use of `stdIn` will feed it the contents of `fname`. To finish, `redirectIn` reinstalls the original `stdIn` stream.

8.2.3   Functional stream input (`STREAM_IO`)

In keeping with the functional style of the SML programming language, we may not wish to use the imperative I/O operations that say, "read characters from stream `s` re-moving them from `s` in the process."

The `TextIO.StreamIO` structure provides a functional (declarative) view of in-put streams, that is, "read a character from stream `s`, yielding an element `c` and the remainder of the stream `s'`, all without destroying the value of `s`."

We can extract a functional input stream from a `TextIO.instream` by applying `TextIO.getInstream`:

```
fun openStream filename : TextIO.StreamIO.instream =
        TextIO.getInstream(TextIO.openIn filename)
```

For the remainder of this chapter we shall assume the following binding:

```
structure TS = TextIO.StreamIO
```

Here are the functional stream versions of the programs shown in the previous section to read all the characters in a file.

```
(* Reading the whole stream at once *)
fun getContents (filename: string) = let
    val f = TextIO.getInstream(TextIO.openIn filename)
    val (s, _) = TS.inputAll f
    in
      TS.closeIn f; s
    end

(* Reading one character at a time *)
fun getContents(filename: string) = let
    val f = TextIO.getInstream(TextIO.openIn filename)
    fun loop(accum, f) = (case TS.input1 f
            of NONE => (TS.closeIn f; accum)
             | SOME(c,f') => loop(c::accum, f')
            (* end case *))
    in
      String.implode(rev(loop([], f)))
    end
```

```
(* Reading a chunk at a time *)
fun getContents(filename: string) = let
    val f = TextIO.getInstream(TextIO.openIn filename)
    fun loop (accum, f) =
        case TS.input f of
            ("",f') => (TS.closeIn f'; accum)
          | (chunk,f') => loop(chunk::accum, f')
    in
      String.concat(rev(loop([], f)))
    end
```

The stream I/O layer also has functions corresponding to the `inputN` and `input-Line` functions found in `TextIO`.

The magical thing about functional input streams is that one can read from the same stream value again and again. For example, we can write a function that eats the word `"thousand"` if it appears at the current file location and otherwise leaves the stream where it was:

```
fun eatThousand (f: TS.instream) : TS.instream = (
    case TS.inputN(f, size "thousand")
     of ("thousand",f') => f'
      | _ => f
    (* end case *))
```

Similarly, we can skip past any whitespace that appears at the current point in a file:

```
fun skipWhiteSpace(f: TS.instream) : TS.instream = (
    case TS.input1 f
     of SOME(c, f') =>
        if Char.isSpace c then skipWhiteSpace f'
        else f
      | NONE => f
    (* end case *))
```

Skipping over whitespace is sufficiently common that the Library provides the function `StringCvt.skipWS` for this purpose.

Reading a pattern from a stream

Suppose one wants to read a string that matches a certain pattern. Instead of reading the pieces one at a time and then concatenating them all together, one can read the pattern and throw away the pieces, and then use `inputN` to pick up the string from the starting point.

For example, an implementation of `inputLine` might work like this:

```
fun inputLine (f : TS.instream) = let
    fun count (n, g) = (case TS.input1 g
            of SOME(#"\n", g') => SOME(TS.inputN(f, n+1))
             | SOME(_, g') => count(n+1, g')
             | NONE => if (n = 0)
                 then NONE
                 else let val (s, g') = TS.inputN(f, n)
                   in
                     SOME(s^"\n", g')
                   end
        (* end case *))
    in
       count (0, f)
    end
```

The `count` function counts (and discards) each character until the newline is found and then uses `inputN` on the original stream `f` to efficiently grab the whole line.

Library functions for scanning input streams

A powerful way to use functional input streams is with the `StringCvt` structure, and with the `scan` functions provided in `Int`, `Real`, `Date`, and other structures. The `StringCvt.reader` type is

```
type ('elem,'stream) reader = 'stream -> ('elem,'stream) option
```

This type is used to denote a function that takes a source of input and, if possible, reads a value of type `'elem` from the beginning of the input, returning the value read and the remainder of the input. Note that `TextIO.StreamIO.input1` is already a `(char,instream) reader`, which means that any function that uses a `reader` can operate directly on a functional input stream. The `scan` functions convert a reader of one type of element into a reader of another type. Thus, to scan an integer in decimal format one can use

```
val scanInt =
      Int.scan StringCvt.DEC TextIO.StreamIO.input1
```

where `Int.scan` changes the character reader `input1` into an integer reader. Here is a larger example. We wish to read a sequence of ten real numbers from an input file:

```
fun read10 (infile : string) = let
    val f = TextIO.getInstream(TextIO.openIn infile)
    val cr = TS.input1    (* character reader *)
    val rr = Real.scan cr (* real reader *)
    fun getN (0, xs, f) = (rev xs,f)
      | getN (n, xs, f) = let
          val (x,f') = valOf (rr f)
          in
            getN (n-1, x::xs, f')
          end
    in
       getN(10,[],f)
    end
```

Note that this code raises the `Option` exception if there are fewer than ten reals in the input stream.

Relationship of imperative streams to functional streams

An imperative input stream (e.g., `TextIO.stdIn`) behaves as if it were a reference to a functional stream. The functional stream can be extracted using `getInstream`, and a new functional stream can be inserted using `setInstream`. Therefore, a function such as `TextIO.input` could be implemented as follows:

```
fun input (ins : TextIO.instream) = let
    val f = TextIO.getInstream ins
    val (s,f') = TextIO.StreamIO.input f
    in
        TextIO.setInstream(ins, f');
        s
    end
```

The `getInstream` and `setInstream` operations make it possible to switch back and forth between the imperative and functional views of the same input stream. In general, given `strm` of type `TextIO.instream`, one can call `getInstream(strm)` to obtain the stream I/O component, use it functionally to obtain a sequence of inputs and new streams, and then reinstall the final result stream `f'` back into `strm` using `setInstream(strm,f')`.

To generate a new imperative `TextIO.instream` from a `TextIO.StreamIO.-instream`, use `TextIO.mkInstream`.

Getting characters without blocking

When processing interactive input from keyboards or sockets, one sometimes wishes to get all the characters that have been typed, without knowing how many are available, and without the risk of "blocking," that is, waiting for more characters to be typed. This goal can be accomplished using the `canInput` function: if `canInput` returns `SOME(n)`, then reading n characters is guaranteed not to block.

```
fun getAllAvailable (f : TS.instream) = let
    fun count (n, f': TS.instream) = (case TS.canInput(f',1)
        of SOME 0 => n
         | NONE => n
         | SOME _ => let val (s,f'') = TS.input f'
             in
                 count(n + size s, f'')
             end
        (* end case *))
    in
        TS.inputN(f, count(0,f))
    end
```

For more sophisticated use of non-blocking I/O, the `PRIM_IO` interface provides non-blocking primitives.

Random access input

There are two models of random access input. The stream I/O (`TextIO.StreamIO`) layer supports lazy functional streams. Once one has a stream value, one can always go back and read it again. This mechanism is an in-memory, seek-to-previous-position kind of random access, and it is efficient and appropriate for many uses.

The other form of random access allows seeking forward and back, and keeps the file in secondary storage (disk) instead of in memory. The stream I/O layer does not support this technique directly. Instead, one must use `StreamIO.getReader` to extract the underlying reader, perform a random access operation on the reader, and then build a new stream using `StreamIO.mkInstream`; see Section 8.2.5 below.

8.2.4   Stream output

Stream output in SML also comes in two flavors, provided by `TextIO.outstream` and `TextIO.StreamIO.outstream`, but they are both imperative! The difference between these two layers is that a `TextIO.outstream` can be made to point to different output streams dynamically, as will be explained below.

Opening and using an output stream is straightforward. For example, the following function writes to the file specified by its argument:

```
fun hello (myfile : string) = let
    val f = TextIO.openOut myfile
    in
      TextIO.output(f, "Hello, ");
      TextIO.output(f, "world!\n");
      TextIO.closeOut f
    end
```

Buffering

Individual calls to `output` and `output1` are buffered within the Library, so that fewer (expensive) calls are made to the operating system. When the buffer is full, or when the stream is closed, or when the program explicitly requests it, the buffer is flushed or written to the device. For interactive text output streams, writing a newline character (`#"\n"`) also causes the buffer to be flushed, which mostly achieves the expected interactive behavior. Sometimes, the Library may not know when an output stream is being used interactively, or the output string may be intended as a prompt, and therefore not end in a newline. To force the buffer to be written to the outside world, one can use the `TextIO.flushOut` function.

Random access output

Random access for output streams is a bit different than for input streams. `getPosOut` returns an `out_pos` value, representing the current position in the output. If, at some

```
fun withOutstream (f, g) func = let
    val f' = TextIO.getOutstream f
    val g' = TextIO.getOutstream g
  in
    TextIO.setOutstream(f, g');
    func () before TextIO.setOutstream(f, f')
      handle e => (TextIO.setOutstream(f, f'); raise e)
  end

fun sayHello () = TextIO.output(TextIO.stdOut, "Hello!\n")

fun redirect logfile = let
    val s = TextIO.openOut logfile
  in
    withOutstream (TextIO.stdOut, s) sayHello;
    TextIO.closeOut s
  end
```

Listing 8.2: Generating an endless stream of blank characters

later time, the program wishes to return to that position, for example, to overwrite the text there, it can call setPosOut with the out_pos value. This operation will reset the output stream to that position.

Because the out_pos type is abstract, one cannot add or subtract integers to move n characters forward or back. As with input streams, one can only return to a position previously visited. Also as with input, to use more powerful forms of random access, it is necessary to go down to the primitive I/O layer of the I/O system; see Section 8.2.5 below.

Dynamic binding of output streams

Each TextIO.outstream behaves like a reference to a TextIO.StreamIO.-outstream. It is possible to extract the latter from the former using getOutstream and then, using setOutstream, insert a different StreamIO.outstream.

It is not unusual for an I/O function to be written relying on the standard I/O streams. A programmer may wish to use the function, but the source is not available and the output, say, needs to go into a specified file. We present a solution to this problem in Listing 8.2, by rebinding the standard output stream stdOut to a different underlying stream. The function redirect runs the sayHello function with stdOut temporarily redirected to the file logfile. Note that withOutstream first saves the underlying functional stream as f' and then restores it into f before returning.

8.2.5 Readers and writers (`PRIM_IO`)

The primitive I/O layer of the I/O system provides unbuffered input and output independent of the operating system. A `reader` is an object supporting primitive input operations, and a `writer` supports primitive output operations. (Note that the primitive I/O `reader` has no connection with `StringCvt.reader`.) Typically, each read or write operation at this level corresponds to an operating system call.

A `StreamIO.instream` contains a `reader`, along with a buffer of characters that have been read using the `reader` but which have not yet been returned from the input stream. This (`reader`, `buffer`) pair can be extracted using `StreamIO.get-Reader`:

```
fun getPrim filename = let
    val f = TextIO.getInstream(TextIO.openIn filename)
    val (reader,buffer) = TS.getReader f
    in
        (reader,buffer)
    end
```

In this case, since the file has just been opened and no I/O operations have been performed, the buffer should be empty and the second value returned by the function will be the empty string `""`.

A reader is basically a record of various operations, in particular, various functions for reading input, all wrapped in a RD data constructor. We could, for example, read 1024 characters and then rebuild an `instream` (using `mkInstream`, the inverse of `getReader`):

```
fun read1024 filename = let
    val (rdr,_) = getPrim filename
    val TextPrimIO.RD{readVec=SOME(read),...} = rdr
    val s = read 1024
    in
        (s, TS.mkInstream(rdr,""))
    end
```

The first character in the returned input stream will be the 1025th character of the file.

Sometimes the programmer might need to create an open `reader` for a given file. The Library does not provide a operating-system independent mechanism for creating readers and writers directly, but the result can be obtained using the functions available:

```
fun openReader fname = let
    val ins = TextIO.openIn fname
    in
        #1(TextIO.StreamIO.getReader(TextIO.getInstream ins))
    end
```

```
local
  structure BIO = BinIO
  structure PIO = BinPrimIO
in
  fun read10 filename = let
        val fIn = BIO.getInstream (BIO.openIn filename)
        val (rd,buf) = BIO.StreamIO.getReader fIn
        val PIO.RD{setPos=SOME setPosIn,readVec=SOME read,...}
            = rd
      in
        setPosIn 1000;
        read 10
      end
end
```

Listing 8.3: Binary random access

Random access seeking, reading, and writing

Moving from the stream I/O layer to the primitive I/O layer and back gives one the power to do sophisticated random access on files. Readers and writers have several (optional) random access functions:

```
type pos
val reader = RD{ . . .
  getPos : (unit->pos) option,
  setPos : (pos->unit) option,
  endPos : (unit->pos) option,
  . . .
}

val writer = WR{ . . .
  getPos : (unit->pos) option,
  setPos : (pos->unit) option,
  endPos : (unit->pos) option,
  . . .
}
```

The `TextPrimIO.pos` type is an abstract type, but `BinPrimIO.pos` must be `Position.int`. This requirement allows flexible random access on binary readers and writers. Suppose we want to read ten bytes from a file at location 1000. Listing 8.3 shows how this goal might be achieved. First, it uses `BinIO` to open the file and extract the reader. Then it employs `PRIM_IO` operations to accomplish the task.

It is even possible to use the primitive I/O layer to do the seeking and then revert to the stream I/O layer to do the reading and writing, using `mkInstream` and mk-

```
local
  structure BIO = BinIO
  structure BSIO = BIO.StreamIO
  structure PIO = BinPrimIO
in
  fun read10 filename = let
        val fIn = BIO.getInstream (BIO.openIn filename)
        val (rd,buf) = BIO.StreamIO.getReader fIn
        val PIO.RD{setPos=SOME setPosIn, ...} = rd
        val _ = setPosIn 1000
        val f = BSIO.mkInstream(rd,Word8Vector.fromList[])
        val (s,f') = BSIO.inputN(f,10)
        in
          s
        end
end
```

Listing 8.4: Binary random access followed by stream reading

Outstream. Listing 8.4 shows how to modify the previous example to use this technique.

To do random access input and output on the same file, it is necessary to obtain a reader and a writer that operate on the same operating system open file descriptor, which is possible to do by constructing a reader and writer that call the underlying operating system's I/O operations (e.g., the functions in the Posix.IO structure). Any buffering layered on top needs to be implemented so as to coordinate reads and writes, to ensure that both input and output have the same view of the data. Typically, this coordination requires some form of resynchronizing of the stream I/O streams with the underlying file whenever the code switches between seeking, reading, and writing. Existing stream I/O streams need to be truncated or terminated, and StreamIO.mkInstream or StreamIO.mkOutstream are used to create new buffered views of the file.

Random access with text I/O

Random access with integer positions in a text file is problematic because, on many systems, text has different representations in external files than in SML strings. For example, newlines are one character in memory but may be two characters in disk files, or Unicode characters may have different external and in-memory representations.

In general, one can use the same approaches as described above for binary I/O, based on a reader or writer from BinPrimIO. From the BinPrimIO object, one then creates a reader or writer for TextPrimIO by integrating the components with the desired byte-to-char translation algorithm. For files and systems where no translation

```
fun infiniteBlanks () : TS.instream = let
      val someBlanks = CharVector.tabulate(1024, fn _ => #" ")
      fun read n = if n >= 1024 then someBlanks
                    else substring(someBlanks, 0, n)
      val rd = TextPrimIO.RD {
                  name = "blanks", chunkSize = 1024,
                  readVec = SOME read,
                  readArr = NONE,
                  readVecNB = SOME(fn n => SOME(read n)),
                  readArrNB = NONE,
                  block = SOME(fn() => ()),
                  canInput = SOME(fn() => true),
                  avail = fn() => NONE,
                  getPos = NONE,
                  setPos = NONE,
                  endPos = NONE,
                  verifyPos = NONE,
                  close = fn() => (),
                  ioDesc = NONE
               }
   in
         TS.mkInstream(rd, "")
   end
```

Listing 8.5: Generating an endless stream of blank characters

is done, e.g., standard Unix I/O, one can use the facilities provided by the `Byte` structure to provide the trivial conversions.

Algorithmic streams

In some cases one may want an `instream` that is not connected to any operating system resource but which generates characters on demand. One can create such a stream by constructing a reader and then using `mkInstream`. For example, Listing 8.5 exhibits a function that creates an input stream generating an infinite stream of blank characters.

One occasionally useful type of algorithmic stream, especially for writing, is the null stream. Anything written to a null stream disappears; a read on a null stream always returns an end-of-stream. This behavior is the abstraction provided by the `/dev/null` file in Unix. The `PRIM_IO` interface defines the functions `nullRd` and `nullWr`, which can be used to generate a reader and writer with null semantics. To get a higher-level stream, one uses the usual techniques, e.g.,

```
fun nullOut () =
      TS.mkOutstream (TextPrimIO.nullWr(), IO.NO_BUF)
```

returns a null output stream for writing text.

8.2.6   Comparison of I/O functions

This chapter has presented many ways of reading and writing, some more efficient than others. Although the absolute and relative speeds of these operations will vary with implementation and hardware, we can note a few general characteristics.

- Stream I/O input is modestly more efficient than imperative I/O input if an implementation constructs the latter employing the reference semantics of a `ref` cell. More sophisticated implementations, however, can be significantly faster than stream I/O, avoiding the bookkeeping and memory management overhead implicit in the functional approach.

- The time spent per element in input tends to increase as the size of the input requested decreases.

- In principle, the most efficient mechanism is to obtain the entire input at once using `StreamIO.inputAll` and then process the input using array, vector, or string operations, especially the higher-level functions provided by the "slice" structures `MONO_ARRAY_SLICE`, `MONO_VECTOR_SLICE`, and `SUBSTRING`. This approach is not always feasible because of the need for interactive I/O or the requirements of library functions.

- If `inputAll` is not appropriate, `input` is a good substitute. It typically returns the result of a single operating system read. For disk files, the result usually will be a sizable chunk. For interactive text I/O, the result will usually be the next input line or character, depending on the mode of the operating system device.

- The `input1` function, especially in its stream I/O form, is convenient for text scanning, but it can also be more expensive than expected. This fact should be kept in mind by C programmers who are used to the negligible cost of the analogous C function `getc`.

- The above comments concern just the basic reading of input. The particular task at hand can have a dramatic effect on the relative speeds. For example, if one simply wishes to count the number of newlines in a file, a function using `input1` may well be the fastest.

- If efficiency is particularly important, the programmer can use the facilities provided by the `reader` at the primitive I/O level, or operating system functions, if available and portability is not of concern. In particular, if the `readArr` or `readArrNB` is available in the `reader`, the code can avoid additional copying of the input.

Similar remarks hold for the output functions.

9
Systems programming

The SML Basis Library provides significant support for accessing low-level operating system features from SML. This support includes an extensive collection of abstract systems modules that allow one to write portable, system-independent applications as well as system-dependent support for accessing services on both Microsoft Windows and Unix systems. These modules do not provide access to higher-level services, such as graphical user interfaces, as such features are outside the scope of the SML Basis Library.

9.1 Portable systems programming

The I/O subsystem described in the previous chapter provides support for input and output using SML that is largely independent of the underlying implementation and operating system. This section discusses the SML Basis Library support for other aspects of systems programming, such as file systems, process management, I/O descriptors, and time and date manipulations. The interfaces provided by the SML Basis Library for these tasks are operating-system independent and can be used to develop "write once, run everywhere" applications.

9.1.1 File system pathnames

The SML Basis Library provides support for working with the hierarchical file systems supported by most operating systems. This support is split into two modules: `OS.-Path`, which provides routines for the portable manipulation of hierarchical paths or pathnames, and `OS.FileSys`, which provides routines for the portable manipulation of a hierarchical file system.

Modern operating systems share the same logical organization of file systems into hierarchical trees of directories and files but differ significantly in the syntax used to name objects in the hierarchy (e.g., Unix uses the '/' character as a path separator, while

Microsoft Windows uses '\'). The OS.Path structure provides an abstract interface to pathnames. Using this module, one can write pathname code that will port across multiple systems. One important aspect of the OS.Path structure is that the functions in it are independent of any underlying file system.

A *pathname* is a string that specifies an object in a hierarchical file system. A pathname can be characterized by the following four aspects:

- A path is either *absolute* or *relative* to some directory (e.g., the current working directory).

- The *volume* on which the object resides. Some systems (e.g., Unix) do not distinguish between volumes in pathnames, in which case this component is the empty string.

- A list of directory names, called *arcs*, that specify the ancestors or parent directories of the object.

- The name of the object relative to its parent directory.

Many systems support the convention that a given pathname suffix or extension, usually beginning with a #"." character, indicates the format or type of the file. Thus, C source files usually end with ".c" while SML files are terminated with ".sml". This convention is common enough that it is part of the pathname abstraction.

To give the flavor of using the functions in OS.Path to manage pathnames independent of the operating system, the following function takes the pathname of a C file and returns the conventional name for the object file obtained by compilation; i.e., we replace the ".c" suffix with ".o".

```
fun objectFileName file = (case OS.Path.splitBaseExt file
        of {base, ext=SOME "c"} =>
            OS.Path.joinBaseExt{base=base, ext=SOME "o"}
         | _ => raise Fail "missing/unrecognized extension"
      (* end case *))
```

Applications that manage collections of files often need to determine whether two pathnames refer to the same filesystem location. One way to achieve this goal is to map pathnames to canonical absolute paths, which we can do as follows:

```
fun cvtPath path = OS.Path.mkAbsolute {
        path = path,
        relativeTo = OS.FileSys.getDir()
      }
```

Note that the effect of this function will change if the application's working directory changes.

9.1.2 File system operations

The `OS.FileSys` structure provides a collection of operations for manipulating a hierarchical file system in an operating system. These operations include reading directories, getting and setting the current working directory, and testing and setting various file properties.

Directories are the internal nodes of the file system hierarchy and, as such, contain references to other files. The `OS.FileSys` structure supports a *directory stream* abstraction for getting the list of files in a directory. For example, the following function takes a path to a directory and returns the list of files in it:

```
fun listDir dirName = let
      val dir = OS.FileSys.openDir dirName
      fun read files = (case OS.FileSys.readDir dir
            of NONE => List.rev files
             | SOME file => read (file::files)
          (* end case *))
      in
        read [] before closeDir dir
      end
```

One important property of the `readDir` function is that it does not return either the current or parent directory arcs (some systems, such as Unix, include these in the directory list). This behavior means that it is trivial to write a recursive traversal of a file system. For example, the following function applies its first argument to the pathname of each non-directory file in the tree rooted at its second argument:

```
fun apply (f, root) = let
      fun walk path = let
            val files = listDir path
            fun walkFile file = let
                  val longName = OS.Path.concat(path, file)
                  in
                    if OS.FileSys.isDir longName
                      then walk longName
                      else f longName
                  end
            in
              List.app walkFile files
            end
      in
        if OS.FileSys.isDir root then walk root else f root
      end
```

This code also illustrates the use of the `isDir` predicate, which tests its argument to see if it is a directory.

Part of the state of a process on most operating systems is the *current working directory*, which is used to interpret relative pathnames. The function `getDir` returns the current working directory of the SML process and the function `chDir` can be used to change it.

The `OS.FileSys` structure provides operations for manipulating *symbolic links*, which are file system objects that specify a path to another file system object. The `isLink` function tests a path to see if it names a symbolic link, and the `readLink` function returns the value of the link (i.e., the path of the object referred to by the link). Note that the path returned by `readLink` may be either absolute or relative to the directory containing the path. These functions may be used safely on systems that do not have a notion of symbolic link, since in that case they treat all file system objects as not being links.

The manipulation of pathnames supported by the `OS.Path` structure is file-system independent. The `OS.FileSys` structure provides two additional pathname operations that work with respect to the underlying file system. The `fullPath` function returns a canonical, absolute pathname that names the same file as its argument. This function expands symbolic links and interprets relative paths with respect to the current working directory. This canonical pathname can be used to test the equivalence of two paths, although the file ID mechanism described below is usually more efficient. A related function is `realPath`, which also expands symbolic links but preserves relative paths.

The `OS.FileSys` structure supports a number of other functions for examining file system properties. In addition to the `isLink` and `isDir` functions described above, one can determine the modification time of a file using the `modTime` function and the size of a file using the `fileSize` function. One of the most useful functions is `access`, which can be used to test the permissions of a file. For example, here is a portable function for finding the location of an executable program given a list of directory paths to search.

```sml
fun findExe (paths, prog) = let
    fun test path =
        OS.FileSys.access(path, [OS.FileSys.A_EXEC])
        andalso not(OS.FileSys.isDir path)
    fun find [] = NONE
      | find (dir::r) = let
        val dir' = if dir = "" then OS.FileSys.getDir()
                   else dir
        val path = OS.Path.joinDirFile{dir=dir', file=prog}
        in
           if test path then SOME path else find r
        end
    in
       find paths
    end
```

This function uses the `access` function to test for the existence of an executable file, and it uses the `isDir` predicate to filter out directories (which are executable on some systems). It also uses the portable pathname function `joinDirFile` to construct candidate pathnames to be tested. The `access` function can also be used to test the existence of a file by passing it an empty access mode list.

Coining temporary filenames is supported by the `OS.FileSys.tmpName` function, which returns a new filename that is not in use. To avoid race conditions, where two applications pick the same temporary filename, this function creates an empty file with a unique name. Temporary files are useful for generating an output file for processing by another program. Here is an example of using `tmpName`:

```
fun withTmpFile (producer, consumer) = let
      val file = OS.FileSys.tmpName()
      val strm = TextIO.openOut file
      in
        (producer strm)
          handle ex => (
            TextIO.closeOut strm; OS.FileSys.remove file;
            raise ex);
        TextIO.closeOut strm;
        consumer file;
        OS.FileSys.remove file
      end
```

The `withTmpFile` function creates a temporary filename, opens it for writing, and passes the output stream to the `producer` function. Once the `producer` function has finished, the output stream is closed and the name of the temporary file is passed to the `consumer` function, which presumably runs a program on the output file (see Section 9.1.3). Finally, the temporary file is removed.

The `OS.FileSys.file_id` equality type represents an abstract unique file ID (i.e., similar to a Unix *inode*). Because of symbolic links and non-canonical paths, a single file may be referred to by many different names, but it has a single unique file ID. Thus, a file ID is an efficient way to test if two paths refer to the same file. Hashing and comparison operations are supported on file IDs, so they can be used as keys in lookup structures.

9.1.3 Processes

Operating systems vary wildly in what support they provide for processes; for example, older PC operating systems do not provide any support for multitasking. For this reason, the OS-independent support for programming with processes is limited to the synchronous execution of a child process and the management of its exit status. For more advanced process management, see Section 9.2.

Processes typically maintain a set of environment variables, which allow the user to tailor certain aspects of programs. Unlike command line arguments, which can be expected to change from invocation to invocation, environment variables tend to remain fixed for a given user during a given session. For example, one might set the `"PRINTER"` variable to `"d22color"`, with the expectation that any print commands will send the job to printer `"d22color"` by default.

How environment variables are set depends on the operating system. Getting the value of an environment variable, however, is provided by the function `OS.Process.get-Env`. Thus, using our example, the expression `getEnv("PRINTER")` would return `SOME("d22color")`. The function returns a value of `NONE` if the variable is not defined.

9.1.4   I/O descriptors

The `OS.IO` structure provides support for working with I/O descriptors, which are an abstraction of system-specific I/O handles (e.g., open file descriptors on Unix systems). One can extract the I/O descriptor for a stream by accessing the `ioDesc` field in the underlying primitive I/O `reader` or `writer`. Getting the I/O descriptor from an input stream is a bit tricky, since getting the reader has the side-effect of truncating the stream. We get around this problem by replacing the original stream by a newly created one.

```
fun getIODesc inStrm = let
      val inStrm' = TextIO.getInstream inStrm
      val (rd as TextPrimIO.RD{ioDesc, ...}, buf) =
            TextIO.StreamIO.getReader inStrm'
      in
        TextIO.setInstream (inStrm,
          TextIO.StreamIO.mkInstream(rd, buf));
        ioDesc
      end
```

I/O descriptors can also be created from file descriptors using the POSIX APIs. I/O descriptors serve three purposes: they provide a way to uniquely identify open I/O handles; they can be used to query the kind of underlying I/O object (e.g., file vs. directory vs. socket); and they can be used to support *polling*.

Applications that manage communication with multiple input sources (e.g., ttys, pipes, and sockets) need a mechanism to avoid getting stuck waiting for one source of input while ignoring input available from the other sources. The SML Basis Library provides a general polling mechanism on I/O descriptors as a way to avoid this problem. The `poll_desc` type represents the combination of an I/O descriptor and a set of conditions to check (e.g., input available). The `poll` operation takes a list of poll descriptors and a timeout and waits until at least one of the specified conditions is met or the timeout expires. The result of the `poll` operation is a list of `poll_info` values, one for each poll descriptor that had a condition satisfied. To make it possible to map from the resulting `poll_info` values back to the argument poll descriptors, the `infoToPoll-Desc` function returns the poll descriptor that a given `poll_info` value corresponds to. Furthermore, the list of `poll_info` values respects the original order of the poll descriptors. For example, the following code implements a higher-level polling mechanism that takes a list of poll descriptor/value pairs and a timeout, and returns a list of values that correspond to the enabled descriptors:

```
fun poll' (pds : (OS.IO.poll_desc * 'a) list, timeOut) = let
      val pis = OS.IO.poll(List.map #1 pds, timeOut)
      fun select ([], [], l) = List.rev l
        | select (pi::pis, (pd, x)::pds, l) =
            if (OS.IO.infoToPollDesc pi = pd)
              then select (pis, pds, x::l)
              else select (pi::pis, pds, l)
    in
      select (pis, pds, [])
    end
```

Notice that the `select` function uses the ordering property of the result list to efficiently project out the selected items.

Poll descriptors are constructed from I/O descriptors using the `pollDesc` function. Since not all devices support polling on all systems, the result of this function is an option, where NONE signifies that polling is not supported. Polling conditions are added by functional update of the poll descriptor using the `pollIn`, `pollOut`, and `pollPr` functions. The last function tests for *high-priority* events, such as exceptional conditions. To illustrate, the following function builds on the previous `getIODesc` to map an input stream to a pair of a poll descriptor that tests for input and the stream:

```
fun getPollDesc strm = (case getIODesc strm
        of SOME iod => (case OS.IO.pollDesc iod
              of SOME pd => (OS.IO.pollIn pd, strm)
               | _ => raise Fail "no polling"
            (* end case *))
         | _ => raise Fail "no desc"
      (* end case *))
```

This function raises an exception if either the stream does not have an I/O descriptor or if it does not support polling.

Finally, we can put these pieces together in the following function, which takes a list of streams and returns a function for reading from those streams that currently have input available. Note that it uses the `getPollDesc` function from above, as well as the specialized version of polling.

```
fun inputMerge strms = let
        val choices = List.map getPollDesc strms
        fun input () = let
              val availStrms = poll' (choices, SOME Time.zeroTime)
              in
                 List.map TextIO.input availStrms
              end
     in
        input
     end
```

9.1.5 Time and dates

Computing with time and date values and execution timing are all supported by the SML Basis Library. The SML Basis Library defines an abstract type `Time.time` to represent both durations and absolute times (which can be thought of as the duration from some epoch). The `Time` structure provides arithmetic and comparison operations on time values. For example, the following code prints the real (or wall clock) time that it takes to run a function on its argument:

```
fun timeIt f x = let
        val t0 = Time.now()
        val result = f x
        val t1 = Time.now()
        in
           print(concat[
               "It took ", Time.toString(Time.-(t1, t0)),
               " seconds\n"
              ]);
           result
        end
```

This function illustrates a couple of other features of the `Time` structure. The function `Time.now` returns the current time of day and the function `Time.toString` converts a time value to a decimal string representation. In addition to the `toString` function, the `Time` structure also provides the standard `fromString`, `fmt`, and `scan` functions.

The `Time` structure also provides operations for converting between concrete numbers and abstract time values. For example, a time value representing 10 milliseconds can be constructed using any of the following expressions:

```
Time.fromReal 0.01
Time.fromMilliseconds 10
Time.fromMicroseconds 10000
```

Going in the other direction, the `Time.toReal` function converts a time value to a real-valued number of seconds. Likewise, there are functions, such as `Time.toMilliseconds`, that convert a time value to an integer number of units (milliseconds in this case). If the result of these functions is too large to be represented as a `Large-Int.int`, then the `Overflow` exception is raised.

As mentioned above, time values can represent absolute times (e.g., 10am GMT on May 10th, 2004). The `Date` structure provides functions for converting time values to and from dates. The abstract type `Date.date` represents a date with respect to some time zone. A date value can be constructed from whole cloth using the `Date.date` function. For example, the expression

```
Date.date {
    year = 2004, month = Date.May, day = 10,
    hour = 10, minute = 0, second = 0,
    offset = SOME Time.zeroTime
}
```

constructs a representation of "10am GMT on May 10th, 2004." The `offset` argument to this function specifies the time zone by the number of seconds west of *Coordinated Universal Time* (UTC), formerly known as *Greenwich Mean Time* (GMT). If we had given `NONE` as the `offset` field value, then the resulting date would be with respect to the local time zone. The offset of the local time zone can be determined by calling the `Date.localOffset` function.

We can also construct date values from time values using the functions `Date.from-TimeLocal` and `Date.fromTimeUniv`. In both cases, the argument time value is interpreted relative to UTC. For example, the expression

```
Date.fromTimeLocal (Time.now ())
```

returns the current date in the local time zone, while

```
Date.fromTimeUniv (Time.now ())
```

returns the current date in Greenwich, England. The `Date.toTime` function converts a date value back to a time value in UTC. This function can be used to convert from one time zone to another. For example, any date can be converted to the local time zone using the following function:

```
fun toLocalTZ d = Date.fromTimeLocal (Date.toTime d)
```

One of the main uses of dates is to convert to and from string representations. The `Date.fmt` operation provides fine control over the string representation of a date value using a format string. For example, the expression

```
Date.fmt "%A %B %d, %Y" (Date.fromTimeLocal (Time.now ()))
```

produces a string representation of the current date with the form

```
"Monday May 10, 2004"
```

while

```
Date.fmt "%Y-%m-%d" (Date.fromTimeLocal (Time.now ()))
```

produces a string representation of the current date with the form

```
"2004-05-10"
```

The format string follows the ISO/IEC 9899:1990 Standard for the C `strftime` function [ISO90] (see the `Date` manual page for details). The `Date.toString` function
produces a date value in fixed 24-character format with the form

```
"Mon May 10 10:00:00 2004"
```

The `toString` function is equivalent to

```
Date.fmt "%a %b %d %H:%M:%S %Y"
```

The `Date.scan` and `Date.fromString` functions convert strings in the `toString`
format to date values.

Time values are also used to represent durations, such as the amount of time it takes
to complete some computation. We have already seen an example of measuring the
real time taken by a computation, but the SML Basis Library also provides support for
measuring the processing time over an interval. The `Timer` structure provides support
for measuring the real, CPU, and garbage-collection time used by a computation. For
example, the following code measures the CPU and garbage-collection (GC) time that
it takes to run a function on its argument:

```
fun timeIt f x = let
    val tmr = Timer.startCPUTimer ()
    fun pr (msg, {usr, sys}) = print (concat [
            msg, Time.toString usr, "u+",
            Time.toString sys, "s\n"
          ]);
    val result = f x
    val {nongc, gc} = Timer.checkCPUTimes tmr
    in
      pr ("non-gc time = ", nongc);
      pr ("gc time = ", gc);
      result
    end
```

9.2   Operating-system specific programming

While the generic, portable facilities described above are complete enough so that most
applications can perform their tasks using just them, there are times when a program

can be more easily written by making use of the richer facilities of a given operating system. In this case, the programmer may know that the program will only be run on that system, or decide to impose that limitation. Even here, good software practice is to develop a system-independent interface for the desired functions and then provide system-dependent implementations.

The remainder of this section will focus on the three system-specific interfaces defined in the Basis.

9.2.1 The `Unix` structure

Despite its name, the `Unix` structure does not define the system calls expected in a Unix, POSIX, or Linux environment. Those functions appear in the `Posix` structure described below. Rather, this structure encapsulates a standard Unix idiom, that of creating a separate process, with streams for reading from and writing to the new process. This idiom is similar to the `OS.Process.system` function, but it provides a richer level of control. There are also related functions for signaling or terminating the child process and reclaiming system resources.

Running a new program in Unix typically consists of using the `dup()` and `pipe()` system calls to set up the file connections between the parent and child processes, calling `fork()` to create a child process, releasing the unnecessary open file descriptors, and finally having the child process run the new program with a call to `execv()`. The `execute` function provides a wrapper for these sequences of actions. In addition, it uses the operating system file descriptors to create Basis library `instream` and `outstream` values.

The following example presents a trivial, but typical, use of the `Unix` structure.

```
fun countWords (text : string list) = let
    val proc = Unix.execute ("/bin/wc", ["-w"])
    val (ins, outs) = Unix.streamsOf proc
    val _ = app (fn s => TextIO.output (outs, s)) text
    val _ = TextIO.closeOut outs
    val cnt = TextIO.inputAll ins
in
    Unix.reap proc;
    valOf (Int.fromString cnt)
end
```

The function counts the number of whitespace-separated words in the string `concat text`. It is implemented by invoking the standard Unix program `wc` with the `-w` flag, which reads its input and writes the number of words in the input stream onto its output stream. Next, the function uses `streamsOf` to extract the input and output streams connected to the child process. From the child's point of view, these correspond to its `stdOut` and `stdIn` streams, respectively. The function then writes the argument strings to the child, after which it closes the output stream. This implementation relies on knowing how `wc` works. Given no file arguments, `wc` acts as a filter, reading and processing input until it sees an end-of-stream. By closing the stream, the function generates an end-of-stream state for the child. The function then asks for all output produced by the child process, knowing that the child process, once it detects the end-of-stream, will write its output and then exit, thereby closing the parent's input stream. The function binds this string to `cnt`.

Just before returning, the function calls the `Unix.reap` function, which is necessary since, in Unix, if someone does not reap a terminated process, certain process resources remain allocated. If `execute` is called frequently enough without performing a `reap`, the parent process will run out of file descriptors and the operating system will generate an exception.

The first argument to `execute` should be the absolute pathname of an executable file, not a command name. To turn a command name such as `"date"` into a pathname such as `"/bin/date"`, the convention is to use `OS.Process.getEnv` to obtain the value of the `PATH` variable, which will be a colon-separated list of directory pathnames, to be searched in order from left to right, looking for the command. Here is a simple implementation.

```
fun findPath cmd = (case OS.Process.getEnv "PATH"
        of NONE => NONE
         | SOME path =>
            findExe (String.fields (fn c => c = #":") path, cmd)
      (* end case *))
```

where `findExe` was defined in Section 9.1.1. Note that the function `Windows.-findExecutable` provides this service for a Microsoft Windows environment.

A simpler mechanism to accomplish command searching is to let a shell or scripting language handle it. As an example, the function

```
fun execute (cmd, args) = let
    val newargs = foldr (fn (a,l) => " "::a::l) [] args
    val newcmd = concat (cmd::newargs)
    in
      Unix.execute ("/bin/sh", ["-c",newcmd])
    end
```

invokes the standard shell with two arguments, the first, `"-c"`, indicating the shell should execute the second argument as a command. The second argument is a string composed of the command and its arguments, all separated by spaces.

One obvious advantage of using `execute` rather than `OS.Process.system` is that the parent program can provide input to the child process, as well as read its output. In simple cases such as the above example, one could use the file system to provide the communication. If there are multiple exchanges between the parent and child, using the file system becomes difficult, if not impossible. For example, the parent process might not know when to read the child's output file because it cannot ascertain when the child process has completed its output. With a direct stream from the child when using `execute`, the parent process can know what the child has written and what more to expect.

In more serious applications, the code should provide appropriate checks and exception handlers for errors. Besides the usual variety of simple errors, `execute` makes it possible for more subtle errors to arise. Consider a case where the parent process writes constantly to the child, while the child reads some input and then writes to its output. Since the parent is not reading the child's output, at some point the child's output buffer becomes full, so the child process blocks trying to write. Since the parent process is still writing, but the child is no longer reading, the parent's output buffer becomes full, at which point the parent process blocks while trying to write, and the system is deadlocked.

Another aspect the programmer needs to consider is when to call `reap`, which closes the pipes connecting the two processes. If the child process is still using them for reading or writing, it may terminate prematurely due to receiving a broken pipe signal `Posix.-Signal.pipe`. The programmer should also consider the effect of buffering in the stream library, which may require explicit flushing of a buffer.

As these examples indicate, effective use of `execute` depends on the parent application knowing what the child process expects for input and what it produces for output. For simple uses, it is usually possible to rely on documentation concerning the child process. For extended interaction between the two processes, it is helpful if there is a well-defined protocol between the two processes. Otherwise, it is too easy for the child to produce unexpected output, perhaps in response to an error, after which the parent process may no longer know how to read the ensuing child output. Even in the simple cases, it can happen that the same command on two different versions of Unix will produce output in two different formats.

In Section 9.1, we discussed the notion of environment variables as they exist in the execution environment. The `executeInEnv` function is identical to `execute`, except that it gives the parent process the ability to alter the child's environment. For example, if the child process is a Unix shell program invoked to run a script provided by a user, it may be desirable, for security reasons, to reset the `PATH` variable to a restricted set of paths such as `"/bin:/usr/bin"`.

In the portable interface defined by the `OS` structure, a process can stop with success or not. Unix-like operating systems provide a finer distinction as to how a process stopped and, in case of an error, what the error was. The `Unix` structure makes this extra information available. In the Unix operating system, when a process finishes, it returns a small integer value to its parent, with a zero value representing success, by convention. This form of termination is provided by the `Unix.exit` function. As for what the parent process sees, it can convert the process status, provided by `reap` or

`OS.Process.system` or some other function, into a `Unix.exit_status` value using the `fromStatus` function. The `W_EXITED` value of `exit_status` corresponds to `OS.Process.success`. If the status is (`W_EXITSTATUS w`), the child process called (`exit w`), where *w* is non-zero.

The operating system will sometimes terminate a process because it was sent a signal by some other process. The `kill` function gives this ability to the parent process. If a process terminates because of a signal, its exit status will be (`W_SIGNALED s`), where *s* is the signal sent. Note that the `Unix` structure does not provide signal values explicitly. These will usually come from a lower-level structure. Thus, if an implementation provides the `Posix` structure, the `Unix.signal` type must be identical to the `Posix.Signal.signal` type. Finally, it is possible for a signal, such as `Posix.-` `Signal.tstp`, to cause a process to be suspended rather than terminated. Notification of this suspension to the parent process has the form (`W_STOPPED s`), where *s* is the signal sent. That `W_STOPPED` has the `exit_status` type is something of a misnomer, as the signaled process has not exited and can be restarted by being sent the `Posix.Signal.cont` signal. Note also that a parent process using only the `Unix` structure will never see this value, since the `reap` function only returns when the child process has indeed terminated. The constructor is included here because of the type equivalence between `exit_status` and `Posix.Process.exit_status`.

9.2.2   System flags

System calls sometimes have a parameter that represents a small set of non-exclusive options. For example, the third argument to the function `Posix.FileSys.openf` allows the user to specify that the operation should fail if someone else has already opened the file, and, when the file is opened, it should be truncated to an empty file. In C, the set is usually represented by the bits of an integer, with supported flags defined by preprocessor variables and combinations of flags formed by bit-wise or.

To support these options in SML, the Library defines a `BIT_FLAGS` signature, which provides an abstract representation for the setting and clearing of bits. We consider this design a flexible and convenient compromise between an explicit use of words and a list of abstract flag values. There is no structure matching the `BIT_FLAGS` signature. Rather, structures have substructures that use an **include** `BIT_FLAGS` specification in their signature. In addition, the substructure defines a basic set of flags. As the underlying operating system may well accept additional flags than those specified in the Library, the `BIT_FLAGS` interface provides the `fromWord` function to produce arbitrary flag values.

The operations in `BIT_FLAGS` form a boolean algebra, with `flags` serving for union (∪) and `intersect` serving for set intersection (∩). The empty set can be expressed using `flags []` while `all` and `intersect []` denote everything. Since an implementation may define more flags than are specified by the Library, `all` may be a superset of the union of the defined flags. Set difference is provided by `clear`, and one can test set inclusion using `allSet`.

9.2.3 POSIX Programming

The structure `Posix` and its substructures provide SML bindings for the types and functions specified in the POSIX standard 1003.1,1996 [POS96]. This specification defines operating system facilities based on a Unix operating system model. There are many systems that provide conforming implementations of POSIX, such as Linux, Free BSD, Solaris, Irix, and OS X, though POSIX is usually a subset of what the systems actually provide. In these cases, an implementation of the `Posix` structure involves little more than calling the underlying C functions.

The major substructures of `Posix` correspond closely to specific sections in the POSIX document.

`Posix.Process`	Section 3
`Posix.ProcEnv`	Section 4
`Posix.FileSys`	Section 5
`Posix.IO`	Section 6
`Posix.TTY`	Section 7
`Posix.SysDB`	Section 9

To leverage the familiarity of Unix names and the available documentation, most of the components of the `Posix` structures retain the traditional names, ignoring capitalization. When the traditional names rely on a prefix convention to get around the lack of modules in C, we usually create a substructure whose name is the prefix. For example, the `struct stat` in C describes information about the status of a file. A typical field would be `st_nlink`. In the Basis module `Posix.FileSys`, we use a substructure `Posix.FileSys.ST` with a value `nlink`. Thus, instead of using `st_nlink` in C, one uses `ST.nlink` in SML. Since the `Posix` structure is a near literal translation of POSIX from C to SML, we refer the reader to any reference on Unix or POSIX to learn how to use the structure or to understand the detailed semantics of the operations.

One programming difference to keep in mind is that, to check for errors in C, the code looks for a negative return value and then consults the value of the global variable `errno` to determine the specific error. In SML, errors in using `Posix` are indicated by the raised exception `OS.SysErr`. Because of the many different errors (see `Posix.-Error`) and the many reasons for their occurrence, the Basis library does not specify which exceptions are raised and when. Again, the reader is referred to POSIX documentation. Typically, if an error causes `errno` to be set to `EABC` in C, the Library will raise the exception

```
OS.SysErr (OS.errorMsg Posix.Error.abc, SOME Posix.Error.abc)
```

for the same error.

9.2.4   The `Windows` structure

The `Windows` structure provides rudimentary access to functions and types specific
to the Microsoft Windows operating system. In flavor, it is somewhere between the
`Unix` and `Posix` structures. The `execute` and `reap` functions are analogues of the
ones in `Unix`, while the remaining functions and substructures expose some lower-level
Windows features that have broad use. On the other hand, whereas the `Posix` structure
makes available almost all POSIX features, the `Windows` structure does not come close
to providing all of the operating system calls available in Microsoft Windows.

The various functions for obtaining system directories and configuration information
in the `Config` substructure are useful for writing system-sensitive code. For example,
the command interpreter is `cmd.exe` in the system directory in Windows NT, but it is
`command.com` in the Windows directory in Windows 95.

The structure provides several methods for creating child processes or subprocesses.
They differ in the way the subprocesses are created, in the degree of communication
between the parent process and the child process, and in whether they are synchronous
or asynchronous.

The simplest and most portable method is to use `OS.Process.system`. The code

```
fun generateAndCompile (txt : string) = let
    val gcc = (case Windows.findExecutable "gcc.exe"
                of SOME gcc => gcc
                 | NONE => raise Fail "Cannot find gcc"
               (* end case *))
    val cmd = concat ["echo '", txt, "' > foo.c"]
    in
        ignore (OS.Process.system cmd);
        OS.Process.system (gcc ^ " -c foo.c")
    end
```

exhibits its use to create and compile a file. It interprets a string as if it were a shell command. It is fully synchronous; the parent process waits until the command is completed.
The child process returns its exit status to the caller. If the subprocess uses the standard
streams, and the parent process is a console process, then the two processes share their
standard streams. If the parent process is a Windows process, then the child process is
allocated a console of its own.

This method has the disadvantage that the Windows shell restricts the maximum
length that the command line may have — if this limit is exceeded, the command
crashes, and Microsoft Windows pops up a box explaining the error. On the other hand,
it is the only method that can run a batch script as a subprocess.

If the restriction on the maximum length of the command line causes problems, or if the subprocess I/O is not relevant, one can use the `simpleExecute` function provided by the `Windows` structure. This function calls the executable directly, avoiding the limitation on the length of the command, and also connects the standard input and output to the null device, so that any input or output is ignored.

```
fun mkArchive (archive, files) = let
    val ar = (case Windows.findExecutable "ar.exe"
                of SOME x => x
                 | NONE => raise Fail "Cannot find ar.exe" )
    val args = concatWith " " ("cr"::archive::files)
    in
       Windows.simpleExecute (ar, args)
    end
```

The `Windows` structure also provides a completely asynchronous function for creating subprocesses, called `launchApplication`. Like `simpleExecute`, it takes the name of an executable and an argument string. It runs the executable with the argument provided. If the subprocess is a console application, the standard streams are not redirected. This command is completely asynchronous; once the subprocess is running, there is no further communication between the two processes.

```
fun runNotepad file = launchApplication ("notepad", file)
```

Another simple method provided by the `Windows` structure for spawning a subprocess is the `openDocument` command. This function takes a pathname of a file and opens that file using the application registered in Microsoft Windows for files of that type. For example, if called with an HTML file, it will open that file in one's browser.

```
fun getHelp () = openDocument ("c:\\help\\index.htm");
```

Sometimes more communication is needed between the parent process and the child process. The `Windows` structure provides two ways of supporting this communication. The first is the `execute` function, which is for running a console subprocess. It creates streams that are linked to the standard input and output streams of that subprocess (the standard error stream of the subprocess is merged with that of the parent process). This linkage allows the parent process to send input to the subprocess, and read the resulting output. This method is asynchronous, but the calling process can call the `reap` function to wait for the subprocess to finish. Note that if the subprocess attempts to read from standard input or write to standard input, then the parent process must provide or consume this information. Otherwise, the subprocess will hang indefinitely. Also, the handle of the subprocess remains open until the subprocess is reaped.

```
fun runCmd (cmd : string, args : string) = let
      val p = Windows.execute (cmd, args)
      val ins = Windows.textInstreamOf p
      val outs = Windows.textOutstreamOf p
   in
      TextIO.output (outs, "Test input\n");
      print (TextIO.inputLine ins);
      Windows.reap p
   end
```

For more information about using `Windows.execute`, `Windows.reap`, and the related stream functions, the reader should consult the description of their `Unix` analogues in Section 9.2.1. Note that the Unix version of `execute` takes a string list as its second argument.

Another way of communicating with subprocesses is to use dynamic data exchange (DDE). The `Windows` structure provides a simple, high-level interface for basic DDE programming. This interface allows the parent process to send commands to the child process, which is typically a windowing process. The DDE interface does not itself create the subprocess.

```
fun openFile file = let
      val busyRetries = 20   (* max number of busy retries *)
      val delay = Time.fromMilliseconds 200
      val ddeInfo =
          Windows.DDE.startDialog ("PFE32", "Editor")
      val cmd = concat ["[FileOpen(\"", file, "\")]"]
   in
      Windows.DDE.executeString (
        ddeInfo, cmd, busyRetries, delay);
      Windows.DDE.stopDialog ddeInfo
   end
```

The `Windows.fromStatus` and `Windows.exit` functions are identical to their `Unix` counterparts, the only real difference being the Windows-specific exit values defined in the `Windows.Status` substructure.

10

Network programming with sockets

10.1 Overview

Sockets are an abstraction for interprocess communication (IPC) that were introduced as part of the Berkeley version of Unix in 1982. They have become a *de facto* standard for network communication and are supported by most major operating systems (including PC systems). The SML Basis Library provides an optional collection of modules for programming with sockets. The interface provided by the Basis follows the C interface for the most part; the major difference is that the SML interface is more *strongly typed*. In particular, the type system distinguishes between passive and active sockets, between sockets in different domains, and between sockets of different protocols.

The Berkeley Socket API supports two styles of communication: *stream* sockets provide *virtual circuits* between pairs of processes, and *datagram* sockets provide *connectionless* packet-based communication. In stream-based interactions, the server allocates a master socket that is used to accept connections from clients. The server then listens on the master socket for connection requests from clients; each request is allocated a new socket that the server uses to communicate with that particular client. As the name suggests, stream-based communication is done as a stream of bytes, not as discrete packets. Connectionless communication is more symmetric: messages are sent to a specific port at a specific address. While datagram sockets provide better performance, messages may be lost or received out of order, which requires additional programming by the client. For this reason, stream sockets are more commonly used than datagram sockets.

10.1.1 Socket-related modules

The SML Basis Library organizes support for socket-based network programming into three related groups of modules.

- The `Socket` structure provides the basic socket types and operations.

- The `NetHostDB`, `NetProtDB`, and `NetServDB` structures provide support for determining the addresses of hosts, protocols, and services on the network.

- The `GenericSock`, `INetSock`, and `UnixSock` structures provide support for socket creation.

10.1.2 Socket-related types

Because some operations apply only to stream sockets, others apply only to datagram sockets, and some apply to either kind, it is convenient to use SML type polymorphism for the socket type. Type `('af,'sock_type) Socket.socket` is parameterized by an address family and a (datagram or stream) socket type. The `'mode Socket.-stream` socket type itself is parameterized by a mode (*active*, for an ordinary communication stream, or *passive*, to accept connections). Thus we have:

Type	Description
`(inet, active stream) socket`	Internet-domain active stream socket.
`(inet, passive stream) socket`	Internet-domain passive stream socket.
`(inet, dgram) socket`	Internet-domain datagram socket.
`(unix, active stream) socket`	Unix-domain active stream socket.
`(unix, passive stream) socket`	Unix-domain passive stream socket.
`(unix, dgram) socket`	Unix-domain datagram socket.

Note that in this table, structure qualifiers are omitted; for example, the Internet active stream socket type is really

```
(INetSock.inet, Socket.active Socket.stream) Socket.socket
```

The types `inet`, `active`, etc. have been dubbed "phantom types" by Leijen and Meijer [LM99]), since they do not have any values.

10.1.3 Socket I/O operations

The `Socket` structure provides a large collection of I/O operations on sockets (32 to be exact). These operations are organized into stream-socket operations (`send` and `recv` in various flavors) and datagram-socket operations (`sendTo` and `recvFrom` in various flavors). For each basic I/O operation, there are eight distinct versions based on the type of data (array vs. vector), synchronization (blocking vs. non-blocking), and options (common case vs. general case). We use a uniform naming convention, with the type denoted by "`Vec`" or "`Arr`", non-blocking denoted by "`NB`", and the general-case form denoted by a prime. For example, `sendArrToNB` is the non-blocking `sendTo` operation on datagram sockets that takes its message from an byte-array slice. Likewise, the `recvVec'` function is the blocking `recv` operation on stream sockets that returns its result as a byte vector and accepts option flags (`peek` and `oob`).

10.2   Socket addresses

To use a socket for communication requires creating an address for the other end of the communication. For datagram sockets, this address is used to address each individual message, while for stream sockets it is used to create the connection. A socket address consists of a pair of a domain-specific host address and a port number.

For each address family or domain supported by an implementation, there is a corresponding module that supports the creation of addresses and sockets in the domain. The SML Basis Library specifies the signature of the `INetSock` structure for creating Internet-domain sockets and the `UnixSock` structure for creating Unix-domain sockets. Each of these structures has two substructures, `UDP` and `TCP`, which contain the socket creation functions for datagram and stream sockets, respectively. In addition, the `INetSock` and `UnixSock` structures define mechanisms to create socket addresses from a host address and port.

For the Internet domain, host addresses are supported by the `NetHostDB` structure, which provides an interface to the network database. This interface allows one to lookup address information by hostname (using `getByName`) or by address (using `getByAddr`). The network-database records contain information about the address family of the host (usually internet domain), the primary name and address of the host, and any aliases and alternative addresses for the host. The `NetHostDB` structure also provides functions for converting between strings and addresses.

10.3   Internet-domain stream sockets

The most common use of sockets is to implement connection-based protocols (e.g., HTTP, FTP, and TELNET) using TCP/IP (i.e., stream sockets). The two participants in a connection-based protocol are called the client, who initiates the connection, and the server. While many times these names reflect an asymmetry in the relationship between the two participants (e.g., the client might be a web browser and the server an HTTP server), it is possible for the relationship to be symmetric. One participant, however, must serve as client and initiate the connection, while the other must be willing to accept the connection. In this section, we describe how to program both the server and client sides of an Internet-domain stream socket.

We start with the client side of the connection, since it is simpler. In order to establish a connection to a server, the client must form a socket address from the server's host and port and then use the address to connect to the server. The following function creates an Internet-domain address for the given port at the given host:

```sml
fun inetAddr {host, port} = let
    val addr = (case NetHostDB.getByName host
            of NONE => raise Fail "unknown host"
             | SOME ent => NetHostDB.addr ent
            (* end case *))
    in
      INetSock.toAddr(addr, port)
    end
```

Using this function, we can create a TCP socket and connect it to the given address in the following code:

```sml
fun connectToPort {host, port} = let
    val addr = inetAddr {host=host, port=port}
    val sock = INetSock.TCP.socket ()
    in
      Socket.connect (sock, addr);
      sock
    end
```

This function first looks up the target host in the network database by calling getBy-Name. If the host is known, then the function gets the host's address from the host's database entry (ent) and combines it with the port to compute the socket address. It then creates a TCP socket and connects it to the server's address. Finally, the new socket is returned and can be used for communication.

Often one uses a symbolic name for a service, instead of an explicit port number. The NetServDB structure provides an interface to the network service database that can be used to look up port numbers based on service names. For example, the inetAddr function from above can be generalized to take a service name instead of a port number as follows:

```sml
fun inetServAddr {host, service} = let
    val addr = (
            case NetHostDB.getByName host
             of NONE => raise Fail "unknown host"
              | SOME ent => NetHostDB.addr ent
            (* end case *))
    val port = (
            case NetServDB.getByName(service, SOME("tcp"))
             of NONE => raise Fail "unknown service"
              | SOME ent => NetServDB.port ent
            (* end case *))
    in
      INetSock.toAddr(addr, port)
    end
```

The SOME("tcp") argument specifies that we want the port associated with the stream version of the service. For example, we can get the address of the HTTP service at standardml.org using the following expression:

```
inetServAddr {host="standardml.org", service="http"}
```

Once a connection is established, one can use the various functions provided by the `Socket` structure for socket I/O. One issue to be aware of is that socket I/O operations can result in only a part of the data being transmitted. To avoid this problem, one should check the number of bytes transmitted. For example, the following function sends a complete vector over the given socket:

```
fun sendAll (sock, v) = let
    fun lp vs = if Word8VectorSlice.isEmpty vs
        then ()
        else let
          val n = Socket.sendVec (sock, vs)
          in
            lp (Word8VectorSlice.subslice(vs, n, NONE))
          end
    in
      lp (Word8VectorSlice.full v)
    end
```

Setting up the server side of a connection is a two-stage process. First, the server must create a passive socket, bind it to the port it is using, and enable it for accepting connections. The second stage is to accept connections. The following function sets up a passive socket on the given port and returns the socket:

```
fun initServerSocket (port : int) = let
    val sock = INetSock.TCP.socket()
    in
      Socket.bind (sock, INetSock.any port);
      Socket.listen (sock, 5);
      sock
    end
```

Note that we use the `any` function to create an address that matches any sender.

To establish a connection, the server must use the `accept` function, which returns a new active socket for communicating with the client and the address of the client. For example, the following function implements a simple echo server that can handle a single client:

```
fun echoServer port = let
      val passiveSock = initServerSocket port
      val (sock, _) = Socket.accept passiveSock
      fun echoLoop () = let
            val data = Socket.recvVec(sock, 1024)
          in
            if (Word8Vector.length data = 0)
              then ()
              else (
                sendAll (sock, data);
                echoLoop ())
          end
   in
      Socket.close passiveSock;
      echoLoop ();
      Socket.close sock
   end
```

Note that when the client closes its end of the connection, the server's call to `recvVec` will return the empty vector and the server will terminate. To generalize this code to support multiple clients requires monitoring both the passive socket for new clients and the currently open active sockets for new data. We monitor both sockets simultaneously by using the `select` function, which is described below in Section 10.6.1.

10.4 Internet-domain datagram sockets

Datagram communication is *connectionless*, so addresses are used on a per-message basis. To illustrate this model of network communication, we use the example of an echo server that sends any message it receives back to its source. For the client, we define a function that measures and reports the round-trip time to send a 128-byte message and receive its echo.

The client uses the `inetAddr` function from above to construct the server's address from a hostname and port number, but instead of using this address to establish a connection to the server, the client uses it to address the message. Here is the client-side function:

```
fun pingClient {host, port} = let
      val sock = INetSock.UDP.socket ()
      val toAddr = inetAddr {host=host, port=port}
      val msg = Word8VectorSlice.full (
            Word8Vector.tabulate(128, fn _ => 0w0))
      val t0 = Time.now()
   in
      Socket.sendVecTo (sock, toAddr, msg);
      ignore (Socket.recvVecFrom (sock, 1024));
      print (Time.fmt 6 (Time.-(Time.now(), t0))
        ^ " seconds\n")
   end
```

Note that we are ignoring the message and address values returned from `recvVec-From`.

The server-side code is similar in structure to the `echoServer` function above. The main difference is that we do not listen for connections, but instead just use `recvVec-From` to wait for messages from clients. Here is the server-side code:

```
fun pingServer port = let
      val sock = INetSock.UDP.socket ()
      val addr = INetSock.any port
      val _ = Socket.bind (sock, addr)
      fun echoLp () = let
            val (msg, fromAddr) = Socket.recvVecFrom (sock, 1024)
            in
              Socket.sendVecTo (sock, fromAddr,
                Word8VectorSlice.full msg);
              echoLp ()
            end
      in
        echoLp ()
      end
```

Because the server can never know if its clients are done (in fact, new clients may start at any time), it is programmed as an infinite loop.

10.5 Unix-domain sockets

Unix-domain sockets provide an efficient mechanism for programs running on the same local system to communicate using socket operations (essentially, they are a form of interprocess communication built into the networking library). A Unix pathname is used to specify the address of a Unix-domain socket; in fact, when a socket is bound to an address, a special file is created with the given address. For example, the X Window System uses the filename `"/tmp/.X11-unix/X0"` for its default Unix-domain connection. Thus, the following function connects a socket to the default X Window System server:

```
fun connectToX11Server () = let
      val addr = UnixSock.toAddr "/tmp/.X11-unix/X0"
      val sock = UnixSock.Strm.socket ()
      in
        Socket.connect (sock, addr);
        sock
      end
```

The `UnixSock.Strm` and `UnixSock.DGrm` structures also provide functions to create connected pairs of sockets. These functions can be used to create a communication channel for communicating with a forked subprocess.

```
fun initServerConnection (port : int, limit) = let
    val sock = INetSock.TCP.socket()
in
    Socket.bind (sock, INetSock.any port);
    Socket.listen (sock, 5);
    fn () => let
      val sd = Socket.sockDesc sock
      val {rds, ...} = Socket.select {
              rds=[sd], wrs=[], exs=[],
              timeout=SOME limit
            }
    in
       if List.null rds
          then NONE
          else SOME(Socket.accept sock)
    end
end
```

Listing 10.1: Building a socket connection with a time limit

10.6   Advanced topics

In the remainder of this chapter, we examine additional techniques for programming with sockets using the SML Basis Library.

10.6.1   Polling sockets

A server that supports multiple client sockets must use some form of polling to check for pending requests. The SML Basis Library provides two mechanisms for polling on sockets. The `Socket.select` function is specific to sockets, while the `IO.poll` function can be used to poll a mix of different kinds of I/O devices including sockets. The `poll` function is discussed in Section 9.1.4, so we focus on the use of `select` here.

The `select` function takes three lists of *socket descriptors* and a timeout value as arguments.

Polling can also be used to check for pending connections without indefinite blocking. For example, the function in Listing 10.1 offers a connection on the given port but limits the time spent waiting for a connection. The function returns NONE when no connection is available before the timeout.

10.6.2 More socket I/O

The socket operations allow reading and writing of bytes, but it is a simple matter to support I/O of strings on stream sockets. For example, the following function reads a string from a stream socket:

```
fun recvString sock = let
        val n = Socket.Ctl.getRCVBUF sock
        in
           Byte.bytesToString(Socket.recvVec(sock, n))
        end
```

Note that the recvString function uses the getRCVBUF function to determine the maximum number of bytes that might be available. We can support sending a string on a socket by modifying the sendAll function given above in Section 10.3:

```
fun sendString (sock, s) = let
      fun lp vs = if Word8VectorSlice.isEmpty vs
            then ()
            else let
              val n = Socket.sendVec (sock, vs)
              in
                 lp (Word8VectorSlice.subslice(vs, n, NONE))
              end
      in
         lp (Word8VectorSlice.full(Byte.stringToBytes s))
      end
```

It is also possible to build full-fledged I/O streams on top of sockets using the techniques described in Section 8.2.5. For example, the function mkStreams defined in Listing 10.2 returns a pair of binary input and output streams built on top of the given socket.

10.6.3 Supporting multiple domains in an application

Some applications need to be able to support connections to a server over multiple domains; for example, the *X Window System* [SG97] supports both Internet-domain and Unix-domain stream sockets. Although sockets from different domains have different types (because of the phantom type discipline),it is possible to structure the code in such a way that common code can be used to communicate over multiple domains. The key is to parameterize the communication code over the socket. For example, the following function applies its argument f to either a Unix-domain or Internet-domain socket:

```sml
fun mkStreams (sock : Socket.active INetSock.stream_sock) = let
    val (haddr, port) =
          INetSock.fromAddr(Socket.Ctl.getSockName sock)
    val sockName = String.concat[
            NetHostDB.toString haddr, ":", Int.toString port
          ]
    val rd = BinPrimIO.RD{
            name = sockName,
            chunkSize = Socket.Ctl.getRCVBUF sock,
            readVec =
              SOME(fn sz => Socket.recvVec(sock, sz)),
            readArr =
              SOME(fn buffer => Socket.recvArr(sock, buffer)),
            readVecNB = NONE, readArrNB = NONE,
            block = NONE,
            canInput = NONE,
            avail = fn () => NONE,
            getPos = NONE, setPos = NONE,
            endPos = NONE, verifyPos = NONE,
            close = fn () => Socket.close sock,
            ioDesc = NONE
          }
    val wr = BinPrimIO.WR{
            name = sockName,
            chunkSize = Socket.Ctl.getSNDBUF sock,
            writeVec =
              SOME(fn buffer => Socket.sendVec(sock, buffer)),
            writeArr =
              SOME(fn buffer => Socket.sendArr(sock, buffer)),
            writeVecNB = NONE, writeArrNB = NONE,
            block = NONE,
            canOutput = NONE,
            getPos = NONE, setPos = NONE,
            endPos = NONE, verifyPos = NONE,
            close = fn () => Socket.close sock,
            ioDesc = NONE
          }
    val inStrm = BinIO.mkInstream(
          BinIO.StreamIO.mkInstream(rd,
            Word8Vector.fromList[]))
    val outStrm = BinIO.mkOutstream (
          BinIO.StreamIO.mkOutstream(wr, IO.BLOCK_BUF))
    in
      (inStrm, outStrm)
    end
```

Listing 10.2: Building binary I/O streams from a socket

```
datatype address = Unix of string | INet of string

fun withSocket (Unix path, port, f) = let
        val addr = UnixSock.toAddr path
        val sock = connectUnixSock {addr = addr, port = port}
    in
        f sock
    end
  | withSocket (INet host, port, f) =
        f (connectINetSock {host = host, port = port})
```

10.6.4 Creating sockets in other domains

The SML Basis Library provides a generic mechanism for creating sockets of any supported domain, although without the same degree of static typing. For example, we can create a "RAW" socket (assuming the application has sufficient permissions) in the Internet domain using the following code:

```
fun rawSocket () = let
        val SOME sockTy = Socket.SOCK.fromString "RAW"
    in
        GenericSock.socket (INetSock.inetAF, sockTy)
    end
```

network communication and are supported

11
Manual pages

11.1   The `Array` structure

The `Array` structure defines polymorphic arrays, which are mutable sequences with constant-time access and update.

Arrays have a special equality property: two arrays are equal if they are the same array, i.e., created by the same call to a primitive array constructor such as `array`, `fromList`, etc.; otherwise they are not equal. This property also holds for arrays of zero length. Thus, the type `ty array` admits equality even if `ty` does not.

Synopsis

```
signature ARRAY
structure Array :> ARRAY
```

Interface

```
eqtype 'a array = 'a array
type 'a vector = 'a Vector.vector

val maxLen : int
val array : int * 'a -> 'a array
val fromList : 'a list -> 'a array
val vector : 'a array -> 'a vector
val tabulate : int * (int -> 'a) -> 'a array

val length : 'a array -> int
val sub : 'a array * int -> 'a
val update : 'a array * int * 'a -> unit
val copy     : {src : 'a array, dst : 'a array, di : int}
                  -> unit
val copyVec : {src : 'a vector, dst : 'a array, di : int}
                  -> unit

val appi : (int * 'a -> unit) -> 'a array -> unit
val app  : ('a -> unit) -> 'a array -> unit
val modifyi : (int * 'a -> 'a) -> 'a array -> unit
val modify  : ('a -> 'a) -> 'a array -> unit
val foldli : (int * 'a * 'b -> 'b) -> 'b -> 'a array -> 'b
val foldri : (int * 'a * 'b -> 'b) -> 'b -> 'a array -> 'b
val foldl  : ('a * 'b -> 'b) -> 'b -> 'a array -> 'b
val foldr  : ('a * 'b -> 'b) -> 'b -> 'a array -> 'b
val findi : (int * 'a -> bool)
                  -> 'a array -> (int * 'a) option
val find  : ('a -> bool) -> 'a array -> 'a option
val exists : ('a -> bool) -> 'a array -> bool
val all : ('a -> bool) -> 'a array -> bool
val collate : ('a * 'a -> order)
                  -> 'a array * 'a array -> order
```

Description

val maxLen : int

> The maximum length of arrays supported by this implementation. Attempts to create larger arrays will result in the Size exception being raised.

val array : int * 'a -> 'a array

> array (n, init) creates a new array of length n; each element is initialized to the value init. If $n < 0$ or maxLen $< n$, then the Size exception is raised.

val fromList : 'a list -> 'a array

> fromList l creates a new array from l. The length of the array is length l and the ith element of the array is the ith element of the the list. If the length of the list is greater than maxLen, then the Size exception is raised.

val vector : 'a array -> 'a vector

> vector arr generates a vector from arr. Specifically, the result is equivalent to
> $$\text{Vector.tabulate (length } arr, \textbf{fn } i \Rightarrow \text{sub } (arr, i))$$

val tabulate : int * (int -> 'a) -> 'a array

> tabulate (n, f) creates an array of n elements, where the elements are defined in order of increasing index by applying f to the element's index. This expression is equivalent to:
> $$\text{fromList (List.tabulate } (n, f))$$
> If $n < 0$ or maxLen $< n$, then the Size exception is raised.

val length : 'a array -> int

> length arr returns $|arr|$, the length of the array arr.

val sub : 'a array * int -> 'a

> sub (arr, i) returns the ith element of the array arr. If $i < 0$ or $|arr| \leq i$, then the Subscript exception is raised.

val update : 'a array * int * 'a -> unit

> update (arr, i, x) sets the ith element of the array arr to x. If $i < 0$ or $|arr| \leq i$, then the Subscript exception is raised.

```
val copy : {src : 'a array, dst : 'a array, di : int}
              -> unit
val copyVec : {src : 'a vector, dst : 'a array, di : int}
                -> unit
```

copy {*src, dst, di*}
copyVec {*src, dst, di*}
These functions copy the entire array or vector *src* into the array *dst*, with the ith element in *src*, for $0 \le i < |src|$, being copied to position $di + i$ in the destination array. If $di < 0$ or if $|dst| < di + |src|$, then the Subscript exception is raised.

Implementation note: In copy, if *dst* and *src* are equal, we must have $di = 0$ to avoid an exception, and copy is then the identity.

```
val appi : (int * 'a -> unit) -> 'a array -> unit
val app : ('a -> unit) -> 'a array -> unit
```

appi *f arr*
app *f arr*
These functions apply the function *f* to the elements of the array *arr* in order of increasing indices. The more general form appi supplies *f* with the array index of the corresponding element.

```
val modifyi : (int * 'a -> 'a) -> 'a array -> unit
val modify : ('a -> 'a) -> 'a array -> unit
```

modifyi *f arr*
modify *f arr*
These functions apply the function *f* to the elements of the array *arr* in order of increasing indices and replace each element with the result. The more general modifyi supplies *f* with the array index of the corresponding element. The expression modify *f arr* is equivalent to modifyi (*f* o #2) *arr*.

```
val foldli : (int * 'a * 'b -> 'b) -> 'b -> 'a array -> 'b
val foldri : (int * 'a * 'b -> 'b) -> 'b -> 'a array -> 'b
val foldl : ('a * 'b -> 'b) -> 'b -> 'a array -> 'b
val foldr : ('a * 'b -> 'b) -> 'b -> 'a array -> 'b
```

foldli *f init arr*
foldri *f init arr*
foldl *f init arr*
foldr *f init arr*
These fold the function *f* over all the elements of the array *arr*, using the value *init* as the initial value. The functions foldli and foldl apply the function *f* from left to right (increasing indices), while the functions foldri and foldr work from right to left (decreasing indices). The more general functions foldli and foldri supply *f* with the array index of the corresponding element.

Refer to the MONO_ARRAY manual pages for reference implementations of the indexed versions.

The expression `foldl f init arr` is equivalent to:

```
foldli (fn (_, a, x) => f(a, x)) init arr
```

The analogous equivalences hold for `foldri` and `foldr`.

```
val findi : (int * 'a -> bool)
                -> 'a array -> (int * 'a) option
val find : ('a -> bool) -> 'a array -> 'a option
```

```
findi pred arr
find pred arr
```
These functions apply *pred* to each element of the array *arr*, from left to right (i.e., increasing indices), until a `true` value is returned. These functions return the first such element, if it exists; otherwise, they return NONE. The more general version `findi` also supplies *pred* with the array index of the element and, upon finding an entry satisfying the predicate, returns that index with the element.

```
val exists : ('a -> bool) -> 'a array -> bool
```

`exists` *pred arr* applies *pred* to each element *x* of the array *arr*, from left to right (i.e., increasing indices), until *pred x* evaluates to `true`; it returns `true` if such an *x* exists and `false` otherwise.

```
val all : ('a -> bool) -> 'a array -> bool
```

`all` *pred arr* applies *pred* to each element *x* of the array *arr*, from left to right (i.e., increasing indices), until *pred x* evaluates to `false`; it returns `false` if such an *x* exists and `true` otherwise. It is equivalent to `not(exists (not o pred) arr))`.

```
val collate : ('a * 'a -> order)
                -> 'a array * 'a array -> order
```

`collate` *cmp* (*a1, a2*) performs a lexicographic comparison of the two arrays using the ordering of elements defined by the function *cmp*.

See also

`ArraySlice` (§11.3; p. 122), MONO_ARRAY (§11.23; p. 193), `Vector` (§11.64; p. 401)

11.2   The `Array2` structure

The `Array2` structure provides polymorphic mutable two-dimensional arrays. As with one-dimensional arrays, these arrays have the equality property that two arrays are equal if, and only if, they are the same array, i.e., created by the same call to a primitive array constructor such as `array`, `fromList`, etc. This property also holds for arrays of zero length. Thus, the type `ty array` admits equality even if `ty` does not.

The elements of two-dimensional arrays are indexed by pair of integers (i, j), where i gives the row index and i gives the column index. As usual, indices start at 0, with increasing indices going from left to right and, in the case of rows, from top to bottom.

Synopsis

```
signature ARRAY2
structure Array2 :> ARRAY2
```

Interface

```
eqtype 'a array
type 'a region = {
                    base : 'a array,
                    row : int,
                    col : int,
                    nrows : int option,
                    ncols : int option
                  }
datatype traversal = RowMajor | ColMajor

val array : int * int * 'a -> 'a array
val fromList : 'a list list -> 'a array
val tabulate : traversal
                  -> int * int * (int * int -> 'a)
                  -> 'a array

val sub : 'a array * int * int -> 'a
val update : 'a array * int * int * 'a -> unit

val dimensions : 'a array -> int * int
val nCols      : 'a array -> int
val nRows      : 'a array -> int
val row : 'a array * int -> 'a Vector.vector
val column : 'a array * int -> 'a Vector.vector

val copy : {
              src : 'a region,
              dst : 'a array,
              dst_row : int,
              dst_col : int
           } -> unit
```

```
val appi : traversal
                -> (int * int * 'a -> unit)
                   -> 'a region -> unit
val app  : traversal -> ('a -> unit) -> 'a array -> unit
val foldi : traversal
                -> (int * int * 'a * 'b -> 'b)
                   -> 'b -> 'a region -> 'b
val fold  : traversal
                -> ('a * 'b -> 'b) -> 'b -> 'a array -> 'b
val modifyi : traversal
                -> (int * int * 'a -> 'a)
                   -> 'a region -> unit
val modify  : traversal -> ('a -> 'a) -> 'a array -> unit
```

Description

```
type 'a region = {
                base : 'a array,
                row : int,
                col : int,
                nrows : int option,
                ncols : int option
             }
```

This type specifies a rectangular subregion of a two-dimensional array. If ncols equals SOME(w), with $0 \leq w$, the region includes only those elements in columns with indices in the range from col to $col + (w - 1)$, inclusively. If ncols is NONE, the region includes only those elements lying on or to the right of column col. A similar interpretation holds for the row and nrows fields. Thus, the region corresponds to all those elements with position (i, j) such that i lies in the specified range of rows and j lies in the specified range of columns.

A region reg is said to be *valid* if it denotes a legal subarray of its base array. More specifically, reg is *valid* if

$$0 \leq \#row\ reg \leq nRows\ (\#base\ reg)$$

when #nrows reg = NONE, or

$$0 \leq \#row\ reg \leq (\#row\ reg) + nr \leq nRows\ (\#base\ reg)$$

when #nrows reg = SOME(nr), and the analogous conditions hold for columns.

datatype traversal = RowMajor | ColMajor

This type specifies a way of traversing a region. Specifically, RowMajor indicates that, given a region, the rows are traversed from left to right (smallest column index to largest column index), starting with the first row in the region, then the second, and so on until the last row is traversed. ColMajor reverses the roles of row and column, traversing the columns from the top down (smallest row index to largest row index), starting with the first column, then the second, and so on until the last column is traversed.

val array : int * int * 'a -> 'a array

> array (r, c, *init*) creates a new array with r rows and c columns, with each element initialized to the value *init*. If $r < 0$, $c < 0$ or the resulting array would be too large, the Size exception is raised.

val fromList : 'a list list -> 'a array

> fromList *l* creates a new array from a list of rows, each of which is a list of elements. Thus, the elements are given in row major order, i.e., hd *l* gives the first row, hd (tl *l*) gives the second row, etc. This function raises the Size exception if the resulting array would be too large or if the lists in *l* do not all have the same length.

val tabulate : traversal
                 -> int * int * (int * int -> 'a)
                 -> 'a array

> tabulate trv (r, c, f) creates a new array with r rows and c columns, with the $(i,j)^{th}$ element initialized to f (i, j). The elements are initialized in the traversal order specified by *trv*. If $r < 0$, $c < 0$ or the resulting array would be too large, the Size exception is raised.

val sub : 'a array * int * int -> 'a

> sub (arr, i, j) returns the $(i,j)^{th}$ element of the array arr. If $i < 0$, $j < 0$, nRows $arr \leq i$, or nCols $arr \leq j$, then the Subscript exception is raised.

val update : 'a array * int * int * 'a -> unit

> update (arr, i, j, a) sets the $(i,j)^{th}$ element of the array arr to a. If $i < 0$, $j < 0$, nRows $arr \leq i$, or nCols $arr \leq j$, then the Subscript exception is raised.

val dimensions : 'a array -> int * int
val nCols : 'a array -> int
val nRows : 'a array -> int

> These functions return size information concerning an array. nCols returns the number of columns, nRows returns the number of rows, and dimension returns a pair containing the number of rows and the number of columns of the array. The functions nRows and nCols are respectively equivalent to #1 o dimensions and #2 o dimensions

val row : 'a array * int -> 'a Vector.vector

> row (arr, i) returns row i of arr. If (nRows arr) $\leq i$ or $i < 0$, then this function raises Subscript.

val column : 'a array * int -> 'a Vector.vector

column (*arr*, *j*) returns column *j* of *arr*. This function raises Subscript if $j < 0$ or nCols *arr* $\leq j$.

val copy : {
                src : 'a region,
                dst : 'a array,
                dst_row : int,
                dst_col : int
        } -> unit

copy {*src*, *dst*, *dst_row*, *dst_col*} copies the region *src* into the array *dst*, with the element at position (#row *src*, #col *src*) copied into the destination array at position (*dst_row*, *dst_col*). If the source region is not valid, then the Subscript exception is raised. Similarly, if the derived destination region (the source region *src* translated to (*dst_row*, *dst_col*)) is not valid in *dst*, then the Subscript exception is raised.

Implementation note: The copy function must correctly handle the case in which the #base *src* and the *dst* arrays are equal and the source and destination regions overlap.

val appi : traversal
             -> (int * int * 'a -> unit)
               -> 'a region -> unit
val app : traversal -> ('a -> unit) -> 'a array -> unit

appi *tr f reg*
app *tr f arr*
These functions apply the function *f* to the elements of an array in the order specified by *tr*. The more general appi function applies *f* to the elements of the region *reg* and supplies both the element and the element's coordinates in the base array to the function *f*. If *reg* is not valid, then the exception Subscript is raised.

The function app applies *f* to the whole array and does not supply the element's coordinates to *f*. Thus, the expression app *tr f arr* is equivalent to:
```
let
  val range = {base=arr,row=0,col=0,nrows=NONE,ncols=NONE}
in
  appi tr (f o #3) range
end
```

```
val foldi : traversal
               -> (int * int * 'a * 'b -> 'b)
                  -> 'b -> 'a region -> 'b
val fold : traversal
               -> ('a * 'b -> 'b) -> 'b -> 'a array -> 'b
```

```
foldi tr f init reg
fold tr f init arr
```
These functions fold the function f over the elements of an array arr, traversing the elements in tr order, and using the value $init$ as the initial value. The more general foldi function applies f to the elements of the region reg and supplies both the element and the element's coordinates in the base array to the function f. If reg is not valid, then the exception Subscript is raised.

The function fold applies f to the whole array and does not supply the element's coordinates to f. Thus, the expression fold tr f $init$ arr is equivalent to:
```
foldi tr (fn (_,_,a,b) => f (a,b)) init
          {base=arr, row=0, col=0, nrows=NONE, ncols=NONE}
```

```
val modifyi : traversal
               -> (int * int * 'a -> 'a)
                  -> 'a region -> unit
val modify : traversal -> ('a -> 'a) -> 'a array -> unit
```

```
modifyi tr f reg
modify tr f arr
```
These functions apply the function f to the elements of an array in the order specified by tr and replace each element with the result of f. The more general modifyi function applies f to the elements of the region reg and supplies both the element and the element's coordinates in the base array to the function f. If reg is not valid, then the exception Subscript is raised.

The function modify applies f to the whole array and does not supply the element's coordinates to f. Thus, the expression modify tr f arr is equivalent to:
```
let
  val range = {base=arr,row=0,col=0,nrows=NONE,ncols=NONE}
in
  modifyi tr (f o #3)
end
```

Discussion

Note that the indices passed to argument functions in appi, foldi, and modifyi are with respect to the underlying matrix and not based on the region. This convention is different from that of the analogous functions on one-dimensional slices.

Rationale: It was clear that two-dimensional arrays needed to be provided, but the interface is fairly rudimentary, because of the lack of experience with their use in SML programs. Thus, we kept regions concrete, as opposed to the abstract slice types, their one-dimensional cousins. In addition, we felt it best, at this time, to avoid picking among the vast number of possible matrix functions (e.g., matrix multiplication).

Implementation note: Unlike one-dimensional types, the signature for two-dimensional arrays does not specify any bounds on possible arrays. Implementations should support a total number of elements that is at least as large as the total number of elements in the corresponding one-dimensional array type.

See also

Array (§11.1; p. 112), MONO_ARRAY2 (§11.24; p. 199)

11.3   The `ArraySlice` structure

The `ArraySlice` structure provides an abstraction of subarrays for polymorphic arrays. A `slice` value can be viewed as a triple (a, i, n), where a is the underlying array, i is the starting index, and n is the length of the subarray, with the constraint that $0 \le i \le i + n \le |a|$. Slices provide a convenient notation for specifying and operating on a contiguous subset of elements in an array.

Synopsis

```
signature ARRAY_SLICE
structure ArraySlice :> ARRAY_SLICE
```

Interface

```
type 'a slice

val length : 'a slice -> int
val sub : 'a slice * int -> 'a
val update : 'a slice * int * 'a -> unit
val full : 'a Array.array -> 'a slice
val slice : 'a Array.array * int * int option -> 'a slice
val subslice : 'a slice * int * int option -> 'a slice
val base : 'a slice -> 'a Array.array * int * int
val vector : 'a slice -> 'a Vector.vector
val copy     : {
                  src : 'a slice,
                  dst : 'a Array.array,
                  di : int
               } -> unit
val copyVec : {
                  src : 'a VectorSlice.slice,
                  dst : 'a Array.array,
                  di : int
               } -> unit
val isEmpty : 'a slice -> bool
val getItem : 'a slice -> ('a * 'a slice) option

val appi : (int * 'a -> unit) -> 'a slice -> unit
val app  : ('a -> unit) -> 'a slice -> unit
val modifyi : (int * 'a -> 'a) -> 'a slice -> unit
val modify  : ('a -> 'a) -> 'a slice -> unit
val foldli : (int * 'a * 'b -> 'b) -> 'b -> 'a slice -> 'b
val foldri : (int * 'a * 'b -> 'b) -> 'b -> 'a slice -> 'b
val foldl  : ('a * 'b -> 'b) -> 'b -> 'a slice -> 'b
val foldr  : ('a * 'b -> 'b) -> 'b -> 'a slice -> 'b
val findi : (int * 'a -> bool)
               -> 'a slice -> (int * 'a) option
val find  : ('a -> bool) -> 'a slice -> 'a option
val exists : ('a -> bool) -> 'a slice -> bool
val all : ('a -> bool) -> 'a slice -> bool
```

```
val collate : ('a * 'a -> order)
                  -> 'a slice * 'a slice -> order
```

Description

```
val length : 'a slice -> int
```

length sl returns $|sl|$, the length (i.e., number of elements) of the slice. This expression is equivalent to #3 (base sl).

```
val sub : 'a slice * int -> 'a
```

sub (sl, i) returns the ith element of the slice sl. If $i < 0$ or $|sl| \leq i$, then the Subscript exception is raised.

```
val update : 'a slice * int * 'a -> unit
```

update (sl, i, a) sets the ith element of the slice sl to a. If $i < 0$ or $|sl| \leq i$, then the Subscript exception is raised.

```
val full : 'a Array.array -> 'a slice
```

full arr creates a slice representing the entire array arr. It is equivalent to

$$slice(arr, 0, NONE)$$

```
val slice : 'a Array.array * int * int option -> 'a slice
```

slice (arr, i, sz) creates a slice based on the array arr starting at index i of the array. If sz is NONE, the slice includes all of the elements to the end of the array, i.e., $arr[i..|arr| - 1]$. This function raises Subscript if $i < 0$ or $|arr| < i$. If sz is SOME(j), the slice has length j, that is, it corresponds to $arr[i..i+j-1]$. It raises Subscript if $i < 0$ or $j < 0$ or $|arr| < i + j$. Note that, if defined, slice returns an empty slice when $i = |arr|$.

```
val subslice : 'a slice * int * int option -> 'a slice
```

subslice (sl, i, sz) creates a slice based on the given slice sl starting at index i of sl. If sz is NONE, the slice includes all of the elements to the end of the slice, i.e., $sl[i..|sl| - 1]$. This function raises Subscript if $i < 0$ or $|sl| < i$. If sz is SOME(j), the slice has length j, that is, it corresponds to $sl[i..i+j-1]$. It raises Subscript if $i < 0$ or $j < 0$ or $|sl| < i + j$. Note that, if defined, subslice returns an empty slice when $i = |sl|$.

```
val base : 'a slice -> 'a Array.array * int * int
```

base sl returns a triple (arr, i, n) representing the concrete representation of the slice. arr is the underlying array, i is the starting index, and n is the length of the slice.

val vector : 'a slice -> 'a Vector.vector

> vector *sl* generates a vector from the slice *sl*. Specifically, the result is equivalent to
> Vector.tabulate (length *sl*, **fn** i => sub (*sl*, i))

val copy : {src : 'a slice, dst : 'a Array.array, di : int}
>   -> unit

val copyVec : {
>   src : 'a VectorSlice.slice,
>   dst : 'a Array.array,
>   di : int
>   } -> unit

> copy {*src, dst, di*}
> copyVec {*src, dst, di*}
> These functions copy the given slice into the array *dst*, with the ith element of *src*, for
> $0 \le i < |src|$, being copied to position $di + i$ in the destination array. If $di < 0$ or if
> $|dst| < di + |src|$, then the Subscript exception is raised.

> **Implementation note:**   The copy function must correctly handle the case in which
> *dst* and the base array of *src* are equal and the source and destination slices overlap.

val isEmpty : 'a slice -> bool

> isEmpty *sl* returns true if *sl* has length 0.

val getItem : 'a slice -> ('a * 'a slice) option

> getItem *sl* returns the first item in *sl* and the rest of the slice, or NONE if *sl* is
> empty.

val appi : (int * 'a -> unit) -> 'a slice -> unit
val app : ('a -> unit) -> 'a slice -> unit

> appi *f sl*
> app *f sl*
> These functions apply the function *f* to the elements of a slice in order of increasing
> indices. The more general appi function supplies *f* with the index of the corresponding
> element in the slice. The expression app *f sl* is equivalent to appi (*f* o #2) *sl*.

val modifyi : (int * 'a -> 'a) -> 'a slice -> unit
val modify : ('a -> 'a) -> 'a slice -> unit

> modifyi *f sl*
> modify *f sl*
> These functions apply the function *f* to the elements of a slice in order of increasing
> indices and replace each element with the result. The more general modifyi supplies *f*
> with the index of the corresponding element in the slice. The expression modify *f sl*
> is equivalent to modifyi (*f* o #2) *sl*.

```
val foldli : (int * 'a * 'b -> 'b) -> 'b -> 'a slice -> 'b
val foldri : (int * 'a * 'b -> 'b) -> 'b -> 'a slice -> 'b
val foldl : ('a * 'b -> 'b) -> 'b -> 'a slice -> 'b
val foldr : ('a * 'b -> 'b) -> 'b -> 'a slice -> 'b
```

```
foldli f init sl
foldri f init sl
foldl f init sl
foldr f init sl
```

These functions fold the function *f* over the elements of a slice, using the value *init* as the initial value. The functions `foldli` and `foldl` apply the function *f* from left to right (increasing indices), while the functions `foldri` and `foldr` work from right to left (decreasing indices). The more general functions `foldli` and `foldri` supply *f* with the index of the corresponding element in the slice.

Refer to the MONO_ARRAY manual pages for reference implementations of the indexed versions.

The expression `foldl` *f init sl* is equivalent to:

```
foldli (fn (_, a, x) => f(a, x)) init sl
```

The analogous equivalence holds for `foldri` and `foldr`.

```
val findi : (int * 'a -> bool)
              -> 'a slice -> (int * 'a) option
val find : ('a -> bool) -> 'a slice -> 'a option
```

```
findi pred sl
find pred sl
```

These functions apply *pred* to each element of the slice *sl*, in order of increasing indices, until a `true` value is returned. These functions return the first such element, if it exists; otherwise, they return NONE. The more general version `findi` also supplies *f* with the index of the element in the slice and, upon finding an entry satisfying the predicate, returns that index with the element.

```
val exists : ('a -> bool) -> 'a slice -> bool
```

`exists` *pred sl* applies *pred* to each element *x* of the slice *sl*, in order of increasing indices, until *pred x* evaluates to `true`; it returns `true` if such an *x* exists and `false` otherwise.

```
val all : ('a -> bool) -> 'a slice -> bool
```

`all` *pred sl* applies *pred* to each element *x* of the slice *sl*, from left to right (i.e., increasing indices), until *pred x* evaluates to `false`; it returns `false` if such an *x* exists and `true` otherwise. It is equivalent to `not(exists (not o pred) l))`.

```
val collate : ('a * 'a -> order)
                -> 'a slice * 'a slice -> order
```

`collate` *cmp (sl, sl2)* performs lexicographic comparison of the two slices using the given ordering *cmp* on elements.

See also

Array (§11.1; p. 112), MONO_ARRAY_SLICE (§11.25; p. 205),
Vector (§11.64; p. 401), VectorSlice (§11.65; p. 405)

11.4 The BinIO structure

The structure `BinIO` provides input/output of binary data (8-bit bytes). The semantics of the various I/O operations can be found in the description of the `IMPERATIVE_IO` signature. The `openIn` and `openOut` functions allow the creation of binary streams to read and write file data. Certain implementations may provide other ways to open files in structures specific to an operating system.

Synopsis

```
signature BIN_IO
structure BinIO :> BIN_IO
```

Interface

```
include IMPERATIVE_IO
  where type StreamIO.vector = Word8Vector.vector
  where type StreamIO.elem = Word8.word
  where type StreamIO.reader = BinPrimIO.reader
  where type StreamIO.writer = BinPrimIO.writer
  where type StreamIO.pos = BinPrimIO.pos
val openIn   : string -> instream
val openOut  : string -> outstream
val openAppend : string -> outstream
```

Description

```
val openIn : string -> instream
val openOut : string -> outstream
```

> `openIn name`
> `openOut name`
> These functions open the file named *name* for input and output, respectively. If *name* is a relative pathname, the file opened depends on the current working directory. With `openOut`, the file is created if it does not already exist and truncated to length zero otherwise. These raise `Io` if a stream cannot be opened on the given file or, in the case of `openIn`, the file *name* does not exist.

```
val openAppend : string -> outstream
```

> `openAppend name` opens the file named *name* for output in append mode, creating it if it does not already exist. If the file already exists, it sets the current position at the end of the file. It raises `Io` if a stream cannot be opened on the given file.
>
> Beyond having the initial file position at the end of the file, any additional properties are system and implementation dependent. On operating systems (e.g., Unix) that support "atomic append mode," each (flushed) output operation to the file will be appended to the end, even if there are other processes writing to the file simultaneously. Due to buffering, however, writing on an `outstream` need not be atomic, i.e., output from a different process may interleave the output of a single write using the stream library. On certain

other operating systems, having the file open for writing prevents any other process from opening the file for writing.

Discussion

All streams created by `mkInstream`, `mkOutstream`, and the open functions in `BinIO` will be closed (and the output streams among them flushed) when the SML program exits.

Note that the `BinIO.StreamIO.pos` type, equal to the `BinPrimIO.pos` type, is concrete, being a synonym for `Position.int`.

See also

`IMPERATIVE_IO` (§11.14; p. 158), `OS.Path` (§11.35; p. 241), `Posix.FileSys` (§11.41; p. 263), `Posix.IO` (§11.42; p. 276), `TextIO` (§11.58; p. 382)

11.5 The **BIT_FLAGS** signature

The BIT_FLAGS signature defines a generic set of operations on an abstract representation of system flags. It is typically included as part of the signature of substructures that implement sets of options.

Synopsis

```
signature BIT_FLAGS
```

Interface

```
eqtype flags
val toWord   : flags -> SysWord.word
val fromWord : SysWord.word -> flags
val all : flags
val flags : flags list -> flags
val intersect : flags list -> flags
val clear : flags * flags -> flags
val allSet : flags * flags -> bool
val anySet : flags * flags -> bool
```

Description

```
eqtype flags
```

> This type is the abstract representation of a set of system flags.

```
val toWord : flags -> SysWord.word
val fromWord : SysWord.word -> flags
```

> These functions convert between the abstract flags type and a bit-vector that is represented as a system word. The interpretation of the bits is system-dependent but follows the C language binding for the host operating system. Note that there is no error checking on the fromWord function's argument.

```
val all : flags
```

> all represents the union of all flags. Note that this set may well be a superset of the flags value defined in a matching structure. For example, BIT_FLAGS is used to define the flags specified by the POSIX standard; a POSIX-conforming operating system may provide additional flags that will not be defined in the Posix structure but could be set in the all value.

```
val flags : flags list -> flags
```

> flags *l* returns a value that represents the union of the flags in the list *l*. The expression flags [] denotes the empty set.

val intersect : flags list -> flags

> intersect *l* returns a value that represents the intersection of the sets of flags in the list *l*. The expression intersect [] denotes all.

val clear : flags * flags -> flags

> clear (*fl1*, *fl2*) returns the set of those flags in *fl2* that are not set in *fl1*, i.e., the set difference *fl2* \ *fl1*. It is equivalent to the expression:
> ```
>     fromWord(
>         SysWord.andb(SysWord.notb (toWord fl1), toWord fl2))
> ```

val allSet : flags * flags -> bool

> allSet (*fl1*, *fl2*) returns true if all of the flags in *fl1* are also in *fl2* (i.e., it tests for inclusion of *fl1* in *fl2*).

val anySet : flags * flags -> bool

> anySet (*fl1*, *fl2*) returns true if any of the flags in *fl1* are also in *fl2* (i.e., it tests for non-empty intersection).

Discussion

> The number of distinct flags in an implementation of the BIT_FLAGS interface must be less than or equal to the number of bits in the SysWord.word type. In addition, from-Word o toWord must be the identity function, and toWord o fromWord must be equivalent to
>
> $$\textbf{fn } w \texttt{ => SysWord.andb(w, toWord all)}$$

See also

11.6 The `Bool` structure

The `Bool` structure provides some basic operations on boolean values.

Synopsis

```
signature BOOL
structure Bool :> BOOL
```

Interface

```
datatype bool = false | true
val not : bool -> bool
val toString : bool -> string
val scan        : (char, 'a) StringCvt.reader
                       -> (bool, 'a) StringCvt.reader
val fromString : string -> bool option
```

Description

```
val not : bool -> bool
```

> `not` `b` returns the logical negation of the boolean value `b`.

```
val toString : bool -> string
```

> `toString` `b` returns the string representation of `b`, either `"true"` or `"false"`.

```
val scan : (char, 'a) StringCvt.reader
              -> (bool, 'a) StringCvt.reader
val fromString : string -> bool option
```

> `scan` *getc strm*
> `fromString` *s*
> These scan a character source for a boolean value. The first takes a character stream reader *getc* and a stream *strm*. Ignoring case and initial whitespace, the sequences `"true"` and `"false"` are converted to the corresponding boolean values. On successful scanning of a boolean value, `scan` returns `SOME(`*b*`, ` *rest*`)`, where *b* is the scanned value and *rest* is the remaining character stream.
>
> The second form scans a boolean from a string *s*. It returns `SOME(`*b*`)` for a scanned value *b*; otherwise it returns `NONE`. The function `fromString` is equivalent to `String-Cvt.scanString scan`.

Discussion

> The `bool` type is considered primitive and is defined in the top-level environment. It is rebound here for consistency.
>
> In addition to the `not` function presented here, the language defines the special operators **andalso** and **orelse**, which provide short-circuit evaluation of the AND and OR of two boolean expressions. The semantics of strict AND and OR operators, which would

evaluate both expressions before applying the operator, are rarely needed and can easily be obtained using the **andalso** and **orelse** operators.

See also

StringCvt (§11.55; p. 366)

11.7 The Byte structure

Bytes are 8-bit integers as provided by the `Word8` structure but they serve the dual role as the elements of the extended ASCII character set. The `Byte` structure provides functions for converting values between these two roles.

Synopsis

```
signature BYTE
structure Byte :> BYTE
```

Interface

```
val byteToChar : Word8.word -> char
val charToByte : char -> Word8.word
val bytesToString : Word8Vector.vector -> string
val stringToBytes : string -> Word8Vector.vector
val unpackStringVec : Word8VectorSlice.slice -> string
val unpackString : Word8ArraySlice.slice -> string
val packString : Word8Array.array * int * substring -> unit
```

Description

```
val byteToChar : Word8.word -> char
```

byteToChar *i* returns the character whose code is *i*.

```
val charToByte : char -> Word8.word
```

charToByte *c* returns an 8-bit word holding the code for the character *c*.

```
val bytesToString : Word8Vector.vector -> string
val stringToBytes : string -> Word8Vector.vector
```

These functions convert between a vector of character codes and the corresponding string. Note that these functions do not perform end-of-line or other character translations. The semantics of these functions can be defined as follows, although one expects actual implementations will be more efficient:

```
fun bytesToString bv =
    CharVector.tabulate(
        Word8Vector.length bv,
        fn i => byteToChar(Word8Vector.sub(bv, i)))
fun stringToBytes s =
    Word8Vector.tabulate(
        String.size s,
        fn i => charToByte(String.sub(s, i)))
```

Implementation note: For implementations where the underlying representation of the `Word8Vector.vector` and `string` types are the same, these functions should be constant-time operations.

val `unpackStringVec` **:** `Word8VectorSlice.slice` `->` `string`

unpackStringVec *slice* returns the string consisting of characters whose codes are held in the vector slice *slice*.

val `unpackString` **:** `Word8ArraySlice.slice` `->` `string`

This function returns the string consisting of characters whose codes are held in the array slice *slice*.

val `packString` **:** `Word8Array.array` `*` `int` `*` `substring` `->` `unit`

packString (*arr*, *i*, *s*) puts the substring s into the array *arr* starting at offset i. It raises `Subscript` if $i < 0$ or $\text{size } s + i > |arr|$.

See also

Char ($\S11.8$; p. 135), String ($\S11.54$; p. 360), Substring ($\S11.56$; p. 372), WORD ($\S11.67$; p. 420), Word8 ($\S11.67$; p. 420), Word8Vector ($\S11.26$; p. 211), Word8VectorSlice ($\S11.27$; p. 215), Word8Array ($\S11.23$; p. 193), Word8ArraySlice ($\S11.25$; p. 205)

11.8 The CHAR signature

The CHAR signature defines a type char of characters and provides basic operations and predicates on values of that type. There is a linear ordering defined on characters. In addition, there is an encoding of characters into a contiguous range of non-negative integers that preserves the linear ordering.

The SML Basis Library defines two structures matching the CHAR signature. The required Char structure provides the extended ASCII 8-bit character set and locale-independent operations on them. For this structure, Char.maxOrd = 255.

The optional WideChar structure defines wide characters, which are represented by a fixed number of 8-bit words (bytes). If the WideChar structure is provided, it is distinct from the Char structure.

Synopsis

```
signature CHAR
structure Char :> CHAR
  where type char = char
  where type string = String.string
structure WideChar :> CHAR
  where type string = WideString.string
```

Interface

```
eqtype char
eqtype string

val minChar : char
val maxChar : char
val maxOrd : int

val ord : char -> int
val chr : int -> char
val succ : char -> char
val pred : char -> char

val compare : char * char -> order
val <  : char * char -> bool
val <= : char * char -> bool
val >  : char * char -> bool
val >= : char * char -> bool

val contains : string -> char -> bool
val notContains : string -> char -> bool

val isAscii : char -> bool
val toLower : char -> char
val toUpper : char -> char
```

```
val isAlpha : char -> bool
val isAlphaNum : char -> bool
val isCntrl : char -> bool
val isDigit : char -> bool
val isGraph : char -> bool
val isHexDigit : char -> bool
val isLower : char -> bool
val isPrint : char -> bool
val isSpace : char -> bool
val isPunct : char -> bool
val isUpper : char -> bool

val toString : char -> String.string
val scan         : (Char.char, 'a) StringCvt.reader
                       -> (char, 'a) StringCvt.reader
val fromString : String.string -> char option
val toCString : char -> String.string
val fromCString : String.string -> char option
```

Description

```
val minChar : char
```

The least character in the ordering. It always equals `chr 0`.

```
val maxChar : char
```

The greatest character in the ordering; it equals `chr maxOrd`.

```
val maxOrd : int
```

The greatest character code; it equals `ord maxChar`.

```
val ord : char -> int
```

`ord c` returns the (non-negative) integer code of the character c.

```
val chr : int -> char
```

`chr i` returns the character whose code is i; it raises `Chr` if $i < 0$ or $i >$ maxOrd.

```
val succ : char -> char
```

`succ c` returns the character immediately following c in the ordering or raises `Chr` if $c = $ maxChar. When defined, `succ c` is equivalent to `chr(ord c + 1)`.

val pred : char -> char

> pred c returns the character immediately preceding c or raises Chr if c = minChar. When defined, pred c is equivalent to chr(ord c - 1).

val compare : char * char -> order

> compare (c, d) returns LESS, EQUAL, or GREATER, depending on whether c precedes, equals, or follows d in the character ordering.

val < : char * char -> bool
val <= : char * char -> bool
val > : char * char -> bool
val >= : char * char -> bool

> These compare characters in the character ordering. Note that the functions ord and chr preserve orderings. For example, if we have x < y for characters x and y, then it is also true that ord x < ord y.

val contains : string -> char -> bool

> contains s c returns true if character c occurs in the string s; otherwise it returns false.

> **Implementation note:**   In some implementations, the partial evaluation of contains to s may build a table, which is used by the resulting function to decide whether a given character is in the string or not. Hence val p = contains s may be expensive to compute, but p c might be fast for any given character c.

val notContains : string -> char -> bool

> notContains s c returns true if character c does not occur in the string s; it returns false otherwise. It is equivalent to not(contains s c).

> **Implementation note:**   As with contains, notContains may be implemented via table lookup.

val isAscii : char -> bool

> isAscii c returns true if c is a (7-bit) ASCII character, i.e., $0 \leq$ ord $c \leq 127$. Note that this function is independent of locale.

```
val toLower : char -> char
val toUpper : char -> char
```

> toLower c
> toUpper c
> These functions return the lowercase (respectively, uppercase) letter corresponding to c if
> c is a letter; otherwise it returns c.

```
val isAlpha : char -> bool
```

> isAlpha c returns true if c is a (lowercase or uppercase).

```
val isAlphaNum : char -> bool
```

> isAlphaNum c returns true if c is alphanumeric (a letter or a decimal digit).

```
val isCntrl : char -> bool
```

> isCntrl c returns true if c is a control character.

```
val isDigit : char -> bool
```

> isDigit c returns true if c is a decimal digit $[0-9]$.

```
val isGraph : char -> bool
```

> isGraph c returns true if c is a graphical character, that is, it is printable and not a
> whitespace character.

```
val isHexDigit : char -> bool
```

> isHexDigit c returns true if c is a hexadecimal digit $[0-9a-fA-F]$.

```
val isLower : char -> bool
```

> isLower c returns true if c is a lowercase letter.

```
val isPrint : char -> bool
```

> isPrint c returns true if c is a printable character (space or visible), i.e., not a
> control character.

```
val isSpace : char -> bool
```

> isSpace c returns true if c is a whitespace character (space, newline, tab, carriage
> return, vertical tab, formfeed).

val isPunct : char -> bool

> isPunct *c* returns true if *c* is a punctuation character: graphical but not alphanumeric.

val isUpper : char -> bool

> isUpper *c* returns true if *c* is an uppercase letter.

val toString : char -> String.string

> toString *c* returns a printable string representation of the character, using, if necessary, SML escape sequences. Printable characters, except for #"\\" and #"\"", are left unchanged. Backslash #"\\" becomes "\\\\"; double quote #"\"" becomes "\\\"". The common control characters are converted to two-character escape sequences:

Alert (ASCII 0x07)	"\\a"
Backspace (ASCII 0x08)	"\\b"
Horizontal tab (ASCII 0x09)	"\\t"
Linefeed or newline (ASCII 0x0A)	"\\n"
Vertical tab (ASCII 0x0B)	"\\v"
Form feed (ASCII 0x0C)	"\\f"
Carriage return (ASCII 0x0D)	"\\r"

> The remaining characters whose codes are less than 32 are represented by three-character strings in "control character" notation, e.g., #"\000" maps to "\\^@", #"\001" maps to "\\^A", etc. For characters whose codes are greater than 999, the character is mapped to a six-character string of the form "\\uxxxx", where xxxx are the four hexadecimal digits corresponding to a character's code. All other characters (i.e., those whose codes are greater than 126 but less than 1000) are mapped to four-character strings of the form "\\ddd", where ddd are the three decimal digits corresponding to a character's code.

> To convert a character to a length-one string containing the character, use the function String.str.

val scan : (Char.char, 'a) StringCvt.reader
           -> (char, 'a) StringCvt.reader
val fromString : String.string -> char option

> scan *getc strm*
> fromString *s*
> These functions scan a character (including possibly a space) or an SML escape sequence representing a character from the prefix of a character stream or a string of printable characters, as allowed in an SML program. After a successful conversion, scan returns the remainder of the stream along with the character, whereas fromString ignores any additional characters in *s* and just returns the character. If the first character is non-printable (i.e., not in the ASCII range [0x20,0x7E]) or starts an illegal escape sequence (e.g., "\q"), no conversion is possible and NONE is returned. The function fromString is equivalent to StringCvt.scanString scan.

> The allowable escape sequences are given in the following table:

\a	Alert (ASCII 0x07)
\b	Backspace (ASCII 0x08)
\t	Horizontal tab (ASCII 0x09)
\n	Linefeed or newline (ASCII 0x0A)
\v	Vertical tab (ASCII 0x0B)
\f	Form feed (ASCII 0x0C)
\r	Carriage return (ASCII 0x0D)
\\	Backslash
\"	Double quote
\^*c*	A control character whose encoding is ord *c* - 64, with the character *c* having ord *c* in the range [64,95]; for example, \^H (control-H) is the same as \b (backspace)
ddd	The character whose encoding is the number *ddd*, three decimal digits denoting an integer in the range [0,255]
\u*xxxx*	The character whose encoding is the number *xxxx*, four hexadecimal digits denoting an integer in the ordinal range of the alphabet
f...f\	This sequence is ignored, where *f...f* stands for a sequence of one or more formatting (space, newline, tab, etc.) characters

In the escape sequences involving decimal or hexadecimal digits, if the resulting value cannot be represented in the character set, NONE is returned. As the table indicates, escaped formatting sequences (\f...f\) are passed over during scanning. Such sequences are successfully scanned, so that the remaining stream returned by scan will never have a valid escaped formatting sequence as its prefix.

Here are some sample conversions:

Input string *s*	fromString *s*
"\\q"	NONE
"a\^D"	SOME #"a"
"a\\ \\\q"	SOME #"a"
"\\ \\"	NONE
" "	NONE
"\\ \\\^D"	NONE
"\\ a"	NONE

val toCString : char -> String.string

toCString *c* returns a printable string corresponding to *c*, with non-printable characters replaced by C escape sequences. Specifically, printable characters, except for #"\\", #"\"", #"?", and #"'", are left unchanged. Backslash (#"\\") becomes "\\\\"; double quote (#"\"") becomes "\\\"", question mark (#"?") becomes "\\?", and single quote (#"'") becomes "\\'". The common control characters are converted to two-character escape sequences:

Alert (ASCII 0x07)	"\\a"
Backspace (ASCII 0x08)	"\\b"
Horizontal tab (ASCII 0x09)	"\\t"
Linefeed or newline (ASCII 0x0A)	"\\n"
Vertical tab (ASCII 0x0B)	"\\v"
Form feed (ASCII 0x0C)	"\\f"
Carriage return (ASCII 0x0D)	"\\r"

All other characters are represented by three octal digits, corresponding to a character's code, preceded by a backslash.

val `fromCString : String.string -> char option`

`fromCString` `s` scans a character (including possibly a space) or a C escape sequence representing a character from the prefix of a string. After a successful conversion, `from-CString` ignores any additional characters in `s`. If no conversion is possible, e.g., if the first character is non-printable (i.e., not in the ASCII range [0x20-0x7E] or starts an illegal escape sequence, `NONE` is returned.

The allowable escape sequences are given below (*cf.* Section 6.1.3.4 of the ISO C standard ISO/IEC 9899:1990 [ISO90]).

`\a`	Alert (ASCII 0x07)
`\b`	Backspace (ASCII 0x08)
`\t`	Horizontal tab (ASCII 0x09)
`\n`	Linefeed or newline (ASCII 0x0A)
`\v`	Vertical tab (ASCII 0x0B)
`\f`	Form feed (ASCII 0x0C)
`\r`	Carriage return (ASCII 0x0D)
`\?`	Question mark
`\\`	Backslash
`\"`	Double quote
`\'`	Single quote
`\^c`	A control character whose encoding is `ord` `c` `-` `64`, with the character `c` having `ord` `c` in the range [64,95]. For example, `\^H` (control-H) is the same as `\b` (backspace).
`\ooo`	The character whose encoding is the number `ooo`, where `ooo` consists of one to three octal digits
`\xhh`	The character whose encoding is the number `hh`, where `hh` is a sequence of hexadecimal digits.

Note that `fromCString` accepts an unescaped single quote character, but does not accept an unescaped double quote character.

In the escape sequences involving octal or hexadecimal digits, the sequence of digits is taken to be the longest sequence of such characters. If the resulting value cannot be represented in the character set, `NONE` is returned.

Discussion

In `WideChar`, the functions `toLower`, `toLower`, `isAlpha`,..., `isUpper` and, in general, the definition of a "letter" are locale-dependent. In `Char`, these functions are locale-independent, with the following semantics:

isUpper *c*	#"A" <= *c* **andalso** *c* <= #"Z"
isLower *c*	#"a" <= *c* **andalso** *c* <= #"z"
isDigit *c*	#"0" <= *c* **andalso** *c* <= #"9"
isAlpha *c*	isUpper *c* **orelse** isLower *c*
isAlphaNum *c*	isAlpha *c* **orelse** isDigit *c*
isHexDigit *c*	isDigit *c*
	orelse (#"a" <= *c* **andalso** *c* <= #"f")
	orelse (#"A" <= *c* **andalso** *c* <= #"F")
isGraph *c*	#"!" <= *c* **andalso** *c* <= #"~"
isPrint *c*	isGraph *c* **orelse** *c* = #" "
isPunct *c*	isGraph *c* **andalso** not (isAlphaNum *c*)
isCntrl *c*	isAscii *c* **andalso** not (isPrint *c*)
isSpace *c*	(#"\t" <= *c* **andalso** *c* <= #"\r")
	orelse *c* = #" "
isAscii *c*	0 <= ord *c* **andalso** ord *c* <= 127
toLower *c*	**if** isUpper *c* **then** chr (ord *c* + 32) **else** *c*
toUpper *c*	**if** isLower *c* **then** chr (ord *c* - 32) **else** *c*

See also

STRING (§11.54; p. 360), TEXT (§11.57; p. 380)

11.9   The CommandLine structure

The CommandLine structure provides access to the name and arguments used to invoke the currently running program.

Synopsis

```
signature COMMAND_LINE
structure CommandLine :> COMMAND_LINE
```

Interface

```
val name : unit -> string
val arguments : unit -> string list
```

Description

```
val name : unit -> string
```

The name used to invoke the current program.

```
val arguments : unit -> string list
```

The argument list used to invoke the current program.

Implementation note: The arguments returned may be only a subset of the arguments actually supplied by the user, since an implementation's runtime system may consume some of them.

Discussion

The precise semantics of the above operations are operating-system and implementation specific. For example, name might return a full pathname or just the base name. See also the comment under arguments.

11.10   The `Date` structure

The `Date` structure provides functions for converting between times and dates, and formatting and scanning dates.

Synopsis

```
signature DATE
structure Date :> DATE
```

Interface

```
datatype weekday = Mon | Tue | Wed | Thu | Fri | Sat | Sun
datatype month
  = Jan | Feb | Mar | Apr | May | Jun
  | Jul | Aug | Sep | Oct | Nov | Dec
type date

exception Date

val date : {
                  year : int,
                  month : month,
                  day : int,
                  hour : int,
                  minute : int,
                  second : int,
                  offset : Time.time option
              } -> date

val year    : date -> int
val month   : date -> month
val day     : date -> int
val hour    : date -> int
val minute  : date -> int
val second  : date -> int
val weekDay : date -> weekday
val yearDay : date -> int
val offset  : date -> Time.time option
val isDst   : date -> bool option

val localOffset : unit -> Time.time

val fromTimeLocal : Time.time -> date
val fromTimeUniv  : Time.time -> date
val toTime : date -> Time.time

val compare : date * date -> order

val fmt      : string -> date -> string
val toString : date -> string
```

```
val scan        : (char, 'a) StringCvt.reader
                    -> (date, 'a) StringCvt.reader
val fromString : string -> date option
```

Description

type `date`

An abstract type whose values represent an instant in a specific time zone.

exception `Date`

This exception is raised when converting a date value to a `string` or `time` value and either the date is invalid or unrepresentable.

val `date` : {
```
                year : int,
                month : month,
                day : int,
                hour : int,
                minute : int,
                second : int,
                offset : Time.time option
        } -> date
```

This function creates a canonical date from the given date information. If the resulting date is outside the range supported by the implementation, the `Date` exception is raised.

Seconds outside the range [0,59] are converted to the equivalent minutes and added to the minutes argument. Similar conversions are performed for minutes to hours, hours to days, days to months, and months to years. Negative values are similarly translated into a canonical range, with the extra borrowed from the next larger unit. Thus, `minute = 10, second = ~140` becomes `minute = 7, second = 40`.

The `offset` argument provides time zone information. A value of NONE represents the local time zone. A value of SOME(t) corresponds to time t west of UTC. In particular, SOME(`Time.zeroTime`) is UTC. Negative offsets denote time zones to the east of UTC, as is traditional. Offsets are taken modulo 24 hours. That is, we express t, in hours, as $sgn(t)(24 * d + r)$, where d and r are non-negative, d is integral, and $r < 24$. The offset then becomes $sgn(t)*r$, and $sgn(t)(24*d)$ is added to the hours (before converting hours to days).

Leap years follow the Gregorian calendar. Leap seconds may or may not be ignored. In an implementation that takes account of leap seconds, the `second` function may return 60 or 61 in the rare cases that it is appropriate.

```
val year : date -> int
val month : date -> month
val day : date -> int
val hour : date -> int
val minute : date -> int
val second : date -> int
val weekDay : date -> weekday
val yearDay : date -> int
val offset : date -> Time.time option
val isDst : date -> bool option
```

These functions extract the attributes of a date value. The year returned by `year` uses year 0 as its base. Thus, the date Robin Milner received the Turing award would have year 1991. The function `yearDay` returns the day of the year, starting from 0, i.e., 1 January is day 0. The value returned by `offset` reports time zone information as the amount of time west of UTC. A value of `NONE` represents the local time zone. The function `isDst` returns `NONE` if the system has no information concerning daylight savings time. Otherwise, it returns `SOME(dst)`, where *dst* is `true` if daylight savings time is in effect.

```
val localOffset : unit -> Time.time
```

The offset from UTC for the local time zone.

```
val fromTimeLocal : Time.time -> date
val fromTimeUniv : Time.time -> date
```

```
fromTimeLocal t
fromTimeUniv t
```
These convert the (UTC) time *t* into a corresponding date. `fromTimeLocal` represents the date in the local time zone; it is the analogue of the ISO C function `localtime`. The returned date will have `offset=NONE`. `fromTimeUniv` returns the date in the UTC time zone; it is the analogue of the ISO C function `gmtime`. The returned date will have `offset=SOME(0)`.

If these functions are applied to the same time value, the resulting dates will differ by the offset of the local time zone from UTC.

```
val toTime : date -> Time.time
```

`toTime date` returns the (UTC) time corresponding to the date *date*. It raises `Date` if the date *date* cannot be represented as a `Time.time` value. It is the analogue of the ISO C function `mktime`.

```
val compare : date * date -> order
```

`compare (date1, date2)` returns `LESS`, `EQUAL`, or `GREATER`, according as *date1* precedes, equals, or follows *date2* in time. It lexicographically compares the dates, using the year, month, day, hour, minute, and second information but ignoring the offset and daylight savings time information. It does not detect invalid dates.

In order to compare dates in two different time zones, the user would have to handle the normalization.

val fmt : string -> date -> string
val toString : date -> string

> fmt *s date*
> toString *date*

These functions return a string representation of the date *date*. The result may be wrong if the date is outside the representable Time.time range. They raise Date if the given date is invalid.

The former formats the date according to the format string *s*, following the semantics of the ISO C function strftime. In particular, fmt is locale-dependent. The allowed formats are given by the following table:

%a	locale's abbreviated weekday name
%A	locale's full weekday name
%b	locale's abbreviated month name
%B	locale's full month name
%c	locale's date and time representation (e.g., "Dec 2 06:55:15 1979")
%d	day of month [01-31]
%H	hour [00-23]
%I	hour [01-12]
%j	day of year [001-366]
%m	month number [01-12]
%M	minutes [00-59]
%p	locale's equivalent of the AM/PM designation
%S	seconds [00-61]
%U	week number of year [00-53], with the first Sunday as the first day of week 01
%w	day of week [0-6], with 0 representing Sunday
%W	week number of year [00-53], with the first Monday as the first day of week 01
%x	locale's appropriate date representation
%X	locale's appropriate time representation
%y	year of century [00-99]
%Y	year including century (e.g., 1997)
%Z	time zone name or abbreviation, or the empty string if no time zone information exists
%%	the percent character
%*c*	the character *c*, if *c* is not one of the format characters listed above

For instance, fmt "%A" *date* returns the full name of the weekday specified by *date* (e.g., "Monday"). For a full description of the format-string syntax, consult a description of strftime. Note, however, that, unlike strftime, the behavior of fmt is defined for the directive %*c* for any character *c*.

toString returns a 24-character string representing the date *date* in the following format:

```
                        "Wed Mar 08 19:06:45 1995"
```
The function is equivalent to `Date.fmt "%a %b %d %H:%M:%S %Y"`.

val `scan : (char, 'a) StringCvt.reader`
             `-> (date, 'a) StringCvt.reader`
val `fromString : string -> date option`

> `scan getc strm`
> `fromString s`

These scan a 24-character date from a character source after ignoring possible initial whitespace. The format of the string must be precisely as produced by `toString`. In particular, the functions do not parse time zone abbreviations. No check of the consistency of the date (weekday, date in the month, ...) is performed. If the scanning fails, NONE is returned.

The function `scan` takes a character stream reader `getc` and a stream `strm`. In case of success, it returns `SOME(date, rest)`, where `date` is the scanned date and `rest` is the remainder of the stream.

The function `fromString` takes a string `s` as its source of characters. It is equivalent to `StringCvt.scanString scan`.

Discussion

In the `Date` structure, the `time` type is used to represent intervals starting from a fixed reference point. These times are always measured in Coordinated Universal Time (UTC), also known as Greenwich Mean Time. The implementation of time values, however, is system-dependent, so time values are not portable across implementations.

A conforming `Date` structure should support date values ranging from around 1900 to 2200, although they may be inaccurate with respect to daylight savings time outside the range of dates supported by time values.

Implementation note: Implementations of this structure might use the ISO C `mktime` function. Some implementations of this function, when given dates that are out of range, wrap around instead of returning -1. Thus, implementations using `mktime` need to check the validity of a date before invoking the function.

See also

`StringCvt` (§11.55; p. 366), `Time` (§11.60; p. 387)

11.11 The General structure

The structure General defines exceptions, datatypes, and functions that are used throughout the SML Basis Library, and are useful in a wide range of programs.

All of the types and values defined in General are available unqualified at the top level.

Synopsis

```
signature GENERAL
structure General :> GENERAL
```

Interface

```
eqtype unit
type exn = exn

exception Bind
exception Match
exception Chr
exception Div
exception Domain
exception Fail of string
exception Overflow
exception Size
exception Span
exception Subscript

val exnName : exn -> string
val exnMessage : exn -> string

datatype order = LESS | EQUAL | GREATER
val ! : 'a ref -> 'a
val := : 'a ref * 'a -> unit
val o : ('b -> 'c) * ('a -> 'b) -> 'a -> 'c
val before : 'a * unit -> 'a
val ignore : 'a -> unit
```

Description

```
eqtype unit
```

    The type containing a single value denoted (), which is typically used as a trivial argument or as a return value for a side-effecting function.

```
type exn = exn
```

    The type of values transmitted when an exception is raised and handled. This type is special in that it behaves like a datatype with an extensible set of data constructors, where new constructors are created by exception declarations.

exception Bind

> This exception is raised when there is a pattern-match failure in a **val** binding.

exception Match

> This exception is raised when there is a pattern-match failure in a **case** expression or function application.

exception Chr

> The exception indicating an attempt to create a character with a code outside the range supported by the underlying character type (see CHAR.chr).

exception Div

> The exception indicating an attempt to divide by zero.

exception Domain

> The exception indicating that the argument of a mathematical function is outside the domain of the function. It is raised by functions in structures matching the MATH or INT_INF signatures.

exception Fail **of** string

> A general-purpose exception used to signify the failure of an operation. It is not raised by any function in the SML Basis Library but is provided for use by users and user-defined libraries.

exception Overflow

> The exception indicating that the result of an arithmetic function is not representable, in particular, is too large.

exception Size

> The exception indicating an attempt to create an aggregate data structure (such as an array, string, or vector) whose size is too large or negative.

exception Span

> The exception indicating an attempt to apply SUBSTRING.span to two incompatible substrings.

exception Subscript

The exception indicating that an index is out of range, typically arising when the program is accessing an element in an aggregate data structure (such as a list, string, array, or vector).

val exnName : exn -> string

exnName *ex* returns a name for the exception *ex*. The name returned may be that of any exception constructor aliasing with *ex*. For instance,

let exception E1; **exception** E2 = E1 **in** exnName E2 **end**

might evaluate to "E1" or "E2".

val exnMessage : exn -> string

exnMessage *ex* returns a message corresponding to exception *ex*. The precise format of the message may vary between implementations and locales but will at least contain the string exnName *ex*.

Example:
```
exnMessage Div = "Div"
exnMessage (OS.SysErr ("No such file", NONE)) =
  "OS.SysErr \"No such file\""
```

datatype order = LESS | EQUAL | GREATER

Values of type order are used when comparing elements of a type that has a linear ordering.

val ! : 'a ref -> 'a

! *re* returns the value referred to by the reference *re*.

val := : 'a ref * 'a -> unit

re := *a* makes the reference *re* refer to the value *a*.

val o : ('b -> 'c) * ('a -> 'b) -> 'a -> 'c

f o *g* is the function composition of *f* and *g*. Thus, (*f* o *g*) *a* is equivalent to *f* (*g a*).

val before : 'a * unit -> 'a

e1 before *e2* returns the result of the expression *e1* after evaluating *e2*. It provides a notational shorthand for the expression

let val tmp = e1 **in** e2; tmp **end**

(assuming tmp is not free in *e2*). Also, it requires that the type of its right-hand-side argument be unit.

val ignore : 'a -> unit

> ignore *a* returns (). The purpose of ignore is to discard the result of a computation, returning () instead. This function is useful when a higher-order function, such as List.-app, requires a function returning unit, but the function to be used returns values of some other type.

11.12 The `GenericSock` structure

Implementations may provide the `GenericSock` structure as a way to provide access to additional address families socket types (beyond those supported by `INetSock` and `UnixSock`).

Synopsis

```
signature GENERIC_SOCK
structure GenericSock :> GENERIC_SOCK
```

Interface

```
val socket : Socket.AF.addr_family * Socket.SOCK.sock_type
                -> ('af, 'sock_type) Socket.sock
val socketPair : Socket.AF.addr_family
                * Socket.SOCK.sock_type
                -> ('af, 'sock_type) Socket.sock
                * ('af, 'sock_type) Socket.sock
val socket' : Socket.AF.addr_family
                * Socket.SOCK.sock_type
                * int -> ('af, 'sock_type) Socket.sock
val socketPair' : Socket.AF.addr_family
                * Socket.SOCK.sock_type
                * int
                -> ('af, 'sock_type) Socket.sock
                * ('af, 'sock_type) Socket.sock
```

Description

```
val socket : Socket.AF.addr_family * Socket.SOCK.sock_type
                -> ('af, 'sock_type) Socket.sock
```

> `socket` (*af*, *sockTy*) creates a socket in the address family specified by *af* and the socket type specified by *sockTy*, with the default protocol. This function raises `Sys-Err` when the any of the following happen: the address family *af* is not supported, the protocol *prot* is not supported, or there are insufficient resources.

```
val socketPair : Socket.AF.addr_family
                * Socket.SOCK.sock_type
                -> ('af, 'sock_type) Socket.sock
                * ('af, 'sock_type) Socket.sock
```

> `socketPair` (*af*, *sockTy*) creates an unnamed pair of connected sockets in the address family specified by *af* and the socket type specified by *sockTy*, with the default protocol. This function raises `SysErr` when the any of the following happen: the address family *af* is not supported, the protocol *prot* is not supported or does not support socket pairs, socket pairs are not supported, or there are insufficient resources.

val socket' : Socket.AF.addr_family
                        * Socket.SOCK.sock_type
                        * int -> ('af, 'sock_type) Socket.sock

socket' (*af*, *sockTy*, *prot*) creates a socket in the address family specified by
af and the socket type specified by *sockTy*, with protocol number *prot*. This function raises SysErr when the any of the following happen: the address family *af* is not
supported, the protocol *prot* is not supported, or there are insufficient resources.

val socketPair' : Socket.AF.addr_family
                        * Socket.SOCK.sock_type
                        * int
                        -> ('af, 'sock_type) Socket.sock
                        * ('af, 'sock_type) Socket.sock

socketPair' (*af*, *sockTy*, *prot*) creates an unnamed pair of connected sockets in the address family specified by *af* and the socket type specified by *sockTy*, with
protocol number *prot*. This function raises SysErr when the any of the following happen: the address family *af* is not supported, the protocol *prot* is not supported or does
not support socket pairs, socket pairs are not supported, or there are insufficient resources.

Discussion

Note that one can use the Socket.AF.list and Socket.SOCK.list functions to
get lists of the address families and socket types that the implementation knows about,
although they are not guaranteed to be supported.

See also

INetSock (§11.16; p. 166), NetProtDB (§11.29; p. 223), Socket (§11.51; p. 330),
UnixSock (§11.63; p. 398)

11.13 The `IEEEReal` structure

The `IEEEReal` structure defines types associated with an IEEE implementation of floating-point numbers. In addition, it provides control for the floating-point hardware's rounding mode. Refer to the IEEE standard 754-1985 [IEE85] and the ANSI/IEEE standard 854-1987 [IEE87] for additional information.

Synopsis

```
signature IEEE_REAL
structure IEEEReal :> IEEE_REAL
```

Interface

```
exception Unordered
datatype real_order = LESS | EQUAL | GREATER | UNORDERED
datatype float_class
  = NAN
  | INF
  | ZERO
  | NORMAL
  | SUBNORMAL
datatype rounding_mode
  = TO_NEAREST
  | TO_NEGINF
  | TO_POSINF
  | TO_ZERO
val setRoundingMode : rounding_mode -> unit
val getRoundingMode : unit -> rounding_mode
type decimal_approx = {
                        class : float_class,
                        sign : bool,
                        digits : int list,
                        exp : int
                      }
val toString : decimal_approx -> string
val scan       : (char, 'a) StringCvt.reader
                  -> (decimal_approx, 'a) StringCvt.reader
val fromString : string -> decimal_approx option
```

Description

`exception` Unordered

> This exception is raises by the `compare` operations on real numbers when the numbers are unordered.

```
val setRoundingMode : rounding_mode -> unit
val getRoundingMode : unit -> rounding_mode
```

These set and get the rounding mode of the underlying hardware. The IEEE standard requires TO_NEAREST as the default rounding mode.

Implementation note: Some platforms do not support all of the rounding modes. An SML implementation built on these platforms will necessarily be non-conforming with, presumably, setRoundingMode raising an exception for the unsupported modes.

```
type decimal_approx = {
                    class : float_class,
                    sign : bool,
                    digits : int list,
                    exp : int
                }
```

This type provides a structured decimal representation of a real. The class field indicates the real class. If sign is true, the number is negative. The integers in the digits list must be digits, i.e., between 0 and 9.

When class is NORMAL or SUBNORMAL, a value of type decimal_approx with digits $= [d_1, d_2, ..., d_n]$ corresponds to the real number $s * 0.d_1d_2...d_n 10^{exp}$, where s is -1 if sign is true and 1 otherwise. When class is ZERO or INF, the value corresponds to zero or infinity, respectively, with its sign determined by sign. When class is NAN, the value corresponds to an unspecified NaN value.

```
val toString : decimal_approx -> string
```

toString d returns a string representation of d. Assuming digits $= [d_1, d_2, ..., d_n]$ and ignoring the sign and exp fields, toString generates the following strings, depending on the class field:

ZERO	`"0.0"`
NORMAL	$"0.d_1d_2...d_n"$
SUBNORMAL	$"0.d_1d_2...d_n"$
INF	`"inf"`
NAN	`"nan"`

If the sign field is true, a `#"~"` is prepended. If the exp field is non-zero and the class is NORMAL or SUBNORMAL, the string `"E"^(Integer.toString exp)` is appended.

The composition toString o REAL.toDecimal is equivalent to REAL.fmt String-Cvt.EXACT.

```
val scan : (char, 'a) StringCvt.reader
             -> (decimal_approx, 'a) StringCvt.reader
val fromString : string -> decimal_approx option
```

scan *getc strm*
fromString *s*

These functions scan a decimal approximation from a prefix of a character source. Initial whitespace is ignored. The first reads from the character stream *strm* using the character input function *getc*. It returns SOME(*d*, *rest*) if the decimal approximation *d* can be parsed; *rest* is the remainder of the character stream. NONE is returned otherwise.

The second form uses the string *s* as input. It returns the decimal approximation on success and NONE otherwise. The fromString function is equivalent to StringCvt.-scanString scan.

The functions accept real numbers with the following format:

$$[+\mbox{\textasciitilde}-]^?([0-9]^+(.[0-9]^+)^?\mid.[0-9]^+)((e\mid E)[+\mbox{\textasciitilde}-]^?[0-9]^+)^?$$

The optional sign determines the value of the sign field, with a default of false. Initial zeros are stripped from the integer part and trailing zeros are stripped from the fractional part, yielding two lists, *il* and *fl*, respectively, of digits. If *il* is non-empty, then class is set to NORMAL, digits is set to *il@fl* with any trailing zeros removed, and exp is set to the length of *il* plus the value of the scanned exponent, if any. If *il* is empty and so is *fl*, then class is set to ZERO, digits = [], and exp = 0. Finally, if *il* is empty but *fl* is not, let m be the number of leading zeros in *fl* and let *fl'* be *fl* after the leading zeros are removed. Then, class is set to NORMAL, digits is set to *fl'*, and exp is set to $-m$ plus the value of the scanned exponent, if any.

These functions also accept the following string representations of non-finite values:

$$[+\mbox{\textasciitilde}-]^?(\mbox{inf}\mid\mbox{infinity}\mid\mbox{nan})$$

where the alphabetic characters are case-insensitive. The optional sign determines the value of the sign field, with a default of false. In the first and second cases, *d* will have class set to INF. In the third case, class is set to NAN. In all these cases, *d* will have digits = [] and exp = 0.

If the exponent is too large to fit into an Int.int value, then the representation is rounded to either zero or infinity according to the following rules:

- If either the mantissa is zero or the exponent is negative, then the result will be
  {class=ZERO, sign=s, digits=[], exp=0}
  where s is true if the mantissa is negative zero.
- If the exponent is positive, then the result will be
  {class=INF, sign=s digits=[], exp=0}
  where s is true if the mantissa is negative.

Discussion

Note that values of type decimal_approx are independent of any floating-point representation.

See also

REAL (§11.50; p. 318), MATH (§11.22; p. 189)

11.14   The `IMPERATIVE_IO` signature

The `IMPERATIVE_IO` signature defines the interface of the *imperative I/O* layer in the I/O stack. This layer provides buffered I/O using mutable, redirectable streams.

Synopsis

```
signature IMPERATIVE_IO
```

Interface

```
structure StreamIO : STREAM_IO

type vector = StreamIO.vector
type elem = StreamIO.elem

type instream
type outstream

val input : instream -> vector
val input1 : instream -> elem option
val inputN : instream * int -> vector
val inputAll : instream -> vector
val canInput : instream * int -> int option
val lookahead : instream -> elem option
val closeIn : instream -> unit
val endOfStream : instream -> bool

val output : outstream * vector -> unit
val output1 : outstream * elem -> unit
val flushOut : outstream -> unit
val closeOut : outstream -> unit

val mkInstream : StreamIO.instream -> instream
val getInstream : instream -> StreamIO.instream
val setInstream : instream * StreamIO.instream -> unit

val mkOutstream : StreamIO.outstream -> outstream
val getOutstream : outstream -> StreamIO.outstream
val setOutstream : outstream * StreamIO.outstream -> unit
val getPosOut : outstream -> StreamIO.out_pos
val setPosOut : outstream * StreamIO.out_pos -> unit
```

Description

```
structure StreamIO : STREAM_IO
```

This substructure provides lower-level stream I/O, as defined by the `STREAM_IO` interface, which is compatible with the `instream` and `outstream` types, in the sense that the conversion functions `mkInstream`, `getInstream`, `mkOutstream`, and `get-Outstream` allow the programmer to convert between low-level streams and redirectable streams. Typically, the redirectable streams are implemented in terms of low-level streams. Note that `StreamIO.outstream` is not a functional stream. The *only* difference between a `StreamIO.outstream` and an `outstream` is that the latter can be redirected.

```
type vector = StreamIO.vector
type elem = StreamIO.elem
```

These are the abstract types of stream elements and vectors of elements. For text streams, these are `Char.char` and `String.string`, while for binary streams they correspond to `Word8.word` and `Word8Vector.vector`.

```
type instream
```

The type of redirectable imperative input streams. Two imperative streams may share an underlying functional stream or reader. Closing one of them effectively closes the underlying functional stream, which will affect subsequent operations on the other.

```
type outstream
```

The type of redirectable output streams. Two or more streams may share an underlying stream or writer, in which case writing or positioning the file pointer on one of them, or closing it, also affects the other.

```
val input : instream -> vector
```

`input strm` attempts to read from *strm*, starting from the current input file position. When elements are available, it returns a `vector` of at least one element. When *strm* is at the end-of-stream or is closed or truncated, it returns an empty vector. Otherwise, `input` blocks until one of these conditions is met and returns accordingly. It may raise the exception `Io`.

```
val input1 : instream -> elem option
```

`input1 strm` reads one element from *strm*. It returns `SOME(e)` if one element is available; it returns `NONE` if at the end-of-stream. Otherwise, `input1` blocks until one of these conditions is met and returns accordingly. It may raise the exception `Io`.

After a call to `input1` returning `NONE` to indicate an end-of-stream, the input stream should be positioned after the end-of-stream.

```
val inputN : instream * int -> vector
```

`inputN (strm, n)` reads at most n elements from *strm*. It returns a vector containing n elements if at least n elements are available before the end-of-stream; it returns a shorter (and possibly empty) vector of all elements remaining before the end-of-stream otherwise. Otherwise, `inputN` blocks until one of these conditions is met and returns accordingly. It raises `Size` if $n < 0$ or if n is greater than the `maxLen` value for the `vector` type. It may also raise the exception `Io`.

val inputAll : instream -> vector

> inputAll *strm* returns all elements of *strm* up to the end-of-stream. It raises Size if the amount of data exceeds the maxLen of the vector type. It may also raise the exception Io.

val canInput : instream * int -> int option

> canInput (*strm*, *n*) returns NONE if any attempt at input would block. It returns SOME(*k*), where $0 \leq k \leq n$, if a call to input would return immediately with at least *k* characters. Note that $k = 0$ corresponds to the stream being at the end-of-stream.
>
> Some streams may not support this operation, in which case the Io exception will be raised. This function also raises the Io exception if there is an error in the underlying system calls. It raises the Size exception if $n < 0$.
>
> **Implementation note:** It is suggested that implementations of canInput should attempt to return as large a *k* as possible. For example, if the buffer contains 10 characters and the user calls canInput (*f*, 15), canInput should call readVecNB(5) to see if an additional 5 characters are available.

val lookahead : instream -> elem option

> lookahead *strm* determines whether one element is available on *strm* before the end-of-stream and returns SOME(e) in this case; it returns NONE if at the end-of-stream. In the former case, the element e is not removed from *strm* but stays available for further input operations. It may block waiting for an element and it may raise the exception Io.
>
> The underlying STREAM_IO stream can be used to easily implement arbitrary lookahead.

val closeIn : instream -> unit

> closeIn *strm* closes the input stream *strm*, freeing resources of the underlying I/O layers associated with it. Closing an already closed stream will be ignored. Other operations on a closed stream will behave as if the stream is at the end-of-stream. The function should be implemented in terms of StreamIO.closeIn. It may also raise Io when another error occurs.

val endOfStream : instream -> bool

> endOfStream *strm* returns true if *strm* is at the end-of-stream and false if elements are still available. It may block until one of these conditions is determined and may raise the exception Io.
>
> When endOfStream returns true on an untruncated stream, this result denotes the *current* situation. After a read from *strm* to consume the end-of-stream, it is possible that the next call to endOfStream *strm* may return false, and input operations will deliver new elements. For further information, consult the description of STREAM_IO.endOf-Stream.

val `output : outstream * vector -> unit`

> `output (strm, vec)` attempts to write the contents of `vec` to `strm`, starting from the current output file position. It may block until the underlying layers (and eventually the operating system) can accept all of `vec`. It may raise the exception `Io`. In that case, it is unspecified how much of `vec` was actually written.

val `output1 : outstream * elem -> unit`

> `output1 (strm, el)` writes exactly one element `el` to `strm`. It may block and may raise the exception `Io` if an error occurs. In that case, it is unspecified how much of `el` was actually written, especially if its physical representation is larger than just one byte. At this level, more than this cannot be guaranteed. Programs that need more control over this possibility need to make use of more primitive or OS-specific I/O routines.

val `flushOut : outstream -> unit`

> `flushOut strm` causes any buffers associated with `strm` to be written out. It is implemented in terms of `StreamIO.flushOut`. The function may block and may raise the exception `Io` when an error occurs.

val `closeOut : outstream -> unit`

> `closeOut strm` flushes any buffers associated with `strm` and then closes `strm`, freeing resources of the underlying I/O layers associated with it. It is implemented in terms of `StreamIO.closeOut`. A write attempt on a closed `outstream` will cause the exception `Io{cause=ClosedStream,...}` to be raised. It may also raise `Io` if another error occurs (e.g., buffers cannot be flushed out).

val `mkInstream : StreamIO.instream -> instream`

> `mkInstream strm` constructs a redirectable input stream from a functional one. The current version of `strm` returned by input operations will be kept internally and used for the next input. They can be obtained by `getInstream`.

val `getInstream : instream -> StreamIO.instream`

> `getInstream strm` returns the current version of the underlying functional input stream of `strm`. Using `getInstream`, it is possible to get input directly from the underlying functional stream. After having done so, it may be necessary to reassign the newly obtained functional stream to `strm` using `setInstream`; otherwise, the previous input will be read again when reading from `strm` the next time.

val setInstream : instream * StreamIO.instream -> unit

> setInstream (*strm*, *strm'*) assigns a new functional stream *strm'* to *strm*.
> Future input on *strm* will be read from *strm'*. This function is useful for redirecting
> input or interleaving input from different streams, e.g., when handling nested include files
> in a lexer.

val mkOutstream : StreamIO.outstream -> outstream

> mkOutstream *strm* constructs a redirectable output stream from a low-level func-
> tional one. Output to the imperative stream will be redirected to *strm*.

val getOutstream : outstream -> StreamIO.outstream

> getOutstream *strm* flushes *strm* and returns the underlying StreamIO output
> stream. Using getOutstream, it is possible to write output directly to the underlying
> stream or to save it and restore it using setOutstream after *strm* has been redirected.

val setOutstream : outstream * StreamIO.outstream -> unit

> setOutstream (*strm*, *strm'*) flushes the stream underlying *strm* and then as-
> signs a new low-level stream *strm'* to it. Future output on *strm* will be redirected to
> *strm'*.

val getPosOut : outstream -> StreamIO.out_pos

> getPosOut *strm* returns the current position in the stream *strm*. This function raises
> the exception Io if the stream does not support the operation, among other reasons. See
> StreamIO.getPosOut.

val setPosOut : outstream * StreamIO.out_pos -> unit

> setPosOut (*strm*, *pos*) sets the current position of the stream *strm* to be *pos*.
> This function raises the exception Io if the stream does not support the operation, among
> other reasons. See StreamIO.setPosOut.

Discussion

> A word is in order concerning I/O nomenclature. We refer to the I/O provided by the
> IMPERATIVE_IO signature as imperative I/O, while the I/O provided by the STREAM_IO
> signature is called stream I/O. On the other hand, the type of buffered I/O handled by both
> of these layers is typically considered "stream I/O," which explains why the I/O objects
> defined in both levels are called instream and outstream. To avoid confusion, we
> sometimes refer to the stream I/O layer as "functional I/O," focusing on the functional
> flavor of the input streams at that level. This term, however, glosses over the imperative
> nature of output at the same level. The principal distinction between the two layers is that
> I/O using IMPERATIVE_IO can be redirected, while I/O using STREAM_IO cannot.

The semantics of imperative I/O operations are (almost) all defined in terms of the operations provided by the underlying STREAM_IO substructure. Specifically, we have the reference implementations:

```
fun input(f) = let
        val (s,g) = StreamIO.input(getInstream f)
        in setInstream(f,g); s
        end
fun inputAll(f)= let
        val (s,g) = StreamIO.inputAll(getInstream f)
        in setInstream(f,g); s
        end
fun endOfStream(f)= StreamIO.endOfStream(getInstream f)
fun output(f,s) = StreamIO.output(getOutStream f, s)
fun flushOut(f) = StreamIO.flushOut(getOutStream f)
```

with similar implementations for other imperative I/O operations.

Alternatively, we can consider imperative I/O streams as reference cells referring to STREAM_IO streams:

```
type instream = StreamIO.instream ref
type outstream = StreamIO.outstream ref

fun input strm = let
        val (v, strm') = StreamIO.input(!strm)
        in
          strm := strm'; v
        end
fun output (strm, v) = StreamIO.output(!strm, v)
```

etc.

The one exception to the above approaches is input1. If an implementation relies solely on StreamIO.input1, input1 could never advance beyond an end-of-stream. The following reference implementation of input1 illustrates one approach to avoiding this problem:

```
fun input1 f = let
        val (s,g) = StreamIO.inputN(getInstream f, 1)
        in setInstream(f,g);
          if length s = 0 then NONE
          else SOME(sub(s,0))
        end
```

Limited random access on input streams — that is, returning to a previously scanned position — can be accomplished using getInstream and the underlying stream I/O layer:

```
fun reread (f : instream, n : int) = let
        val g = getInstream(f)
        val s = inputN (f,n)
        in
          setInstream(f,g);
          (s, inputN (f,n))
        end
```

The pair of vectors returned by `reread` will always be identical. Similarly, limited random access on output streams can be done directly using `getPosOut` and `setPosOut`. More general random access is only available at the primitive I/O level.

Implementation note: Input on a closed or truncated stream behaves as though the stream is permanently at the end-of-stream. Thus, in addition to closing the underlying functional stream, the `closeIn` function must also replace the functional stream with an empty stream.

See also

BinIO (§11.4; p. 127), ImperativeIO (§11.15; p. 165),
STREAM_IO (§11.52; p. 346), TextIO (§11.58; p. 382)

11.15 The `ImperativeIO` functor

The optional `ImperativeIO` functor can be used to implement (derive) an imperative-style stream I/O facility in terms of a lazy functional stream I/O facility. In the imperative style, input and output operations do not return a new stream each time but cause side effects on their arguments. Most functions can raise the `Io` exception for various reasons, including illegal or inconsistent parameters, IO failures, and attempts to do I/O on closed output streams.

The `ImperativeIO` functor is not often needed, as the required `BinIO` and `Text-IO` structures supply imperative-style I/O for most situations. It plays a useful role when the programmer needs to construct I/O facilities with element types other than `char` or `Word8.word`, or ones based on user-specified I/O primitives.

Synopsis

```
signature IMPERATIVE_IO
functor ImperativeIO (...): IMPERATIVE_IO
  where type StreamIO.elem = StreamIO.elem
  where type StreamIO.vector = StreamIO.vector
  where type StreamIO.instream = StreamIO.instream
  where type StreamIO.outstream = StreamIO.outstream
  where type StreamIO.out_pos = StreamIO.out_pos
  where type StreamIO.reader = StreamIO.reader
  where type StreamIO.writer = StreamIO.writer
  where type StreamIO.pos = StreamIO.pos
```

Functor Argument Interface

```
structure StreamIO : STREAM_IO
structure Vector : MONO_VECTOR
structure Array : MONO_ARRAY
sharing type StreamIO.elem = Vector.elem = Array.elem
sharing type StreamIO.vector = Vector.vector = Array.vector
```

Description

```
structure StreamIO : STREAM_IO
```

> The particular functional stream I/O facility from which this imperative I/O facility is derived. Most functions just call functions in `StreamIO` and do a little extra bookkeeping.

See also

IMPERATIVE_IO (§11.14; p. 158), MONO_ARRAY (§11.23; p. 193),
MONO_VECTOR (§11.26; p. 211), PrimIO (§11.49; p. 317),
STREAM_IO (§11.52; p. 346), StreamIO (§11.53; p. 358)

11.16   The `INetSock` structure

This structure provides operations for creating and manipulating Internet-domain addresses and sockets.

Synopsis

```
signature INET_SOCK
structure INetSock :> INET_SOCK
```

Interface

```
type inet
type 'sock_type sock = (inet, 'sock_type) Socket.sock
type 'mode stream_sock = 'mode Socket.stream sock
type dgram_sock = Socket.dgram sock
type sock_addr = inet Socket.sock_addr
val inetAF : Socket.AF.addr_family
val toAddr : NetHostDB.in_addr * int -> sock_addr
val fromAddr : sock_addr -> NetHostDB.in_addr * int
val any : int -> sock_addr
structure UDP : sig
    val socket : unit -> dgram_sock
    val socket' : int -> dgram_sock
  end
structure TCP : sig
    val socket : unit -> 'mode stream_sock
    val socket' : int -> 'mode stream_sock
    val getNODELAY : 'mode stream_sock -> bool
    val setNODELAY : 'mode stream_sock * bool -> unit
  end
```

Description

`type` inet

> The witness type of the INet address family. There are no values of this type.

`type` 'mode stream_sock = 'mode Socket.stream sock

> The type-scheme of Internet-domain stream sockets. The type parameter *'mode* can be instantiated to either `Socket.active` or `Socket.passive`.

`type` dgram_sock = Socket.dgram sock

> The type of Internet-domain datagram sockets.

type `sock_addr = inet Socket.sock_addr`

The type of Internet-domain socket addresses.

val `inetAF : Socket.AF.addr_family`

The address family value that represents the Internet domain.

val `toAddr : NetHostDB.in_addr * int -> sock_addr`

`toAddr (ia, i)` converts an Internet address `ia` and a port number `i` into a socket address (in the INet address family).

val `fromAddr : sock_addr -> NetHostDB.in_addr * int`

This function converts a socket address (in the INet address family) into a pair `(ia,i)` of an Internet address `ia` and a port number `i`.

val `any : int -> sock_addr`

`any port` creates a socket address that fixes the port to `port` but leaves the Internet address unspecified. This function corresponds to the `INADDR_ANY` constant in the C Sockets API. The values created by this function are used to `bind` a socket to a specific port.

structure `UDP` **: sig ... end**

This structure contains functions for creating datagram sockets in the Internet domain.

> **val** `socket : unit -> dgram_sock`
>
> This function creates a datagram socket in the INet address family with the default protocol. It raises `SysErr` if there are too many sockets in use.
>
> **val** `socket' : int -> dgram_sock`
>
> `socket' prot` creates a datagram socket in the INet address family with the protocol number `prot`. The interpretation of `prot` is system-dependent, but a value of 0 is equivalent to `socket()`. It raises `SysErr` if there are too many sockets in use.

structure `TCP` **: sig ... end**

This structure contains functions for creating stream sockets in the Internet domain.

> **val** `socket : unit -> 'mode stream_sock`
>
> This function creates a stream socket in the INet address family with the default protocol. It raises `SysErr` if there are too many sockets in use.

val `socket' : int -> 'mode stream_sock`

`socket'` *`prot`* creates a stream socket in the INet address family with the protocol number *`prot`*. The interpretation of *`prot`* is system dependent, but a value of 0 is equivalent to `socket()`.

val `getNODELAY : 'mode stream_sock -> bool`
val `setNODELAY : 'mode stream_sock * bool -> unit`

These functions query and set the `TCP_NODELAY` flag on the socket. When set to `false` (the default), there is only a single small packet allowed to be outstanding on a given TCP connection at any time, thereby reducing small packet traffic on slower WANs. When set to `true`, packets are sent as fast as possible, which reduces the latency of the response (see [Ste98] for more information).

See also

`GenericSock` (§11.12; p. 153), `NetHostDB` (§11.28; p. 220), `Socket` (§11.51; p. 330), `UnixSock` (§11.63; p. 398)

11.17   The `INTEGER` signature

Instances of the `INTEGER` signature provide a type of signed integers of either a fixed or arbitrary precision, and arithmetic and conversion operations. For fixed precision implementations, most arithmetic operations raise the exception `Overflow` when their result is not representable.

Synopsis

```
signature INTEGER
structure Int :> INTEGER
  where type int = int
structure FixedInt :> INTEGER
structure LargeInt :> INTEGER
structure IntN :> INTEGER
structure Position :> INTEGER
```

Interface

```
eqtype int

val toLarge    : int -> LargeInt.int
val fromLarge : LargeInt.int -> int
val toInt    : int -> Int.int
val fromInt : Int.int -> int

val precision : Int.int option
val minInt : int option
val maxInt : int option

val + : int * int -> int
val - : int * int -> int
val * : int * int -> int
val div : int * int -> int
val mod : int * int -> int
val quot : int * int -> int
val rem : int * int -> int

val compare : int * int -> order
val <  : int * int -> bool
val <= : int * int -> bool
val >  : int * int -> bool
val >= : int * int -> bool

val ~ : int -> int
val abs : int -> int
val min : int * int -> int
val max : int * int -> int
val sign : int -> Int.int
val sameSign : int * int -> bool
```

```
val fmt       : StringCvt.radix -> int -> string
val toString : int -> string
val scan       : StringCvt.radix
                   -> (char, 'a) StringCvt.reader
                     -> (int, 'a) StringCvt.reader
val fromString : string -> int option
```

Description

```
val toLarge : int -> LargeInt.int
val fromLarge : LargeInt.int -> int
```

These convert between integer values of types `int` and `LargeInt.int`. The latter raises `Overflow` if the value does not fit.

$Int M.$ `fromLarge` o $Int N.$ `toLarge` converts an integer from type $Int N.$ `int` to $Int M.$ `int`.

```
val toInt : int -> Int.int
val fromInt : Int.int -> int
```

These convert between integer values of types `int` and the default integer type. They raise `Overflow` if the value does not fit.

```
val precision : Int.int option
```

If `SOME (n)`, this value denotes the number n of significant bits in type `int`, including the sign bit. If it is `NONE`, `int` has arbitrary precision. The precision need not necessarily be a power of 2.

```
val minInt : int option
val maxInt : int option
```

The minimum (most negative) and the maximum (most positive) integers, respectively, representable by `int`. If a value is `NONE`, `int` can represent all negative (respectively, positive) integers, within the limits of the heap size.

If `precision` is `SOME (n)`, then we have `minInt` $= -2^{n-1}$ and `maxInt` $= 2^{n-1}-1$.

```
val + : int * int -> int
val - : int * int -> int
val * : int * int -> int
```

These functions return the sum, difference, and product, respectively, of the arguments. They raise `Overflow` when the result is not representable.

val div : int * int -> int

> *i* div *j* returns the greatest integer less than or equal to the quotient of *i* by *j*, i.e., $\lfloor (i/j) \rfloor$. It raises Overflow when the result is not representable and Div when $j = 0$. Note that rounding is toward negative infinity, not zero.

val mod : int * int -> int

> *i* mod *j* returns the remainder of the division of *i* by *j*. It raises Div when $j = 0$. When defined, (*i* mod *j*) has the same sign as *j*, and
> $$(i \text{ div } j) \text{ * } j + (i \text{ mod } j) = i$$

val quot : int * int -> int

> quot (*i*, *j*) returns the truncated quotient of the division of *i* by *j*, i.e., it computes (i/j) and then drops any fractional part of the quotient. It raises Overflow when the result is not representable and Div when $j = 0$. Note that, unlike div, quot rounds toward zero. In addition, unlike div and mod, neither quot nor rem are infix by default; an appropriate infix declaration would be infix 7 quot rem.

> **Implementation note:** Rounding toward zero is the semantics of most hardware divide instructions, so quot may be faster than div.

val rem : int * int -> int

> *i* rem *j* returns the remainder of the division of *i* by *j*. It raises Div when $j = 0$. (*i* rem *j*) has the same sign as *i*, and it holds that
> $$(i \text{ quot } j) \text{ * } j + (i \text{ rem } j) = i$$
> This behavior matches the semantics of most hardware divide instructions, so rem may be faster than mod.

val compare : int * int -> order

> compare (*i*, *j*) returns LESS, EQUAL, or GREATER when *i* is less than, equal to, or greater than *j*, respectively.

val < : int * int -> bool
val <= : int * int -> bool
val > : int * int -> bool
val >= : int * int -> bool

> These functions return true if the corresponding relation holds between the two integers.

val ˜ : int -> int

> ˜ *i* returns the negation of *i*, i.e., $(0 - i)$. It raises Overflow when the result is not representable. Overflow can occur, for example, when int is an n-bit 2's-complement integer type and ˜ is applied to -2^{n-1}.

val abs : int -> int

> abs *i* returns the absolute value (magnitude) of *i*. It raises Overflow when the result is not representable.

val min : int * int -> int
val max : int * int -> int

> These functions return the smaller (respectively, larger) of the arguments.

val sign : int -> Int.int

> sign *i* returns ~1, 0, or 1 when *i* is less than, equal to, or greater than 0, respectively.

val sameSign : int * int -> bool

> sameSign (*i*, *j*) returns true if *i* and *j* have the same sign. It is equivalent to (sign *i* = sign *j*).

val fmt : StringCvt.radix -> int -> string
val toString : int -> string

> fmt *radix i*
> toString *i*
> These functions return a string containing a representation of *i* with # " ~ " used as the sign for negative numbers. The former formats the string according to *radix*. The hexadecimal digits 10 through 15 are represented as # "A" through # "F", respectively. No prefix "0x" is generated for the hexadecimal representation. The second form is equivalent to fmt StringCvt.DEC *i*.

val scan : StringCvt.radix
                 -> (char, 'a) StringCvt.reader
                -> (int, 'a) StringCvt.reader
val fromString : string -> int option

> scan *radix getc strm*
> fromString *s*
> The first expression returns SOME(*i*, *rest*) if an integer in the format denoted by *radix* can be parsed from a prefix of the character stream *strm* after skipping initial whitespace, where *i* is the value of the integer parsed and *rest* is the rest of the character stream. NONE is returned otherwise. This function raises Overflow when an integer can be parsed but is too large to be represented by type int.
>
> The format that scan accepts depends on the *radix* argument. Regular expressions defining these formats are as follows:

Radix	Format
StringCvt.BIN	$[+\,\tilde{}\,-]^?[0-1]^+$
StringCvt.OCT	$[+\,\tilde{}\,-]^?[0-7]^+$
StringCvt.DEC	$[+\,\tilde{}\,-]^?[0-9]^+$
StringCvt.HEX	$[+\,\tilde{}\,-]^?(\texttt{0x}\mid\texttt{0X})^?[0-9a-fA-F]^+$

Note that strings such as `"0xg"` and `"0x 123"` are scanned as SOME(0), even when using a hexadecimal radix.

The second expression returns SOME(*i*) if an integer *i* in the format $[+\,\tilde{}\,-]^?[0-9]^+$ can be parsed from a prefix of the string *s*, ignoring initial whitespace; NONE is returned otherwise. The function `fromString` raises `Overflow` when an integer can be parsed but is too large to fit in type `int`. It is equivalent to the expression `StringCvt.scanString (scan StringCvt.DEC)`.

Discussion

Fixed precision representations are required to be 2's-complement. Implementations of arbitrary precision should appear as 2's-complement under conversion to and from words.

If an implementation provides the `IntInf` structure, then `LargeInt` must be the same structure as `IntInf` (viewed through a thinning INTEGER signature). Otherwise, if `LargeInt` is not the same as `Int`, then there must be a structure Int*N* equal to `Large-Int`.

The type `FixedInt.int` is the largest fixed precision integer supported, while the type `LargeInt.int` is the largest integer supported. A structure Int*N* implements N-bit integers. The type `Position.int` is used to represent positions in files and I/O streams.

Implementation note: It is recommended that compilers recognize the idiom of converting between integers of differing precisions using an intermediate representation (e.g., `Int31.fromLarge o Int8.toLarge`) and optimize these compositions.

See also

IntInf (§11.18; p. 174), StringCvt (§11.55; p. 366)

11.18   The `IntInf` structure

The optional `IntInf` structure is one of the possible implementations of the `INTEGER`
interface. In addition to the `INTEGER` operations, it provides some operations useful
for programming with arbitrarily large integers. Operations in `IntInf` that return a
value of type `IntInf.int` should never raise the `Overflow` exception. Note that,
as it extends the `INTEGER` interface, `IntInf` defines a type `int`. Any use of this type
below, unmodified by a structure, refers to the local type `int` defined in `IntInf`.

Synopsis

```
signature INT_INF
structure IntInf :> INT_INF
```

Interface

```
include INTEGER
val divMod : int * int -> int * int
val quotRem : int * int -> int * int
val pow : int * Int.int -> int
val log2 : int -> Int.int
val orb  : int * int -> int
val xorb : int * int -> int
val andb : int * int -> int
val notb : int -> int
val << : int * Word.word -> int
val ~>> : int * Word.word -> int
```

Description

`val` divMod : int * int -> int * int

    divMod (i, j) returns the pair $(i$ div j, i mod $j)$ but is likely to be more
efficient than computing both components separately. It raises `Div` if $j = 0$.

`val` quotRem : int * int -> int * int

    quotRem (i, j) returns the pair (quot(i, j), rem(i, j) but is likely to be
more efficient than computing both components separately. It raises `Div` if $j = 0$.

`val` pow : int * Int.int -> int

    pow (i, j) returns the result of raising i to the jth power. This application is well
defined when $j > 0$. When $j = 0$, pow(i, j) is 1; in particular, pow$(0, 0)$ is 1.
When $j < 0$, we define the following exceptional cases:

i	$\text{pow}(i,j)$
0	Raise Div
$|i| = 1$	i^j
$|i| > 1$	0

val log2 : int -> Int.int

> log2 i returns the truncated base-2 logarithm of its argument, i.e., the largest integer k for which $\text{pow}(2, k) \leq i$. It raises Domain if $i \leq 0$ and Overflow if the result is not representable as an Int.int.

val orb : int * int -> int
val xorb : int * int -> int
val andb : int * int -> int

> These functions return the bit-wise OR, bit-wise exclusive OR, and bit-wise AND, respectively, of the arguments.

val notb : int -> int

> notb i returns the bit-wise complement (NOT) of i. It is equivalent to ~(i + 1).

val << : int * Word.word -> int

> << (i, n) shifts i to the left by n bit positions, filling in zeros from the right. When i and n are interpreted as integers, with the latter non-negative, this expression evaluates to $(i * 2^n)$.

val ~>> : int * Word.word -> int

> ~>> (i, n) shifts i to the right by n bit positions. When i and n are interpreted as integers, with the latter non-negative, this expression evaluates to $\lfloor (i/2^n) \rfloor$.

Discussion

If an implementation provides the IntInf structure, then the type LargeInt.int must be the same as the type IntInf.int.

The bit-wise operations (andb, orb, notb, <<, etc.) treat the integer arguments as having 2's-complement representation. In particular, if we let $bit = 2^n$, we have, for all sufficiently large values of n,

$$\begin{array}{l} \text{andb}(i, bit) = 0 \text{ if } i \geq 0 \\ \text{andb}(i, bit) = bit \text{ if } i < 0 \end{array}$$

Rationale: It is useful to have a module providing bit-wise operations on an unbounded domain. Such a module can serve as the basis for implementing sets or bit-vectors. These operations seemed to naturally fit into the specification of the IntInf module, rather than requiring an additional WordInf structure.

Implementation note: Having this structure as part of the basis allows implementations to provide compiler or runtime support to optimize integer representation and operations.

See also

INTEGER (§11.17; p. 169), LargeInt (§11.17; p. 169)

11.19   The IO structure

The IO structure contains types and values common to all the input/output structures and functors. In particular, it defines the Io exception, which is used to provide structured information for any errors occurring during I/O.

Synopsis

```
signature IO
structure IO :> IO
```

Interface

```
exception Io of {
  name : string,
  function : string,
  cause : exn
}
exception BlockingNotSupported
exception NonblockingNotSupported
exception RandomAccessNotSupported
exception ClosedStream
datatype buffer_mode = NO_BUF | LINE_BUF | BLOCK_BUF
```

Description

```
exception Io of {
  name : string,
  function : string,
  cause : exn
}
```

This exception is the principal exception raised when an error occurs in the I/O subsystem. The components of Io are as follows:

name The name component of the reader or writer.

function The name of the function raising the exception.

cause The underlying exception raised by the reader or writer, or detected at the stream I/O level.

Some of the standard causes are

- OS.SysErr if an actual system call was done and failed.
- Subscript if ill-formed arguments are given.
- BlockingNotSupported.
- NonblockingNotSupported.
- ClosedStream.

The cause field of Io is not limited to these particular exceptions. Users who create their own readers or writers may raise any exception they like, which will be reported as the cause field of the resulting Io exception.

exception `BlockingNotSupported`

The exception used in the `output`, `outputSubstr`, `output1`, and `flushOut` I/O operations if the underlying writer does not support blocking writes, or in the `input`, `inputN`, and `input1` I/O operations if the underlying reader does not support blocking reads. It should never be raised within the I/O system; it should only be used in the `cause` field of an `Io` exception.

exception `NonblockingNotSupported`

The exception used by the `canInput` I/O operation if the underlying stream does not support non-blocking input. It should never be raised within the I/O system; it should only be used in the `cause` field of an `Io` exception.

exception `RandomAccessNotSupported`

The exception used by the `STREAM_IO` position operations to indicate that random access operations are not supported by the underlying device. It should never be raised within the I/O system; it should only be used in the `cause` field of an `Io` exception.

exception `ClosedStream`

This exception is used by the output I/O operations if the underlying object is closed or terminated. It should never be raised within the I/O system; it should only be used in the `cause` field of an `Io` exception.

datatype `buffer_mode = NO_BUF | LINE_BUF | BLOCK_BUF`

These values specify the type of buffering used on output streams. If an output stream has mode `BLOCK_BUF`, the implementation should store output in a buffer, actually writing the buffer's content to the device only when the buffer is full. If an output stream has mode `NO_BUF`, the implementation should write the argument bytes of any output function directly to the corresponding device. If an output stream has mode `LINE_BUF`, output bytes should be buffered until a newline character (`#"\n"`) is seen, at which point the buffer should be flushed, including the newline character. For binary streams, the `LINE_BUF` mode should be treated as a synonym for `BLOCK_BUF`.

Implementation note: Output buffering is provided for efficiency, to reduce the number of writes to the underlying device, which may be an expensive operation. The I/O subsystem should select the initial buffer mode based on the output device. By default, output should be buffered. The optimum buffer size is specified by the `chunkSize` field in the underlying `writer` value. Output to `TextIO.stdErr` should be unbuffered. Output to a terminal-like device should be line-buffered. A simple test for a terminal-like device is the following expression:

```
OS.IO.kind iod = OS.IO.Kind.tty
```

where `iod` is the I/O descriptor associated with the open stream.

Discussion

The SML Basis Library I/O modules will never raise a bare BlockingNotSupported, NonblockingNotSupported, RandomAccessNotSupported, or ClosedStream exception; these exceptions are only used in the cause field of the Io exception. Any module, however, may raise Subscript directly if given ill-formed arguments, or may raise Io with Subscript as the cause.

It is possible that multiple error conditions hold when an I/O function is called. For example, a random access call may be made on a closed stream corresponding to a device that does not support random access. The cause reported in the generated Io exception is implementation-dependent.

See also

BinIO (§11.4; p. 127), IMPERATIVE_IO (§11.14; p. 158), PRIM_IO (§11.48; p. 308), STREAM_IO (§11.52; p. 346), TextIO (§11.58; p. 382)

11.20   The `List` structure

The `List` structure provides a collection of utility functions for manipulating polymorphic lists, traditionally an important datatype in functional programming.

Following the concrete syntax provided by the list : : operator, the head of a list appears leftmost. Thus, a traversal of a list from left to right starts with the head and then recurses on the tail. In addition, as a sequence type, a list has an indexing of its elements, with the head having index 0, the second element having index 1, etc.

Synopsis

```
signature LIST
structure List :> LIST
```

Interface

```
datatype 'a list = nil | :: of 'a * 'a list

exception Empty

val null : 'a list -> bool
val length : 'a list -> int
val @ : 'a list * 'a list -> 'a list
val concat : 'a list list -> 'a list
val revAppend : 'a list * 'a list -> 'a list
val tabulate : int * (int -> 'a) -> 'a list
val hd : 'a list -> 'a
val tl : 'a list -> 'a list
val last : 'a list -> 'a
val getItem : 'a list -> ('a * 'a list) option
val nth : 'a list * int -> 'a
val take : 'a list * int -> 'a list
val drop : 'a list * int -> 'a list
val rev : 'a list -> 'a list

val app : ('a -> unit) -> 'a list -> unit
val map : ('a -> 'b) -> 'a list -> 'b list
val mapPartial : ('a -> 'b option) -> 'a list -> 'b list
val find : ('a -> bool) -> 'a list -> 'a option
val filter : ('a -> bool) -> 'a list -> 'a list
val partition : ('a -> bool)
                    -> 'a list -> 'a list * 'a list
val foldl : ('a * 'b -> 'b) -> 'b -> 'a list -> 'b
val foldr : ('a * 'b -> 'b) -> 'b -> 'a list -> 'b

val exists : ('a -> bool) -> 'a list -> bool
val all : ('a -> bool) -> 'a list -> bool

val collate : ('a * 'a -> order)
                    -> 'a list * 'a list -> order
```

Description

exception Empty

> This exception indicates that an empty list was given as an argument to a function requiring a non-empty list.

val null : 'a list -> bool

> null l returns true if the list l is empty.

val length : 'a list -> int

> length l returns the number of elements in the list l.

val @ : 'a list * 'a list -> 'a list

> $l1$ @ $l2$ returns the list that is the concatenation of $l1$ and $l2$.

val concat : 'a list list -> 'a list

> concat l returns the list that is the concatenation of all the lists in l in order.
>> concat$[l1,l2,\ldots ln]$ = $l1$ @ $l2$ @ $\ldots$ @ ln

val revAppend : 'a list * 'a list -> 'a list

> revAppend $(l1, l2)$ returns (rev l1) @ l2.

val tabulate : int * (int -> 'a) -> 'a list

> tabulate (n, f) returns a list of length n equal to $[f(0), f(1), \ldots, f(n\text{-}1)]$, created from left to right. It raises Size if $n < 0$.

val hd : 'a list -> 'a

> hd l returns the first element of l. It raises Empty if l is nil.

val tl : 'a list -> 'a list

> tl l returns all but the first element of l. It raises Empty if l is nil.

val last : 'a list -> 'a

> last l returns the last element of l. It raises Empty if l is nil.

val getItem : 'a list -> ('a * 'a list) option

> getItem l returns NONE if the list is empty and SOME(hd l,tl l) otherwise. This function is particularly useful for creating value readers from lists of characters. For example, Int.scan StringCvt.DEC getItem has the type
>
> $$\text{(int,char list) StringCvt.reader}$$
>
> and can be used to scan decimal integers from lists of characters.

val nth : 'a list * int -> 'a

> nth (l, i) returns the ith element of the list l, counting from 0. It raises Subscript if $i < 0$ or $i \geq$ length l. We have nth(l,0) = hd l, ignoring exceptions.

val take : 'a list * int -> 'a list

> take (l, i) returns the first i elements of the list l. It raises Subscript if $i < 0$ or $i >$ length l. We have take(l, length l) = l.

val drop : 'a list * int -> 'a list

> drop (l, i) returns what is left after dropping the first i elements of the list l. It raises Subscript if $i < 0$ or $i >$ length l. It holds that take(l, i) @ drop(l, i) = l when $0 \leq i \leq$ length l. We also have drop(l, length l) = [].

val rev : 'a list -> 'a list

> rev l returns a list consisting of l's elements in reverse order.

val app : ('a -> unit) -> 'a list -> unit

> app f l applies f to the elements of l, from left to right.

val map : ('a -> 'b) -> 'a list -> 'b list

> map f l applies f to each element of l from left to right, returning the list of results.

val mapPartial : ('a -> 'b option) -> 'a list -> 'b list

> mapPartial f l applies f to each element of l from left to right, returning a list of results, with SOME stripped, where f was defined. f is not defined for an element of l if f applied to the element returns NONE. The above expression is equivalent to:
>
> $$\text{((map valOf) o (filter isSome) o (map } f\text{)) } l$$

val find : ('a -> bool) -> 'a list -> 'a option

find *pred l* applies *pred* to each element *x* of the list *l*, from left to right, until *pred x* evaluates to true. This function returns the first such element, if it exists; otherwise, it returns NONE.

val filter : ('a -> bool) -> 'a list -> 'a list

filter *pred l* applies *pred* to each element *x* of *l*, from left to right, and returns the list of those *x* for which *pred x* evaluated to true, in the same order as they occurred in the argument list.

val partition : ('a -> bool)
                    -> 'a list -> 'a list * 'a list

partition *pred l* applies *pred* to each element *x* of *l*, from left to right, and returns a pair (*pos, neg*), where *pos* is the list of those *x* for which *pred x* evaluated to true, and *neg* is the list of those for which *pred x* evaluated to false. The elements of *pos* and *neg* retain the same relative order they possessed in *l*.

val foldl : ('a * 'b -> 'b) -> 'b -> 'a list -> 'b

foldl *f init* [*x1, x2, ..., xn*] returns
            f(*xn*,...,*f*(*x2, f*(*x1, init*))...)
or *init* if the list is empty.

val foldr : ('a * 'b -> 'b) -> 'b -> 'a list -> 'b

foldr *f init* [*x1, x2, ..., xn*] returns
            f(*x1, f*(*x2, ..., f*(*xn, init*)...))
or *init* if the list is empty.

val exists : ('a -> bool) -> 'a list -> bool

exists *pred l* applies *pred* to each element *x* of the list *l*, from left to right, until *pred x* evaluates to true; it returns true if such an *x* exists and false otherwise.

val all : ('a -> bool) -> 'a list -> bool

all *pred l* applies *pred* to each element *x* of the list *l*, from left to right, until *pred x* evaluates to false; it returns false if such an *x* exists and true otherwise. It is equivalent to not(exists (not o *pred*) *l*)).

val collate : ('a * 'a -> order)
                    -> 'a list * 'a list -> order

collate *cmp* (*l1, l2*) performs a lexicographic comparison of the two lists using the given ordering *cmp* on the list elements.

Discussion

The list type is considered primitive and is defined in the top-level environment. It is rebound here for consistency.

Rationale: Lists are usually supported with a large collection of library functions. Here, we provide a somewhat smaller collection of operations that reflect common usage. We feel the collection is moderately complete, in that most programs will not need to define additional list operations. We have tried to adopt names that reflect a consensus from various existing libraries and texts. We have avoided functions relying on equality types.

See also

General (§11.11; p. 149), ListPair (§11.21; p. 185)

11.21 The `ListPair` structure

The `ListPair` structure provides operations on pairs of lists. The operations fall into two categories. Those in the first category, whose names do not end in `"Eq"`, do not require that the lists have the same length. When the lists are of uneven lengths, the excess elements from the tail of the longer list are ignored. The operations in the second category, whose names have the suffix `"Eq"`, differ from their similarly named operations in the first category only when the list arguments have unequal lengths, in which case they typically raise the `UnequalLengths` exception.

Synopsis

```
signature LIST_PAIR
structure ListPair :> LIST_PAIR
```

Interface

```
exception UnequalLengths

val zip   : 'a list * 'b list -> ('a * 'b) list
val zipEq : 'a list * 'b list -> ('a * 'b) list
val unzip : ('a * 'b) list -> 'a list * 'b list

val app   : ('a * 'b -> unit) -> 'a list * 'b list -> unit
val appEq : ('a * 'b -> unit) -> 'a list * 'b list -> unit
val map   : ('a * 'b -> 'c) -> 'a list * 'b list -> 'c list
val mapEq : ('a * 'b -> 'c) -> 'a list * 'b list -> 'c list
val foldl   : ('a * 'b * 'c -> 'c)
                -> 'c -> 'a list * 'b list -> 'c
val foldr   : ('a * 'b * 'c -> 'c)
                -> 'c -> 'a list * 'b list -> 'c
val foldlEq : ('a * 'b * 'c -> 'c)
                -> 'c -> 'a list * 'b list -> 'c
val foldrEq : ('a * 'b * 'c -> 'c)
                -> 'c -> 'a list * 'b list -> 'c

val all    : ('a * 'b -> bool) -> 'a list * 'b list -> bool
val exists : ('a * 'b -> bool) -> 'a list * 'b list -> bool
val allEq : ('a * 'b -> bool) -> 'a list * 'b list -> bool
```

Description

```
exception UnequalLengths
```

This exception is raised by those functions that require arguments of identical length.

val zip : 'a list * 'b list -> ('a * 'b) list
val zipEq : 'a list * 'b list -> ('a * 'b) list

> zip (*l1*, *l2*)
> zipEq (*l1*, *l2*)
> These functions combine the two lists *l1* and *l2* into a list of pairs, with the first element of each list comprising the first element of the result, the second elements comprising the second element of the result, and so on. If the lists are of unequal lengths, zip ignores the excess elements from the tail of the longer one, while zipEq raises the exception UnequalLengths.

val unzip : ('a * 'b) list -> 'a list * 'b list

> unzip *l* returns a pair of lists formed by splitting the elements of *l*. This function is the inverse of zip for equal length lists.

val app : ('a * 'b -> unit) -> 'a list * 'b list -> unit
val appEq : ('a * 'b -> unit) -> 'a list * 'b list -> unit

> app *f* (*l1*, *l2*)
> appEq *f* (*l1*, *l2*)
> These apply the function *f* to the list of pairs of elements generated from left to right from the lists *l1* and *l2*. If the lists are of unequal lengths, the former ignores the excess elements from the tail of the longer one and the latter raises UnequalLengths. The above expressions are respectively equivalent to:
> $$\text{List.app } f \text{ (zip } (l1, l2))$$
> $$\text{List.app } f \text{ (zipEq } (l1, l2))$$
> ignoring possible side effects of the function *f*.

val map : ('a * 'b -> 'c) -> 'a list * 'b list -> 'c list
val mapEq : ('a * 'b -> 'c) -> 'a list * 'b list -> 'c list

> map *f* (*l1*, *l2*)
> mapEq *f* (*l1*, *l2*)
> These map the function *f* over the list of pairs of elements generated from left to right from the lists *l1* and *l2*, returning the list of results. If the lists are of unequal lengths, the former ignores the excess elements from the tail of the longer one and the latter raises UnequalLengths. The above expressions are respectively equivalent to:
> $$\text{List.map } f \text{ (zip } (l1, l2))$$
> $$\text{List.map } f \text{ (zipEq } (l1, l2))$$
> ignoring possible side effects of the function *f*.

```
val foldl : ('a * 'b * 'c -> 'c)
                -> 'c -> 'a list * 'b list -> 'c
val foldr : ('a * 'b * 'c -> 'c)
                -> 'c -> 'a list * 'b list -> 'c
val foldlEq : ('a * 'b * 'c -> 'c)
                -> 'c -> 'a list * 'b list -> 'c
val foldrEq : ('a * 'b * 'c -> 'c)
                -> 'c -> 'a list * 'b list -> 'c
```

> foldl *f init* (*l1*, *l2*)
> foldr *f init* (*l1*, *l2*)
> foldlEq *f init* (*l1*, *l2*)
> foldrEq *f init* (*l1*, *l2*)

These functions return the result of folding the function *f* in the specified direction over the pair of lists *l1* and *l2* starting with the value *init*. They are respectively equivalent to:

> List.foldl *f' init* (zip (*l1*, *l2*))
> List.foldr *f' init* (zip (*l1*, *l2*))
> List.foldl *f' init* (zipEq (*l1*, *l2*))
> List.foldr *f' init* (zipEq (*l1*, *l2*))

where *f'* is fn ((a,b),c) => f(a,b,c) and the possible side-effects of the function *f* are ignored.

```
val all : ('a * 'b -> bool) -> 'a list * 'b list -> bool
val exists : ('a * 'b -> bool) -> 'a list * 'b list -> bool
```

> all *pred* (*l1*, *l2*)
> exists *pred* (*l1*, *l2*)

These functions provide short-circuit testing of a predicate over a pair of lists. They are respectively equivalent to:

> List.all *pred* (zip (*l1*, *l2*))
> List.exists *pred* (zip (*l1*, *l2*))

```
val allEq : ('a * 'b -> bool) -> 'a list * 'b list -> bool
```

allEq *pred* (*l1*, *l2*) returns true if *l1* and *l2* have equal length and all pairs of elements satisfy the predicate *pred*. That is, the expression is equivalent to:

> (List.length *l1* = List.length *l2*) **andalso**
> (List.all *pred* (zip (*l1*, *l2*)))

This function does not appear to have any nice algebraic relation with the other functions, but it is included because it provides a useful notion of equality, which is analogous to the notion of equality of lists over equality types.

Implementation note: The implementation is simple:

```
fun allEq p ([], []) = true
  | allEq p (x::xs, y::ys) = p(x,y) andalso allEq p (xs,ys)
  | allEq _ _ = false
```

Discussion

Note that a function that requires equal length arguments should check this condition lazily, i.e., it should act as though the lists have equal length and invoke the user-supplied function argument but raise the exception `UnequalLengths` if it arrives at the end of one list before the end of the other.

See also

List (§11.20; p. 180)

11.22 The MATH signature

The signature MATH specifies basic mathematical constants, the square root function, and trigonometric, hyperbolic, exponential, and logarithmic functions based on a real type. The functions defined here have roughly the same semantics as their counterparts in ISO C's math.h.

The top-level structure Math provides these functions for the default real type Real.-real.

In the functions below, unless specified otherwise, if any argument is a NaN, the return value is a NaN. In a list of rules specifying the behavior of a function in special cases, the first matching rule defines the semantics.

Synopsis

```
signature MATH
structure Math :> MATH
  where type real = Real.real
```

Interface

```
type real

val pi : real
val e  : real

val sqrt : real -> real
val sin  : real -> real
val cos  : real -> real
val tan  : real -> real
val asin : real -> real
val acos : real -> real
val atan : real -> real
val atan2 : real * real -> real
val exp  : real -> real
val pow  : real * real -> real
val ln    : real -> real
val log10 : real -> real
val sinh : real -> real
val cosh : real -> real
val tanh : real -> real
```

Description

```
val pi : real
```

An approximation of the constant π (3.141592653...).

val e : real

An approximation of the base e (2.718281828...) of the natural logarithm.

val sqrt : real -> real

sqrt x returns the square root of x. sqrt (~0.0) = ~0.0. If $x < 0$, it returns NaN.

val sin : real -> real
val cos : real -> real
val tan : real -> real

sin x
cos x
tan x
These functions return the sine, cosine, and tangent, respectively, of x, measured in radians. If x is an infinity, these functions return NaN. Note that tan will produce infinities at various finite values, roughly corresponding to the singularities of the tangent function.

val asin : real -> real
val acos : real -> real

asin x
acos x
These functions return the arc sine and arc cosine, respectively, of x. asin is the inverse of sin. Its result is guaranteed to be in the closed interval $[-\pi/2, \pi/2]$. acos is the inverse of cos. Its result is guaranteed to be in the closed interval $[0, \pi]$. If the magnitude of x exceeds 1.0, they return NaN.

val atan : real -> real

atan x returns the arc tangent of x. atan is the inverse of tan. For finite arguments, the result is guaranteed to be in the open interval $(-\pi/2, \pi/2)$. If x is $+\infty$, it returns $\pi/2$; if x is $-\infty$, it returns $-\pi/2$.

val atan2 : real * real -> real

atan2 (y, x) returns the arc tangent of (y/x) in the closed interval $[-\pi, \pi]$, corresponding to angles within ± 180 degrees. The quadrant of the resulting angle is determined using the signs of both x and y and is the same as the quadrant of the point (x,y). When $x = 0$ (i.e., an angle of 90 degrees), the result is (real (sign y)) * pi/2.0. It holds that

$$sign(\cos(atan2(y, x))) = sign(x)$$

and

$$sign(\sin(atan2(y, x))) = sign(y)$$

except for inaccuracies incurred by the finite precision of `real` and the approximation algorithms used to compute the mathematical functions.

Rules for exceptional cases are specified in the following table.

y	x	atan2(y,x)
± 0	$0 < x$	± 0
± 0	$+0$	± 0
± 0	$x < 0$	$\pm \pi$
± 0	-0	$\pm \pi$
$y, 0 < y$	± 0	$\pi/2$
$y, y < 0$	± 0	$-\pi/2$
$\pm y$, finite $y > 0$	$+\infty$	± 0
$\pm y$, finite $y > 0$	$-\infty$	$\pm \pi$
$\pm\infty$	finite x	$\pm\pi/2$
$\pm\infty$	$+\infty$	$\pm\pi/4$
$\pm\infty$	$-\infty$	$\pm 3\pi/4$

val exp : real -> real

exp x returns e^x, i.e., e raised to the xth power. If x is $+\infty$, it returns $+\infty$; if x is $-\infty$, it returns 0.

val pow : real * real -> real

pow (x, y) returns x^y, i.e., x raised to the yth power. For finite x and y, this function is well defined when $x > 0$ or when $x < 0$ and y is integral. Rules for exceptional cases are specified below.

x	y	pow(x,y)
x, including NaN	0	1
$\lvert x \rvert > 1$	$+\infty$	$+\infty$
$\lvert x \rvert < 1$	$+\infty$	$+0$
$\lvert x \rvert > 1$	$-\infty$	$+0$
$\lvert x \rvert < 1$	$-\infty$	$+\infty$
$+\infty$	$y > 0$	$+\infty$
$+\infty$	$y < 0$	$+0$
$-\infty$	$y > 0$, odd integer	$-\infty$
$-\infty$	$y > 0$, not odd integer	$+\infty$
$-\infty$	$y < 0$, odd integer	-0
$-\infty$	$y < 0$, not odd integer	$+0$
x	NaN	NaN
NaN	$y \neq 0$	NaN
± 1	$\pm\infty$	NaN
finite $x < 0$	finite non-integer y	NaN
± 0	$y < 0$, odd integer	$\pm\infty$
± 0	finite $y < 0$, not odd integer	$+\infty$
± 0	$y > 0$, odd integer	± 0
± 0	$y > 0$, not odd integer	$+0$

val `ln : real -> real`
val `log10 : real -> real`

> `ln` x
> `log10` r
> These functions return the natural logarithm (base e) and decimal logarithm (base 10), respectively, of x. If $x < 0$, they return NaN; if $x = 0$, they return $-\infty$; if x is ∞, they return ∞.

val `sinh : real -> real`
val `cosh : real -> real`
val `tanh : real -> real`

> `sinh` x
> `cosh` x
> `tanh` x
> These functions return the hyperbolic sine, hyperbolic cosine, and hyperbolic tangent, respectively, of x, that is, the values $(e^x - e^{-x})/2$, $(e^x + e^{-x})/2$, and `(sinh x)/(cosh x)`.
>
> These functions have the following properties:

$\sinh \pm 0$	$=$	± 0
$\sinh \pm \infty$	$=$	$\pm \infty$
$\cosh \pm 0$	$=$	1
$\cosh \pm \infty$	$=$	$\pm \infty$
$\tanh \pm 0$	$=$	± 0
$\tanh \pm \infty$	$=$	± 1

See also

> REAL (§11.50; p. 318)

11.23   The `MONO_ARRAY` signature

The `MONO_ARRAY` signature is a generic interface to monomorphic arrays, which are mutable sequences with constant-time access and update. Monomorphic arrays allow more compact representations than the analogous polymorphic arrays over the same element type.

Arrays have a special equality property: two arrays are equal if they are the same array, i.e., created by the same call to a primitive array constructor such as `array`, `fromList`, etc.; otherwise they are not equal. This property also holds for arrays of zero length.

Synopsis

```
signature MONO_ARRAY
structure Word8Array :> MONO_ARRAY
  where type vector = Word8Vector.vector
  where type elem = Word8.word
structure CharArray :> MONO_ARRAY
  where type vector = CharVector.vector
  where type elem = char
structure WideCharArray :> MONO_ARRAY
  where type vector = WideCharVector.vector
  where type elem = WideChar.char
structure BoolArray :> MONO_ARRAY
  where type vector = BoolVector.vector
  where type elem = bool
structure IntArray :> MONO_ARRAY
  where type vector = IntVector.vector
  where type elem = int
structure WordArray :> MONO_ARRAY
  where type vector = WordVector.vector
  where type elem = word
structure RealArray :> MONO_ARRAY
  where type vector = RealVector.vector
  where type elem = real
structure LargeIntArray :> MONO_ARRAY
  where type vector = LargeIntVector.vector
  where type elem = LargeInt.int
structure LargeWordArray :> MONO_ARRAY
  where type vector = LargeWordVector.vector
  where type elem = LargeWord.word
structure LargeRealArray :> MONO_ARRAY
  where type vector = LargeRealVector.vector
  where type elem = LargeReal.real
structure IntNArray :> MONO_ARRAY
  where type vector = Int{N}Vector.vector
  where type elem = Int{N}.int
```

```
structure WordNArray :> MONO_ARRAY
  where type vector = Word{N}Vector.vector
  where type elem = Word{N}.word
structure RealNArray :> MONO_ARRAY
  where type vector = Real{N}Vector.vector
  where type elem = Real{N}.real
```

Interface

```
eqtype array
type elem
type vector

val maxLen : int
val array : int * elem -> array
val fromList : elem list -> array
val vector : array -> vector
val tabulate : int * (int -> elem) -> array

val length : array -> int
val sub : array * int -> elem
val update : array * int * elem -> unit
val copy    : {src : array, dst : array, di : int} -> unit
val copyVec : {src : vector, dst : array, di : int} -> unit

val appi : (int * elem -> unit) -> array -> unit
val app  : (elem -> unit) -> array -> unit
val modifyi : (int * elem -> elem) -> array -> unit
val modify  : (elem -> elem) -> array -> unit
val foldli : (int * elem * 'b -> 'b) -> 'b -> array -> 'b
val foldri : (int * elem * 'b -> 'b) -> 'b -> array -> 'b
val foldl  : (elem * 'b -> 'b) -> 'b -> array -> 'b
val foldr  : (elem * 'b -> 'b) -> 'b -> array -> 'b
val findi : (int * elem -> bool)
                    -> array -> (int * elem) option
val find  : (elem -> bool) -> array -> elem option
val exists : (elem -> bool) -> array -> bool
val all : (elem -> bool) -> array -> bool
val collate : (elem * elem -> order)
                    -> array * array -> order
```

Description

type vector

> The corresponding monomorphic vector type. We denote the length of a vector *vec* of
> type vector by |*vec*|.

val maxLen : int

> The maximum length of arrays supported by this implementation. Attempts to create larger arrays will result in the Size exception being raised.

val array : int * elem -> array

> array (n, init) creates a new array of length n; each element is initialized to the value init. If $n < 0$ or maxLen $< n$, then the Size exception is raised.

val fromList : elem list -> array

> fromList l creates a new array from l, whose length is length l and with the ith element of l used as the ith element of the array. If the length of the list is greater than maxLen, then the Size exception is raised.

val vector : array -> vector

> vector arr generates a vector from arr. Specifically, if vec is the resulting vector, we have $|vec| = |arr|$ and, for $0 \le i < |arr|$, element i of vec is sub (arr, i).

val tabulate : int * (int -> elem) -> array

> tabulate (n, f) creates an array of n elements, where the elements are defined in order of increasing index by applying f to the element's index. This expression is equivalent to the following:
>
> $$\text{fromList (List.tabulate } (n, f))$$
>
> If $n < 0$ or maxLen $< n$, then the Size exception is raised.

val length : array -> int

> length arr returns $|arr|$, the number of elements in the array arr.

val sub : array * int -> elem

> sub (arr, i) returns the ith element of the array arr. If $i < 0$ or $|arr| \le i$, then the Subscript exception is raised.

val update : array * int * elem -> unit

> update (arr, i, x) sets the ith element of the array arr to x. If $i < 0$ or $|arr| \le i$, then the Subscript exception is raised.

```
val copy : {src : array, dst : array, di : int} -> unit
val copyVec : {src : vector, dst : array, di : int} -> unit
```

> `copy {src, dst, di}`
> `copyVec {src, dst, di}`
> These functions copy the entire array or vector src into the array dst, with the ith
> element in src, for $0 \leq i < |src|$, being copied to position $di + i$ in the destination
> array. If $di < 0$ or if $|dst| < di + |src|$, then the Subscript exception is raised.
>
> **Implementation note:**   In copy, if dst and src are equal, we must have di = 0 to
> avoid an exception, and copy is then the identity.

```
val appi : (int * elem -> unit) -> array -> unit
val app : (elem -> unit) -> array -> unit
```

> `appi f arr`
> `app f arr`
> These functions apply the function f to the elements of an array in left-to-right order (i.e.,
> increasing indices). The more general appi function supplies both the element and the
> element's index to the function f. The expression app f arr is equivalent to:
> $$\text{appi } (f \text{ o } \#2) \text{ } arr$$

```
val modifyi : (int * elem -> elem) -> array -> unit
val modify : (elem -> elem) -> array -> unit
```

> `modifyi f arr`
> `modify f arr`
> These functions apply the function f to the elements of an array in left-to-right order
> (i.e., increasing indices) and replace each element with the result of applying f. The
> more general modifyi function supplies both the element and the element's index to the
> function f. The expression modify f arr is equivalent to:
> $$\text{modifyi } (f \text{ o } \#2) \text{ } arr$$

```
val foldli : (int * elem * 'b -> 'b) -> 'b -> array -> 'b
val foldri : (int * elem * 'b -> 'b) -> 'b -> array -> 'b
val foldl : (elem * 'b -> 'b) -> 'b -> array -> 'b
val foldr : (elem * 'b -> 'b) -> 'b -> array -> 'b
```

> `foldli f init arr`
> `foldri f init arr`
> `foldl f init arr`
> `foldr f init arr`
> These fold the function f over all the elements of an array, using the value $init$ as the
> initial value. The functions foldli and foldl apply the function f from left to right
> (increasing indices), while the functions foldri and foldr work from right to left (de-
> creasing indices). The more general functions foldli and foldri supply f with the
> array index of the corresponding element.
>
>   The indexed versions could be implemented as:

```
fun foldli f init seq = let
    val len = length seq
    fun loop (i, b) =
        if i = len then b
        else loop(i+1,f(i,sub(seq,i),b))
    in
      loop(0,init)
    end

fun foldri f init seq = let
    val len = length seq
    fun loop (i, b) =
        if i = ~1 then b
        else loop(i-1,f(i,sub(seq,i),b))
    in
      loop(len-1,init)
    end
```

The expression `foldl` *f init arr* is equivalent to:

```
foldli (fn (_, a, x) => f(a, x)) init arr
```

The analogous equivalences hold for `foldri` and `foldr`.

val `findi` : (int * elem -> bool)
                -> array -> (int * elem) option
val `find` : (elem -> bool) -> array -> elem option

`findi` *pred arr*
`find` *pred arr*
These functions apply *pred* to each element of the array *arr*, from left to right (i.e., increasing indices), until a `true` value is returned. These functions return the first such element, if it exists; otherwise, they return NONE. The more general version `findi` also supplies *pred* with the array index of the element and, upon finding an entry satisfying the predicate, returns that index with the element.

val `exists` : (elem -> bool) -> array -> bool

`exists` *pred arr* applies *pred* to each element x of the array *arr*, from left to right (i.e., increasing indices), until *pred* x evaluates to `true`; it returns `true` if such an x exists and `false` otherwise.

val `all` : (elem -> bool) -> array -> bool

`all` *pred arr* applies *pred* to each element x of the array *arr*, from left to right (i.e., increasing indices), until *pred* x evaluates to `false`; it returns `false` if such an x exists and `true` otherwise. It is equivalent to `not(exists (not o` *pred*`) arr))`.

val `collate` : (elem * elem -> order)
                -> array * array -> order

`collate` *cmp* (*a1*, *a2*) performs a lexicographic comparison of the two arrays using the given ordering *cmp* on elements.

Discussion

If an implementation provides a structure matching `MONO_ARRAY` for some element type `ty`, it must provide the corresponding monomorphic structure matching `MONO_VECTOR` with the vector types in the two structures identified.

See also

`Array` (§11.1; p. 112), `MONO_ARRAY_SLICE` (§11.25; p. 205),
`MONO_VECTOR` (§11.26; p. 211), `MONO_VECTOR_SLICE` (§11.27; p. 215)

11.24   The `MONO_ARRAY2` signature

The `MONO_ARRAY2` signature is a generic interface to mutable two-dimensional arrays. As usual, arrays have the equality property that two arrays are equal only if they are the same array, i.e., created by the same call to a primitive array constructor such as `array`, `fromList`, etc.; otherwise they are not equal. This property also holds for arrays of zero length.

The elements of two-dimensional arrays are indexed by a pair of integers (i, j), where i gives the row index and i gives the column index. As usual, indices start at 0, with increasing indices going from left to right and, in the case of rows, from top to bottom.

Synopsis

```
signature MONO_ARRAY2
structure Word8Array2 :> MONO_ARRAY2
  where type vector = Word8Vector.vector
  where type elem = Word8.word
structure CharArray2 :> MONO_ARRAY2
  where type vector = CharVector.vector
  where type elem = char
structure WideCharArray2 :> MONO_ARRAY2
  where type vector = WideCharVector.vector
  where type elem = WideChar.char
structure BoolArray2 :> MONO_ARRAY2
  where type vector = BoolVector.vector
  where type elem = bool
structure IntArray2 :> MONO_ARRAY2
  where type vector = IntVector.vector
  where type elem = int
structure WordArray2 :> MONO_ARRAY2
  where type vector = WordVector.vector
  where type elem = word
structure RealArray2 :> MONO_ARRAY2
  where type vector = RealVector.vector
  where type elem = real
structure LargeIntArray2 :> MONO_ARRAY2
  where type vector = LargeIntVector.vector
  where type elem = LargeInt.int
structure LargeWordArray2 :> MONO_ARRAY2
  where type vector = LargeWordVector.vector
  where type elem = LargeWord.word
structure LargeRealArray2 :> MONO_ARRAY2
  where type vector = LargeRealVector.vector
  where type elem = LargeReal.real
structure IntNArray2 :> MONO_ARRAY2
  where type vector = Int{N}Vector.vector
  where type elem = Int{N}.int
```

```
structure WordNArray2 :> MONO_ARRAY2
  where type vector = Word{N}Vector.vector
  where type elem = Word{N}.word
structure RealNArray2 :> MONO_ARRAY2
  where type vector = Real{N}Vector.vector
  where type elem = Real{N}.real
```

Interface

```
eqtype array
type elem
type vector
type region = {
                base : array,
                row : int,
                col : int,
                nrows : int option,
                ncols : int option
              }
datatype traversal = datatype Array2.traversal

val array : int * int * elem -> array
val fromList : elem list list -> array
val tabulate : traversal
                  -> int * int * (int * int -> elem)
                    -> array

val sub : array * int * int -> elem
val update : array * int * int * elem -> unit

val dimensions : array -> int * int
val nCols      : array -> int
val nRows      : array -> int

val row : array * int -> vector
val column : array * int -> vector

val copy : {
             src : region,
             dst : array,
             dst_row : int,
             dst_col : int
           } -> unit

val appi : traversal
              -> (int * int * elem -> unit)
                -> region -> unit
val app  : traversal -> (elem -> unit) -> array -> unit
```

```
val foldi : traversal
                -> (int * int * elem * 'b -> 'b)
                -> 'b -> region -> 'b
val fold  : traversal
                -> (elem * 'b -> 'b) -> 'b -> array -> 'b
val modifyi : traversal
                -> (int * int * elem -> elem)
                -> region -> unit
val modify  : traversal -> (elem -> elem) -> array -> unit
```

Description

type vector

The type of one-dimensional immutable vectors of the underlying element type.

```
type region = {
                base : array,
                row : int,
                col : int,
                nrows : int option,
                ncols : int option
            }
```

This type specifies a rectangular subregion of a two-dimensional array. If ncols equals SOME(w), the region includes only those elements in columns with indices in the range from w to $col + (w - 1)$, inclusively. If ncols = NONE, the region includes only those elements lying on or to the right of column col. A similar interpretation holds for the row and nrows fields. Thus, the region corresponds to all those elements with position (i, j) such that i lies in the specified range of rows and j lies in the specified range of columns.

A region reg is said to be *valid* if it denotes a legal subarray of its base array. More specifically, reg is *valid* if

$$0 \leq \#\text{row } reg \leq \text{nRows } (\#\text{base } reg)$$

when #nrows reg = NONE, or

$$0 \leq \#\text{row } reg \leq (\#\text{row } reg) + nr \leq \text{nRows } (\#\text{base } reg)$$

when #nrows reg = SOME(nr), and the analogous conditions hold for columns.

datatype traversal = **datatype** Array2.traversal

This type specifies ways of traversing an array or region. For more complete information, see the entry for Array2.traversal.

val array : int * int * elem -> array

array (r, c, $init$) creates a new array with r rows and c columns, with each element initialized to the value $init$. If $r < 0$, $c < 0$, or the resulting array size is too large, the Size exception is raised.

val fromList : elem list list -> array

> fromList *l* creates a new array from a list of rows, each of which is a list of elements. Thus, the elements are given in row major order, i.e., hd *l* gives the first row, hd (tl *l*) gives the second row, etc. This function raises the Size exception if the resulting array would be too large or if the lists in *l* do not all have the same length.

val tabulate : traversal
>   -> int * int * (int * int -> elem)
>   -> array

> tabulate tr (*r*, *c*, *f*) creates a new array with r rows and c columns, with the $(i,j)^{th}$ element initialized to *f* (*i*,*j*). The elements are initialized in the traversal order specified by *tr*. If $r < 0$, $c < 0$, or the resulting array size is too large, the Size exception is raised.

val sub : array * int * int -> elem

> sub (*arr*, *i*, *j*) returns the $(i,j)^{th}$ element of the array *arr*. If $i < 0$, $j < 0$, nRows *arr* $\leq i$, or nCols *arr* $\leq j$, then the Subscript exception is raised.

val update : array * int * int * elem -> unit

> update (*arr*, *i*, *j*, *a*) sets the $(i,j)^{th}$ element of the array *arr* to *a*. If $i < 0$, $j < 0$, nRows *arr* $\leq i$, or nCols *arr* $\leq j$, then the Subscript exception is raised.

val dimensions : array -> int * int
val nCols : array -> int
val nRows : array -> int

> dimensions *arr*
> nCols *arr*
> nRows *arr*
> These functions return size information concerning the array *arr*. nCols returns the number of columns, nRows returns the number of rows, and dimension returns a pair containing the number of rows and columns of the array. The functions nRows and nCols are respectively equivalent to #1 o dimensions and #2 o dimensions

val row : array * int -> vector

> row (*arr*, *i*) returns row *i* of *arr*. It raises Subscript if $i < 0$ or nRows *arr* $\leq$ *i*.

val column : array * int -> vector

> column (*arr*, *j*) returns column *j* of *arr*. It raises Subscript if $j < 0$ or nCols *arr* $\leq j$.

```
val copy : {
                src : region,
                dst : array,
                dst_row : int,
                dst_col : int
            } -> unit
```

copy {*src*, *dst*, *dst_row*, *dst_col*} copies the region *src* into the array *dst*, with the (#row *src*, #col *src*)th element being copied into the destination array at position (*dst_row*, *dst_col*). If the source region is not valid, then the Subscript exception is raised. Similarly, if the derived destination region (the source region *src* translated to (*dst_row*, *dst_col*)) is not valid in *dst*, then the Subscript exception is raised.

Implementation note: The copy function must correctly handle the case in which *src* and *dst* are equal and the source and destination regions overlap.

```
val appi : traversal
              -> (int * int * elem -> unit)
                 -> region -> unit
val app : traversal -> (elem -> unit) -> array -> unit
```

appi *tr f reg*
app *tr f arr*
These apply the function *f* to the elements of an array in the order specified by *tr*. The more general appi function applies *f* to the elements of the region *reg* and supplies both the element and the element's coordinates in the base array to the function *f*. If *reg* is not valid, then the exception Subscript is raised.

The function app applies *f* to the whole array and does not supply the element's coordinates to *f*. Thus the expression app *tr f arr* is equivalent to:
appi *tr* (*f* o #3) (*arr*, {row=0,col=0,nrows=NONE,ncols=NONE})

```
val foldi : traversal
              -> (int * int * elem * 'b -> 'b)
                 -> 'b -> region -> 'b
val fold : traversal
              -> (elem * 'b -> 'b) -> 'b -> array -> 'b
```

foldi *tr f init reg*
fold *tr f init arr*
These fold the function *f* over the elements of an array *arr*, traversing the elements in *tr* order and using the value *init* as the initial value. The more general foldi function applies *f* to the elements of the region *reg* and supplies both the element and the element's coordinates in the base array to the function *f*. If *reg* is not valid, then the exception Subscript is raised.

The function fold applies *f* to the whole array and does not supply the element's coordinates to *f*. Thus the expression fold *tr f init arr* is equivalent to:
foldi *tr* (**fn** (_,_,a,b) => *f* (a,b)) *init*
    (*arr*, {row=0, col=0, nrows=NONE, ncols=NONE})

```
val modifyi : traversal
                  -> (int * int * elem -> elem)
                     -> region -> unit
val modify : traversal -> (elem -> elem) -> array -> unit
```

```
modifyi tr f reg
modify tr f arr
```
These apply the function `f` to the elements of an array in the order specified by `tr` and replace each element with the result of `f`. The more general `modifyi` function applies `f` to the elements of the region `reg` and supplies both the element and the element's coordinates in the base array to the function `f`. If `reg` is not valid, then the exception `Subscript` is raised.

The function `modify` applies `f` to the whole array and does not supply the element's coordinates to `f`. Thus the expression `modify f arr` is equivalent to:

```
modifyi (f o #3) (arr, {row=0,col=0,nrows=NONE,ncols=NONE})
```

Discussion

If an implementation provides any structure matching `MONO_ARRAY2`, it must also supply the structure `Array2` and its signature `ARRAY2`.

Note that the indices passed to argument functions in `appi`, `foldi`, and `modifyi` are with respect to the underlying matrix and not based on the region. This convention is different from that of the analogous functions on one-dimensional slices.

Implementation note: Unlike one-dimensional types, the signature for two-dimensional arrays does not specify any bounds on possible arrays. Implementations should support a total number of elements that is at least as large as the total number of elements in the corresponding one-dimension array type.

See also

Array2 (§11.2; p. 116)

11.25 The `MONO_ARRAY_SLICE` signature

The `MONO_ARRAY_SLICE` signature provides an abstraction of subarrays for monomorphic arrays. A `slice` value can be viewed as a triple `(a, i, n)`, where a is the underlying array, i is the starting index, and n is the length of the subarray, with the constraint that $0 \leq i \leq i + n \leq |a|$, where $|a|$ is the length of the array a. Slices provide a convenient notation for specifying and operating on a contiguous subset of elements in an array.

Synopsis

```
signature MONO_ARRAY_SLICE
structure Word8ArraySlice :> MONO_ARRAY_SLICE
  where type vector = Word8Vector.vector
  where type vector_slice = Word8VectorSlice.slice
  where type array = Word8Array.array
  where type elem = Word8.word
structure CharArraySlice :> MONO_ARRAY_SLICE
  where type vector = CharVector.vector
  where type vector_slice = CharVectorSlice.slice
  where type array = CharArray.array
  where type elem = char
structure WideCharArraySlice :> MONO_ARRAY_SLICE
  where type vector = WideCharVector.vector
  where type vector_slice = WideCharVectorSlice.slice
  where type array = WideCharArray.array
  where type elem = WideChar.char
structure BoolArraySlice :> MONO_ARRAY_SLICE
  where type vector = BoolVector.vector
  where type vector_slice = BoolVectorSlice.slice
  where type array = BoolArray.array
  where type elem = bool
structure IntArraySlice :> MONO_ARRAY_SLICE
  where type vector = IntVector.vector
  where type vector_slice = IntVectorSlice.slice
  where type array = IntArray.array
  where type elem = int
structure WordArraySlice :> MONO_ARRAY_SLICE
  where type vector = WordVector.vector
  where type vector_slice = WordVectorSlice.slice
  where type array = WordArray.array
  where type elem = word
structure RealArraySlice :> MONO_ARRAY_SLICE
  where type vector = RealVector.vector
  where type vector_slice = RealVectorSlice.slice
  where type array = RealArray.array
  where type elem = real
```

```
structure LargeIntArraySlice :> MONO_ARRAY_SLICE
  where type vector = LargeIntVector.vector
  where type vector_slice = LargeIntVectorSlice.slice
  where type array = LargeIntArray.array
  where type elem = LargeInt.int
structure LargeWordArraySlice :> MONO_ARRAY_SLICE
  where type vector = LargeWordVector.vector
  where type vector_slice = LargeWordVectorSlice.slice
  where type array = LargeWordArray.array
  where type elem = LargeWord.word
structure LargeRealArraySlice :> MONO_ARRAY_SLICE
  where type vector = LargeRealVector.vector
  where type vector_slice = LargeRealVectorSlice.slice
  where type array = LargeRealArray.array
  where type elem = LargeReal.real
structure IntNArraySlice :> MONO_ARRAY_SLICE
  where type vector = Int{N}Vector.vector
  where type vector_slice = Int{N}VectorSlice.slice
  where type array = Int{N}Array.array
  where type elem = Int{N}.int
structure WordNArraySlice :> MONO_ARRAY_SLICE
  where type vector = Word{N}Vector.vector
  where type vector_slice = Word{N}VectorSlice.slice
  where type array = Word{N}Array.array
  where type elem = Word{N}.word
structure RealNArraySlice :> MONO_ARRAY_SLICE
  where type vector = Real{N}Vector.vector
  where type vector_slice = Real{N}VectorSlice.slice
  where type array = Real{N}Array.array
  where type elem = Real{N}.real
```

Interface

```
type elem
type array
type slice
type vector
type vector_slice
val length : slice -> int
val sub : slice * int -> elem
val update : slice * int * elem -> unit
val full : array -> slice
val slice : array * int * int option -> slice
val subslice : slice * int * int option -> slice
val base : slice -> array * int * int
val vector : slice -> vector
val copy    : {src : slice, dst : array, di : int} -> unit
val copyVec : {src : vector_slice, dst : array, di : int}
                 -> unit
val isEmpty : slice -> bool
val getItem : slice -> (elem * slice) option
```

```
val appi : (int * elem -> unit) -> slice -> unit
val app  : (elem -> unit) -> slice -> unit
val modifyi : (int * elem -> elem) -> slice -> unit
val modify  : (elem -> elem) -> slice -> unit
val foldli : (int * elem * 'b -> 'b) -> 'b -> slice -> 'b
val foldr  : (elem * 'b -> 'b) -> 'b -> slice -> 'b
val foldl  : (elem * 'b -> 'b) -> 'b -> slice -> 'b
val foldri : (int * elem * 'b -> 'b) -> 'b -> slice -> 'b
val findi : (int * elem -> bool)
                -> slice -> (int * elem) option
val find  : (elem -> bool) -> slice -> elem option
val exists : (elem -> bool) -> slice -> bool
val all : (elem -> bool) -> slice -> bool
val collate : (elem * elem -> order)
                -> slice * slice -> order
```

Description

type array

> The underlying monomorphic array type. We denote the length of an array `arr` of type array by $|arr|$.

type vector

> The underlying monomorphic vector type. We denote the length of a vector `vec` of type vector by $|vec|$.

type vector_slice

> Slices of the monomorphic vector type.

val length : slice -> int

> length `sl` returns $|sl|$, the length (i.e., number of elements) of the slice.

val sub : slice * int -> elem

> sub (`sl`, `i`) returns the ith element of the slice `sl`. If $i < 0$ or $|sl| \leq i$, then the Subscript exception is raised.

val update : slice * int * elem -> unit

> update (`sl`, `i`, `a`) sets the ith element of the slice `sl` to `a`. If $i < 0$ or $|sl| \leq i$, then the Subscript exception is raised.

val `full : array -> slice`

> `full` `arr` creates a slice representing the entire array `arr`. It is equivalent to the expression `slice(arr, 0, NONE)`.

val `slice : array * int * int option -> slice`

> `slice (arr, i, sz)` creates a slice based on the array `arr` starting at index i of the array `arr`. If `sz` is `NONE`, the slice includes all of the elements to the end of the array, i.e., $arr[i..|arr|-1]$. This function raises `Subscript` if $i < 0$ or $|arr| < i$. If `sz` is `SOME(j)`, the slice has length j, that is, it corresponds to $arr[i..i+j-1]$. It raises `Subscript` if $i < 0$ or $j < 0$ or $|arr| < i + j$. Note that, if defined, `slice` returns an empty slice when $i = |arr|$.

val `subslice : slice * int * int option -> slice`

> `subslice (sl, i, sz)` creates a slice based on the given slice `sl` starting at index i of `sl`. If `sz` is `NONE`, the slice includes all of the elements to the end of the slice, i.e., $sl[i..|sl|-1]$. This function raises `Subscript` if $i < 0$ or $|sl| < i$. If `sz` is `SOME(j)`, the slice has length j, that is, it corresponds to $sl[i..i+j-1]$. It raises `Subscript` if $i < 0$ or $j < 0$ or $|sl| < i + j$. Note that, if defined, `slice` returns an empty slice when $i = |sl|$.

val `base : slice -> array * int * int`

> `base sl` returns a triple `(arr, i, n)` representing the concrete representation of the slice. `arr` is the underlying array, i is the starting index, and n is the length of the slice.

val `vector : slice -> vector`

> `vector sl` generates a vector from the slice `sl`. Specifically, if `vec` is the resulting vector, we have $|vec| = $ `length sl` and, for $0 \le i < $ `length sl`, element i of `vec` is `sub (sl, i)`.

val `copy : {src : slice, dst : array, di : int} -> unit`
val `copyVec : {src : vector_slice, dst : array, di : int}`
                       `-> unit`

> `copy {src, dst, di}`
> `copyVec {src, dst, di}`
> These functions copy the given slice into the array `dst`, with element `sub (src, i)`, for $0 \le i < |src|$, being copied to position $di + i$ in the destination array. If $di < 0$, or if $|dst| < di + |src|$, then the `Subscript` exception is raised.

Implementation note: The `copy` function must correctly handle the case in which `dst` and the base array of `src` are equal and the source and destination slices overlap.

```
val isEmpty : slice -> bool
```

isEmpty *sl* returns true if *sl* has length 0.

```
val getItem : slice -> (elem * slice) option
```

getItem *sl* returns the first item in *sl* and the rest of the slice, or NONE if *sl* is empty.

```
val appi : (int * elem -> unit) -> slice -> unit
val app : (elem -> unit) -> slice -> unit
```

appi *f sl*
app *f sl*
These functions apply the function *f* to the elements of a slice in left-to-right order (i.e., increasing indices). The more general appi function supplies *f* with the index of the corresponding element in the slice. The expression app *f sl* is equivalent to appi (*f* o #2) *sl*.

```
val modifyi : (int * elem -> elem) -> slice -> unit
val modify : (elem -> elem) -> slice -> unit
```

modifyi *f sl*
modify *f sl*
These functions apply the function *f* to the elements of an array slice in left-to-right order (i.e., increasing indices) and replace each element with the result. The more general modifyi supplies *f* with the index of the corresponding element in the slice. The expression modify *f sl* is equivalent to modifyi (*f* o #2) *sl*.

```
val foldli : (int * elem * 'b -> 'b) -> 'b -> slice -> 'b
val foldr : (elem * 'b -> 'b) -> 'b -> slice -> 'b
val foldl : (elem * 'b -> 'b) -> 'b -> slice -> 'b
val foldri : (int * elem * 'b -> 'b) -> 'b -> slice -> 'b
```

foldli *f init sl*
foldr *f init sl*
foldl *f init sl*
foldri *f init sl*
These fold the function *f* over all the elements of an array slice, using the value *init* as the initial value. The functions foldli and foldl apply the function *f* from left to right (increasing indices), while the functions foldri and foldr work from right to left (decreasing indices). The more general functions foldli and foldri supply *f* with the index of the corresponding element in the slice.

Refer to the MONO_ARRAY manual pages for reference implementations of the indexed versions.

The expression foldl *f init sl* is equivalent to:

```
            foldli (fn (_, a, x) => f(a, x)) init sl
```

The analogous equivalence holds for foldri and foldr.

```
val findi : (int * elem -> bool)
                 -> slice -> (int * elem) option
val find : (elem -> bool) -> slice -> elem option
```

    findi *pred sl*
    find *pred sl*
    These functions apply *pred* to each element of the slice *sl*, from left to right (i.e., increasing indices), until a true value is returned. These functions return the first such element, if it exists; otherwise, they return NONE. The more general version findi also supplies *pred* with the index of the element in the slice and, upon finding an entry satisfying the predicate, returns that index with the element.

```
val exists : (elem -> bool) -> slice -> bool
```

    exists *pred sl* applies *pred* to each element *x* of the slice *sl*, from left to right (i.e., increasing indices), until *pred x* evaluates to true; it returns true if such an *x* exists and false otherwise.

```
val all : (elem -> bool) -> slice -> bool
```

    all *pred sl* applies *pred* to each element *x* of the slice *sl*, from left to right (i.e., increasing indices), until *pred x* evaluates to false; it returns false if such an *x* exists and true otherwise. It is equivalent to not(exists (not o *pred*) *l*)).

```
val collate : (elem * elem -> order)
                  -> slice * slice -> order
```

    collate *cmp* (*sl*, *sl2*) performs a lexicographic comparison of the two slices using the given ordering *cmp* on elements.

Discussion

    If an implementation provides a structure matching MONO_ARRAY_SLICE for some element type ty, then it must also provide the corresponding monomorphic structures matching the signatures MONO_VECTOR_SLICE, MONO_ARRAY, and MONO_VECTOR, with the vector, array, and vector slice types all respectively identified.

See also

    ArraySlice (§11.3; p. 122), MONO_ARRAY (§11.23; p. 193),
    MONO_VECTOR (§11.26; p. 211), MONO_VECTOR_SLICE (§11.27; p. 215)

11.26   The `MONO_VECTOR` signature

The `MONO_VECTOR` signature is a generic interface to monomorphic vectors, which are immutable sequences with constant-time access. Monomorphic vectors allow more compact representations than the analogous polymorphic vectors over the same element type.

Synopsis

```
signature MONO_VECTOR
structure Word8Vector :> MONO_VECTOR
  where type elem = Word8.word
structure CharVector :> MONO_VECTOR
  where type vector = String.string
  where type elem = char
structure WideCharVector :> MONO_VECTOR
  where type vector = WideString.string
  where type elem = WideChar.char
structure BoolVector :> MONO_VECTOR
  where type elem = bool
structure IntVector :> MONO_VECTOR
  where type elem = int
structure WordVector :> MONO_VECTOR
  where type elem = word
structure RealVector :> MONO_VECTOR
  where type elem = real
structure LargeIntVector :> MONO_VECTOR
  where type elem = LargeInt.int
structure LargeWordVector :> MONO_VECTOR
  where type elem = LargeWord.word
structure LargeRealVector :> MONO_VECTOR
  where type elem = LargeReal.real
structure IntNVector :> MONO_VECTOR
  where type elem = Int{N}.int
structure WordNVector :> MONO_VECTOR
  where type elem = Word{N}.word
structure RealNVector :> MONO_VECTOR
  where type elem = Real{N}.real
```

Interface

```
type vector
type elem

val maxLen : int
val fromList : elem list -> vector
val tabulate : int * (int -> elem) -> vector
val length : vector -> int
val sub : vector * int -> elem
```

```
val update : vector * int * elem -> vector
val concat : vector list -> vector
val appi : (int * elem -> unit) -> vector -> unit
val app  : (elem -> unit) -> vector -> unit
val mapi : (int * elem -> elem) -> vector -> vector
val map  : (elem -> elem) -> vector -> vector
val foldli : (int * elem * 'a -> 'a) -> 'a -> vector -> 'a
val foldri : (int * elem * 'a -> 'a) -> 'a -> vector -> 'a
val foldl  : (elem * 'a -> 'a) -> 'a -> vector -> 'a
val foldr  : (elem * 'a -> 'a) -> 'a -> vector -> 'a
val findi : (int * elem -> bool)
                    -> vector -> (int * elem) option
val find  : (elem -> bool) -> vector -> elem option
val exists : (elem -> bool) -> vector -> bool
val all : (elem -> bool) -> vector -> bool
val collate : (elem * elem -> order)
                    -> vector * vector -> order
```

Description

val maxLen : int

> The maximum length of vectors supported by this implementation. Attempts to create larger vectors will result in the Size exception being raised.

val fromList : elem list -> vector

> fromList l creates a new vector from l, whose length is length l and with the ith element of l used as the ith element of the vector. If the length of the list is greater than maxLen, then the Size exception is raised.

val tabulate : int * (int -> elem) -> vector

> tabulate (n, f) creates a vector of n elements, where the elements are defined in order of increasing index by applying f to the element's index. This is expression to the following:
>
> $$fromList\ (List.tabulate\ (n,\ f))$$
>
> If $n < 0$ or maxLen $< n$, then the Size exception is raised.

val length : vector -> int

> length vec returns $|vec|$, the length (i.e., the number of elements) of the vector vec.

val sub : vector * int -> elem

> sub $(vec,\ i)$ returns the ith element of the vector vec. If $i < 0$ or $|vec| \leq i$, then the Subscript exception is raised.

```
val update : vector * int * elem -> vector
```

> update (*vec, i, x*) returns a new vector, identical to *vec*, except the ith element of *vec* is set to *x*. If $i < 0$ or $|vec| \leq i$, then the Subscript exception is raised.

```
val concat : vector list -> vector
```

> concat *l* returns the vector that is the concatenation of the vectors in the list *l*. If the total length of these vectors exceeds maxLen, then the Size exception is raised.

```
val appi : (int * elem -> unit) -> vector -> unit
val app  : (elem -> unit) -> vector -> unit
```

> appi *f vec*
> app *f vec*
> These functions apply the function *f* to the elements of a vector in left-to-right order (i.e., increasing indices). The more general appi function supplies both the element and the element's index to the function *f*. The expression app *f vec* is equivalent to:
> $$\text{appi } (f \text{ o } \#2) \text{ } vec$$

```
val mapi : (int * elem -> elem) -> vector -> vector
val map  : (elem -> elem) -> vector -> vector
```

> mapi *f vec*
> map *f vec*
> These functions produce new vectors by mapping the function *f* from left to right over the argument vector. The more general mapi function supplies both the element and the element's index to the function *f*. The expression mapi *f vec* is equivalent to:
> ```
> fromList (
>     List.map f (foldri (fn (i,a,l) => (i,a)::l) [] vec))
> ```
> The expression map *f vec* is equivalent to:
> $$\text{mapi } (f \text{ o } \#2) \text{ } vec$$

```
val foldli : (int * elem * 'a -> 'a) -> 'a -> vector -> 'a
val foldri : (int * elem * 'a -> 'a) -> 'a -> vector -> 'a
val foldl  : (elem * 'a -> 'a) -> 'a -> vector -> 'a
val foldr  : (elem * 'a -> 'a) -> 'a -> vector -> 'a
```

> foldli *f init vec*
> foldri *f init vec*
> foldl *f init vec*
> foldr *f init vec*
> These fold the function *f* over all the elements of a vector, using the value *init* as the initial value. The functions foldli and foldl apply the function *f* from left to right (increasing indices), while the functions foldri and foldr work from right to left (decreasing indices). The more general functions foldli and foldri supply both the element and the element's index to the function *f*.

Refer to the MONO_ARRAY manual pages for reference implementations of the indexed versions.

The expression foldl f is equivalent to:

$$\texttt{foldli (fn (\_, } a, \; x) \texttt{ => } f(a, \; x))$$

A similar relation holds between foldr and foldri.

---

val findi : (int * elem -> bool)
                -> vector -> (int * elem) option
val find : (elem -> bool) -> vector -> elem option

    findi *pred vec*
    find *pred vec*
These functions apply *pred* to each element of the vector *vec*, from left to right (i.e., increasing indices), until a true value is returned. These functions return the first such element, if it exists; otherwise, they return NONE. The more general version findi also supplies *pred* with the vector index of the element and, upon finding an entry satisfying the predicate, returns that index with the element.

---

val exists : (elem -> bool) -> vector -> bool

    exists *pred vec* applies *pred* to each element *x* of the vector *vec*, from left to right (i.e., increasing indices), until *pred* *x* evaluates to true; it returns true if such an *x* exists and false otherwise.

---

val all : (elem -> bool) -> vector -> bool

    all *pred vec* applies *pred* to each element *x* of the vector *vec*, from left to right (i.e., increasing indices), until *pred* *x* evaluates to false; it returns false if such an *x* exists and true otherwise. It is equivalent to not(exists (not o *pred*) *vec*)).

---

val collate : (elem * elem -> order)
                -> vector * vector -> order

    collate *cmp* (*v1*, *v2*) performs a lexicographic comparison of the two vectors using the given ordering *cmp* on elements.

Discussion

The type String.string is identical to CharVector.vector.

See also

MONO_ARRAY (§11.23; p. 193), MONO_ARRAY_SLICE (§11.25; p. 205),
MONO_VECTOR_SLICE (§11.27; p. 215), Vector (§11.64; p. 401)

11.27 The `MONO_VECTOR_SLICE` signature

The `MONO_VECTOR_SLICE` signature provides an abstraction of subarrays for monomorphic immutable arrays or vectors. A `slice` value can be viewed as a triple (*v*, *i*, *n*), where *v* is the underlying vector, *i* is the starting index, and *n* is the length of the subarray, with the constraint that $0 \le i \le i + n \le |v|$, where $|v|$ is the length of the vector *v*. Slices provide a convenient notation for specifying and operating on a contiguous subset of elements in a vector.

Synopsis

```
signature MONO_VECTOR_SLICE
structure Word8VectorSlice :> MONO_VECTOR_SLICE
  where type vector = Word8Vector.vector
  where type elem = Word8.word
structure CharVectorSlice :> MONO_VECTOR_SLICE
  where type slice = Substring.substring
  where type vector = String.string
  where type elem = char
structure WideCharVectorSlice :> MONO_VECTOR_SLICE
  where type slice = WideSubstring.substring
  where type vector = WideString.string
  where type elem = WideChar.char
structure BoolVectorSlice :> MONO_VECTOR_SLICE
  where type vector = BoolVector.vector
  where type elem = bool
structure IntVectorSlice :> MONO_VECTOR_SLICE
  where type vector = IntVector.vector
  where type elem = int
structure WordVectorSlice :> MONO_VECTOR_SLICE
  where type vector = WordVector.vector
  where type elem = word
structure RealVectorSlice :> MONO_VECTOR_SLICE
  where type vector = RealVector.vector
  where type elem = real
structure LargeIntVectorSlice :> MONO_VECTOR_SLICE
  where type vector = LargeIntVector.vector
  where type elem = LargeInt.int
structure LargeWordVectorSlice :> MONO_VECTOR_SLICE
  where type vector = LargeWordVector.vector
  where type elem = LargeWord.word
structure LargeRealVectorSlice :> MONO_VECTOR_SLICE
  where type vector = LargeRealVector.vector
  where type elem = LargeReal.real
structure IntNVectorSlice :> MONO_VECTOR_SLICE
  where type elem = Int{N}.int
  where type vector = Int{N}Vector.vector
structure WordNVectorSlice :> MONO_VECTOR_SLICE
  where type elem = Word{N}.word
  where type vector = Word{N}Vector.vector
```

```
structure RealNVectorSlice :> MONO_VECTOR_SLICE
  where type elem = Real{N}.real
  where type vector = Real{N}Vector.vector
```

Interface

```
type elem
type vector
type slice

val length : slice -> int
val sub : slice * int -> elem
val full : vector -> slice
val slice : vector * int * int option -> slice
val subslice : slice * int * int option -> slice
val base : slice -> vector * int * int
val vector : slice -> vector
val concat : slice list -> vector
val isEmpty : slice -> bool
val getItem : slice -> (elem * slice) option
val appi : (int * elem -> unit) -> slice -> unit
val app  : (elem -> unit) -> slice -> unit
val mapi : (int * elem -> elem) -> slice -> vector
val map  : (elem -> elem) -> slice -> vector
val foldli : (int * elem * 'b -> 'b) -> 'b -> slice -> 'b
val foldr  : (elem * 'b -> 'b) -> 'b -> slice -> 'b
val foldl  : (elem * 'b -> 'b) -> 'b -> slice -> 'b
val foldri : (int * elem * 'b -> 'b) -> 'b -> slice -> 'b
val findi : (int * elem -> bool)
                  -> slice -> (int * elem) option
val find  : (elem -> bool) -> slice -> elem option
val exists : (elem -> bool) -> slice -> bool
val all : (elem -> bool) -> slice -> bool
val collate : (elem * elem -> order)
                  -> slice * slice -> order
```

Description

```
type vector
```

The underlying monomorphic vector type. We denote the length of a vector *vec* of type vector by |*vec*|.

```
val length : slice -> int
```

length *sl* returns |*sl*|, the length (i.e., number of elements) of the slice.

val sub : slice * int -> elem

> sub (*sl*, *i*) returns the ith element of the slice *sl*. If $i < 0$ or $|sl| \leq i$, then the Subscript exception is raised.

val full : vector -> slice

> full *vec* creates a slice representing the entire vector *vec*. It is equivalent to the expression slice(*vec*, 0, NONE).

val slice : vector * int * int option -> slice

> slice (*vec*, *i*, *sz*) creates a slice based on the vector *vec* starting at index *i* of the vector *vec*. If *sz* is NONE, the slice includes all of the elements to the end of the vector, i.e., $vec[i..|vec| - 1]$. This function raises Subscript if $i < 0$ or $|vec| < i$. If *sz* is SOME(*j*), the slice has length *j*, that is, it corresponds to $vec[i..i+j-1]$. It raises Subscript if $i < 0$ or $j < 0$ or $|vec| < i + j$. Note that, if defined, slice returns an empty slice when $i = |vec|$.

val subslice : slice * int * int option -> slice

> subslice (*sl*, *i*, *sz*) creates a slice based on the given slice *sl* starting at index *i* of *sl*. If *sz* is NONE, the slice includes all of the elements to the end of the slice, i.e., $sl[i..|sl| - 1]$. This function raises Subscript if $i < 0$ or $|sl| < i$. If *sz* is SOME(*j*), the slice has length *j*, that is, it corresponds to $sl[i..i+j-1]$. It raises Subscript if $i < 0$ or $j < 0$ or $|sl| < i + j$. Note that, if defined, slice returns an empty slice when $i = |sl|$.

val base : slice -> vector * int * int

> base *sl* returns a triple (*vec*, *i*, *n*) representing the concrete representation of the slice. *vec* is the underlying vector, *i* is the starting index, and *n* is the length of the slice.

val vector : slice -> vector

> vector *sl* extracts a vector from the slice *sl*. Specifically, if *vec* is the resulting vector, we have $|vec| = |sl|$, and element *i* of *vec* is sub (*sl*, i), for $0 \leq i < |sl|$.

val concat : slice list -> vector

> concat *l* is the concatenation of all the vectors in *l*. This function raises Size if the sum of all the lengths is greater than the maximum length allowed by vectors of type vector.

val isEmpty : slice -> bool

    isEmpty *sl*   returns true if *sl* has length 0.

val getItem : slice -> (elem * slice) option

    getItem *sl*   returns the first item in *sl* and the rest of the slice, or NONE if *sl* is empty.

val appi : (int * elem -> unit) -> slice -> unit
val app : (elem -> unit) -> slice -> unit

    appi *f sl*
    app *f sl*
These functions apply the function *f* to the elements of a slice in left-to-right order (i.e., increasing indices). The more general appi function supplies *f* with the index of the corresponding element in the slice. The expression app *f sl* is equivalent to appi (*f* o #2) *sl*.

val mapi : (int * elem -> elem) -> slice -> vector
val map : (elem -> elem) -> slice -> vector

    mapi *f sl*
    map *f sl*
These functions generate new vectors by mapping the function *f* from left to right over the argument slice. The more general mapi function supplies both the element and the element's index in the slice to the function *f*. The latter expression is equivalent to:

$$\text{mapi } (f \text{ o \#2) } sl$$

val foldli : (int * elem * 'b -> 'b) -> 'b -> slice -> 'b
val foldr : (elem * 'b -> 'b) -> 'b -> slice -> 'b
val foldl : (elem * 'b -> 'b) -> 'b -> slice -> 'b
val foldri : (int * elem * 'b -> 'b) -> 'b -> slice -> 'b

    foldli *f init sl*
    foldr *f init sl*
    foldl *f init sl*
    foldri *f init sl*
These fold the function *f* over all the elements of a vector slice, using the value *init* as the initial value. The functions foldli and foldl apply the function *f* from left to right (increasing indices), while the functions foldri and foldr work from right to left (decreasing indices). The more general functions foldli and foldri supply *f* with the index of the corresponding element in the slice.

    Refer to the MONO_ARRAY manual pages for reference implementations of the indexed versions.

    The expression foldl *f init sl* is equivalent to:

        foldli (**fn** (_, *a*, *x*) => *f*(*a*, *x*)) *init sl*
The analogous equivalence holds for foldri and foldr.

```
val findi : (int * elem -> bool)
                -> slice -> (int * elem) option
val find : (elem -> bool) -> slice -> elem option
```

> findi *pred sl*
> find *pred sl*
> These functions apply *pred* to each element of the slice *sl*, from left to right (i.e., increasing indices), until a `true` value is returned. These functions return the first such element, if it exists; otherwise, they return `NONE`. The more general version `findi` also supplies *pred* with the index of the element in the slice and, upon finding an entry satisfying the predicate, returns that index with the element.

```
val exists : (elem -> bool) -> slice -> bool
```

> `exists` *pred sl* applies *pred* to each element *x* of the slice *sl*, from left to right (i.e., increasing indices), until *pred* *x* evaluates to `true`; it returns `true` if such an *x* exists and `false` otherwise.

```
val all : (elem -> bool) -> slice -> bool
```

> `all` *pred sl* applies *pred* to each element *x* of the slice *sl*, from left to right (i.e., increasing indices), until *pred* *x* evaluates to `false`; it returns `false` if such an *x* exists and `true` otherwise. It is equivalent to `not(exists (not o` *pred*`) sl))`.

```
val collate : (elem * elem -> order)
                -> slice * slice -> order
```

> `collate` *cmp* (*sl*, *sl2*) performs a lexicographic comparison of the two slices using the given ordering *cmp* on elements.

Discussion

If an implementation provides a structure matching `MONO_VECTOR_SLICE` for some element type `ty`, it must provide the corresponding monomorphic structure matching `MONO_VECTOR` with the vector types in the two structures identified.

See also

`MONO_ARRAY` (§11.23; p. 193), `MONO_ARRAY_SLICE` (§11.25; p. 205),
`MONO_VECTOR` (§11.26; p. 211), `VectorSlice` (§11.65; p. 405)

11.28   The `NetHostDB` structure

This structure accesses the information contained in the network host database. The data might be retrieved from a file such as `/etc/hosts` on older Unix systems or dynamically via some network communication. The structure can be used to convert host names (e.g., `"cs.uchicago.edu"`) to Internet addresses (e.g., `"128.135.11.87"`).

Synopsis

```
signature NET_HOST_DB
structure NetHostDB :> NET_HOST_DB
```

Interface

```
eqtype in_addr
eqtype addr_family
type entry

val name : entry -> string
val aliases : entry -> string list
val addrType : entry -> addr_family
val addr : entry -> in_addr
val addrs : entry -> in_addr list
val getByName : string -> entry option
val getByAddr : in_addr -> entry option
val getHostName : unit -> string

val toString : in_addr -> string
val scan        : (char, 'a) StringCvt.reader
                      -> (in_addr, 'a) StringCvt.reader
val fromString : string -> in_addr option
```

Description

```
eqtype in_addr
```

> The type representing an Internet address.

```
eqtype addr_family
```

> The type representing address families (also known as domains).

```
type entry
```

> The type representing an entry from the host database.

```
val name : entry -> string
```

> `name` *en* returns the official name of the host described by entry *en*.

val aliases : entry -> string list

> aliases *en* returns the alias list of the host described by entry *en*.

val addrType : entry -> addr_family

> addrType *en* returns the address family of the host described by entry *en*.

val addr : entry -> in_addr

> addr *en* returns the main Internet address of the host described by entry *en*, which is the first address of the list returned by addrs.

val addrs : entry -> in_addr list

> addrs *en* returns the list of Internet addresses of the host described by entry *en*. The list is guaranteed to be non-empty.

val getByName : string -> entry option

> getByName *s* reads the network host database for a host with name *s*. If successful, it returns SOME(en), where en is the corresponding database entry; otherwise, it returns NONE.

val getByAddr : in_addr -> entry option

> getByAddr *ia* reads the network host database for a host with Internet address *ia*. If successful, it returns SOME(en), where en is the corresponding database entry; otherwise, it returns NONE.

val getHostName : unit -> string

> The standard hostname for the current processor.

val toString : in_addr -> string

> toString *ia* returns a string representation of the Internet address *ia* in the form "*a.b.c.d*".

```
val scan : (char, 'a) StringCvt.reader
           -> (in_addr, 'a) StringCvt.reader
val fromString : string -> in_addr option
```

scan *getc strm*
fromString *s*

These functions scan Internet addresses from a character source. The first returns the result SOME(ia,rest) if an Internet address can be parsed from a prefix of the character stream *strm* after skipping initial whitespace, where ia is the resulting address, and rest is the remainder of the character stream. NONE is returned otherwise.

The second form returns SOME(ia) if an Internet address ia can be parsed from a prefix of string *s*. NONE is returned otherwise. It is equivalent to StringCvt.scanString scan.

Addresses in this notation have one of the following forms:

a,   where *a* is a 32-bit unsigned integer constant.

a.b,   where *a* is an 8-bit unsigned integer constant, and *b* is a 24-bit integer constant.

a.b.c,   where *a* and *b* are 8-bit unsigned integer constants, and *c* is a 16-bit integer constant.

a.b.c.d,   where *a*, *b*, *c*, and *d* are 8-bit integer constants.

The integer constants may be decimal, octal, or hexadecimal, as specified in the C language.

See also

GenericSock (§11.12; p. 153), INetSock (§11.16; p. 166),
NetProtDB (§11.29; p. 223), Socket (§11.51; p. 330)

11.29 The `NetProtDB` structure

This structure accesses the information contained in the network protocol database. The data may be retrieved from a file, such as `/etc/protocols` on many Unix systems, or via the NIS protocols map.

Synopsis

```
signature NET_PROT_DB
structure NetProtDB :> NET_PROT_DB
```

Interface

```
type entry
val name : entry -> string
val aliases : entry -> string list
val protocol : entry -> int
val getByName : string -> entry option
val getByNumber : int -> entry option
```

Description

`type entry`

    The type of a network protocol database entry.

`val name : entry -> string`

    `name` *en* returns the official name of the protocol described by entry *en* (e.g., `"ip"`).

`val aliases : entry -> string list`

    `aliases` *en* returns the alias list of the protocol described by entry *en*.

`val protocol : entry -> int`

    `protocol` *en* returns the protocol number of the protocol described by entry *en*.

`val getByName : string -> entry option`

    `getByName` *s* reads the network protocol database for a protocol with name *s*. If successful, it returns `SOME(en)`, where en is the corresponding database entry; otherwise, it returns `NONE`.

`val getByNumber : int -> entry option`

    `getByNumber` *i* reads the network protocol database for a protocol with protocol number *i*. If successful, it returns `SOME(en)`, where en is the corresponding database entry; otherwise, it returns `NONE`.

See also

NetHostDB (§11.28; p. 220)

11.30   The `NetServDB` structure

This structure accesses the information contained in the network services database. This data may be retrieved from the file `/etc/services` on many Unix systems, or from some other database.

Synopsis

```
signature NET_SERV_DB
structure NetServDB :> NET_SERV_DB
```

Interface

```
type entry
val name : entry -> string
val aliases : entry -> string list
val port : entry -> int
val protocol : entry -> string
val getByName : string * string option -> entry option
val getByPort : int * string option -> entry option
```

Description

`type entry`

>   The abstract type of a network service database entry.

`val name : entry -> string`

>   name *ent* returns the official name of the service described by entry *ent* (e.g., `"ftp"`, `"telnet"`, etc.).

`val aliases : entry -> string list`

>   aliases *ent* returns the alias list of the service described by entry *ent*.

`val port : entry -> int`

>   port *ent* returns the port number of the service described by entry *ent*.

`val protocol : entry -> string`

>   protocol *ent* returns the name of the protocol to use for the service described by the entry *ent* (e.g., `"tcp"` or `"udp"`).

val getByName : string * string option -> entry option

> getByName (*s, prot*) reads the network service database for a service with name
> *s*. If *prot* is SOME(protname), the protocol of the service must also match protname;
> if *prot* is NONE, no protocol restriction is imposed. If successful, it returns SOME(en),
> where en is the corresponding database entry; otherwise, it returns NONE.

val getByPort : int * string option -> entry option

> getByPort (*i, prot*) reads the network service database for a service with port
> number *i*. If *prot* is SOME(protname), the protocol of the service must also match
> protname; if *prot* is NONE, no protocol restriction is imposed. If successful, it returns
> SOME(en), where en the corresponding database entry; otherwise, it returns NONE.

See also

> Socket (§11.51; p. 330), NetHostDB (§11.28; p. 220), NetProtDB (§11.29; p. 223)

11.31 The `Option` structure

The `Option` structure defines the `option` type, used for handling partial functions and optional values, and provides a collection of common combinators.

The type, the `Option` exception, and the functions `getOpt`, `valOf`, and `isSome` are available in the top-level environment.

Synopsis

```
signature OPTION
structure Option :> OPTION
```

Interface

```
datatype 'a option = NONE | SOME of 'a
exception Option
val getOpt : 'a option * 'a -> 'a
val isSome : 'a option -> bool
val valOf : 'a option -> 'a
val filter : ('a -> bool) -> 'a -> 'a option
val join : 'a option option -> 'a option
val app : ('a -> unit) -> 'a option -> unit
val map : ('a -> 'b) -> 'a option -> 'b option
val mapPartial : ('a -> 'b option)
                       -> 'a option -> 'b option
val compose : ('a -> 'b) * ('c -> 'a option)
                  -> 'c -> 'b option
val composePartial : ('a -> 'b option) * ('c -> 'a option)
                          -> 'c -> 'b option
```

Description

```
datatype 'a option = NONE | SOME of 'a
```

> The type `option` provides a distinction between some value and no value and is often used for representing the result of partially defined functions. It can be viewed as a typed version of the C convention of returning a `NULL` pointer to indicate no value.

```
exception Option
```

> This exception is raised by the `valOf` function when applied to `NONE`.

```
val getOpt : 'a option * 'a -> 'a
```

> `getOpt (opt, a)` returns v if *opt* is `SOME(v)`; otherwise, it returns *a*.

```
val isSome : 'a option -> bool
```

> `isSome opt` returns `true` if *opt* is `SOME(v)`; otherwise it returns `false`.

val valOf : 'a option -> 'a

>   valOf *opt* returns v if *opt* is SOME(v); otherwise, it raises the Option exception.

val filter : ('a -> bool) -> 'a -> 'a option

>   filter *f a* returns SOME(*a*) if *f(a)* is true and NONE otherwise.

val join : 'a option option -> 'a option

>   The join function maps NONE to NONE and SOME(v) to v.

val app : ('a -> unit) -> 'a option -> unit

>   app *f opt* applies the function *f* to the value v if *opt* is SOME(v) and otherwise
>   does nothing.

val map : ('a -> 'b) -> 'a option -> 'b option

>   map *f opt* maps NONE to NONE and SOME(v) to SOME(*f* v).

val mapPartial : ('a -> 'b option)
                           -> 'a option -> 'b option

>   mapPartial *f opt* maps NONE to NONE and SOME(v) to *f*(v). The expression
>   mapPartial *f* is equivalent to join o (map *f*).

val compose : ('a -> 'b) * ('c -> 'a option)
                      -> 'c -> 'b option

>   compose (*f*, *g*) *a* returns NONE if *g*(*a*) is NONE; otherwise, if *g*(*a*) is SOME(v),
>   it returns SOME(*f* v). Thus, the compose function composes *f* with the partial function
>   *g* to produce another partial function. The expression compose (*f*, *g*) is equivalent
>   to (map *f*) o *g*.

val composePartial : ('a -> 'b option) * ('c -> 'a option)
                            -> 'c -> 'b option

>   composePartial (*f*, *g*) *a* returns NONE if *g*(*a*) is NONE; otherwise, if *g*(*a*)
>   is SOME(v), it returns *f*(v). Thus, the composePartial function composes the two
>   partial functions *f* and *g* to produce another partial function. The expression compose-
>   Partial (*f*, *g*) is equivalent to (mapPartial *f*) o *g*.

11.32   The OS structure

The OS structure is a container for a collection of structures for interacting with the operating system's file system, directory paths, processes, and I/O subsystem. The types and functions provided by the OS substructures are meant to present a model for handling these resources that is largely independent of the operating system.

The structure also declares the SysErr exception used to report operating system error conditions.

Synopsis

```
signature OS
structure OS :> OS
```

Interface

```
structure FileSys : OS_FILE_SYS
structure IO : OS_IO
structure Path : OS_PATH
structure Process : OS_PROCESS

eqtype syserror

exception SysErr of string * syserror option

val errorMsg : syserror -> string
val errorName : syserror -> string
val syserror  : string -> syserror option
```

Description

```
structure FileSys : OS_FILE_SYS
```

    File system: files and directories and their attributes.

```
structure IO : OS_IO
```

    I/O polling.

```
structure Path : OS_PATH
```

    Syntactic manipulation of pathnames.

```
structure Process : OS_PROCESS
```

    Process control, exit status, and environment.

eqtype syserror

> The type representing errors that arise when making calls to the runtime or operating system. These values are usually transmitted by the `SysErr` exception.

exception SysErr **of** string * syserror option

> This exception is raised when a call to the runtime system or host operating system results in an error. The first argument is a descriptive string explaining the error, and the second argument optionally specifies the system error condition. The form and content of the description strings are operating system and implementation dependent, but if a SysErr exception has the form `SysErr(s, SOME e)`, then we have `errorMsg e = s`. System errors that do not have a corresponding `syserror` value will result in `SysErr` being raised with a second argument of NONE.

val errorMsg : syserror -> string

> `errorMsg err` returns a string describing the system error identified by the error code *err*. The form and content of the description strings are operating system and implementation dependent.

val errorName : syserror -> string
val syserror : string -> syserror option

> errorName *err*
> syserror *s*
> These functions provide conversions between the abstract `syserror` type and their operating system dependent string names. The primary purpose of these functions is to provide a mechanism for dealing with error codes that might not have symbolic names defined for them in the operating-system specific modules. The former function returns a unique name used for the `syserror` value, while the latter returns the `syserror` whose name is *s*, if it exists. If *e* is a `syserror`, then it should be the case that
>
>   SOME *e* = syserror(errorName *e*)

See also

> OS.FileSys (§11.33; p. 231), OS.IO (§11.34; p. 237), OS.Path (§11.35; p. 241),
> OS.Process (§11.36; p. 250)

11.33 The OS.FileSys structure

The OS.FileSys structure provides facilities for accessing and operating on the file system. These functions are designed to be portable across operating systems. They raise OS.SysErr with an argument in case of errors.

Except for fullPath and realPath, functions taking a string argument will raise the OS.SysErr exception if the argument string is empty.

It is expected that all functions taking a pathname as an argument (e.g., modTime or OS.Process.system) will resolve any components corresponding to symbolic links. The obvious exceptions to this rule are isLink and readLink, where only symbolic links appearing as directory components of the pathname are resolved.

Synopsis
```
signature OS_FILE_SYS
structure OS.FileSys : OS_FILE_SYS
```

Interface
```
type dirstream

val openDir : string -> dirstream
val readDir : dirstream -> string option
val rewindDir : dirstream -> unit
val closeDir : dirstream -> unit

val chDir : string -> unit
val getDir : unit -> string
val mkDir : string -> unit
val rmDir : string -> unit
val isDir : string -> bool
val isLink : string -> bool
val readLink : string -> string
val fullPath : string -> string
val realPath : string -> string
val modTime : string -> Time.time
val fileSize : string -> Position.int
val setTime : string * Time.time option -> unit
val remove : string -> unit
val rename : {old : string, new : string} -> unit

datatype access_mode = A_READ | A_WRITE | A_EXEC

val access : string * access_mode list -> bool

val tmpName : unit -> string

eqtype file_id
```

```
val fileId : string -> file_id
val hash : file_id -> word
val compare : file_id * file_id -> order
```

Description

val openDir : string -> dirstream

> openDir *path* opens the directory specified by *path* and returns a directory stream
> for use with readDir, rewindDir, and closeDir. The stream reads the directory
> entries off the file system in some unspecified order. It raises SysErr if, for example, the
> directory does not exist or is not accessible.

val readDir : dirstream -> string option

> readDir *dir* returns and removes one filename from the directory stream *dir*. When
> the directory stream is empty (that is, when all entries have been read from the stream),
> NONE is returned. readDir filters out the names corresponding to the current and parent
> arcs.

val rewindDir : dirstream -> unit

> rewindDir *dir* resets the directory stream *dir*, as if it had just been opened. It
> raises SysErr in case of an operating system error, though, since the directory stream has
> already been opened, an error should not be likely.

val closeDir : dirstream -> unit

> closeDir *dir* closes the directory stream *dir*, releasing any system resources asso-
> ciated with it. Any subsequent read or rewind on the stream will raise exception SysErr.
> Closing a closed directory stream, however, has no effect.

val chDir : string -> unit

> chDir *s* changes the current working directory to *s*, which affects future calls to all
> functions that access the file system. These include the input/output functions such as
> TextIO.openIn and TextIO.openOut and functions defined in this structure. It
> raises SysErr if, for example, the directory does not exist or is not readable.
>
> The chDir function will also change the current volume (on systems with volumes)
> if one is specified. This function does not allow the user to change the current working
> directory of another volume than the current volume, even on systems where this concept
> is otherwise supported.

val getDir : unit -> string

> An absolute canonical pathname of the current working directory. This pathname includes
> the current volume on those systems that support volumes.

val mkDir : string -> unit

> mkDir *s* creates a directory *s* on the file system. If *s* has multiple arcs, each of the ancestor directories must exist or else will need to be created first, if they do not already exist. This function raises SysErr if, for example, the directory in which *s* is to be created does not exist or is not writable.

val rmDir : string -> unit

> rmDir *s* removes directory *s* from the file system. It raises SysErr if, for example, *s* does not exist or if the directory in which *s* resides is not writable or if the directory is not empty.

val isDir : string -> bool

> isDir *s* tests whether *s* is a directory. It raises SysErr if, for example, *s* does not exist or if the directory in which *s* resides is not accessible.

val isLink : string -> bool

> isLink *s* returns true if *s* names a symbolic link. It raises SysErr if, for example, *s* does not exist or there is an access violation. On operating systems without symbolic links, it will always return false unless an exception is raised first.

val readLink : string -> string

> readLink *s* returns the contents of the symbolic link *s*. It raises SysErr if, for example, *s* does not exist or is not a symbolic link, or there is an access violation. On operating systems without symbolic links, it raises SysErr unconditionally.
>
> The precise form of the returned string, in particular, whether it corresponds to an absolute or relative path, is system-dependent.

val fullPath : string -> string

> fullPath *path* returns an absolute canonical path that names the same file system object as *path*. The resulting path will have a volume prefix (on systems supporting volumes); all occurrences of the current, parent, and empty arcs will have been expanded or removed; and any symbolic links will have been fully expanded. An empty *path* is treated as ".". It raises SysErr if, for example, a directory on the path, or the file or directory named, does not exist or is not accessible or if there is a link loop.

val realPath : string -> string

> realPath *path* returns a canonical path that names the same file system object as *path*. If *path* is an absolute path, then realPath acts like fullPath. If *path* is relative and on the same volume as the current working directory, then it returns a path that is relative to the current working directory but in which the symbolic links have been expanded. Otherwise, it raises OS.Path.Path.

Implementation note: This function can be implemented as follows:

```
fun realPath p = if OS.Path.isAbsolute p
         then fullPath p
         else OS.Path.mkRelative{
             path=fullPath p, relativeTo=fullPath(getDir())
           }
```

val modTime : string -> Time.time

modTime *path* returns the modification time of file *path*. It raises SysErr if, for example, *path* does not exist or if the directory in which *path* resides is not accessible.

val fileSize : string -> Position.int

fileSize *path* returns the size of file *path* in bytes. It raises SysErr if, for example, *path* does not exist or if the directory in which *path* resides is not accessible.

val setTime : string * Time.time option -> unit

setTime (*path*, *opt*) sets the modification and access time of file *path*. If *opt* is SOME(*t*), then the time *t* is used; otherwise, the current time (i.e., Time.now()) is used. It raises SysErr if *path* does not exist, the directory in which *path* resides is not accessible, or the user does not have the appropriate permission.

val remove : string -> unit

remove *path* deletes the file *path* from the file system. It raises SysErr if *path* does not exist or is not writable, if the directory in which *path* resides is not writable, or if *file* is a directory. Use the rmDir function to delete directories.

If one removes a file that has been opened for reading or writing, the behavior of subsequent reads and writes is undefined. For example, removing the file may close all existing streams or generate an exception. The Unix idiom of opening a file and then removing it is not portable.

val rename : {old : string, new : string} -> unit

rename {*old*, *new*} changes the name of file *old* to *new*. If *new* and *old* refer to the same file, rename does nothing. If a file called *new* exists, it is removed. It raises SysErr if, for example, *old* does not exist or if one of the directories in which *old* or *new* reside is not writable. This function may also fail if *old* refers to an open file or if *old* and *new* are on different file systems, i.e., if a copy is required.

val access : string * access_mode list -> bool

access (*path*, *accs*) tests the permissions of file *path*, expanding symbolic links as necessary. If the list *accs* of required access modes is empty, it tests whether *path* exists. If *accs* contains A_READ, A_WRITE, or A_EXEC, respectively, it tests whether the user process has read, write, or execute permission for the file, testing their conjunction if more than one is present. Note that `access` is also implicitly testing the user's access to the parent directories of the file. The function will only raise `OS.SysErr` for errors unrelated to resolving the pathname and the related permissions, such as being interrupted by a signal during the system call.

Implementation note: On systems that do not support a notion of execution permissions, the `access` should accept but ignore the `A_EXEC` value.

val `tmpName : unit -> string`

This function creates a new empty file with a unique name and returns the full pathname of the file. The named file will be readable and writable by the creating process but, if the host operating systems supports it, not accessible by other users. This function can be used to create a temporary file that will not collide with other applications.

This function raises `SysErr` if it cannot create the unique file or filename.

eqtype `file_id`

A unique identifier associated with a file system object. A value of this type is not persistent across changes in the file system (e.g., mount/unmount), but it is better than pathnames for uniquely identifying files. A `file_id` value should not be confused with the open file identifier `OS.IO.iodesc`.

val `fileId : string -> file_id`

`fileId` *path* returns the unique `file_id` value associated with the file system object designated by the pathname *path*. In particular, if `fileId` *p* = `fileId` *p'*, then the paths *p* and *p'* refer to the same file system object. Note that if *p* is a symbolic link, then `fileId` *p* = `fileId(readLink` *p*) .

val `hash : file_id -> word`

`hash` *fid* returns a hash value associated with *fid*.

Implementation note: `hash` must have the property that values produced are well distributed when taken modulo 2^n for any *n*.

val `compare : file_id * file_id -> order`

`compare` (*fid*, *fid'*) returns LESS, EQUAL, or GREATER when *fid* is less than, equal to, or greater than *fid'*, respectively, in some underlying total ordering of `file_id` values.

Discussion

For functions dealing with file attributes, such as `fileSize` or `rename`, the arguments can be directories as well as ordinary files.

See also

> BinIO (§11.4; p. 127), OS (§11.32; p. 229), OS.Path (§11.35; p. 241),
> TextIO (§11.58; p. 382)

11.34 The OS.IO structure

The OS.IO structure provides a general interface for polling I/O devices. This interface has been modeled after the Unix SVR4 poll interface. A poll_desc created from an I/O descriptor can be used to test for various polling conditions.

Synopsis

```
signature OS_IO
structure OS.IO : OS_IO
```

Interface

```
eqtype iodesc
val hash : iodesc -> word
val compare : iodesc * iodesc -> order
eqtype iodesc_kind
val kind : iodesc -> iodesc_kind
structure Kind : sig
    val file    : iodesc_kind
    val dir     : iodesc_kind
    val symlink : iodesc_kind
    val tty     : iodesc_kind
    val pipe    : iodesc_kind
    val socket  : iodesc_kind
    val device  : iodesc_kind
  end
eqtype poll_desc
type poll_info
val pollDesc : iodesc -> poll_desc option
val pollToIODesc : poll_desc -> iodesc
exception Poll
val pollIn  : poll_desc -> poll_desc
val pollOut : poll_desc -> poll_desc
val pollPri : poll_desc -> poll_desc
val poll : poll_desc list * Time.time option
              -> poll_info list
val isIn  : poll_info -> bool
val isOut : poll_info -> bool
val isPri : poll_info -> bool
val infoToPollDesc : poll_info -> poll_desc
```

Description

eqtype iodesc

> An iodesc is an abstraction for an opened OS object that supports I/O (e.g., a file, console, or socket). In Unix, an iodesc corresponds to a file descriptor, while in Microsoft Windows it corresponds to a file handle.

Since `iodesc` values correspond to low-level, OS-specific objects, they are not typi-cally created explicitly by the user but are generated as a side-effect of the creation of a high-level abstraction. For example, `TextIO.openIn` creates an `instream` value from which the underlying `PrimIO.reader` can be accessed. This latter value may contain the corresponding `iodesc` value.

If the underlying operating system is known, there will usually be mechanisms for con-verting between `iodesc` values and the type of value used by the operating system. For example, the functions `Posix.FileSys.fdToIOD` and `Posix.FileSys.iodTo-FD` provide this service for POSIX implementations, translating between `iodesc`s and open file descriptors.

val `hash : iodesc -> word`

`hash` *iod* returns a hash value for the I/O descriptor *iod*.

Implementation note: `hash` must have the property that values produced are well distributed when taken modulo 2^n for any n.

val `compare : iodesc * iodesc -> order`

`compare (`*iod*`, `*iod'*`)` returns LESS, EQUAL, or GREATER when *iod* is less than, equal to, or greater than *iod'*, respectively, in some underlying linear ordering on `iodesc` values.

eqtype `iodesc_kind`

This abstract type is used to represent the *kind* of system object that an `iodesc` represents. The possible values are defined in the `Kind` substructure.

val `kind : iodesc -> iodesc_kind`

`kind` *iod* returns the kind of system object that the I/O descriptor *iod* represents. This function raises `SysErr` if, for example, *iod* refers to a closed file.

structure `Kind :` **sig ... end**

      val `file : iodesc_kind`
      val `dir : iodesc_kind`
      val `symlink : iodesc_kind`
      val `tty : iodesc_kind`
      val `pipe : iodesc_kind`
      val `socket : iodesc_kind`
      val `device : iodesc_kind`

These values represent the various kinds of system objects that an I/O descriptor might represent. The following list summarizes the intended meaning of these val-ues:

file A regular file in the file system. The I/O descriptor associated with a stream produced by one of the `BinIO` or `TextIO` file opening operations will always have this kind.

dir A directory in the file system. I/O descriptors associated with file system objects for which `OS.FileSys.isDir` returns `true` will have this kind.

symlink A symbolic link or file system alias. I/O descriptors associated with file system objects for which `OS.FileSys.isLink` returns `true` will have this kind.

tty A terminal console.

pipe A pipe to another system process.

socket A network socket.

device A logical or physical hardware device.

Note that a given implementation may define other `iodesc` values not covered by these definitions.

eqtype `poll_desc`

An abstract representation of a polling operation on an I/O descriptor.

type `poll_info`

An abstract representation of the per-descriptor information returned by the `poll` operation.

val `pollDesc : iodesc -> poll_desc option`

`pollDesc` *iod* create a polling operation on the given descriptor; `NONE` is returned when no polling is supported by the I/O device.

val `pollToIODesc : poll_desc -> iodesc`

`pollToIODesc` *pd* returns the I/O descriptor that is being polled using *pd*.

exception `Poll`

This exception is raised when an attempt is made to add an inappropriate polling condition to a poll descriptor.

val `pollIn : poll_desc -> poll_desc`
val `pollOut : poll_desc -> poll_desc`
val `pollPri : poll_desc -> poll_desc`

`pollIn` *pd*
`pollOut` *pd*
`pollPri` *pd*
These functions return a poll descriptor that has input (respectively, output, high-priority) polling added to the poll descriptor *pd*. It raises `Poll` if input (respectively, output, high-priority events) is not appropriate for the underlying I/O device.

val poll : poll_desc list * Time.time option
                    -> poll_info list

> poll (*l, timeout*) polls a collection of I/O devices for the conditions specified by
> the list of poll descriptors *l*. The argument *timeout* specifies the timeout where:
>
> - NONE means wait indefinitely.
> - SOME(Time.zeroTime) means do not block.
> - SOME(t) means timeout after time t.
>
> This function returns a list of poll_info values corresponding to those descriptors in *l*
> whose conditions are enabled. The returned list respects the order of the argument list, and
> a value in the returned list will reflect a (non-empty) subset of the conditions specified in
> the corresponding argument descriptor. The poll function will raise OS.SysErr if, for
> example, one of the file descriptors refers to a closed file.

val isIn : poll_info -> bool
val isOut : poll_info -> bool
val isPri : poll_info -> bool

> isIn *info*
> isOut *info*
> isPri *info*
> These functions return true if input (respectively, output, priority information) is present
> in *info*.

val infoToPollDesc : poll_info -> poll_desc

> infoToPollDesc *pi* returns the underlying poll descriptor from poll information *pi*.

See also

> PRIM_IO (§11.48; p. 308), OS (§11.32; p. 229)

11.35 The OS.Path structure

The OS.Path structure provides support for manipulating the *syntax* of file system paths independent of the underlying file system. It is purposely designed not to rely on any file system operations: none of the functions accesses the actual file system. There are two reasons for this design: many systems support multiple file systems that may have different semantics, and applications may need to manipulate paths that do not exist in the underlying file system.

Before discussing the model of paths and the semantics of the individual operations, we need to define some terms:

- An *arc* denotes a directory or file relative to the directory in which it is recorded. In a path string, arcs are separated by the arc separator character. This character is #"/" in Unix and in Microsoft Windows both #"\\" and #"/" are allowed. For example, in Unix, the path "abc/def" contains two arcs: "abc" and "def". There are two special arcs: parentArc and currentArc. Under both Unix and Windows, the parentArc is ".." and currentArc is ".". An empty arc corresponds to an empty string.

  Although represented concretely as a string, an arc should be viewed as an abstraction in the context of the OS.Path structure, with a limited set of valid representations. In particular, a non-empty string *a* is a *valid arc* only if fromString *a* returns {isAbs=false, vol="", arcs=[a]}.

- A *path* corresponds to a list of arcs, with an optional root, that denotes the path of directories leading to a file or directory in the file system hierarchy.

- An *absolute path* has a root. Unix examples include "/" and "/a/b"; Microsoft Windows examples include "\", "\a\b", and "A:\a\b".

- A *relative path* is one without a root. Unix examples include ".." and "a/b"; Windows examples include "..", "a\b", and "A:a\b".

- A *canonical path* contains no occurrences of the empty arc, no occurrences of the current arc unless the current arc is the only arc in the path, and contains parent arcs only at the beginning and only if the path is relative. Some examples of canonical paths, using Unix syntax, are as follows: ".", "/.", "/", "a", "a/b/c", "..", "../a", "../../a/b/c", and "/a/b/c".

  In a Microsoft Windows implementation, canonical paths are entirely lowercase.

- A path has an associated *volume*. Under Unix, there is only one volume, whose name is "". Under Microsoft Windows, example volume names are "", "A:", and "C:".

In addition to operations for canonicalizing paths and computing relative paths, the
`Path` structure supports path manipulations relative to three different views of a path:

1. A navigation oriented view, where a path is broken down into its root and a non-
   empty list of arcs. A path is either absolute or relative. The root of a path specifies
   the volume to which the path is taken to be relative. For Unix, there is only the
   `" "` volume.

2. A directory/file view, where a path is broken down into a directory specifier and a
   filename.

3. A base/extension view, where a path is broken down into a base filename and
   an extension. We make the assumption that the extension separator character is
   `#"."`, which works for most operating systems.

Our main design principle is that the functions should behave in a natural fashion
when applied to *canonical* paths. All functions, except `concat`, preserve canonical
paths, i.e., if all arguments are canonical, then so is the result.

Note that, although the model of path manipulation provided by the `Path` structure is operating-system independent, the analysis of strings is not. In particular, any
given implementation of the `Path` structure has an implicit notion of what the arc separator character is. Thus, on a Microsoft Windows system, `Path` will treat the string
`"\\d\\e"` as representing an absolute path with two arcs, whereas on a Unix system
it will correspond to a relative path with one arc.

Synopsis

```
signature OS_PATH
structure OS.Path : OS_PATH
```

Interface

```
exception Path
exception InvalidArc

val parentArc : string
val currentArc : string

val fromString : string
                 -> {
                     isAbs : bool,
                     vol : string,
                     arcs : string list
                 }
```

```
val toString : {
                   isAbs : bool,
                   vol : string,
                   arcs : string list
               } -> string

val validVolume : {isAbs : bool, vol : string} -> bool

val getVolume : string -> string
val getParent : string -> string

val splitDirFile : string -> {dir : string, file : string}
val joinDirFile : {dir : string, file : string} -> string
val dir  : string -> string
val file : string -> string

val splitBaseExt : string
                       -> {base : string, ext : string option
                          }
val joinBaseExt : {base : string, ext : string option}
                       -> string
val base : string -> string
val ext  : string -> string option

val mkCanonical : string -> string
val isCanonical : string -> bool
val mkAbsolute : {path : string, relativeTo : string}
                       -> string
val mkRelative : {path : string, relativeTo : string}
                       -> string
val isAbsolute : string -> bool
val isRelative : string -> bool
val isRoot : string -> bool

val concat : string * string -> string

val fromUnixPath : string -> string
val toUnixPath : string -> string
```

Description

```
exception Path
exception InvalidArc
```

These exceptions are raised to signify invalid paths and arcs, respectively.

```
val parentArc : string
```

The string denoting the parent directory (e.g., " . . " on Microsoft Windows and Unix).

val currentArc : string

The string denoting the current directory (e.g., " . " on Microsoft Windows and Unix).

val fromString : string
```
                    -> {
                        isAbs : bool,
                        vol : string,
                        arcs : string list
                    }
```

fromString *path* returns the decomposition {*isAbs*, *vol*, *arcs*} of the path specified by *path*. *vol* is the volume name and *arcs* is the list of (possibly empty) arcs of the path. *isAbs* is true if the path is absolute. Under Unix, the volume name is always the empty string; under Microsoft Windows it can have the forms "A:", "C:", etc.

Here are some examples for Unix paths:

path	fromString *path*
" "	{isAbs=false, vol="", arcs=[]}
"/"	{isAbs=true, vol="", arcs=[""]}
"//"	{isAbs=true, vol="", arcs=["", ""]}
"a"	{isAbs=false, vol="", arcs=["a"]}
"/a"	{isAbs=true, vol="", arcs=["a"]}
"//a"	{isAbs=true, vol="", arcs=["","a"]}
"a/"	{isAbs=false, vol="", arcs=["a", ""]}
"a//"	{isAbs=false, vol="", arcs=["a", "", ""]}
"a/b"	{isAbs=false, vol="", arcs=["a", "b"]}

val toString : {
```
                    isAbs : bool,
                    vol : string,
                    arcs : string list
            } -> string
```

toString {*isAbs*, *vol*, *arcs*} makes a string out of a path represented as a list of arcs. *isAbs* specifies whether or not the path is absolute, and *vol* provides a corresponding volume. It returns "" when applied to {isAbs=false, vol="", arcs=[]}. The exception Path is raised if validVolume{*isAbs*, *vol*} is false or if *isAbs* is false and *arcs* has an initial empty arc. The exception InvalidArc is raised if any component in *arcs* is not a valid representation of an arc. The exception Size is raised if the resulting string has size greater than String.maxSize.

toString o fromString is the identity. fromString o toString is also the identity, provided no exception is raised and none of the strings in *arcs* contains an embedded arc separator character. In addition, isRelative(toString {isAbs=false, vol, arcs}) evaluates to true when defined.

val validVolume : {isAbs : bool, vol : string} -> bool

> validVolume {*isAbs*, *vol*} returns true if *vol* is a valid volume name for an absolute or relative path, respectively as *isAbs* is true or false. Under Unix, the only valid volume name is " ". Under Microsoft Windows, the valid volume names have the forms "a:", "A:", "b:", "B:", etc., and, if *isAbs* = false, also "". Under MacOS, *isAbs* can be true if and only if *vol* is " ".

val getVolume : string -> string

> getVolume *path* returns the volume portion of the path *path*.

val getParent : string -> string

> getParent *path* returns a string denoting the parent directory of *path*. It holds that getParent *path* = *path* if and only if *path* is a root. If the last arc is empty or the parent arc, then getParent appends a parent arc. If the last arc is the current arc, then it is replaced with the parent arc. Note that if *path* is canonical, then the result of getParent will also be canonical.
>
> Here are some examples for Unix paths:

path	getParent *path*
"/"	"/"
"a"	"."
"a/"	"a/.."
"a///"	"a///.."
"a/b"	"a"
"a/b/"	"a/b/.."
".."	"../.."
"."	".."
""	".."

val splitDirFile : string -> {dir : string, file : string}

> splitDirFile *path* splits the string path *path* into its directory and file parts, where the file part is defined to be the last arc. The file will be " " if the last arc is " ".
>
> Here are some examples for Unix paths:

path	splitDirFile *path*
""	{dir = "", file = ""}
"."	{dir = "", file = "."}
"b"	{dir = "", file = "b"}
"b/"	{dir = "b", file = ""}
"a/b"	{dir = "a", file = "b"}
"/a"	{dir = "/", file = "a"}

val joinDirFile : {dir : string, file : string} -> string

> joinDirFile {*dir, file*} creates a whole path out of a directory and a file by extending the path *dir* with the arc *file*. If the string *file* does not correspond to an arc, it raises InvalidArc. The exception Size is raised if the resulting string has size greater than String.maxSize.

val dir : string -> string
val file : string -> string

> These functions return the directory and file parts of a path, respectively. They can be defined as
>
> > **val** dir = #dir o splitDirFile
> > **val** file = #file o splitDirFile
>
> Although they are likely to be more efficient.

val splitBaseExt : string
                      -> {base : string, ext : string option
                      }

> splitBaseExt *path* splits the path *path* into its base and extension parts. The extension is a non-empty sequence of characters following the right-most, non-initial, occurrence of " . " in the last arc; NONE is returned if the extension is not defined. The base part is everything to the left of the extension except the final " . ". Note that if there is no extension, a terminating " . " is included with the base part.
>
> Here are some examples for Unix paths:

path	splitBaseExt *path*
" "	{base = " ", ext = NONE}
".login"	{base = ".login", ext = NONE}
"/.login"	{base = "/.login", ext = NONE}
"a"	{base = "a", ext = NONE}
"a."	{base = "a.", ext = NONE}
"a.b"	{base = "a", ext = SOME "b"}
"a.b.c"	{base = "a.b", ext = SOME "c"}
".news/comp"	{base = ".news/comp", ext = NONE}

val joinBaseExt : {base : string, ext : string option}
                    -> string

> joinBaseExt {*base, ext*} returns an arc composed of the base name and the extension (if different from NONE). It is a left inverse of splitBaseExt, i.e., joinBaseExt o splitBaseExt is the identity. The opposite does not hold, since the extension may be empty or may contain extension separators. Note that, although splitBaseExt will never return the extension SOME(" "), joinBaseExt treats this value as equivalent to NONE. The exception Size is raised if the resulting string has size greater than String.maxSize.

```
val base : string -> string
val ext : string -> string option
```

These functions return the base and extension parts parts of a path, respectively. They can be defined as

```
    val base = #base o splitBaseExt
    val ext = #ext o splitBaseExt
```

Although they are likely to be more efficient.

```
val mkCanonical : string -> string
```

mkCanonical *path* returns the canonical path equivalent to *path*. Redundant occurrences of the parent arc, the current arc, and the empty arc are removed. The canonical path will never be the empty string; the empty path is converted to the current directory path (".") under Unix and Microsoft Windows).

Note that the syntactic canonicalization provided by mkCanonical may not preserve the file system meaning of a path in the presence of symbolic links (see concat).

```
val isCanonical : string -> bool
```

isCanonical *path* returns true if *path* is a canonical path. It is equivalent to (*path* = mkCanonical *path*).

```
val mkAbsolute : {path : string, relativeTo : string}
                 -> string
```

mkAbsolute {*path*, *relativeTo*} returns an absolute path that is equivalent to the path *path* relative to the absolute path *relativeTo*. If *path* is already absolute, it is returned unchanged; otherwise, the function returns the canonical concatenation of *relativeTo* with *path*, i.e., mkCanonical (concat (*abs*, *p*)). Thus, if *path* and *relativeTo* are canonical, the result will be canonical. If *relativeTo* is not absolute, or if the two paths refer to different volumes, then the Path exception is raised. The exception Size is raised if the resulting string has size greater than String.-maxSize.

```
val mkRelative : {path : string, relativeTo : string}
                 -> string
```

mkRelative {*path*, *relativeTo*} returns a relative path *p* that, when taken relative to the canonical form of the absolute path *relativeTo*, is equivalent to the path *path*. If *path* is relative, it is returned unchanged. If *path* is absolute, the procedure for computing the relative path is to first compute the canonical form *abs* of *relativeTo*. If *path* and *abs* are equal, then the current arc is the result; otherwise, the common prefix is stripped from *path* and *abs*, giving *p'* and *abs'*. The resulting path is then formed by appending *p'* to a path consisting of one parent arc for each arc in *abs'*. Note that if both paths are canonical, then the result will be canonical.

If *relativeTo* is not absolute, or if *path* and *relativeTo* are both absolute but have different roots, the Path exception is raised. The exception Size is raised if the resulting string has size greater than String.maxSize.

Here are some examples for Unix paths:

path	relativeTo	mkRelative{path, relativeTo}
"a/b"	"/c/d"	"a/b"
"/"	"/a/b/c"	"../../.."
"/a/b/"	"/a/c"	"../b/"
"/a/b"	"/a/c"	"../b"
"/a/b/"	"/a/c/"	"../b/"
"/a/b"	"/a/c/"	"../b"
"/"	"/"	"."
"/"	"/."	"."
"/"	"/.."	"."
"/a/b/../c"	"/a/d"	"../b/../c"
"/a/b"	"/c/d"	"../../a/b"
"/c/a/b"	"/c/d"	"../a/b"
"/c/d/a/b"	"/c/d"	"a/b"

val isAbsolute : string -> bool
val isRelative : string -> bool

    isAbsolute *path*
    isRelative *path*
These functions return true if *path* is, respectively, absolute or relative.

val isRoot : string -> bool

    isRoot *path* returns true if *path* is a canonical specification of a root directory.

val concat : string * string -> string

concat (*path*, t) returns the path consisting of *path* followed by t. It raises the exception Path if t is not a relative path or if *path* and t refer to different volumes. The exception Size is raised if the resulting string has size greater than String.maxSize.
    One possible implementation of concat is

```
fun concat (p1, p2) = (case (fromString p1, fromString p2)
      of (_, {isAbs=true, ...}) => raise Path
       | ({isAbs, vol=v1, arcs=al1},
          {vol=v2, arcs=al2, ...}
         ) => if ((v2 = "") orelse (v1 = v2))
              then toString{
                     isAbs=isAbs, vol=v1,
                     arcs=concatArcs(al1, al2)
                   }
              else raise Path
      (* end case *))
```

where concatArcs is like List.@, except that a trailing empty arc in the first argument is dropped. Note that concat should not be confused with the concatenation of two strings.
    concat does not preserve canonical paths. For example, concat("a/b", "../c")

returns `"a/b/../c"`. The parent arc is not removed because `"a/b/../c"` and `"a/c"` may not be equivalent in the presence of symbolic links.

val `fromUnixPath : string -> string`

> `fromUnixPath s` converts the Unix-style path s to the path syntax of the host operating system. Slash characters are translated to the directory separators of the local system, as are parent arcs and current arcs. This function raises the `InvalidArc` exception if any arc in the Unix path is invalid in the host system's path syntax (e.g., an arc that has a backslash character in it when the host system is Microsoft Windows).
>
> Note that the syntax of Unix pathnames necessarily limits this function. It is not possible to specify paths that have a non-empty volume name or paths that have a slash in one of their arcs using this function.

val `toUnixPath : string -> string`

> `toUnixPath s` converts the path s, which is in the host operating system's syntax, to a Unix-style path. If the path s has a non-empty volume name, then the `Path` exception is raised. Also, if any arc in the pathname contains the slash character, then the `Invalid-Arc` exception is raised.

Discussion

> Syntactically, two paths can be checked for equality by applying string equality to canonical versions of the paths. Since volumes and individual arcs are just special classes of paths, an identical test for equality can be applied to these classes.

See also

> `OS` (§11.32; p. 229), `OS.FileSys` (§11.33; p. 231), `OS.IO` (§11.34; p. 237),
> `OS.Process` (§11.36; p. 250), `Posix.FileSys` (§11.41; p. 263)

11.36   The `OS.Process` structure

The `OS.Process` structure provides functions for manipulating processes in an operating-system independent manner.

Synopsis

```
signature OS_PROCESS
structure OS.Process : OS_PROCESS
```

Interface

```
type status
val success : status
val failure : status
val isSuccess : status -> bool
val system : string -> status
val atExit : (unit -> unit) -> unit
val exit : status -> 'a
val terminate : status -> 'a
val getEnv : string -> string option
val sleep : Time.time -> unit
```

Description

`type status`

>   The `status` type represents various termination conditions for processes. On POSIX-based systems, `status` will typically be an integral value.

`val success : status`

>   The unique `status` value that signifies the successful termination of a process.

`val failure : status`

>   A `status` value that signifies an error during the execution of a process. Note that, in contrast to the success value, there may be other failure values.

`val isSuccess : status -> bool`

>   `isSuccess` *sts* returns `true` if the status denotes success.

>   **Implementation note:**   On implementations supporting the `Unix` structure, this function returns `true` only when `Unix.fromStatus` *sts* is `Unix.W_EXITED`. The analogous condition also holds for implementations providing the `Posix` structure.

val system : string -> status

> system *cmd* passes the command string *cmd* to the operating system's default shell to execute. It returns the termination status resulting from executing the command. It raises SysErr if the command cannot be executed.
>
> Note that, although this function is independent of the operating system, the interpretation of the string *cmd* depends very much on the underlying operating system and shell. On Unix systems, the default shell is "/bin/sh"; on Microsoft Windows systems, the default shell is the Windows shell; on MacOS systems, the command is compiled and executed as an Apple script.

val atExit : (unit -> unit) -> unit

> atExit *act* registers an action *act* to be executed when the current SML program calls exit. Actions will be executed in the reverse order of registration.
>
> Uncaught exceptions raised by the execution of *act* are trapped and ignored. Calls from *act* to atExit are ignored. Calls from *act* to exit do not return, but should cause the remainder of the functions registered with atExit to be executed. Calls to terminate (or similar functions such as Posix.Process.exit) will terminate the process immediately.

val exit : status -> 'a

> exit *st* executes all actions registered with atExit, flushes and closes all I/O streams opened using the Library, and then terminates the SML process with termination status *st*.

> **Implementation note:** If the argument to exit comes from system or some other function (such as Unix.reap) returning a status value, then the implementation should attempt to preserve the meaning of the exit code from the subprocess. For example, on a POSIX system, if Posix.Process.fromStatus *st* yields Posix.Process.‑ W_EXITSTATUS *v*, then *v* should be passed to Posix.Process.exit after all necessary cleanup is done.
>
> If *st* does not connote an exit value, exit should act as though called with failure. For example, on a POSIX system, this situation would occur if Posix.Process.from‑ Status *st* is Posix.Process.W_SIGNALED or Posix.Process.W_STOPPED.

val terminate : status -> 'a

> terminate *st* terminates the SML process with termination status *st*, without executing the actions registered with atExit or flushing open I/O streams.

val getEnv : string -> string option

> getEnv *s* returns the value of the environment variable *s*, if defined; otherwise, it returns NONE.
>
> An environment is associated with each SML process, modeled as a list of pairs of

strings, corresponding to name-value pairs. (The way the environment is established depends on the host operating system.) The `getEnv` function scans the environment for a pair whose first component equals s. If successful, it returns the second component.

val `sleep` **:** `Time.time` **->** `unit`

`sleep` t suspends the calling process for the time specified by t. If t is zero or negative, then the calling process does not sleep but returns immediately. No exception is raised. Note that the granularity of sleeping is operating-system dependent.

See also

OS (§11.32; p. 229), OS.FileSys (§11.33; p. 231), OS.IO (§11.34; p. 237), OS.Path (§11.35; p. 241), Posix.ProcEnv (§11.43; p. 284), Posix.Process (§11.44; p. 289)

11.37   The PACK_REAL signature

The PACK_REAL signature specifies the interface for packing and unpacking floating-point numbers into Word8 vectors and arrays. This interface provides a mechanism for transmitting floating-point values over a network.

For each optional Real*N* structure provided by an implementation, the implementation may also provide a pair of structures PackReal*N*Big and PackReal*N*Little. These structures share the real type defined in Real*N*. The PackReal*N*Big structures perform big-endian packing and unpacking, and the PackReal*N*Little structures perform little-endian packing and unpacking.

In addition, an implementation may provide the structures PackRealBig and Pack-RealLittle, which are aliases for the PACK_REAL structures related to the default Real structure.

Synopsis

```
signature PACK_REAL
structure PackRealBig :> PACK_REAL
  where type real = Real.real
structure PackRealLittle :> PACK_REAL
  where type real = Real.real
structure PackRealNBig :> PACK_REAL
  where type real = Real{N}.real
structure PackRealNLittle :> PACK_REAL
  where type real = Real{N}.real
```

Interface

```
type real

val bytesPerElem : int
val isBigEndian : bool

val toBytes    : real -> Word8Vector.vector
val fromBytes : Word8Vector.vector -> real
val subVec : Word8Vector.vector * int -> real
val subArr : Word8Array.array * int -> real
val update : Word8Array.array * int * real -> unit
```

Description

```
val bytesPerElem : int
```

> The number of bytes per element, sufficient to store a value of type real.

```
val isBigEndian : bool
```

> isBigEndian is true if the structure implements a big-endian view of the data.

```
val toBytes : real -> Word8Vector.vector
val fromBytes : Word8Vector.vector -> real
```

These functions pack and unpack floating-point values into and out of `Word8Vector.-`
`vector` values. The function `fromBytes` raises the `Subscript` exception if the argument vector does not have length at least `bytesPerElem`; otherwise, the first `bytes-`
`PerElem` bytes are used.

```
val subVec : Word8Vector.vector * int -> real
val subArr : Word8Array.array * int -> real
```

subVec (*vec*, *i*)
subArr (*vec*, *i*)
These functions extract the subsequence

$$vec[\text{bytesPerElem}*i..\text{bytesPerElem}*(i+1)-1]$$

of the aggregate *vec* and convert it into a `real` value according to the endianness of the
structure. They raise the `Subscript` exception if $i < 0$ or if $|vec| < \text{bytesPerElem}*$
$(i+1)$.

```
val update : Word8Array.array * int * real -> unit
```

update (*arr*, *i*, *r*) stores r into the bytes `bytesPerElem`*i through `bytes-`
`PerElem`*(i+1)-1 of the array *arr*, according to the structure's endianness. It raises
the `Subscript` exception if $i < 0$ or if $|arr| < \text{bytesPerElem}*(i+1)$.

See also

PACK_WORD (§11.38; p. 255), REAL (§11.50; p. 318)

11.38   The **PACK_WORD** signature

The PackWord$N$Big and PackWord$N$Little structures provide facilities for packing and unpacking N-bit word elements into Word8 vectors. This mechanism allows
word values to be transmitted in binary format over networks. The PackWord$N$Big
structures perform big-endian packing and unpacking, while the PackWord$N$Little
structures perform little-endian packing and unpacking.

Synopsis

```
signature PACK_WORD
structure PackWordNBig :> PACK_WORD
structure PackWordNLittle :> PACK_WORD
```

Interface

```
val bytesPerElem : int
val isBigEndian : bool
val subVec  : Word8Vector.vector * int -> LargeWord.word
val subVecX : Word8Vector.vector * int -> LargeWord.word
val subArr  : Word8Array.array * int -> LargeWord.word
val subArrX : Word8Array.array * int -> LargeWord.word
val update : Word8Array.array * int * LargeWord.word
                 -> unit
```

Description

```
val bytesPerElem : int
```

The number of bytes per element. Most implementations will provide several structures
with values of bytesPerElem that are small powers of two (e.g., 1, 2, 4, and 8, corresponding to N of 8, 16, 32, 64, respectively).

```
val isBigEndian : bool
```

True if the structure implements a big-endian view of the data (most-significant byte first).
Otherwise, the structure implements a little-endian view (least-significant byte first).

```
val subVec : Word8Vector.vector * int -> LargeWord.word
val subVecX : Word8Vector.vector * int -> LargeWord.word
```

subVec (*vec*, *i*)
subVecX (*vec*, *i*)
These extract the subvector

$$vec[\text{bytesPerElem}*i\,..\,\text{bytesPerElem}*(i+1)-1]$$

of the vector *vec* and convert it into a word according to the endianness of the structure. The subVecX version extends the sign bit (most significant bit) when converting
the subvector to a word. The functions raise the Subscript exception if $i < 0$ or if
$|vec| < \text{bytesPerElem} * (i + 1)$.

```
val subArr  : Word8Array.array * int -> LargeWord.word
val subArrX : Word8Array.array * int -> LargeWord.word
```

    subArr (*arr*, *i*)
    subArrX (*arr*, *i*)
    These extract the subarray

$$arr[\texttt{bytesPerElem*}i..\texttt{bytesPerElem*}(i+1)\texttt{-1}]$$

of the array *arr* and convert it into a word according to the endianness of the structure. The subArrX version extends the sign bit (most significant bit) when converting the subarray into a word. The functions raise the Subscript exception if $i < 0$ or if $|arr| <$ $\texttt{bytesPerElem} * (i + 1)$.

```
val update : Word8Array.array * int * LargeWord.word
                -> unit
```

    update (*arr*, *i*, *w*) stores the bytesPerElem low-order bytes of the word *w* into the bytes bytesPerElem*i through bytesPerElem*(i+1)-1 of the array *arr*, according to the structure's endianness. It raises the Subscript exception if $i < 0$ or if Word8Array.length *arr* $< \texttt{bytesPerElem} * (i + 1)$.

See also

    Byte (§11.7; p. 133), LargeWord (§11.67; p. 420), MONO_ARRAY (§11.23; p. 193), MONO_VECTOR (§11.26; p. 211), PACK_REAL (§11.37; p. 253)

11.39   The `Posix` structure

This optional structure contains several substructures that are useful for interfacing to POSIX operating systems. For more complete information on the semantics of the types and functions provided in `Posix`, see the POSIX Standard (1003.1,1996) [POS96].

Synopsis

```
signature POSIX
structure Posix :> POSIX
```

Interface

```
structure Error : POSIX_ERROR
structure Signal : POSIX_SIGNAL
structure Process : POSIX_PROCESS
  where type signal = Signal.signal
structure ProcEnv : POSIX_PROC_ENV
  where type pid = Process.pid
structure FileSys : POSIX_FILE_SYS
  where type file_desc = ProcEnv.file_desc
  where type uid = ProcEnv.uid
  where type gid = ProcEnv.gid
structure IO : POSIX_IO
  where type pid = Process.pid
  where type file_desc = ProcEnv.file_desc
  where type open_mode = FileSys.open_mode
structure SysDB : POSIX_SYS_DB
  where type uid = ProcEnv.uid
  where type gid = ProcEnv.gid
structure TTY : POSIX_TTY
  where type pid = Process.pid
  where type file_desc = ProcEnv.file_desc
```

Description

```
structure Error : POSIX_ERROR
```

>   System error codes and their descriptions.

```
structure Signal : POSIX_SIGNAL
```

>   Signal values and their associated codes.

```
structure Process : POSIX_PROCESS
  where type signal = Signal.signal
```

>   Process creation and management.

```
structure ProcEnv : POSIX_PROC_ENV
  where type pid = Process.pid
```

User and group IDs, process times, environment, etc.


```
structure FileSys : POSIX_FILE_SYS
  where type file_desc = ProcEnv.file_desc
  where type uid = ProcEnv.uid
  where type gid = ProcEnv.gid
```

File system operations.


```
structure IO : POSIX_IO
  where type pid = Process.pid
  where type file_desc = ProcEnv.file_desc
  where type open_mode = FileSys.open_mode
```

Input/output operations.


```
structure SysDB : POSIX_SYS_DB
  where type uid = ProcEnv.uid
  where type gid = ProcEnv.gid
```

System databases, such as the password and group databases.


```
structure TTY : POSIX_TTY
  where type pid = Process.pid
  where type file_desc = ProcEnv.file_desc
```

Terminal (tty) control: speed, attributes, drain, flush, etc.

Discussion

The `Posix` structure and signatures are optional as a group; i.e., they are either all present or all absent. Furthermore, if they are present, then the `SysWord` structure must also be provided by the implementation, but note that an implementation may provide the `SysWord` structure without providing the `Posix` structure.

Most functions in the `Posix` structure can raise `OS.SysErr` for many reasons. The description of an individual function will usually not describe all of the possible causes for raising the exception or all of the system errors (see `OS.syserror` and `Posix.-Error.syserror`) carried by the exception. The programmer will need to consult more detailed POSIX documentation.

See also

`Posix.Error` (§11.40; p. 259), `Posix.FileSys` (§11.41; p. 263),
`Posix.IO` (§11.42; p. 276), `Posix.ProcEnv` (§11.43; p. 284),
`Posix.Process` (§11.44; p. 289), `Posix.Signal` (§11.45; p. 294),
`Posix.SysDB` (§11.46; p. 296), `Posix.TTY` (§11.47; p. 298)

11.40   The `Posix.Error` structure

The structure `Posix.Error` provides symbolic names for errors that may be generated by the POSIX library and various related functions. These values are typically
carried as the second argument to the `SysErr` exception.

Synopsis

```
signature POSIX_ERROR
structure Posix.Error : POSIX_ERROR
```

Interface

```
eqtype syserror = OS.Process.syserror

val toWord    : syserror -> SysWord.word
val fromWord : SysWord.word -> syserror

val errorMsg : syserror -> string
val errorName : syserror -> string
val syserror : string -> syserror option

val acces        : syserror
val again        : syserror
val badf         : syserror
val badmsg       : syserror
val busy         : syserror
val canceled     : syserror
val child        : syserror
val deadlk       : syserror
val dom          : syserror
val exist        : syserror
val fault        : syserror
val fbig         : syserror
val inprogress   : syserror
val intr         : syserror
val inval        : syserror
val io           : syserror
val isdir        : syserror
val loop         : syserror
val mfile        : syserror
val mlink        : syserror
val msgsize      : syserror
val nametoolong : syserror
val nfile        : syserror
val nodev        : syserror
val noent        : syserror
val noexec       : syserror
val nolck        : syserror
val nomem        : syserror
val nospc        : syserror
val nosys        : syserror
```

```
val notdir   : syserror
val notempty : syserror
val notsup   : syserror
val notty    : syserror
val nxio     : syserror
val perm     : syserror
val pipe     : syserror
val range    : syserror
val rofs     : syserror
val spipe    : syserror
val srch     : syserror
val toobig   : syserror
val xdev     : syserror
```

Description

```
eqtype syserror = OS.Process.syserror
```

POSIX error type. This type is identical to the type `OS.syserror`.

```
val toWord : syserror -> SysWord.word
val fromWord : SysWord.word -> syserror
```

These functions convert between `syserror` values and non-zero word representations. Note that there is no validation that a `syserror` value generated using `fromWord` corresponds to an error value supported by the underlying system.

```
val errorMsg : syserror -> string
```

`errorMsg` *sy* returns a string that describes the system error *sy*.

```
val errorName : syserror -> string
```

`errorName` *err* returns a unique name used for the `syserror` value.

```
val syserror : string -> syserror option
```

`syserror` *s* returns the `syserror` whose name is *s*, if it exists. If *e* is a `syserror`, we have `SOME(e) = syserror(errorName e)`.

Discussion

The values defined in this structure represent the standard POSIX errors. The following table provides a brief description of their meanings:

SML name	Description
acces	An attempt was made to access a file in a way that is forbidden by its file permissions.

SML name	Description
again	A resource is temporarily unavailable, and later calls to the same routine may complete normally.
badf	A bad file descriptor was out of range or referred to no open file, or a read (write) request was made to a file that was only open for writing (reading).
badmsg	The implementation has detected a corrupted message.
busy	An attempt was made to use a system resource that was being used in a conflicting manner by another process.
canceled	The associated asynchronous operation was canceled before completion.
child	A `wait` related function was executed by a process that had no existing or unwaited-for child process.
deadlk	An attempt was made to lock a system resource that would have resulted in a deadlock situation.
dom	An input argument was outside the defined domain of a mathematical function.
exist	An existing file was specified in an inappropriate context, for instance, as the new link in a `link` function.
fault	The system detected an invalid address in attempting to use an argument of a system call.
fbig	The size of a file would exceed an implementation-defined maximum file size.
inprogress	An asynchronous process has not yet completed.
intr	An asynchronous signal (such as a `quit` or a `term` (terminate) signal) was caught by the process during the execution of an interruptible function.
inval	An invalid argument was supplied.
io	Some physical input or output error occurred.
isdir	An illegal operation was attempted on a directory, such as opening a directory for writing.
loop	A loop was encountered during pathname resolution due to symbolic links.
mfile	An attempt was made to open more than the maximum number of file descriptors allowed in this process.
mlink	An attempt was made to have the link count of a single file exceed a system-dependent limit.
msgsize	An inappropriate message buffer length was used.
nametoolong	The size of a pathname string, or a pathname component, was longer than the system-dependent limit.
nfile	There were too many open files.
nodev	An attempt was made to apply an inappropriate function to a device, for example, trying to read from a write-only device such as a printer.
noent	A component of a specified pathname did not exist, or the pathname was an empty string.
noexec	A request was made to execute a file that, although it had the appropriate permissions, was not in the format required by the implementation for executable files.

SML name	Description
nolck	A system-imposed limit on the number of simultaneous file and record locks was reached.
nomem	The process image required more memory than was allowed by the hardware or by system-imposed memory management constraints.
nospc	During a `write` operation on a regular file, or when extending a directory, there was no free space left on the device.
nosys	An attempt was made to use a function that is not available in this implementation.
notdir	A component of the specified pathname existed, but it was not a directory, when a directory was expected.
notempty	A directory with entries other than " . " and " . . " was supplied when an empty directory was expected.
notsup	The implementation does not support this feature of the standard.
notty	A control function was attempted for a file or a special file for which the operation was inappropriate.
nxio	Input or output on a special file referred to a device that did not exist or made a request beyond the limits of the device. This error may occur when, for example, a tape drive is not online.
perm	An attempt was made to perform an operation limited to processes with appropriate privileges or to the owner of a file or some other resource.
pipe	A write was attempted on a pipe or FIFO for which there was no process to read the data.
range	The result of a function was too large to fit in the available space.
rofs	An attempt was made to modify a file or directory on a file system that was read-only at that time.
spipe	An invalid seek operation was issued on a pipe or FIFO.
srch	No such process could be found corresponding to that specified by a given process ID.
toobig	The sum of bytes used by the argument list and environment list was greater than the system-imposed limit.
xdev	A link to a file on another file system was attempted.

The string representation of a `syserror` value, as returned by `errorName`, is the name of the error. Thus, `errorName badmsg = "badmsg"`.

The name of a corresponding POSIX error can be derived by capitalizing all letters and adding the character "E" as a prefix. For example, the POSIX error associated with `nodev` is ENODEV. The only exception to this rule is the error `toobig`, whose associated POSIX error is E2BIG.

See also

OS (§11.32; p. 229), Posix (§11.39; p. 257)

11.41 The `Posix.FileSys` structure

The structure `Posix.FileSys` provides access to file system operations as described in Section 5 of the POSIX standard (1003.1,1996) [POS96].

Synopsis
signature POSIX_FILE_SYS
structure Posix.FileSys : POSIX_FILE_SYS

Interface
eqtype uid
eqtype gid
eqtype file_desc

val fdToWord : file_desc -> SysWord.word
val wordToFD : SysWord.word -> file_desc
val fdToIOD : file_desc -> OS.IO.iodesc
val iodToFD : OS.IO.iodesc -> file_desc option

type dirstream

val opendir : string -> dirstream
val readdir : dirstream -> string option
val rewinddir : dirstream -> unit
val closedir : dirstream -> unit

val chdir : string -> unit
val getcwd : unit -> string

val stdin : file_desc
val stdout : file_desc
val stderr : file_desc

structure S : **sig**
    eqtype mode
    include BIT_FLAGS
      where type flags = mode

    val irwxu : mode
    val irusr : mode
    val iwusr : mode
    val ixusr : mode
    val irwxg : mode
    val irgrp : mode
    val iwgrp : mode
    val ixgrp : mode
    val irwxo : mode
    val iroth : mode
    val iwoth : mode
    val ixoth : mode

```
      val isuid : mode
      val isgid : mode
   end

structure O : sig
      include BIT_FLAGS

      val append : flags
      val excl : flags
      val noctty : flags
      val nonblock : flags
      val sync : flags
      val trunc : flags
   end

datatype open_mode
   = O_RDONLY
   | O_WRONLY
   | O_RDWR

val openf   : string * open_mode * O.flags -> file_desc
val createf : string * open_mode * O.flags * S.mode
                    -> file_desc
val creat : string * S.mode -> file_desc

val umask : S.mode -> S.mode
val link : {old : string, new : string} -> unit
val mkdir : string * S.mode -> unit
val mkfifo : string * S.mode -> unit
val unlink : string -> unit
val rmdir : string -> unit
val rename : {old : string, new : string} -> unit
val symlink : {old : string, new : string} -> unit
val readlink : string -> string

eqtype dev

val wordToDev : SysWord.word -> dev
val devToWord : dev -> SysWord.word

eqtype ino

val wordToIno : SysWord.word -> ino
val inoToWord : ino -> SysWord.word

structure ST : sig
      type stat
```

```
      val isDir  : stat -> bool
      val isChr  : stat -> bool
      val isBlk  : stat -> bool
      val isReg  : stat -> bool
      val isFIFO : stat -> bool
      val isLink : stat -> bool
      val isSock : stat -> bool
      val mode : stat -> S.mode
      val ino : stat -> ino
      val dev : stat -> dev
      val nlink : stat -> int
      val uid : stat -> uid
      val gid : stat -> gid
      val size : stat -> Position.int
      val atime : stat -> Time.time
      val mtime : stat -> Time.time
      val ctime : stat -> Time.time
    end

val stat  : string -> ST.stat
val lstat : string -> ST.stat
val fstat : file_desc -> ST.stat

datatype access_mode = A_READ | A_WRITE | A_EXEC

val access : string * access_mode list -> bool

val chmod : string * S.mode -> unit
val fchmod : file_desc * S.mode -> unit
val chown : string * uid * gid -> unit
val fchown : file_desc * uid * gid -> unit
val utime : string
            * {actime : Time.time, modtime : Time.time} option
            -> unit
val ftruncate : file_desc * Position.int -> unit

val pathconf  : string * string -> SysWord.word option
val fpathconf : file_desc * string -> SysWord.word option
```

Description

eqtype uid

    User identifier; identical to `Posix.ProcEnv.uid`.

eqtype gid

    Group identifier; identical to `Posix.ProcEnv.gid`.

eqtype `file_desc`

Open file descriptor.

val `fdToWord : file_desc -> SysWord.word`
val `wordToFD : SysWord.word -> file_desc`

These functions convert between an abstract open file descriptor and the integer representation used by the operating system. These calls should be avoided where possible, for the SML implementation may be able to garbage collect (i.e., automatically close) any `file_desc` value that is not accessible, but it cannot reclaim any `file_desc` that has ever been made concrete by `fdToWord`. Also, there is no validation that the file descriptor created by `wordToFD` corresponds to an actually open file.

val `fdToIOD : file_desc -> OS.IO.iodesc`
val `iodToFD : OS.IO.iodesc -> file_desc option`

These convert between a POSIX open file descriptor and the handle used by the OS subsystem. The function `iodToFD` returns an `option` type because, on certain systems, some open I/O devices are not associated with an underlying open file descriptor.

type `dirstream`

A directory stream opened for reading. A directory stream is an ordered sequence of all the directory entries in a particular directory. This type is identical to `OS.FileSys.-dirstream`.

val `opendir : string -> dirstream`

`opendir` *dirName* opens the directory designated by the *dirName* parameter and associates a directory stream with it. The directory stream is positioned at the first entry.

val `readdir : dirstream -> string option`

`readdir` *dir* returns and removes one filename from the directory stream *dir*. When the directory stream is empty (that is, when all entries have been read from the stream), NONE is returned. Entries for "." (current directory) and ".." (parent directory) are never returned.

Rationale: The reason for filtering out the current and parent directory entries is that it makes recursive walks of a directory tree easier.

val `rewinddir : dirstream -> unit`

`rewinddir` *d* repositions the directory stream *d* for reading at the beginning.

val closedir : dirstream **->** unit

> closedir *d* closes the directory stream *d*. Closing a previously closed dirstream does not raise an exception.

val chdir : string **->** unit

> chdir *s* changes the current working directory to *s*.

val getcwd : unit **->** string

> The absolute pathname of the current working directory.

val stdin : file_desc
val stdout : file_desc
val stderr : file_desc

> The standard input, output, and error file descriptors.

structure S : **sig** ... **end**

> **eqtype** mode
>> A file mode is a set of (read, write, execute) permissions for the owner of the file, members of the file's group, and others.
>
> **val** irwxu : mode
>> Read, write, and execute permission for "user" (the file's owner).
>
> **val** irusr : mode
>> Read permission for "user" (the file's owner).
>
> **val** iwusr : mode
>> Write permission for "user" (the file's owner).
>
> **val** ixusr : mode
>> Execute permission for "user" (the file's owner).
>
> **val** irwxg : mode
>> Read, write, and execute permission for members of the file's group.
>
> **val** irgrp : mode
>> Read permission for members of the file's group.

val iwgrp : mode

Write permission for members of the file's group.

val ixgrp : mode

Execute permission for members of the file's group.

val irwxo : mode

Read, write, and execute permission for "others" (all users).

val iroth : mode

Read permission for "others" (all users).

val iwoth : mode

Write permission for "others" (all users).

val ixoth : mode

Execute permission for "others" (all users).

val isuid : mode

Set-user-ID mode, indicating that the effective user ID of any user executing the file should be made the same as that of the owner of the file.

val isgid : mode

Set-group-ID mode, indicating that the effective group ID of any user executing the file should be made the same as the group of the file.

structure O : **sig** ... **end**

The structure Posix.FileSys.O contains file status flags used in calls to openf.

val append : flags

If set, the file pointer is set to the end of the file prior to each write.

val excl : flags

This flag causes the open to fail if the file already exists.

val noctty : flags

If the path parameter identifies a terminal device, this flag assures that the terminal device does not become the controlling terminal for the process.

val nonblock : flags

Open, read, and write operations on the file will be non-blocking.

val `sync : flags`

> If set, updates and writes to regular files and block devices are synchronous updates. On return from a function that performs a synchronous update (`writeVec`, `write-Arr`, `ftruncate`, `openf` with `trunc`), the calling process is assured that all data for the file have been written to permanent storage, even if the file is also open for deferred update.

val `trunc : flags`

> This flag causes the file to be truncated (to zero length) upon opening.

datatype `open_mode`

> Operations allowed on an open file.

`= O_RDONLY`

> Open a file for reading only.

`| O_WRONLY`

> Open a file for writing only.

`| O_RDWR`

> Open a file for reading and writing.

```
val openf : string * open_mode * O.flags -> file_desc
val createf : string * open_mode * O.flags * S.mode
                -> file_desc
    openf (s, om, f)
    createf (s, om, f, m)
```

> These calls open a file named s for reading, writing, or both (depending on the open mode om). The flags f specify the state of the open file. If the file does not exist, `openf` raises the `OS.SysErr` exception whereas `createf` creates the file, setting its protection mode to m (as modified by the `umask`).
>
> Note that, in C, the roles of `openf` and `createf` are combined in the function `open`. The first acts like `open` without the `O_CREAT` flag; the second acts like `open` with the `O_CREAT` flag and the specified permission mode. Also, the `createf` function should not be confused with the `creat` function below, which behaves like its C namesake.

val `creat : string * S.mode -> file_desc`

> `creat (s, m)` opens a file s for writing. If the file exists, this call truncates the file to zero length. If the file does not exist, it creates the file, setting its protection mode to m (as modified by the `umask`). This expression is equivalent to the following:
>
> $$\texttt{createf}(s,\texttt{O\_WRONLY},\texttt{O.trunc},m)$$

val umask : S.mode -> S.mode

umask *cmask* sets the file mode creation mask of the process to *cmask* and returns the previous value of the mask.

Whenever a file is created (by openf, creat, mkdir, etc.), all file permissions set in the file mode creation mask are removed from the mode of the created file. This clearing allows users to restrict the default access to their files.

The mask is inherited by child processes.

val link : {old : string, new : string} -> unit

link {*old*, *new*} creates an additional hard link (directory entry) for an existing file. Both the old and the new links share equal access rights to the underlying object.

Both *old* and *new* must reside on the same file system. A hard link to a directory cannot be created.

Upon successful completion, link updates the file status change time of the *old* file and updates the file status change and modification times of the directory containing the *new* entry. (See Posix.FileSys.ST.)

val mkdir : string * S.mode -> unit

mkdir (*s*, *m*) creates a new directory named *s* with protection mode *m* (as modified by the umask).

val mkfifo : string * S.mode -> unit

mkfifo (*s*, *m*) makes a FIFO special file (or named pipe) *s*, with protection mode *m* (as modified by the umask).

val unlink : string -> unit

unlink *path* removes the directory entry specified by *path* and, if the entry is a hard link, decrements the link count of the file referenced by the link.

When all links to a file are removed and no process has the file open or mapped, all resources associated with the file are reclaimed, and the file is no longer accessible. If one or more processes has the file open or mapped when the last link is removed, the link is removed before unlink returns, but the removal of the file contents is postponed until all open or map references to the file are removed. If the *path* parameter names a symbolic link, the symbolic link itself is removed.

val rmdir : string -> unit

rmdir *s* removes a directory *s*, which must be empty.

val rename : {old : string, new : string} -> unit

rename {*old*, *new*} changes the name of a file system object from *old* to *new*.

```
val symlink : {old : string, new : string} -> unit
```

symlink {*old*, *new*} creates a symbolic link *new*. Any component of a pathname resolving to *new* will be replaced by the text *old*. Note that *old* may be a relative or absolute pathname and might not be the pathname of any existing file.

```
val readlink : string -> string
```

readlink *s* reads the value of a symbolic link *s*.

eqtype dev

Device identifier. The device identifier and the file serial number (*inode* or ino) uniquely identify a file.

```
val wordToDev : SysWord.word -> dev
val devToWord : dev -> SysWord.word
```

These functions convert between dev values and words by which the operating system identifies a device. There is no verification that a value created by wordToDev corresponds to a valid device identifier.

eqtype ino

File serial number (*inode*).

```
val wordToIno : SysWord.word -> ino
val inoToWord : ino -> SysWord.word
```

These functions convert between ino values and words by which the operating system identifies an inode. There is no verification that a value created by wordToIno corresponds to a to a valid inode.

structure ST : **sig** ... **end**

    type stat

        This type models status information concerning a file.

```
val isDir : stat -> bool
val isChr : stat -> bool
val isBlk : stat -> bool
val isReg : stat -> bool
val isFIFO : stat -> bool
val isLink : stat -> bool
val isSock : stat -> bool
```

These functions return `true` if the file described by the parameter is, respectively, a directory, a character special device, a block special device, a regular file, a FIFO, a symbolic link, or a socket.

```
val mode : stat -> S.mode
```

`mode` `st` returns the protection mode of the file described by `st`.

```
val ino : stat -> ino
val dev : stat -> dev
```

These functions return the file serial number (inode) and the device identifier, respectively, of the corresponding file.

```
val nlink : stat -> int
```

`nlink` `st` returns the number of hard links to the file described by `st`.

```
val uid : stat -> uid
val gid : stat -> gid
```

These functions return the owner and group ID of the file.

```
val size : stat -> Position.int
```

`size` `st` returns the size (number of bytes) of the file described by `st`.

```
val atime : stat -> Time.time
val mtime : stat -> Time.time
val ctime : stat -> Time.time
```

These functions return, respectively, the last access time, the last modification time, or the last status change time of the file.

```
val stat : string -> ST.stat
val lstat : string -> ST.stat
val fstat : file_desc -> ST.stat
```

These functions return information on a file system object. For `stat` and `lstat`, the object is specified by its pathname. Note that an empty string causes an exception. For `fstat`, an open file descriptor is supplied.

`lstat` differs from `stat` in that, if the pathname argument is a symbolic link, the information concerns the link itself, not the file to which the link points.

datatype access_mode = A_READ | A_WRITE | A_EXEC

This type is identical to OS.FileSys.access_mode.

val access : string * access_mode list -> bool

access (s, l) checks the accessibility of file s. If l is the empty list, it checks for the existence of the file; if l contains A_READ, it checks for the readability of s based on the real user and group IDs of the process; and so on.

The value returned depends only on the appropriate privileges of the process and the permissions of the file. A directory may be indicated as writable by access, but an attempt to open it for writing will fail (although files may be created there). A file's permissions may indicate that it is executable, but the exec can fail if the file is not in the proper format. Conversely, if the process has appropriate privileges, access will return true if none of the appropriate file permissions are set.

val chmod : string * S.mode -> unit

chmod (s, mode) changes the permissions of s to mode.

val fchmod : file_desc * S.mode -> unit

fchmod (fd, mode) changes the permissions of the file opened as fd to mode.

val chown : string * uid * gid -> unit

chown (s, uid, gid) changes the owner and group of file s to uid and gid, respectively.

val fchown : file_desc * uid * gid -> unit

fchown (fd, uid, gid) changes the owner and group of the file opened as fd to uid and gid, respectively.

val utime : string
        * {actime : Time.time, modtime : Time.time} option
        -> unit

utime (f, SOME{actime,modtime}) sets the access and modification times of the file f to actime and modtime, respectively.
utime (f, NONE) sets the access and modification times of a file to the current time.

val ftruncate : file_desc * Position.int -> unit

ftruncate (fd, n) changes the length of a file opened as fd to n bytes. If the new length is less than the previous length, all data beyond n bytes are discarded. If the new length is greater than the previous length, the file is extended to its new length by the necessary number of zero bytes.

val pathconf : string * string -> SysWord.word option
val fpathconf : file_desc * string -> SysWord.word option

    pathconf (*s*, *p*)
    fpathconf (*fd*, *p*)
These functions return the value of property *p* of the file system underlying the file specified by *s* or *fd*. For integer-valued properties, if the value is unbounded, NONE is returned.
If the value is bounded, SOME(*v*) is returned, where *v* is the value. For boolean-value
properties, if the value is true, SOME(1) is returned; otherwise, SOME(0) or NONE is
returned. The OS.SysErr exception is raised if something goes wrong, including when
p is not a valid property or when the implementation does not associate the property with
the file.

    In the case of pathconf, read, write, or execute permission of the named file is not
required, but all directories in the path leading to the file must be searchable.

    The properties required by POSIX are described below. A given implementation may
support additional properties.

"CHOWN_RESTRICTED"   True if the use of chown on any files (other than directories)
    in the specified directory is restricted to processes with appropriate privileges. This
    property only applies to directories.

"LINK_MAX"   The maximum value of a file's link count as returned by the ST.nlink
    function.

"MAX_CANON"   The maximum number of bytes that can be stored in an input queue.
    This property only applies to terminal devices.

"MAX_INPUT"   The maximum number of bytes allowed in an input queue before being
    read by a process. This property only applies to terminal devices.

"NAME_MAX"   The maximum number of bytes in a filename. This value may be as small
    as 13 but is never larger than 255. This property only applies to directories, and its
    value applies to filenames within the directory.

"NO_TRUNC"   True if supplying a filename longer than allowed by "NAME_MAX" causes
    an error and false if long filenames are truncated. This property only applies to direc-
    tories.

"PATH_MAX"   The maximum number of bytes in a pathname. This value is never larger
    than 65,535 and is the maximum length of a relative pathname when the specified
    directory is the working directory. This property only applies to directories.

"PIPE_BUF"   Maximum number of bytes guaranteed to be written atomically. This
    value is applicable only to FIFOs. The value returned applies to the referenced object.
    If the path or file descriptor parameter refers to a directory, the value returned applies
    to any FIFO that exists or can be created within the directory.

"VDISABLE"   If defined, the integer code ord(c) of the character c that can be used
    to disable the terminal special characters specified in Posix.TTY.V. This property
    only applies to terminal devices.

"ASYNC_IO"   True if asynchronous input or output operations may be performed on the
    file.

"SYNC_IO"   True if synchronous input or output operations may be performed on the
    file.

"PRIO_IO"   True if prioritized input or output operations may be performed on the file.

Implementation note: An implementation can call the operating system's `pathconf` or `fpathconf` functions, which return an integer. If the returned value is -1 and `errno` has been set, an exception is raised. Otherwise, a returned value of -1 should be mapped to NONE, and other values should be wrapped in SOME and returned.

Rationale: The encoding of boolean values as `int option`, with false having two representations, is an unpleasant choice. It would be preferable to split these two functions into four, with one pair handling integer-valued properties, with the present return type, and the other pair handling boolean-valued properties, returning values of type `bool`. Unfortunately, the nature of the POSIX `pathconf` and `fpathconf` functions would make this approach a nightmare for the implementor.

First, the specification of these functions provides a non-negative integer return value for both booleans and numbers. POSIX header files provide no inherent information as to the type of a property. Although the basic properties specified by POSIX have fixed types, each system is allowed to add its own non-standard properties. Thus, for an SML implementation to make the distinction, it would have to rely on somehow gleaning the information from, e.g., system-specific manual pages.

In addition, the POSIX specification is unclear on how boolean values are encoded. Some systems return 0 for false; others appear to return -1 without setting `errno`. Technically, the latter value may be interpreted as meaning that the property value is unknown or unspecified, which means that, from the programmer's point of view, the property is not usable.

See also

BIT_FLAGS (§11.5; p. 129), OS.FileSys (§11.33; p. 231), Posix (§11.39; p. 257), Posix.IO (§11.42; p. 276), Posix.ProcEnv (§11.43; p. 284), Posix.Process (§11.44; p. 289)

11.42   The `Posix.IO` structure

The structure `Posix.IO` specifies functions that provide the primitive POSIX input/output operations, as described in Section 6 of the POSIX standard (1003.1,1996) [POS96].

Synopsis

```
signature POSIX_IO
structure Posix.IO : POSIX_IO
```

Interface

```
eqtype file_desc
eqtype pid

val pipe : unit -> {infd : file_desc, outfd : file_desc}
val dup : file_desc -> file_desc
val dup2 : {old : file_desc, new : file_desc} -> unit
val close : file_desc -> unit

val readVec : file_desc * int -> Word8Vector.vector
val readArr : file_desc * Word8ArraySlice.slice -> int
val writeVec : file_desc * Word8VectorSlice.slice -> int
val writeArr : file_desc * Word8ArraySlice.slice -> int

datatype whence
  = SEEK_SET
  | SEEK_CUR
  | SEEK_END

structure FD : sig
    include BIT_FLAGS
    val cloexec : flags
  end

structure O : sig
    include BIT_FLAGS
    val append : flags
    val nonblock : flags
    val sync : flags
  end

datatype open_mode
  = O_RDONLY
  | O_WRONLY
  | O_RDWR

val dupfd : {old : file_desc, base : file_desc}
               -> file_desc
val getfd : file_desc -> FD.flags
val setfd : file_desc * FD.flags -> unit
```

```
val getfl : file_desc -> O.flags * open_mode
val setfl : file_desc * O.flags -> unit

val lseek : file_desc * Position.int * whence
                  -> Position.int
val fsync : file_desc -> unit

datatype lock_type
   = F_RDLCK
   | F_WRLCK
   | F_UNLCK

structure FLock : sig
    type flock
    val flock : {
                    ltype : lock_type,
                    whence : whence,
                    start : Position.int,
                    len : Position.int,
                    pid : pid option
                  } -> flock
    val ltype   : flock -> lock_type
    val whence  : flock -> whence
    val start   : flock -> Position.int
    val len     : flock -> Position.int
    val pid     : flock -> pid option
   end

val getlk : file_desc * FLock.flock -> FLock.flock
val setlk : file_desc * FLock.flock -> FLock.flock
val setlkw : file_desc * FLock.flock -> FLock.flock

val mkBinReader  : {
                    fd : file_desc,
                    name : string,
                    initBlkMode : bool
                  } -> BinPrimIO.reader
val mkTextReader : {
                    fd : file_desc,
                    name : string,
                    initBlkMode : bool
                  } -> TextPrimIO.reader
```

```
val mkBinWriter  : {
                        fd : file_desc,
                        name : string,
                        appendMode : bool,
                        initBlkMode : bool,
                        chunkSize : int
                   } -> BinPrimIO.writer
val mkTextWriter : {
                        fd : file_desc,
                        name : string,
                        appendMode : bool,
                        initBlkMode : bool,
                        chunkSize : int
                   } -> TextPrimIO.writer
```

Description

eqtype `file_desc`

> Open file descriptor.

eqtype `pid`

> A process ID, used as an identifier for an operating system process.

val `pipe : unit -> {infd : file_desc, outfd : file_desc}`

> This function creates a pipe (channel) and returns two file descriptors that refer to the read (`infd`) and write (`outfd`) ends of the pipe.

val `dup : file_desc -> file_desc`

> dup `fd` returns a new file descriptor that refers to the same open file, with the same file pointer and access mode, as `fd`. The underlying word (see `Posix.FileSys.fdToWord`) of the returned file descriptor is the lowest one available. It is equivalent to dupfd `{old=fd, base=Posix.FileSys.wordToFD 0w0}`.

val `dup2 : {old : file_desc, new : file_desc} -> unit`

> dup2 `{old, new}` duplicates the open file descriptor `old` as the file descriptor `new`.

val `close : file_desc -> unit`

> close `fd` closes the file descriptor `fd`.

val readVec : file_desc * int -> Word8Vector.vector

> readVec (*fd*, *n*) reads at most *n* bytes from the file referred to by *fd*. The size of the resulting vector is the number of bytes that were successfully read, which may be less than *n*. This function returns the empty vector if end-of-stream is detected (or if *n* is 0). It raises the Size exception if *n*<0.

val readArr : file_desc * Word8ArraySlice.slice -> int

> readArr (*fd*, *slice*) reads bytes from the file specified by *fd* into the array slice *slice* and returns the number of bytes actually read. The end-of-file condition is marked by returning 0, although 0 is also returned if the *slice* is empty. This function will raise OS.SysErr if there is some problem with the underlying system call (e.g., the file is closed).

val writeVec : file_desc * Word8VectorSlice.slice -> int
val writeArr : file_desc * Word8ArraySlice.slice -> int

> writeVec (*fd*, *slice*)
> writeArr (*fd*, *slice*)
> These functions write the bytes of the vector or array slice *slice* to the open file *fd*. Both functions return the number of bytes actually written and will raise OS.SysErr if there is some problem with the underlying system call (e.g., the file is closed or there is insufficient disk space).

structure FD : **sig** ... **end**

> This substructure defines the file-status bit flags that are use by the getfd and setfd operations.
>
> **val** cloexec : flags
>
> > The file descriptor flag that, if set, will cause the file descriptor to be closed should the opening process replace itself (through exec, etc.). If cloexec is not set, the open file descriptor will be inherited by the new process.

structure O : **sig** ... **end**

> This substructure defines the file-status bit flags that are use by the getfl and setfl operations.
>
> **val** append : flags
>
> > The file status flag that forces the file offset to be set to the end of the file prior to each write.
>
> **val** nonblock : flags
>
> > The file status flag used to enable non-blocking I/O.

val sync : flags

> The file status flag enabling writes using "synchronized I/O file integrity comple-
> tion."

datatype open_mode

> Operations allowed on an open file.

> = O_RDONLY

>> Open a file for reading only.

> | O_WRONLY

>> Open a file for writing only.

> | O_RDWR

>> Open a file for reading and writing.

val dupfd : {old : file_desc, base : file_desc}
                   -> file_desc

> dupfd {*old*, *base*} returns a new file descriptor bound to *old*. The returned de-
> scriptor is greater than or equal to the file descriptor *base* based on the underlying integer
> mapping defined by Posix.FileSys.fdToWord and Posix.FileSys.wordTo-
> FD. It corresponds to the POSIX fcntl function with the F_DUPFD command.

val getfd : file_desc -> FD.flags

> getfd *fd* gets the file descriptor flags associated with *fd*. It corresponds to the POSIX
> fcntl function with the F_GETFD command.

val setfd : file_desc * FD.flags -> unit

> setfd (*fd*, *fl*) sets the flags of file descriptor *fd* to *fl*. It corresponds to the
> POSIX fcntl function with the F_SETFD command.

val getfl : file_desc -> O.flags * open_mode

> getfl *fd* gets the file status flags for the open file descriptor *fd* and the access mode
> in which the file was opened. It corresponds to the POSIX fcntl function with the
> F_GETFL command.

val setfl : file_desc * O.flags -> unit

> setfl (*fd*, *fl*) sets the file status flags for the open file descriptor *fd* to *fl*. It
> corresponds to the POSIX fcntl function with the F_SETFL command.

val lseek : file_desc * Position.int * whence
               -> Position.int

> lseek (*fd*, *off*, *wh*) sets the file offset for the open file descriptor *fd* to *off* if *wh* is SEEK_SET, to its current value plus *off* bytes if *wh* is SEEK_CUR, or to the size of the file plus *off* bytes if *wh* is SEEK_END. Note that *off* may be negative.

val fsync : file_desc -> unit

> fsync *fd* indicates that all data for the open file descriptor *fd* are to be transferred to the device associated with the descriptor; it is similar to a "flush" operation.

datatype lock_type
  = F_RDLCK
  | F_WRLCK
  | F_UNLCK

> These constructors denote the kind of lock. F_RDLCK indicates a shared or read lock. F_WRLCK indicates an exclusive or write lock. F_WRLCK indicates a lock is unlocked or inactive.

structure FLock : **sig** ... **end**

> This substructure defines the representation of advisory locks and provides operations on them.

type flock

> > Type representing an advisory lock. It can be considered an abstraction of the record used as the argument to the flock function below.

val flock : {
                   ltype : lock_type,
                   whence : whence,
                   start : Position.int,
                   len : Position.int,
                   pid : pid option
                } -> flock

> > flock {*ltype*, *whence*, *start*, *len*, *pid*} creates a flock value described by the parameters. The *whence* and *start* parameters give the beginning file position as in lseek. The *len* value provides the number of bytes to be locked. If the section starts at the beginning of the file and *len* = 0, then the entire file is locked. Normally, *pid* will be NONE. This value is only used in a flock returned by getlk.

```
val ltype : flock -> lock_type
val whence : flock -> whence
val start : flock -> Position.int
val len : flock -> Position.int
val pid : flock -> pid option
```

These are projection functions for the fields composing a flock value.

val getlk : file_desc * FLock.flock -> FLock.flock

getlk (*fd*, *fl*) gets the first lock that blocks the lock description *fl* on the open file descriptor *fd*. It corresponds to the POSIX fcntl function with the F_GETLK command.

val setlk : file_desc * FLock.flock -> FLock.flock

setlk (*fd*, *fl*) sets or clears a file segment lock according to the lock description *fl* on the open file descriptor *fd*. An exception is raised immediately if a shared or exclusive lock cannot be set. It corresponds to the POSIX fcntl function with the F_SETLK command.

val setlkw : file_desc * FLock.flock -> FLock.flock

This function is similar to the setlk function above, except that setlkw waits on blocked locks until they are released. It corresponds to the POSIX fcntl function with the F_SETLKW command.

```
val mkBinReader : {
                    fd : file_desc,
                    name : string,
                    initBlkMode : bool
                  } -> BinPrimIO.reader
val mkTextReader : {
                     fd : file_desc,
                     name : string,
                     initBlkMode : bool
                   } -> TextPrimIO.reader
```

These functions convert an open POSIX file descriptor into a reader. From this reader, one can then construct an input stream. The functions are comparable to the POSIX function fdopen.

The argument fields have the following meanings:

fd A file descriptor for a file opened for reading.

name The name associated with the file, used in error messages shown to the user.

initBlkMode False if the file is currently in non-blocking mode, i.e., if the flag O.-nonblock is set in #1(getfl fd).

```
val mkBinWriter : {
                    fd : file_desc,
                    name : string,
                    appendMode : bool,
                    initBlkMode : bool,
                    chunkSize : int
              } -> BinPrimIO.writer
val mkTextWriter : {
                    fd : file_desc,
                    name : string,
                    appendMode : bool,
                    initBlkMode : bool,
                    chunkSize : int
              } -> TextPrimIO.writer
```

These functions convert an open POSIX file descriptor into a writer. From this writer, one can then construct an output stream. The functions are comparable to the POSIX function fdopen.

The argument fields have the following meanings:

fd A file descriptor for a file opened for writing.

name The name associated with the file, used in error messages shown to the user.

initBlkMode False if the file is currently in non-blocking mode, i.e., if the flag O.-nonblock is set in #1(getfl fd).

appendMode True if the file is in append mode, i.e., if the flag O.append is set in #1(getfl fd).

chunkSize The recommended size of write operations for efficient writing.

See also

BIT_FLAGS (§11.5; p. 129), OS.IO (§11.34; p. 237), Posix (§11.39; p. 257), Posix.Error (§11.40; p. 259), Posix.FileSys (§11.41; p. 263), Posix.IO (§11.42; p. 276)

11.43   The `Posix.ProcEnv` structure

The structure `Posix.ProcEnv` specifies functions, as described in Section 4 of the
POSIX standard (1003.1,1996) [POS96], that provide primitive POSIX access to the
process environment.

Synopsis

signature POSIX_PROC_ENV
structure Posix.ProcEnv : POSIX_PROC_ENV

Interface

eqtype pid
eqtype uid
eqtype gid
eqtype file_desc

val uidToWord : uid -> SysWord.word
val wordToUid : SysWord.word -> uid
val gidToWord : gid -> SysWord.word
val wordToGid : SysWord.word -> gid

val getpid : unit -> pid
val getppid : unit -> pid
val getuid : unit -> uid
val geteuid : unit -> uid
val getgid : unit -> gid
val getegid : unit -> gid
val setuid : uid -> unit
val setgid : gid -> unit
val getgroups : unit -> gid list
val getlogin : unit -> string
val getpgrp : unit -> pid
val setsid : unit -> pid
val setpgid : {pid : pid option, pgid : pid option} -> unit

val uname : unit -> (string * string) list

val time : unit -> Time.time
val times : unit
                  -> {
                     elapsed : Time.time,
                     utime : Time.time,
                     stime : Time.time,
                     cutime : Time.time,
                     cstime : Time.time
                  }

val getenv : string -> string option
val environ : unit -> string list

```
val ctermid : unit -> string
val ttyname : file_desc -> string
val isatty : file_desc -> bool

val sysconf : string -> SysWord.word
```

Description

eqtype pid

> A process ID, used as an identifier for an operating system process.

eqtype uid

> User identifier.

eqtype gid

> Group identifier.

eqtype file_desc

> Open file descriptor.

```
val uidToWord : uid -> SysWord.word
val wordToUid : SysWord.word -> uid
```

> These functions convert between an abstract user ID and an underlying unique unsigned integer. Note that wordToUid does not ensure that it returns a valid uid.

```
val gidToWord : gid -> SysWord.word
val wordToGid : SysWord.word -> gid
```

> These convert between an abstract group ID and an underlying unique unsigned integer. Note that wordToGid does not ensure that it returns a valid gid.

```
val getpid : unit -> pid
val getppid : unit -> pid
```

> The process ID and the parent process ID, respectively, of the calling process.

```
val getuid : unit -> uid
val geteuid : unit -> uid
```

> The real and effective user IDs, respectively, of the calling process.

val getgid : unit -> gid
val getegid : unit -> gid

    The real and effective group IDs, respectively, of the calling process.

val setuid : uid -> unit

    setuid *u* sets the real user ID and the effective user ID to *u*.

val setgid : gid -> unit

    setgid *g* sets the real group ID and the effective group ID to *g*.

val getgroups : unit -> gid list

    The list of supplementary group IDs of the calling process.

val getlogin : unit -> string

    The user name associated with the calling process, i.e., the login name associated with the calling process.

val getpgrp : unit -> pid

    The process group ID of the calling process.

val setsid : unit -> pid

    This function creates a new session if the calling process is not a process group leader and returns the process group ID of the calling process.

val setpgid : {pid : pid option, pgid : pid option} -> unit

    setpgid (SOME *pid*, SOME *pgid*) sets the process group ID of the process specified by *pid* to *pgid*.
    setpgid (NONE, SOME *pgid*) sets the process group ID of the calling process to *pgid*.
    setpgid (SOME *pid*, NONE) makes the process specified by *pid* become a process group leader.
    setpgid (NONE, NONE) makes the calling process become a process group leader.

val uname : unit -> (string * string) list

    A list of name-value pairs including, at least, the names: "sysname", "nodename", "release", "version", and "machine". (A POSIX implementation may provide additional values beyond this set.) The respective values are strings that describe the named system component.

val `time : unit -> Time.time`

> The elapsed wall clock time since the Epoch.

val `times : unit`
```
        -> {
            elapsed : Time.time,
            utime   : Time.time,
            stime   : Time.time,
            cutime  : Time.time,
            cstime  : Time.time
        }
```

> A record containing the wall clock time (`elapsed`), user time (`utime`), system time (`stime`), user CPU time of terminated child processes (`cutime`), and system CPU time of terminated child processes (`cstime`) for the calling process.

val `getenv : string -> string option`

> `getenv` *name* searches the environment list for a string of the form *name*=*value* and returns `SOME(`*value*`)` if *name* is present; it returns `NONE` if *name* is not present. This function is equivalent to `OS.Process.getEnv`.

val `environ : unit -> string list`

> The environment of the calling process as a list of strings.

val `ctermid : unit -> string`

> A string that represents the pathname of the controlling terminal for the calling process.

val `ttyname : file_desc -> string`

> `ttyname` *fd* produces a string that represents the pathname of the terminal associated with file descriptor *fd*. It raises `OS.SysErr` if *fd* does not denote a valid terminal device.

val `isatty : file_desc -> bool`

> `isatty` *fd* returns `true` if *fd* is a valid file descriptor associated with a terminal. Note that `isatty` will return `false` if *fd* is a bad file descriptor.

val sysconf : string -> SysWord.word

> sysconf s returns the integer value for the POSIX configurable system variable s. It raises OS.SysErr if s does not denote a supported POSIX system variable.
>
> The properties required by POSIX are described below. This list is a minimal set required for POSIX compliance, and an implementation may extend it with additional properties.
>
> **"ARG_MAX"**   Maximum length of arguments, in bytes, for the functions exec, exece, and execp from the Posix.Process module, This limit also applies to environment data.
>
> **"CHILD_MAX"**   Maximum number of concurrent processes associated with a real user ID.
>
> **"CLK_TCK"**   Number of clock ticks per second.
>
> **"NGROUPS_MAX"**   Maximum number of supplementary group IDs associated with a process, in addition to the effective group ID.
>
> **"OPEN_MAX"**   Maximum number of files that one process can have open concurrently.
>
> **"STREAM_MAX"**   Maximum number of streams that one process can have open concurrently.
>
> **"TZNAME_MAX"**   Maximum number bytes allowed for a time zone name.
>
> **"JOB_CONTROL"**   Non-zero if the implementation supports job control.
>
> **"SAVED_IDS"**   Non-zero if each process has a saved set-user-ID and and saved set-group-ID.
>
> **"VERSION"**   A version number.
>
> Consult Section 4.8 of POSIX standard 1003.1,1996 [POS96] for additional information. Note that a property in SML has the same name as the property in C, but without the prefix "_SC_".

See also

> Posix (§11.39; p. 257), Posix.FileSys (§11.41; p. 263),
> Posix.ProcEnv (§11.43; p. 284), Time (§11.60; p. 387)

11.44   The `Posix.Process` structure

The structure `Posix.Process` describes the primitive POSIX operations dealing with processes, as described in Section 3 of the POSIX standard 1003.1,1996[POS96].

Synopsis
```
signature POSIX_PROCESS
structure Posix.Process : POSIX_PROCESS
```

Interface
```
eqtype signal
eqtype pid

val wordToPid : SysWord.word -> pid
val pidToWord : pid -> SysWord.word

val fork : unit -> pid option
val exec  : string * string list -> 'a
val exece : string * string list * string list -> 'a
val execp : string * string list -> 'a

datatype waitpid_arg
  = W_ANY_CHILD
  | W_CHILD of pid
  | W_SAME_GROUP
  | W_GROUP of pid
datatype exit_status
  = W_EXITED
  | W_EXITSTATUS of Word8.word
  | W_SIGNALED of signal
  | W_STOPPED of signal

val fromStatus : OS.Process.status -> exit_status

structure W : sig
    include BIT_FLAGS
    val untraced : flags
  end

val wait : unit -> pid * exit_status
val waitpid : waitpid_arg * W.flags list
                -> pid * exit_status
val waitpid_nh : waitpid_arg * W.flags list
                  -> (pid * exit_status) option

val exit : Word8.word -> 'a
```

```
datatype killpid_arg
  = K_PROC of pid
  | K_SAME_GROUP
  | K_GROUP of pid

val kill : killpid_arg * signal -> unit

val alarm : Time.time -> Time.time
val pause : unit -> unit
val sleep : Time.time -> Time.time
```

Description

eqtype signal

A POSIX signal; an asynchronous notification of an event.

eqtype pid

A process ID, used as an identifier for an operating system process.

```
val wordToPid : SysWord.word -> pid
val pidToWord : pid -> SysWord.word
```

These functions convert between a process ID and the integer representation used by the operating system. Note that there is no validation that a pid value generated using word-ToPid is legal on the given system or that it corresponds to a currently running process.

```
val fork : unit -> pid option
```

This function creates a new process. The new child process is a copy of the calling parent process. After the execution of fork, both the parent and child process execute independently but share various system resources. Upon successful completion, fork returns NONE in the child process and the pid of the child in the parent process. It raises OS.-SysErr on failure.

```
val exec : string * string list -> 'a
val exece : string * string list * string list -> 'a
val execp : string * string list -> 'a
```

```
exec (path, args)
exece (path, args, env)
execp (file, args)
```
These functions replace the current process image with a new process image. There is no return from a successful call, as the calling process image is overlaid by the new process image. In the first two forms, the *path* argument specifies the pathname of the executable file. In the last form, if *file* contains a slash character, it is treated as the pathname for

the executable file; otherwise, an executable file with the name `file` is searched for in the directories specified by the environment variable PATH.

Normally, the new image is given the same environment as the calling program. The `env` argument in `exece` allows the program to specify a new environment.

The `args` argument is a list of string arguments to be passed to the new program. By convention, the first item in `args` is some form of the filename of the new program, usually the last arc in the path or filename.

datatype waitpid_arg

= W_ANY_CHILD

Any child process

| W_CHILD **of** pid

The child process with the given `pid`

| W_SAME_GROUP

Any child process in the same process group as the calling process

| W_GROUP **of** pid

Any child process whose process group ID is given by `pid`.

datatype exit_status
    = W_EXITED
    | W_EXITSTATUS **of** Word8.word
    | W_SIGNALED **of** signal
    | W_STOPPED **of** signal

These values represent the ways in which a process might stop. They correspond to, respectively, terminate successfully, terminate with the given value, terminate upon receipt of the given signal, and stop upon receipt of the given signal. The value carried by W_EXITSTATUS must never be zero.

If an implementation provides both the Posix and Unix structures, then the datatypes Posix.Process.exit_status and Unix.exit_status must be the same.

val fromStatus : OS.Process.status **->** exit_status

fromStatus *sts* returns a concrete view of the given status.

structure W : **sig** ... **end**

> **val** untraced : flags
>
>> This flag is used to request the status of those child processes that are stopped on systems that support job control.

val wait : unit -> pid * exit_status

This function allows a calling process to obtain status information on any of its child processes. The execution of wait suspends the calling process until status information on one of its child processes is available. If status information is available prior to the execution of wait, return is immediate. wait returns the process ID of the child and its exit status.

val waitpid : waitpid_arg * W.flags list
                -> pid * exit_status

waitpid (*procs*, *l*) is identical to wait, except that the status is reported only for child processes specified by *procs*. A set of flags *l* may be used to modify the behavior of waitpid.

val waitpid_nh : waitpid_arg * W.flags list
                   -> (pid * exit_status) option

waitpid_nh (*procs*, *l*) is identical to waitpid, except that the call does not suspend if status information for one of the children specified by *procs* is not immediately available.

Rationale: In C, waitpid_nh is handled by waitpid, using an additional flag to indicate no hanging. In SML the semantics of waitpid_nh requires a different return type from that of waitpid, hence the split into two functions.

val exit : Word8.word -> 'a

exit *i* terminates the calling process. If the parent process is executing a wait related call, the exit status *i* is made available to it. exit does not return to the caller.

Calling exit does not flush or close any open IO streams, nor does it call OS.-Process.atExit. It does close any open POSIX files and performs the actions associated with the C version of exit.

datatype killpid_arg

> = K_PROC **of** pid
>
>> The process with ID pid.

| K_SAME_GROUP

> All processes in the same process group as the calling process.

| K_GROUP **of** pid

> All processes in the process group specified by pid.

val kill : killpid_arg * signal -> unit

> kill (*procs*, *sig*) sends the signal *sig* to the process or group of processes specified by *procs*.

val alarm : Time.time -> Time.time

> alarm *t* causes the system to send an alarm signal (alrm) to the calling process after *t* seconds have elapsed. If there is a previous alarm request with time remaining, the alarm function returns a non-zero value corresponding to the number of seconds remaining on the previous request. Zero time is returned if there are no outstanding calls.

val pause : unit -> unit

> This function suspends the calling process until the delivery of a signal that is either caught or that terminates the process.

val sleep : Time.time -> Time.time

> sleep *t* causes the current process to be suspended from execution until either *t* seconds have elapsed or until the receipt of a signal that is either caught or that terminates the process.

See also

BIT_FLAGS (§11.5; p. 129), OS.Process (§11.36; p. 250), Posix (§11.39; p. 257), Posix.Signal (§11.45; p. 294).

11.45   The `Posix.Signal` structure

The structure `Posix.Signal` defines the symbolic names of all the signals defined in Section 3.3 of the POSIX standard (1003.1,1996) [POS96] and provides conversion functions between them and their underlying representations.

Synopsis

```
signature POSIX_SIGNAL
structure Posix.Signal : POSIX_SIGNAL
```

Interface

```
eqtype signal

val toWord   : signal -> SysWord.word
val fromWord : SysWord.word -> signal

val abrt : signal
val alrm : signal
val bus  : signal
val fpe  : signal
val hup  : signal
val ill  : signal
val int  : signal
val kill : signal
val pipe : signal
val quit : signal
val segv : signal
val term : signal
val usr1 : signal
val usr2 : signal
val chld : signal
val cont : signal
val stop : signal
val tstp : signal
val ttin : signal
val ttou : signal
```

Description

```
eqtype signal
```

    A POSIX signal; an asynchronous notification of an event.

```
val toWord : signal -> SysWord.word
val fromWord : SysWord.word -> signal
```

    These convert between a signal identifier and its underlying integer representation. Note that `fromWord` does not check that the result corresponds to a valid POSIX signal.

Discussion

The values defined in this structure represent the standard POSIX signals. The following table provides a brief description of their meanings.

SML name	Description
abrt	End process (abort).
alrm	Alarm clock.
bus	Bus error.
fpe	Floating-point exception.
hup	Hangup.
ill	Illegal instruction.
int	Interrupt.
kill	Kill. (It cannot be caught or ignored.)
pipe	Write on a pipe when there is no process to read it.
quit	Quit.
segv	Segmentation violation.
term	Software termination signal.
usr1	User-defined signal 1.
usr2	User-defined signal 2.
chld	Sent to parent on child stop or exit.
cont	Continue if stopped. (It cannot be caught or ignored.)
stop	Stop. (It cannot be caught or ignored.)
tstp	Interactive stop.
ttin	Background read attempted from control terminal.
ttou	Background write attempted from control terminal.

The name of the corresponding POSIX signal can be derived by capitalizing all letters and adding the string "SIG" as a prefix. For example, the POSIX signal associated with usr2 is SIGUSR2.

See also

Posix (§11.39; p. 257), Posix.Process (§11.44; p. 289)

11.46   The `Posix.SysDB` structure

The `Posix.SysDB` structure implements operations on the user database and the group database (in POSIX parlance, the password file and the group file). These are the data and operations described in Section 9 of the POSIX standard (1003.1,1996) [POS96].

Synopsis

```
signature POSIX_SYS_DB
structure Posix.SysDB : POSIX_SYS_DB
```

Interface

```
eqtype uid
eqtype gid

structure Passwd : sig
    type passwd
    val name  : passwd -> string
    val uid   : passwd -> uid
    val gid   : passwd -> gid
    val home  : passwd -> string
    val shell : passwd -> string
  end

structure Group : sig
    type group
    val name    : group -> string
    val gid     : group -> gid
    val members : group -> string list
  end

val getgrgid : gid -> Group.group
val getgrnam : string -> Group.group
val getpwuid : uid -> Passwd.passwd
val getpwnam : string -> Passwd.passwd
```

Description

eqtype uid

> User identifier; identical to `Posix.ProcEnv.uid`.

eqtype gid

> Group identifier; identical to `Posix.ProcEnv.gid`.

structure Passwd : **sig** ... **end**

This substructure defines the representation of password-database records and operations for accessing their fields.

type passwd

Information related to a user.

val name : passwd -> string
val uid : passwd -> uid
val gid : passwd -> gid
val home : passwd -> string
val shell : passwd -> string

These functions extract the name, the user ID, the group ID, the path of the initial working, or home, directory, and the initial command shell, respectively, of the user corresponding to the passwd value. The names of the corresponding fields in C are the same but prefixed with "pw_." The one exception is that C uses "pw_dir" for the home directory.

structure Group : **sig** ... **end**

This substructure defines the representation of group-database records and operations for accessing their fields.

type group

Information related to a group.

val name : group -> string
val gid : group -> gid
val members : group -> string list

These extract the name, the group ID, and the names of users belonging to the group, respectively, of the group corresponding to the group value. In C, these fields are named gr_name, gr_gid, and gr_mem, respectively.

val getgrgid : gid -> Group.group
val getgrnam : string -> Group.group
val getpwuid : uid -> Passwd.passwd
val getpwnam : string -> Passwd.passwd

These functions return the group or user database entry associated with the given group ID or name, or user ID or name. It raises OS.SysErr if there is no group or user with the given ID or name.

See also

Posix (§11.39; p. 257)

11.47   The `Posix.TTY` structure

The structure `Posix.TTY` specifies a model of a general terminal interface, as described in Section 7 of the POSIX standard (1003.1,1996) [POS96].

Synopsis

```
signature POSIX_TTY
structure Posix.TTY : POSIX_TTY
```

Interface

```
eqtype pid
eqtype file_desc

structure V : sig
    val eof    : int
    val eol    : int
    val erase  : int
    val intr   : int
    val kill   : int
    val min    : int
    val quit   : int
    val susp   : int
    val time   : int
    val start  : int
    val stop   : int
    val nccs : int
    type cc
    val cc : (int * char) list -> cc
    val update : cc * (int * char) list -> cc
    val sub : cc * int -> char
  end

structure I : sig
    include BIT_FLAGS
    val brkint : flags
    val icrnl  : flags
    val ignbrk : flags
    val igncr  : flags
    val ignpar : flags
    val inlcr  : flags
    val inpck  : flags
    val istrip : flags
    val ixoff  : flags
    val ixon   : flags
    val parmrk : flags
  end
```

```
structure O : sig
    include BIT_FLAGS
    val opost : flags
  end

structure C : sig
    include BIT_FLAGS
    val clocal : flags
    val cread  : flags
    val cs5    : flags
    val cs6    : flags
    val cs7    : flags
    val cs8    : flags
    val csize  : flags
    val cstopb : flags
    val hupcl  : flags
    val parenb : flags
    val parodd : flags
  end

structure L : sig
    include BIT_FLAGS
    val echo   : flags
    val echoe  : flags
    val echok  : flags
    val echonl : flags
    val icanon : flags
    val iexten : flags
    val isig   : flags
    val noflsh : flags
    val tostop : flags
  end

eqtype speed

val compareSpeed : speed * speed -> order
val speedToWord : speed -> SysWord.word
val wordToSpeed : SysWord.word -> speed

val b0    : speed
val b50   : speed
val b75   : speed
val b110  : speed
val b134  : speed
val b150  : speed
val b200  : speed
val b300  : speed
val b600  : speed
val b1200 : speed
val b1800 : speed
```

```
val b2400 : speed
val b4800 : speed
val b9600 : speed
val b19200 : speed
val b38400 : speed

type termios

val termios : {
                iflag : I.flags,
                oflag : O.flags,
                cflag : C.flags,
                lflag : L.flags,
                cc : V.cc,
                ispeed : speed,
                ospeed : speed
             } -> termios
val fieldsOf : termios
                 -> {
                iflag : I.flags,
                oflag : O.flags,
                cflag : C.flags,
                lflag : L.flags,
                cc : V.cc,
                ispeed : speed,
                ospeed : speed
             }
val getiflag : termios -> I.flags
val getoflag : termios -> O.flags
val getcflag : termios -> C.flags
val getlflag : termios -> L.flags
val getcc    : termios -> V.cc

structure CF : sig
    val getospeed : termios -> speed
    val getispeed : termios -> speed
    val setospeed : termios * speed -> termios
    val setispeed : termios * speed -> termios
  end

structure TC : sig
    eqtype set_action

    val sanow   : set_action
    val sadrain : set_action
    val saflush : set_action

    eqtype flow_action
```

```
    val ooff : flow_action
    val oon  : flow_action
    val ioff : flow_action
    val ion  : flow_action

eqtype queue_sel

    val iflush  : queue_sel
    val oflush  : queue_sel
    val ioflush : queue_sel

    val getattr : file_desc -> termios
    val setattr : file_desc * set_action * termios -> unit
    val sendbreak : file_desc * int -> unit
    val drain : file_desc -> unit
    val flush : file_desc * queue_sel -> unit
    val flow : file_desc * flow_action -> unit
    val getpgrp : file_desc -> pid
    val setpgrp : file_desc * pid -> unit
  end
```

Description

eqtype `pid`

>   A process identifier.

eqtype `file_desc`

>   An open file descriptor.

structure `V` : **sig** ... **end**

>   The `V` substructure provides means for specifying the special control characters.

```
    val eof : int
    val eol : int
    val erase : int
    val intr : int
    val kill : int
    val min : int
    val quit : int
    val susp : int
    val time : int
    val start : int
    val stop : int
```

Indices for the special control characters EOF, EOL, ERASE, INTR, KILL, MIN, QUIT, SUSP, TIME, START, and STOP, respectively. These values are the indices used in the functions cc and sub.

val nccs : int

The total number of special characters. Thus, valid indices range from 0 to nccs − 1.

type cc

A vector of special control characters used by the device driver.

val cc : (int * char) list -> cc

cc *l* creates a value of type cc, mapping an index to its paired character. Unspecified indices are associated with #"\000". For example, to have the character #"\^D" (control-D) serve as the EOF (end-of-file) character, one would use
$$cc \ [(V.eof, \ \#"\backslash^D")]$$
to use a cc value, embed it in a termios type, and invoke TC.setattr.

val update : cc * (int * char) list -> cc

update (*cs*, *l*) returns a copy of *cs*, but with the new mappings specified by *l* overwriting the original mappings.

val sub : cc * int -> char

sub (*cs*, *i*) returns the special control character associated in *cs* with the index *i*. It raises Subscript if *i* is negative or *i* ≥ nccs.

structure I : **sig** ... **end**

The I substructure contains flags for specifying input control. The following table provides a brief description of the flags.

Flag name	Description
brkint	Signal interrupt on break.
icrnl	Map CR (#"\^M") to NL (#"\n") on input.
ignbrk	Ignore a break condition.
igncr	Ignore CR characters.
ignpar	Ignore characters with parity errors.
inlcr	Map NL to CR on input.
inpck	Enable input parity check.
istrip	Strip the eighth bit of a byte.
ixoff	Enable start/stop input control.
ixon	Enable start/stop output control.
parmrk	Mark parity errors.

structure O : **sig** ... **end**

The O substructure contains flags for specifying output control.

val opost : flags

> Perform output processing.

structure C : **sig** ... **end**

> The C substructure contains flags for specifying basic terminal hardware control. The following table provides a brief description of the flags.

Flag name	Description
clocal	Ignore modem status lines.
cread	Enable the receiver.
csize	Mask for the number of bits per byte used for both transmission and reception. This value is the union of cs5, cs6, cs7, and cs8.
cs5	5 bits per byte.
cs6	6 bits per byte.
cs7	7 bits per byte.
cs8	8 bits per byte.
cstopb	Specifies sending two stop bits rather than one.
hupcl	Hang up the modem connection when the last process with the port open closes it.
parenb	Enable parity generation and detection.
parodd	Use odd parity rather than even if parenb is set.

structure L : **sig** ... **end**

> The L substructure contains flags for specifying various local control modes. The following table provides a brief description of the flags.

Flag name	Description
echo	Echo input characters back to the terminal.
echoe	Echo the ERASE character on backspace in canonical mode.
echok	Echo the KILL character in canonical mode.
echonl	In canonical mode, echo a NL character even if echo is not set.
icanon	Set canonical mode, enabling erase and kill processing, and providing line-based input.
iexten	Enable extended functions.
isig	Enable input characters to be mapped to signals.
noflsh	Disable the normal input and output flushing connected with the INTR, QUIT, and SUSP characters. (See the Posix.TTY.V substructure.)
tostop	Send Posix.Signal.ttou for background output.

eqtype speed

> Terminal input and output baud rates.

val compareSpeed : speed ***** speed **->** order

> compareSpeed (*sp*, *sp'*) returns LESS, EQUAL, or GREATER when the baud rate *sp* is less than, equal to, or greater than that of *sp'*, respectively.

val speedToWord : speed **->** SysWord.word
val wordToSpeed : SysWord.word **->** speed

> These functions convert between a speed value and its underlying word representation. No checking is performed by wordToSpeed to ensure the resulting value corresponds to an allowed speed in the given system.

type termios

> The attributes associated with a terminal. It acts as an abstract representation of the record used as the argument to the termios function.

val termios : {
                    iflag : I.flags,
                    oflag : O.flags,
                    cflag : C.flags,
                    lflag : L.flags,
                    cc : V.cc,
                    ispeed : speed,
                    ospeed : speed
              } **->** termios

> This function creates a termios value using the given flags, special characters, and speeds.

val fieldsOf : termios
                    -> {
                    iflag : I.flags,
                    oflag : O.flags,
                    cflag : C.flags,
                    lflag : L.flags,
                    cc : V.cc,
                    ispeed : speed,
                    ospeed : speed
              }

> This function returns a concrete representation of a termios value.

```
val getiflag : termios -> I.flags
val getoflag : termios -> O.flags
val getcflag : termios -> C.flags
val getlflag : termios -> L.flags
val getcc : termios -> V.cc
```

These functions are the projection functions from a `termios` value to its constituent fields.

structure CF : **sig** ... **end**

The CF substructure contains functions for getting and setting the input and output baud rates in a `termios` value.

```
val getospeed : termios -> speed
val getispeed : termios -> speed
```

These functions return the output and input baud rates, respectively, of the argument.

```
val setospeed : termios * speed -> termios
val setispeed : termios * speed -> termios
    setospeed (t, speed)
    setispeed (t, speed)
```

These expressions return a copy of *t*, but with the output (input) speed set to *speed*.

structure TC : **sig** ... **end**

The TC substructure contains various types and functions used for handling terminal line control.

eqtype set_action

Values of this type specify the behavior of the `setattr` function.

```
val sanow : set_action
val sadrain : set_action
val saflush : set_action
```

sanow Changes occur immediately.

sadrain Changes occur after all output is transmitted.

saflush Changes occur after all output is transmitted and after all received but unread input is discarded.

eqtype flow_action

Values of this type specify the behavior of the `flow` function.

val ooff : flow_action
val oon : flow_action
val ioff : flow_action
val ion : flow_action

> **ooff** Causes the suspension of output.
>
> **oon** Restarts the suspended output.
>
> **ioff** Causes the transmission of a STOP character to the terminal device, to stop it from transmitting data.
>
> **ion** Causes the transmission of a START character to the terminal device, to restart it transmitting data.

eqtype queue_sel

> Values of this type specify the behavior of the flush function.

val iflush : queue_sel
val oflush : queue_sel
val ioflush : queue_sel

> **iflush** Causes all data received but not read to be flushed.
>
> **oflush** Causes all data written but not transmitted to be flushed.
>
> **ioflush** Discards all data written but not transmitted, or received but not read.

val getattr : file_desc -> termios

> getattr *fd* gets the attributes of the terminal associated with the file descriptor *fd*.

val setattr : file_desc * set_action * termios -> unit

> setattr (*fd*, *action*, *termios*) sets the attributes of the terminal associated with the file descriptor *fd* as specified in *termios*. When the change occurs is specified by *action*.

val sendbreak : file_desc * int -> unit

> sendbreak (*fd*, *t*) causes the transmission of a sequence of zero-valued bits to be sent, if the associated terminal is using asynchronous serial data transmission. If *t* is zero, this function will send zero-valued bits for at least a quarter of a second and no more than half a second. If *t* is not zero, zero-valued bits are transmitted for an implementation-defined period of time.

val drain : file_desc -> unit

> drain *fd* waits for all output written on *fd* to be transmitted.

val flush : file_desc * queue_sel -> unit

> flush (*fd*, *qs*) discards any data written but not transmitted, or received but not read, depending on the value of *qs*.

val flow : file_desc * flow_action -> unit

> flow (*fd*, *action*) suspends and restarts the transmission or reception of data, depending on the value of *action*.

val getpgrp : file_desc -> pid

> getpgrp *fd* returns the process group ID of the foreground process group associated with the terminal attached to *fd*.

val setpgrp : file_desc * pid -> unit

> setpgrp (*fd*, *pid*) sets the foreground process group ID associated with *fd* to *pid*.

Discussion

The values of type speed defined in this structure specify the standard baud rates with the obvious correspondence, i.e., b1200 is 1200 baud, b9600 is 9600 baud, etc. The value b0 indicates "hang up."

See also

BIT_FLAGS (§11.5; p. 129), Posix (§11.39; p. 257), Posix.Error (§11.40; p. 259), Posix.FileSys (§11.41; p. 263), Posix.IO (§11.42; p. 276), Posix.Process (§11.44; p. 289)

11.48   The `PRIM_IO` signature

The `PRIM_IO` signature is an abstraction of the low-level input-output system calls commonly available on file descriptors (`OS.IO.iodesc`). Imperative and stream I/O operations do not access the operating system directly but, instead, use the appropriate primitive I/O `reader` and `writer` operations.

Several operations in the `PRIM_IO` interface will raise exceptions that have been left intentionally unspecified. The actual exception raised is usually operating-system dependent but may depend on the underlying implementation. For example, a `reader` connected to a prime number generator might raise `Overflow`. More typically, the close operation on a reader or writer may cause an exception to be raised if there is a failure in the underlying file system, such as the disk being full or the file server being unavailable. In addition, one would expect `readVec` and `readVecNB` to raise `Size` if the resulting vector would exceed the maximum allowed vector size or if the input parameter is negative. Similarly, one would expect `readArr`, `readArrNB`, `writeArr`, `writeArrNB`, `writeVec`, and `writeVecNB` to raise `Subscript` if array bounds are violated. Readers and writers should not, in general, raise the `IO.Io` exception. It is assumed that the higher levels will catch the exceptions raised at the primitive I/O level and appropriately construct and raise the `IO.Io` exception.

A `reader` is required to raise `IO.Io` if any of its functions, except `close` or `getPos`, is invoked after a call to `close`. A `writer` is required to raise `IO.Io` if any of its functions, except `close`, is invoked after a call to `close`. In both cases, the `cause` field of the exception should be `IO.ClosedStream`.

Synopsis

```
signature PRIM_IO
structure BinPrimIO :> PRIM_IO
  where type array = Word8Array.array
  where type vector = Word8Vector.vector
  where type elem = Word8.word
  where type pos = Position.int
structure TextPrimIO :> PRIM_IO
  where type array = CharArray.array
  where type vector = CharVector.vector
  where type elem = Char.char
structure WideTextPrimIO :> PRIM_IO
  where type array = WideCharArray.array
  where type vector = WideCharVector.vector
  where type elem = WideChar.char
```

Interface

```
type elem
type vector
type vector_slice
type array
type array_slice

eqtype pos

val compare : pos * pos -> order

datatype reader
  = RD of {
    name : string,
    chunkSize : int,
    readVec : (int -> vector) option,
    readArr : (array_slice -> int) option,
    readVecNB : (int -> vector option) option,
    readArrNB : (array_slice -> int option) option,
    block : (unit -> unit) option,
    canInput : (unit -> bool) option,
    avail : unit -> int option,
    getPos : (unit -> pos) option,
    setPos : (pos -> unit) option,
    endPos : (unit -> pos) option,
    verifyPos : (unit -> pos) option,
    close : unit -> unit,
    ioDesc : OS.IO.iodesc option
  }

datatype writer
  = WR of {
    name : string,
    chunkSize : int,
    writeVec : (vector_slice -> int) option,
    writeArr : (array_slice -> int) option,
    writeVecNB : (vector_slice -> int option) option,
    writeArrNB : (array_slice -> int option) option,
    block : (unit -> unit) option,
    canOutput : (unit -> bool) option,
    getPos : (unit -> pos) option,
    setPos : (pos -> unit) option,
    endPos : (unit -> pos) option,
    verifyPos : (unit -> pos) option,
    close : unit -> unit,
    ioDesc : OS.IO.iodesc option
  }

val openVector : vector -> reader
```

```
val nullRd : unit -> reader
val nullWr : unit -> writer

val augmentReader : reader -> reader
val augmentWriter : writer -> writer
```

Description

type elem

> The elem type is an abstraction that represents the "element" of a file (or device, etc.).
> Typically, elements are either characters (char) or bytes (Word8.word).

type vector
type vector_slice
type array
type array_slice

> One typically reads or writes a sequence of elements in one operation. The vector type
> is an immutable vector of elements, the vector_slice type is a slice of a vector, the
> array type is an mutable array of elements, and the array_slice type is a slice of an
> array.

eqtype pos

> This type is an abstraction of a position in a file, usually used for random access.

val compare : pos * pos -> order

> compare (*pos*, *pos'*) returns LESS, EQUAL, or GREATER when *pos* is less than,
> equal to, or greater than *pos'*, respectively, in some underlying linear ordering on pos
> values.

```
datatype reader
  = RD of {
    name : string,
    chunkSize : int,
    readVec : (int -> vector) option,
    readArr : (array_slice -> int) option,
    readVecNB : (int -> vector option) option,
    readArrNB : (array_slice -> int option) option,
    block : (unit -> unit) option,
    canInput : (unit -> bool) option,
    avail : unit -> int option,
    getPos : (unit -> pos) option,
    setPos : (pos -> unit) option,
    endPos : (unit -> pos) option,
    verifyPos : (unit -> pos) option,
    close : unit -> unit,
    ioDesc : OS.IO.iodesc option
  }
```

A reader is an abstraction for a source of items of type elem. Usually, it will correspond to a file or device opened for reading. It can also represent the output of some algorithm or function, not necessarily connected to the outside world, that produces elements. The resulting sequence of elements is potentially unbounded. In the description below, we usually refer to the limit sequence as a "file," as files are the most common instance.

name is the name associated with this reader, used in error messages shown to the user.

chunkSize is the recommended (efficient) size of the read operations on this reader. This value is typically set to the block size of the operating system's buffers. chunkSize = 1 strongly recommends unbuffered reads, but since buffering is handled at a higher level, it cannot guarantee it. chunkSize ≤ 0 is illegal.

readVec(n) when present, reads up to n elements, returning a vector of the elements read. This function returns the empty vector if the end-of-stream is detected (or if n is 0). It blocks, if necessary, until the end-of-stream is detected or at least one element is available.

It is recommended that implementations of this function raise the Size exception if $n<0$.

readArr(slice) when present, reads up to k elements into the array slice slice, where k is the size of the slice. This function returns the number of elements actually read, which will be less than or equal to k. If no elements remain before the end-of-stream, it returns 0 (this function also returns 0 when slice is empty). It blocks, if necessary, until at least one element is available.

readVecNB(n) when present, reads i elements without blocking for $1 \leq i \leq n$, creating a vector v, and returning SOME(v). If the end-of-stream is detected, this operation returns returns SOME(fromList[]). If the read would block, then it returns NONE without blocking.

readArrNB(slice) when present, reads, without blocking, up to k elements into the array slice slice, where k is the size of the slice. If this function would block (i.e. no elements are available and the end-of-stream has no been detected), then it returns

NONE; otherwise, it returns SOME(n), where n is the number of elements actually read (0 on end-of-stream)

block()   when present, blocks until at least one element is available for reading without blocking, or until an end-of-stream condition is detected.

canInput()   when present, returns true if and only if the next read can proceed without blocking.

avail()   returns the number of bytes available on the "device" or NONE if it cannot be determined. For files or strings, this value is the file or string size minus the current position; for most other input sources, this value is probably NONE. This value can be used as a hint by inputAll. Note that this is a byte count, not an element count.

getPos()   when present, returns the current position in the file. The getPos function must be non-decreasing (in the absence of setPos operations or other interference on the underlying object).

setPos(*i*)   when present, moves to position i in the underlying file.

endPos()   when present, returns the position corresponding to the end of the file without actually changing the current position.

verifyPos()   when present, returns the true current position in the file. It is similar to getPos, except that the latter may maintain its own notion of file position for efficiency whereas verifyPos will typically perform a system call to obtain the underlying operating system's value of the file position.

close   marks the reader closed and, if necessary, performs any cleanup and releases any operating system resources. Further operations on the reader (besides close and getPos) raise IO.ClosedStream.

ioDesc   when present, is the abstract operating system descriptor associated with this stream.

One of readVec, readVecNB, readArr, or readArrNB must be provided. Providing more of the optional functions increases the usefulness and/or efficiency of clients.

- Absence of all of readVec, readArr, and block means that blocking input is not possible.
- Absence of all of readVecNB, readArrNB, and canInput means that non-blocking input is not possible.
- Absence of readVecNB means that non-blocking input requires two system calls (using canInput and readVec).
- Absence of readArr or readArrNB means that input into an array requires extra copying. *Note that the "lazy functional stream" model does not use arrays at all.*
- Absence of setPos prevents random access.

Having avail return a value helps the client perform very large input more efficiently, with one system call and no copying.

If the reader can provide more than the minimum set of operations *in a way that is more efficient than the obvious synthesis* (see augmentReader), then by all means it should do so. Providing more than the minimum by just doing the obvious synthesis inside the primitive I/O layer is not recommended because then clients will not get the "hint" about which are the efficient ("recommended") operations. Clients concerned with efficiency will make use of the operations provided natively and may need to choose algorithms depending on which operations are provided; clients not concerned with efficiency or requiring certain operations can use the reader constructed by augmentReader.

```
datatype writer
  = WR of {
    name : string,
    chunkSize : int,
    writeVec : (vector_slice -> int) option,
    writeArr : (array_slice -> int) option,
    writeVecNB : (vector_slice -> int option) option,
    writeArrNB : (array_slice -> int option) option,
    block : (unit -> unit) option,
    canOutput : (unit -> bool) option,
    getPos : (unit -> pos) option,
    setPos : (pos -> unit) option,
    endPos : (unit -> pos) option,
    verifyPos : (unit -> pos) option,
    close : unit -> unit,
    ioDesc : OS.IO.iodesc option
  }
```

A writer is a file (device, etc.) opened for writing. A writer is an abstraction for a store of items of type elem. Usually, it will correspond to a file or device opened for writing. It can also represent input to some algorithm or function, not necessarily connected to the outside world, that consumes the output to guide its computations. The resulting store of elements is potentially unbounded. In the discussion below, we usually refer to the store as a "file," as files are the most common instance.

name is the name associated with this file or device, for use in error messages shown to the user.

chunkSize is the recommended (efficient) size of write operations on this writer. This value is typically set to the block size of the operating system's buffers. chunkSize = 1 strongly recommends unbuffered writes, but since buffering is handled at a higher level, it cannot guarantee it. chunkSize $\leq$ 0 is illegal.

writeVec(*slice*) when present, writes the elements from the vector slice *slice* to the output device and returns the number of elements actually written. If necessary, it blocks until the output device can accept at least one element.

writeArr(*slice*) when present, writes the elements from the array slice *slice* and returns the number of elements actually written. If necessary, it blocks until the underlying device can accept at least one element.

writeVecNB(*slice*) when present, attempts to write the elements from the vector slice *slice* to the output device without blocking. If successful, it returns SOME(n), where n is the number of elements actually written. Otherwise, if it would block, then it returns NONE without blocking.

writeVecNB(*slice*) when present, attempts to write the elements from the array slice *slice* to the output device without blocking. If successful, it returns SOME(n), where n is the number of elements actually written. Otherwise, if it would block, then it returns NONE without blocking.

block() when present, blocks until the writer is guaranteed to be able to write without blocking.

canOutput() when present, returns true if and only if the next write can proceed without blocking.

getPos() when present, returns the current position within the file.

endPos() when present, returns the position corresponding to the end of the file, without actually changing the current position.

setPos(*i*) when present, moves to position *i* in the file, so future writes occur at this position.

verifyPos() when present, returns the true current position in the file. This function is similar to getPos, except that the latter may maintain its own notion of file position for efficiency, whereas verifyPos will typically perform a system call to obtain the underlying operating system's value of the file position.

close() marks the writer closed and, if necessary, performs any cleanup and releases any operating system resources. Further operations (other than close) raise IO.ClosedStream.

ioDesc when present, is the abstract operating system descriptor associated with this stream.

The write operations return the number of full elements that have been written. If the size of an element is greater than 1 byte, it is possible that an additional part of an element might be written. For example, if one tries to write two elements, each of size 3 bytes, the underlying system write operation may report that only 4 of the 6 bytes has been written. Thus, one full element have been written, plus part of the second, so the write operation would return 1.

One of writeVec, writeVecNB, writeArr, or writeArrNB must be provided. Providing more of the optional functions increases the usefulness and/or efficiency of clients.

- Absence of all of writeVec, writeArr, and block means that blocking output is not possible.

- Absence of all of writeVecNB, writeArrNB, and canOutput means that non-blocking output is not possible.

- Absence of writeArr or writeArrNB means that extra copying will be required to write from an array.

- Absence of setPos prevents random access.

val openVector : vector -> reader

openVector *v* creates a reader whose content is *v*.

val nullRd : unit -> reader
val nullWr : unit -> writer

These functions create readers and writers for a null device abstraction. The null reader produced by nullRd acts like a reader that is always at the end-of-stream. The null writer produced by nullWr serves as a sink; any data written using it are thrown away. Null readers and writers may be closed; if closed, they are expected to behave the same as any other closed reader or writer.

val augmentReader : reader -> reader

augmentReader *rd* produces a reader in which as many as possible of readVec, `readArr`, `readVecNB`, and `readArrNB` are provided, by synthesizing these from the operations of `rd`.

For example, `augmentReader` can synthesize `readVec` from `readVecNB` and `block`, synthesize vector reads from array reads, and synthesize array reads from vector reads, as needed. The following table indicates how each synthesis can be accomplished.

Synthesize:	From:
`readVec`	`readVec` or `readArr` or (`block` and (`readVecNB` or `readArrNB`))
`readArr`	`readArr` or `readVec` or (`block` and (`readArrNB` or `readVecNB`))
`readVecNB`	`readVecNB` or `readArrNB` or (`canInput` and (`readVec` or `readArr`))
`readArrNB`	`readArrNB` or `readVecNB` or (`canInput` and (`readArr` or `readVec`))

In each case, the synthesized operation may not be as efficient as a more direct implementation — for example, it is faster to read data directly into an array than it is to read them into a vector and then copy them into the array. But `augmentReader` should do no harm: if a reader *rd* supplies some operation (such as `readArr`), then `augmentReader(rd)` provides the same implementation of that operation, not a synthesized one.

val `augmentWriter : writer -> writer`

`augmentWriter` *wr* produces a writer in which as many as possible of `writeVec`, `writeArr`, `writeVecNB`, and `writeArrNB` are provided, by synthesizing these from the operations of `wr`.

The following table indicates how each synthesis can be accomplished.

Synthesize:	From:
`writeVec`	`writeVec` or `writeArr` or (`block` and (`writeVecNB` or `writeArrNB`))
`writeArr`	`writeArr` or `writeVec` or (`block` and (`writeArrNB` or `writeVecNB`))
`writeVecNB`	`writeVecNB` or `writeArrNB` or (`canOutput` and (`writeVec` or `writeArr`))
`writeArrNB`	`writeArrNB` or `writeVecNB` or (`canOutput` and (`writeArr` or `writeVec`))

The synthesized operation may not be as efficient as a more direct implementation, but if a writer supplies some operation, then the augmented writer provides the same implementation of that operation.

Discussion

It may not be possible to use `augmentReader` or `augmentWriter` to synthesize operations in a way that is thread-safe in concurrent systems.

None of the function components in readers and writers should block, except for the obvious ones: `readVec`, `readArray`, `writeVec`, `writeArray`, and `block`.

The end-of-stream condition at the stream I/O level is an artifact of a read operation at the primitive I/O level returning zero elements. Although this event is maintained in the stream, it is a transient condition at the primitive I/O level. If a call to `readVec` returns an empty vector one time, it is quite possible that another call to `readVec` at the same file position will return elements. The value returned by an `endPos` function should indicate the position after the last element in the file at the time the function is called.

Implementation note: The functions `getPos`, `setPos`, `endPos`, and `verify-Pos` are used to support arbitrary random access on the underlying I/O file or device. On most systems, these operations are well supported only on static objects such as strings or regular files. Typical implementations will therefore set `getPos` and the rest to NONE in both readers and writers for all other file types.

In an implementation where an input stream is represented as a chain of buffers, each buffer may contain, along with its vector of data, a `pos` value indicating where the data came from in the underlying file. As each buffer corresponds to a read operation, the client is likely to call `getPos` on each read operation. Thus, the reader should, if possible, maintain its own version of the file position, to be returned by `getPos`, to avoid extra system calls.

Unlike readers, which can expect their `getPos` functions to be called frequently, writers need not implement `getPos` in a highly efficient manner: a system call for each `get-Pos` is acceptable. Indeed, with a file opened for atomic append, the information cannot be obtained reliably except by a system call using `verifyPos`.

See also

BinIO (§11.4; p. 127), IMPERATIVE_IO (§11.14; p. 158), OS.IO (§11.34; p. 237), Posix.IO (§11.42; p. 276), PrimIO (§11.49; p. 317), STREAM_IO (§11.52; p. 346), TextIO (§11.58; p. 382)

11.49 The `PrimIO` functor

The optional functor `PrimIO` builds an instance of the primitive I/O signature `PRIM_IO`.

Synopsis

```
signature PRIM_IO
functor PrimIO (...): PRIM_IO
  where type elem = Vector.elem
  where type vector = Vector.vector
  where type vector_slice = VectorSlice.slice
  where type array = Array.array
  where type array_slice = ArraySlice.slice
  where type pos = pos
```

Functor Argument Interface

```
structure Vector : MONO_VECTOR
structure VectorSlice : MONO_VECTOR_SLICE
structure Array : MONO_ARRAY
structure ArraySlice : MONO_ARRAY_SLICE
sharing type Vector.elem = VectorSlice.elem = Array.elem
  = ArraySlice.elem
sharing type Vector.vector = VectorSlice.vector
  = Array.vector = ArraySlice.vector
sharing type VectorSlice.slice = ArraySlice.vector_slice
sharing type Array.array = ArraySlice.array
val someElem : Vector.elem
eqtype pos
val compare : pos * pos -> order
```

Description

```
val someElem : Vector.elem
```

> An element that may be read or written by a `reader` or `writer`. The value `someElem` is typically used for the initialization of buffers.

```
val compare : pos * pos -> order
```

> compare (*pos*, *pos'*) returns LESS, EQUAL, or GREATER when *pos* is less than, equal to, or greater than *pos'*, respectively, in some underlying linear ordering on `pos` values.

See also

General (§11.11; p. 149), MONO_ARRAY (§11.23; p. 193), MONO_ARRAY_SLICE (§11.25; p. 205), MONO_VECTOR (§11.26; p. 211), MONO_VECTOR_SLICE (§11.27; p. 215), PRIM_IO (§11.48; p. 308), StreamIO (§11.53; p. 358)

11.50   The REAL signature

The REAL signature specifies structures that implement floating-point numbers. The semantics of floating-point numbers should follow the IEEE standard 754-1985 [IEE85] and the ANSI/IEEE standard 854-1987 [IEE87]. In addition, implementations of the REAL signature are required to use non-trapping semantics. Additional aspects of the design of the REAL and MATH signatures were guided by the Floating-Point C Extensions [FPC95] developed by the X3J11 ANSI committee and the lecture notes [Kah96] by W. Kahan on the IEEE standard 754.

Although there can be many representations for NaN values, the Library models them as a single value and currently provides no explicit way to distinguish among them, ignoring the sign bit. Thus, in the descriptions below and in the Math structure, we just refer to the NaN value.

Synopsis
```
signature REAL
structure Real :> REAL
  where type real = real
structure LargeReal :> REAL
structure RealN :> REAL
```

Interface
```
type real

structure Math : MATH
  where type real = real

val radix : int
val precision : int

val maxFinite    : real
val minPos       : real
val minNormalPos : real

val posInf : real
val negInf : real

val + : real * real -> real
val - : real * real -> real
val * : real * real -> real
val / : real * real -> real
val rem : real * real -> real
val *+ : real * real * real -> real
val *- : real * real * real -> real
val ~ : real -> real
val abs : real -> real
```

```
val min : real * real -> real
val max : real * real -> real

val sign : real -> int
val signBit : real -> bool
val sameSign : real * real -> bool
val copySign : real * real -> real

val compare     : real * real -> order
val compareReal : real * real -> IEEEReal.real_order
val <  : real * real -> bool
val <= : real * real -> bool
val >  : real * real -> bool
val >= : real * real -> bool
val == : real * real -> bool
val != : real * real -> bool
val ?= : real * real -> bool
val unordered : real * real -> bool

val isFinite : real -> bool
val isNan : real -> bool
val isNormal : real -> bool
val class : real -> IEEEReal.float_class

val toManExp : real -> {man : real, exp : int}
val fromManExp : {man : real, exp : int} -> real
val split   : real -> {whole : real, frac : real}
val realMod : real -> real

val nextAfter : real * real -> real
val checkFloat : real -> real

val realFloor : real -> real
val realCeil  : real -> real
val realTrunc : real -> real
val realRound : real -> real
val floor : real -> int
val ceil  : real -> int
val trunc : real -> int
val round : real -> int
val toInt      : IEEEReal.rounding_mode -> real -> int
val toLargeInt : IEEEReal.rounding_mode
                    -> real -> LargeInt.int
val fromInt     : int -> real
val fromLargeInt : LargeInt.int -> real
val toLarge    : real -> LargeReal.real
val fromLarge : IEEEReal.rounding_mode
                    -> LargeReal.real -> real
```

```
val fmt        : StringCvt.realfmt -> real -> string
val toString : real -> string
val scan       : (char, 'a) StringCvt.reader
                     -> (real, 'a) StringCvt.reader
val fromString : string -> real option

val toDecimal   : real -> IEEEReal.decimal_approx
val fromDecimal : IEEEReal.decimal_approx -> real option
```

Description

type real

> Note that, as discussed below, `real` is not an equality type.

structure Math : MATH
  where type real = real

> This substructure contains various constants and mathematical functions for the given `real` type.

val radix : int

> The base of the representation, e.g., 2 or 10 for IEEE floating point.

val precision : int

> The number of digits, each between 0 and `radix-1`, in the mantissa. Note that the precision includes the implicit (or hidden) bit used in the IEEE representation (e.g., the value of `Real64.precision` is 53).

val maxFinite : real
val minPos : real
val minNormalPos : real

> The maximum finite number, the minimum non-zero positive number, and the minimum non-zero normalized number, respectively.

val posInf : real
val negInf : real

> Positive and negative infinity values.

```
val + : real * real -> real
val - : real * real -> real
```

> *r1* + *r2*
> *r1* - *r2*
> These denote the sum and difference of *r1* and *r2*. If one argument is finite and the other infinite, the result is infinite with the correct sign, e.g., $5 - (-\infty) = \infty$. We also have $\infty + \infty = \infty$ and $(-\infty) + (-\infty) = (-\infty)$. Any other combination of two infinities produces NaN.

```
val * : real * real -> real
```

> *r1* * *r2* denotes the product of *r1* and *r2*. The product of zero and an infinity produces NaN. Otherwise, if one argument is infinite, the result is infinite with the correct sign, e.g., $-5 * (-\infty) = \infty$, $\infty * (-\infty) = -\infty$.

```
val / : real * real -> real
```

> *r1* / *r2* denotes the quotient of *r1* and *r2*. We have $0/0 = $ NaN and $\pm\infty / \pm\infty = $ NaN. Dividing a finite, non-zero number by a zero or an infinity by a finite number produces an infinity with the correct sign. (Note that zeros are signed.) A finite number divided by an infinity is 0 with the correct sign.

```
val rem : real * real -> real
```

> rem (*x*, *y*) returns the remainder $x - n * y$, where $n = \text{trunc}(x/y)$. The result has the same sign as x and has absolute value less than the absolute value of y.
>
> If x is an infinity or y is 0, rem returns NaN. If y is an infinity, rem returns x.

```
val *+ : real * real * real -> real
val *- : real * real * real -> real
```

> *+ (*a*, *b*, *c*)
> *- (*a*, *b*, *c*)
> These functions return $a*b + c$ and $a*b - c$, respectively. Their behaviors on infinities follow from the behaviors derived from addition, subtraction, and multiplication.
>
> The precise semantics of these operations depend on the language implementation and the underlying hardware. Specifically, certain architectures provide these operations as a single instruction, possibly using a single rounding operation. Thus, the use of these operations may be faster than performing the individual arithmetic operations sequentially but may also produce different results because of differences in rounding behavior

```
val ~ : real -> real
```

> ~ *r* produces the negation of *r*. $\sim(\pm\infty) = \mp\infty$.

val abs : real -> real

abs r returns the absolute value $|r|$ of r.

$$\mathrm{abs}(\pm 0.0) = +0.0 \quad \mathrm{abs}(\pm\infty) = +\infty \quad \mathrm{abs}(\pm NaN) = +NaN$$

val min : real * real -> real
val max : real * real -> real

These functions return the smaller (respectively, larger) of the arguments. If exactly one argument is NaN, they return the other argument. If both arguments are NaN, they return NaN.

val sign : real -> int

sign r returns ~1 if r is negative, 0 if r is zero, or 1 if r is positive. An infinity returns its sign; a zero returns 0 regardless of its sign. It raises Domain on NaN.

val signBit : real -> bool

signBit r returns true if and only if the sign of r (infinities, zeros, and NaN, included) is negative.

val sameSign : real * real -> bool

sameSign ($r1$, $r2$) returns true if and only if signBit $r1$ equals signBit $r2$.

val copySign : real * real -> real

copySign (x, y) returns x with the sign of y, even if y is NaN.

val compare : real * real -> order
val compareReal : real * real -> IEEEReal.real_order

The function compare returns LESS, EQUAL, or GREATER according to whether its first argument is less than, equal to, or greater than the second. It raises IEEEReal.- Unordered on unordered arguments.

The function compareReal behaves similarly, except that the values it returns have the extended type IEEEReal.real_order and it returns IEEEReal.UNORDERED on unordered arguments (i.e., if one of the arguments is a NaN).

```
val < : real * real -> bool
val <= : real * real -> bool
val > : real * real -> bool
val >= : real * real -> bool
```

These functions return `true` if the corresponding relation holds between the two reals.

Note that these operators return `false` on unordered arguments, i.e., if either argument is NaN, so that the usual reversal of comparison under negation does not hold, e.g., `a < b` is not the same as `not (a >= b)`.

```
val == : real * real -> bool
val != : real * real -> bool
```

```
== (x, y)
!= (x, y)
```
The first returns `true` if and only if neither y nor x is NaN, and y and x are equal, ignoring signs on zeros. This function is equivalent to the IEEE = operator.

The second function `!=` is equivalent to `not o op ==` and the IEEE `?<>` operator.

```
val ?= : real * real -> bool
```

This function returns `true` if either argument is NaN or if the arguments are bitwise equal, ignoring signs on zeros. It is equivalent to the IEEE `?=` operator.

```
val unordered : real * real -> bool
```

`unordered (x, y)` returns `true` if x and y are unordered, i.e., at least one of x and y is NaN.

```
val isFinite : real -> bool
```

`isFinite x` returns `true` if x is neither NaN nor an infinity.

```
val isNan : real -> bool
```

`isNan x` returns `true` if x is NaN.

```
val isNormal : real -> bool
```

`isNormal x` returns `true` if x is normal, i.e., neither zero, subnormal, infinite, nor NaN.

```
val class : real -> IEEEReal.float_class
```

`class x` returns the `IEEEReal.float_class` to which x belongs.

val toManExp : real -> {man : real, exp : int}

toManExp r returns {*man*, *exp*}, where *man* and *exp* are the mantissa and exponent of r, respectively. Specifically, we have the relation

$$r = man * \text{radix}^{exp}$$

where $1.0 \leq man * radix < radix$. This function is comparable to frexp in the C library.

If r is ± 0, *man* is ± 0 and *exp* is $+0$. If r is $\pm\infty$, *man* is $\pm\infty$ and *exp* is unspecified. If r is NaN, *man* is NaN and *exp* is unspecified.

val fromManExp : {man : real, exp : int} -> real

fromManExp {*man*, *exp*} returns $man * \text{radix}^{exp}$. This function is comparable to ldexp in the C library. Note that, even if *man* is a non-zero, finite real value, the result of fromManExp can be zero or infinity because of underflows and overflows.

If *man* is ± 0, the result is ± 0. If *man* is $\pm\infty$, the result is $\pm\infty$. If *man* is NaN, the result is NaN.

val split : real -> {whole : real, frac : real}
val realMod : real -> real

split r
realMod r
The former returns {*whole*, *frac*}, where *frac* and *whole* are the fractional and integral parts of r, respectively. Specifically, *whole* is integral, $|frac| < 1.0$, *whole* and *frac* have the same sign as r, and $r = whole + frac$. This function is comparable to modf in the C library.

If r is $\pm\infty$, *whole* is $\pm\infty$ and *frac* is ± 0. If r is NaN, both *whole* and *frac* are NaN.

realMod is equivalent to #frac o split.

val nextAfter : real * real -> real

nextAfter (r, t) returns the next representable real after r in the direction of t. Thus, if t is less than r, nextAfter returns the largest representable floating-point number less than r. If $r = t$ it returns r, if either argument is NaN it returns NaN, and if r is $\pm\infty$ it returns $\pm\infty$.

val checkFloat : real -> real

checkFloat x raises Overflow if x is an infinity and raises Div if x is NaN. Otherwise, it returns its argument.

This can be used to synthesize trapping arithmetic from the non-trapping operations given here. Note, however, that infinities can be converted to NaNs by some operations, so that if accurate exceptions are required, checks must be done after each operation.

```
val realFloor : real -> real
val realCeil : real -> real
val realTrunc : real -> real
val realRound : real -> real
```

```
realFloor r
realCeil r
realTrunc r
realRound r
```
These functions convert real values to integer-valued reals: `realFloor` produces $\lfloor r \rfloor$, the largest integer not larger than r, `realCeil` produces $\lceil r \rceil$, the smallest integer not less than r, `realTrunc` rounds r toward zero, and `realRound` rounds to the integer-values real value that is *nearest* to r. If r is NaN or an infinity, these functions return r.

```
val floor : real -> int
val ceil : real -> int
val trunc : real -> int
val round : real -> int
```

```
floor r
ceil r
trunc r
round r
```
These functions convert reals to integers. `floor` produces $\lfloor r \rfloor$, the largest `int` not larger than r. `ceil` produces $\lceil r \rceil$, the smallest `int` not less than r. `trunc` rounds r toward zero. `round` yields the integer nearest to r. In the case of a tie, it rounds to the nearest even integer. They raise `Overflow` if the resulting value cannot be represented as an `int`, for example, on infinity. They raise `Domain` on NaN arguments.

These are respectively equivalent to:
```
                toInt IEEEReal.TO_NEGINF r
                toInt IEEEReal.TO_POSINF r
                toInt IEEEReal.TO_ZERO r
                toInt IEEEReal.TO_NEAREST r
```

```
val toInt : IEEEReal.rounding_mode -> real -> int
val toLargeInt : IEEEReal.rounding_mode
                    -> real -> LargeInt.int
```

```
toInt mode x
toLargeInt mode x
```
These functions convert the argument x to an integral type using the specified rounding mode. They raise `Overflow` if the result is not representable, in particular, if x is an infinity. They raise `Domain` if the input real is NaN.

```
val fromInt : int -> real
val fromLargeInt : LargeInt.int -> real
```

```
fromInt i
fromLargeInt i
```
These functions convert the integer i to a `real` value. If the absolute value of i is larger

than `maxFinite`, then the appropriate infinity is returned. If i cannot be exactly represented as a `real` value, then the current rounding mode is used to determine the resulting value. The top-level function `real` is an alias for `Real.fromInt`.

```
val toLarge : real -> LargeReal.real
val fromLarge : IEEEReal.rounding_mode
                    -> LargeReal.real -> real
```

toLarge *r*
fromLarge *r*
These convert between values of type `real` and type `LargeReal.real`. If r is too small or too large to be represented as a `real`, `fromLarge` will convert it to a zero or an infinity.

```
val fmt : StringCvt.realfmt -> real -> string
val toString : real -> string
```

fmt *spec r*
toString *r*
These functions convert reals into strings. The conversion provided by the function `fmt` is parameterized by *spec*, which has the following forms and interpretations.

SCI *arg* Scientific notation has the format:

$$[\tilde{\ }]^?[0-9](.[0-9]^+)^?\mathrm{E}[0-9]^+$$

where there is always one digit before the decimal point, non-zero if the number is nonzero. *arg* specifies the number of digits to appear after the decimal point, with six the default if *arg* is `NONE`. If *arg* is `SOME(0)`, no fractional digits and no decimal point are printed.

FIX *arg* Fixed-point notation has the format:

$$[\tilde{\ }]^?[0-9]^+(.[0-9]^+)^?$$

arg specifies the number of digits to appear after the decimal point, with six the default if *arg* is `NONE`. If *arg* is `SOME(0)`, no fractional digits and no decimal point are printed.

GEN *arg* Adaptive notation: the notation used is either scientific or fixed-point, depending on the value converted. *arg* specifies the maximum number of significant digits used, with 12 the default if *arg* is `NONE`.

EXACT Exact decimal notation: refer to `IEEEReal.toString` for a complete description of this format.

In all cases, positive and negative infinities are converted to `"inf"` and `"~inf"`, respectively, and NaN values are converted to the string `"nan"`.

Refer to `StringCvt.realfmt` for more details concerning these formats, especially the adaptive format GEN.

fmt raises `Size` if *spec* is an invalid precision, i.e., if *spec* is

- SCI (SOME *i*) with $i < 0$
- FIX (SOME *i*) with $i < 0$

- GEN (SOME i) with $i < 1$

The exception should be raised when fmt $spec$ is evaluated.

The fmt function allows the user precise control as to the form of the resulting string. Note, therefore, that it is possible for fmt to produce a result that is not a valid SML string representation of a real value.

The value returned by toString is equivalent to:

$$(\text{fmt (StringCvt.GEN NONE) } r)$$

```
val scan : (char, 'a) StringCvt.reader
              -> (real, 'a) StringCvt.reader
val fromString : string -> real option
```

scan *getc strm*
fromString *s*

These functions scan a real value from a character source. The first version reads from *strm* using reader *getc*, ignoring initial whitespace. It returns SOME($r, rest$) if successful, where r is the scanned real value and *rest* is the unused portion of the character stream *strm*. Values of too large a magnitude are represented as infinities; values of too small a magnitude are represented as zeros.

The second version returns SOME(r) if a real value can be scanned from a prefix of s, ignoring any initial whitespace; otherwise, it returns NONE. This function is equivalent to StringCvt.scanString scan.

The functions accept real numbers with the following format:

$$[+\text{\textasciitilde}-]^?([0-9]^+(.[0-9]^+)^? \mid .[0-9]^+)((e \mid E)[+\text{\textasciitilde}-]^?[0-9]^+)^?$$

They also accept the following string representations of non-finite values:

$$[+\text{\textasciitilde}-]^?(\text{inf} \mid \text{infinity} \mid \text{nan})$$

where the alphabetic characters are case-insensitive.

```
val toDecimal : real -> IEEEReal.decimal_approx
val fromDecimal : IEEEReal.decimal_approx -> real option
```

toDecimal *r*
fromDecimal *d*

These convert between real values and decimal approximations. Decimal approximations are to be converted using the IEEEReal.TO_NEAREST rounding mode. toDecimal should produce only as many digits as are necessary for fromDecimal to convert back to the same number. In particular, for any normal or subnormal real value r, we have the bit-wise equality:

$$\text{fromDecimal (toDecimal } r) = r.$$

For toDecimal, when the r is not normal or subnormal, then the exp field is set to 0 and the digits field is the empty list. In all cases, the sign and class fields capture the sign and class of r.

For fromDecimal, if class is ZERO or INF, the resulting real is the appropriate signed zero or infinity. If class is NAN, a signed NaN is generated. If class is NORMAL or SUBNORMAL, the `sign`, `digits`, and `exp` fields are used to produce a real number whose value is.

$$s * 0.d_1 d_2 ... d_n 10^{exp}$$

where `digits` $= [d_1, d_2, ..., d_n]$ and where s is -1 if `sign` is true and 1 otherwise. Note that the conversion itself should ignore the `class` field, so that the resulting value might have class NORMAL, SUBNORMAL, ZERO, or INF. For example, if `digits` is empty or a list of all zero's, the result should be a signed zero. More generally, very large or small magnitudes are converted to infinities or zeros.

If the argument to `fromDecimal` does not have a valid format, i.e., if the `digits` field contains integers outside the range [0,9], it returns NONE.

Implementation note: Algorithms for accurately and efficiently converting between binary and decimal real representations are readily available, e.g., see the technical report by Gay [Gay90].

Discussion

If `LargeReal` is not the same as `Real`, then there must be a structure `RealN` equal to `LargeReal`.

The sign of a zero is ignored in all comparisons.

Unless specified otherwise, any operation involving NaN will return NaN.

Note that, if x is real, $\tilde{} x$ is equivalent to $\tilde{} (x)$, that is, it is identical to x but with its sign bit flipped. In particular, the literal $\tilde{} 0.0$ is just 0.0 with its sign bit set. On the other hand, this value might not be the same as $0.0-0.0$, in which rounding modes come into play.

Except for the `*+` and `*-` functions, arithmetic should be done in the exact precision specified by the `precision` value. In particular, arithmetic must not be done in some extended precision and then rounded.

The relation between the comparison predicates defined here and those defined by IEEE, ISO C, and FORTRAN is specified in the following table.

SML	IEEE	C	FORTRAN
==	=	==	.EQ.
!=	?<>	!=	.NE.
<	<	<	.LT.
<=	<=	<=	.LE.
>	>	>	.GT.
>=	>=	>=	.GE.
?=	?=	!islessgreater	.UE.
not o ?=	<>	islessgreater	.LG.
unordered	?	isunordered	unordered
not o unordered	<=>	!isunordered	.LEG.
not o op <	?>=	! <	.UGE.
not o op <=	?>	! <=	.UG.
not o op >	?<=	! >	.ULE.
not o op >=	?<	! >=	.UL.

Implementation note: Implementations may choose to provide a debugging mode, in which NaNs and infinities are detected when they are generated.

Rationale: The specification of the default signature and structure for non-integer arithmetic, particularly concerning exceptional conditions, was the source of much debate, given the desire of supporting efficient floating-point modules. If we permit implementations to differ on whether or not, for example, to raise `Div` on division by zero, the user really would not have a standard to program against. Portable code would require adopting the more conservative position of explicitly handling exceptions. A second alternative was to specify that functions in the `Real` structure must raise exceptions, but that implementations so desiring could provide additional structures matching `REAL` with explicit floating-point semantics. This choice was rejected because it meant that the default `real` type would not be the same as a defined floating-point `real` type, which would give a second-class status to the latter while providing the default real with worse performance and involving additional implementation complexity for little benefit.

Deciding if `real` should be an equality type, and, if so, what should equality mean, was also problematic. IEEE specifies that the sign of zeros be ignored in comparisons and that equality evaluate to false if either argument is NaN. These constraints are disturbing to the SML programmer. The former implies that `0 = ~0` is true while `r/0 = r/~0` is false. The latter implies such anomalies as `r = r` is false, or that, for a ref cell `rr`, we could have `rr = rr` but not have `!rr = !rr`. We accepted the unsigned comparison of zeros but felt that the reflexive property of equality, structural equality, and the equivalence of `<>` and `not o =` ought to be preserved. Additional complications led to the decision to not have `real` be an equality type.

The type, signature, and structure identifiers `real`, `REAL`, and `Real`, although misnomers in light of the floating-point-specific nature of the modules, were retained for historical reasons.

See also

IEEEReal (§11.13; p. 155), MATH (§11.22; p. 189), StringCvt (§11.55; p. 366)

11.51   The `Socket` structure

This structure provides the standard socket types, socket management, and I/O operations. The creation of sockets is relegated to domain-specific structures (such as INet-Sock and UnixSock).

Synopsis

```
signature SOCKET
structure Socket :> SOCKET
```

Interface

```
type ('af,'sock_type) sock
type 'af sock_addr
type dgram
type 'mode stream
type passive
type active

structure AF : sig
    type addr_family = NetHostDB.addr_family
    val list : unit -> (string * addr_family) list
    val toString   : addr_family -> string
    val fromString : string -> addr_family option
  end

structure SOCK : sig
    eqtype sock_type
    val stream : sock_type
    val dgram : sock_type
    val list : unit -> (string * sock_type) list
    val toString   : sock_type -> string
    val fromString : string -> sock_type option
  end

structure Ctl : sig
    val getDEBUG : ('af, 'sock_type) sock -> bool
    val setDEBUG : ('af, 'sock_type) sock * bool -> unit
    val getREUSEADDR : ('af, 'sock_type) sock -> bool
    val setREUSEADDR : ('af, 'sock_type) sock * bool
                         -> unit
    val getKEEPALIVE : ('af, 'sock_type) sock -> bool
    val setKEEPALIVE : ('af, 'sock_type) sock * bool
                         -> unit
    val getDONTROUTE : ('af, 'sock_type) sock -> bool
    val setDONTROUTE : ('af, 'sock_type) sock * bool
                         -> unit
    val getLINGER : ('af, 'sock_type) sock
                    -> Time.time option
    val setLINGER : ('af, 'sock_type) sock
                    * Time.time option -> unit
```

```
    val getBROADCAST : ('af, 'sock_type) sock -> bool
    val setBROADCAST : ('af, 'sock_type) sock * bool
                        -> unit
    val getOOBINLINE : ('af, 'sock_type) sock -> bool
    val setOOBINLINE : ('af, 'sock_type) sock * bool
                        -> unit
    val getSNDBUF : ('af, 'sock_type) sock -> int
    val setSNDBUF : ('af, 'sock_type) sock * int -> unit
    val getRCVBUF : ('af, 'sock_type) sock -> int
    val setRCVBUF : ('af, 'sock_type) sock * int -> unit
    val getTYPE : ('af, 'sock_type) sock -> SOCK.sock_type
    val getERROR : ('af, 'sock_type) sock -> bool
    val getPeerName : ('af, 'sock_type) sock
                        -> 'af sock_addr
    val getSockName : ('af, 'sock_type) sock
                        -> 'af sock_addr
    val getNREAD : ('af, 'sock_type) sock -> int
    val getATMARK : ('af, active stream) sock -> bool
  end

val sameAddr : 'af sock_addr * 'af sock_addr -> bool
val familyOfAddr : 'af sock_addr -> AF.addr_family

val bind : ('af, 'sock_type) sock * 'af sock_addr -> unit
val listen : ('af, passive stream) sock * int -> unit
val accept : ('af, passive stream) sock
                -> ('af, active stream) sock * 'af sock_addr
val acceptNB : ('af, passive stream) sock
                -> (('af, active stream) sock
                 * 'af sock_addr) option
val connect : ('af, 'sock_type) sock * 'af sock_addr
                -> unit
val connectNB : ('af, 'sock_type) sock * 'af sock_addr
                -> bool

val close : ('af, 'sock_type) sock -> unit
datatype shutdown_mode
  = NO_RECVS
  | NO_SENDS
  | NO_RECVS_OR_SENDS
val shutdown : ('af, 'mode stream) sock * shutdown_mode
                -> unit

type sock_desc
val sockDesc : ('af, 'sock_type) sock -> sock_desc
val sameDesc : sock_desc * sock_desc -> bool
```

```
val select : {
                rds : sock_desc list,
                wrs : sock_desc list,
                exs : sock_desc list,
                timeout : Time.time option
              }
           -> {
              rds : sock_desc list,
              wrs : sock_desc list,
              exs : sock_desc list
              }
val ioDesc : ('af, 'sock_type) sock -> OS.IO.iodesc

type out_flags = {don't_route : bool, oob : bool}
type in_flags = {peek : bool, oob : bool}

val sendVec : ('af, active stream) sock
              * Word8VectorSlice.slice -> int
val sendArr : ('af, active stream) sock
              * Word8ArraySlice.slice -> int
val sendVec' : ('af, active stream) sock
               * Word8VectorSlice.slice
               * out_flags -> int
val sendArr' : ('af, active stream) sock
               * Word8ArraySlice.slice
               * out_flags -> int
val sendVecNB  : ('af, active stream) sock
                 * Word8VectorSlice.slice -> int option
val sendVecNB' : ('af, active stream) sock
                 * Word8VectorSlice.slice
                 * out_flags -> int option
val sendArrNB  : ('af, active stream) sock
                 * Word8ArraySlice.slice -> int option
val sendArrNB' : ('af, active stream) sock
                 * Word8ArraySlice.slice
                 * out_flags -> int option

val recvVec  : ('af, active stream) sock * int
               -> Word8Vector.vector
val recvVec' : ('af, active stream) sock * int * in_flags
               -> Word8Vector.vector
val recvArr  : ('af, active stream) sock
               * Word8ArraySlice.slice -> int
val recvArr' : ('af, active stream) sock
               * Word8ArraySlice.slice
               * in_flags -> int
```

```
val recvVecNB  : ('af, active stream) sock * int
                    -> Word8Vector.vector option
val recvVecNB' : ('af, active stream) sock * int * in_flags
                    -> Word8Vector.vector option
val recvArrNB  : ('af, active stream) sock
                    * Word8ArraySlice.slice -> int option
val recvArrNB' : ('af, active stream) sock
                    * Word8ArraySlice.slice
                    * in_flags -> int option

val sendVecTo : ('af, dgram) sock
                    * 'af sock_addr
                    * Word8VectorSlice.slice -> unit
val sendArrTo : ('af, dgram) sock
                    * 'af sock_addr
                    * Word8ArraySlice.slice -> unit
val sendVecTo' : ('af, dgram) sock
                    * 'af sock_addr
                    * Word8VectorSlice.slice
                    * out_flags -> unit
val sendArrTo' : ('af, dgram) sock
                    * 'af sock_addr
                    * Word8ArraySlice.slice
                    * out_flags -> unit
val sendVecToNB  : ('af, dgram) sock
                    * 'af sock_addr
                    * Word8VectorSlice.slice -> bool
val sendVecToNB' : ('af, dgram) sock
                    * 'af sock_addr
                    * Word8VectorSlice.slice
                    * out_flags -> bool
val sendArrToNB  : ('af, dgram) sock
                    * 'af sock_addr
                    * Word8ArraySlice.slice -> bool
val sendArrToNB' : ('af, dgram) sock
                    * 'af sock_addr
                    * Word8ArraySlice.slice
                    * out_flags -> bool

val recvVecFrom  : ('af, dgram) sock * int
                    -> Word8Vector.vector
                    * 'sock_type sock_addr
val recvVecFrom' : ('af, dgram) sock * int * in_flags
                    -> Word8Vector.vector
                    * 'sock_type sock_addr
```

```
val recvArrFrom   : ('af, dgram) sock
                          * Word8ArraySlice.slice
                          -> int * 'af sock_addr
val recvArrFrom'  : ('af, dgram) sock
                          * Word8ArraySlice.slice
                          * in_flags -> int * 'af sock_addr
val recvVecFromNB  : ('af, dgram) sock * int
                              -> (Word8Vector.vector
                              * 'sock_type sock_addr) option
val recvVecFromNB' : ('af, dgram) sock * int * in_flags
                              -> (Word8Vector.vector
                              * 'sock_type sock_addr) option
val recvArrFromNB  : ('af, dgram) sock
                          * Word8ArraySlice.slice
                          -> (int * 'af sock_addr) option
val recvArrFromNB' : ('af, dgram) sock
                          * Word8ArraySlice.slice
                          * in_flags
                          -> (int * 'af sock_addr) option
```

Description

type ('af,'sock_type) sock

> The type of a socket. Sockets are polymorphic over both the address family and the socket type. The type parameter 'af is instantiated with the appropriate address family type (INetSock.inet or UnixSock.unix). The type parameter 'sock_type is instantiated with the appropriate socket type (dgram or stream).

type 'af sock_addr

> The type of a socket address. The type parameter 'af describes the address family of the address (INetSock.inet or UnixSock.unix).

type dgram

> The witness type for datagram sockets.

type 'mode stream

> The witness type for stream sockets. The type parameter 'mode describes the mode of the stream socket: active or passive.

structure AF : **sig** ... **end**

> The AF substructure defines an abstract type that represents the different network-address families.

val `list : unit -> (string * addr_family) list`

> This function returns a list of all the available address families. Every element of the list is a pair `(name, af)`, where `name` is the name of the address family and `af` is the actual address family value.
>
> The names of the address families are taken from the symbolic constants used in the C Socket API and stripping the leading "AF_." For example, the Unix-domain address family is named `"UNIX"`, the Internet-domain address family is named `"INET"`, and the *Apple Talk* address family is named `"APPLETALK"`.

val `toString : addr_family -> string`
val `fromString : string -> addr_family option`

> These functions convert between address family values and their names. For example, the expression `toString (INetSock.inetAF)` returns the string `"INET"`. `fromString` returns `NONE` if no family value corresponds to the given name.
>
> If a pair `(name, af)` is in the list returned by `list`, then it is the case that `name` is equal to `toString(af)`.

structure `SOCK :` **sig** `...` **end**

> The `SOCK` substructure provides an abstract type and operations for the different types of sockets. This type is used by the `getTYPE` function.

eqtype `sock_type`

> The type of socket types.

val `stream : sock_type`

> The stream socket type value.

val `dgram : sock_type`

> The datagram socket type value.

val `list : unit -> (string * sock_type) list`

> This function returns a list of the available socket types. Every element of the list is of the form `(name, sty)`, where `name` is the name of the socket type and `sty` is the actual socket type value.
>
> The list of possible socket type names includes `"STREAM"` for stream sockets, `"DGRAM"` for datagram sockets, and `"RAW"` for raw sockets. These names are formed by taking the symbolic constants from the C API and removing the leading "SOCK_."

val `toString : sock_type -> string`
val `fromString : string -> sock_type option`

> These functions convert between a socket type value and its name (e.g., "STREAM"). `fromString` returns `NONE` if no socket type value corresponds to the name.
>
> If a pair `(name, sty)` is in the list returned by `list`, then it is the case that `name` is equal to `toString(sty)`.

structure Ctl : **sig** ... **end**

The Ctl substructure provides support for manipulating the options associated with a socket. These functions raise the SysErr exception when the argument socket has been closed.

val getDEBUG : ('af, 'sock_type) sock **->** bool
val setDEBUG : ('af, 'sock_type) sock ***** bool **->** unit

These functions query and set the SO_DEBUG flag for the socket. This flag enables or disables low-level debugging within the kernel. Enabled, it allows the kernel to maintain a history of the recent packets that have been received or sent.

val getREUSEADDR : ('af, 'sock_type) sock **->** bool
val setREUSEADDR : ('af, 'sock_type) sock ***** bool **->** unit

These functions query and set the SO_REUSEADDR flag for the socket. When true, this flag instructs the system to allow the reuse of local socket addresses in bind calls.

val getKEEPALIVE : ('af, 'sock_type) sock **->** bool
val setKEEPALIVE : ('af, 'sock_type) sock ***** bool **->** unit

These functions query and set the SO_KEEPALIVE flag for the socket. When true, the system will generate periodic transmissions on a connected socket, when no other data are being exchanged.

val getDONTROUTE : ('af, 'sock_type) sock **->** bool
val setDONTROUTE : ('af, 'sock_type) sock ***** bool **->** unit

These functions query and set the SO_DONTROUTE flag for the socket. When this flag is true, outgoing messages bypass the normal routing mechanisms of the underlying protocol, and are instead directed to the appropriate network interface as specified by the network portion of the destination address. Note that this option can be specified on a per message basis by using one of the sendVec', sendArr', sendVecTo', or sendArrTo' functions.

val getLINGER : ('af, 'sock_type) sock **->** Time.time option
val setLINGER : ('af, 'sock_type) sock ***** Time.time option
                         -> unit

These functions query and set the SO_LINGER flag for the socket *sock*. This flag controls the action taken when unsent messages are queued on a socket and a close is performed. If the flag is set to NONE, then the system will close the socket as quickly as possible, discarding data if necessary. If the flag is set to SOME(*t*) and the socket promises reliable delivery, then the system will block the close operation until the data are delivered or the timeout *t* expires. If *t* is negative or too large, then the Time is raised.

val getBROADCAST : ('af, 'sock_type) sock **->** bool
val setBROADCAST : ('af, 'sock_type) sock ***** bool **->** unit

These functions query and set the SO_BROADCAST flag for the socket *sock*, which enables or disables the ability of the process to send broadcast messages over the socket.

val getOOBINLINE : ('af, 'sock_type) sock -> bool
val setOOBINLINE : ('af, 'sock_type) sock * bool -> unit

These functions query and set the SO_OOBINLINE flag for the socket. When set, which indicates that out-of-band data should be placed in the normal input queue of the socket. Note that this option can be specified on a per message basis by using one of the sendVec', sendArr', sendVecTo', or sendArrTo' functions.

val getSNDBUF : ('af, 'sock_type) sock -> int
val setSNDBUF : ('af, 'sock_type) sock * int -> unit

These functions query and set the size of the send queue buffer for the socket.

val getRCVBUF : ('af, 'sock_type) sock -> int
val setRCVBUF : ('af, 'sock_type) sock * int -> unit

These query and set the size of receive queue buffer for the socket.

val getTYPE : ('af, 'sock_type) sock -> SOCK.sock_type

This function returns the socket type of the socket.

val getERROR : ('af, 'sock_type) sock -> bool

This function indicates whether or not an error has occurred.

val getPeerName : ('af, 'sock_type) sock -> 'af sock_addr

This function returns the socket address to which the socket is connected.

val getSockName : ('af, 'sock_type) sock -> 'af sock_addr

This function returns the socket address to which the socket is bound.

val getNREAD : ('af, 'sock_type) sock -> int

This function returns the number of bytes available for reading on the socket.

val getATMARK : ('af, active stream) sock -> bool

This function indicates whether or not the read pointer on the socket is currently at the out-of-band mark.

val sameAddr : 'af sock_addr * 'af sock_addr -> bool

This function tests whether two socket addresses are the same.

val familyOfAddr : 'af sock_addr -> AF.addr_family

familyOfAddr *addr* returns the address family of the socket address *addr*.

val bind : ('af, 'sock_type) sock * 'af sock_addr -> unit

bind (*sock*, *sa*) binds the address *sa* to the passive socket *sock*. This function raises SysErr when the address *sa* is already in use, when *sock* is already bound to an address, or when *sock* has been closed.

val listen : ('af, passive stream) sock * int -> unit

listen (*sock*, *n*) creates a queue (of size *n*) for pending questions associated to the socket *sock*. The size of queue is limited by the underlying system, but requesting a queue size larger than the limit does not cause an error (a typical limit is 128, but older systems use a limit of 5).

This function raises the SysErr exception if *sock* has been closed.

val accept : ('af, passive stream) sock
                -> ('af, active stream) sock * 'af sock_addr

accept *sock* extracts the first connection request from the queue of pending connections for the socket *sock*. The socket must have been bound to an address via bind and enabled for listening via listen. If a connection is present, accept returns a pair (*s*, *sa*) consisting of a new active socket *s* with the same properties as *sock* and the address *sa* of the connecting entity. If no pending connections are present on the queue, then accept blocks until a connection is requested. One can test for pending connection requests by using the select function to test the socket for reading.

This function raises the SysErr exception if *sock* has not been properly bound and enabled or if *sock* has been closed.

val acceptNB : ('af, passive stream) sock
                -> (('af, active stream) sock
                * 'af sock_addr) option

This function is the non-blocking form of the accept operation. If the operation can complete without blocking (i.e., there is a pending connection), then this function returns SOME(*s*,*sa*), where *s* is a new active socket with the same properties as *sock* and *sa* is the the address of the connecting entity. If there are no pending connections, then this function returns NONE.

This function raises the SysErr exception if *sock* has not been properly bound and enabled or if *sock* has been closed.

val connect : ('af, 'sock_type) sock * 'af sock_addr
                -> unit

connect (*sock*, *sa*) attempts to connect the socket *sock* to the address *sa*. If *sock* is a datagram socket, the address specifies the peer with which the socket is to be associated; *sa* is the address to which datagrams are to be sent and the only address from which datagrams are to be received. If *sock* is a stream socket, the address specifies another socket to which to connect.

This function raises the `SysErr` exception when the address specified by `sa` is unreachable, when the connection is refused or times out, when `sock` is already connected, or when `sock` has been closed.

val `connectNB : ('af, 'sock_type) sock * 'af sock_addr`
`                    -> bool`

This function is the non-blocking form of `connect`. If the connection can be established without blocking the caller (which is typically true for datagram sockets but not stream sockets), then `true` is returned. Otherwise, `false` is returned and the connection attempt is started; one can test for the completion of the connection by testing the socket for writing using the `select` function. This function will raise `SysErr` if it is called on a socket for which a previous connection attempt has not yet been completed.

val `close : ('af, 'sock_type) sock -> unit`

`close sock` closes the connection to the socket `sock`. This function raises the `SysErr` exception if the socket has already been closed.

val `shutdown : ('af, 'mode stream) sock * shutdown_mode`
`                    -> unit`

`shutdown (sock, mode)` shuts down all or part of a full-duplex connection on socket `sock`. If `mode` is `NO_RECVS`, further receives will be disallowed. If `mode` is `NO_SENDS`, further sends will be disallowed. If `mode` is `NO_RECVS_OR_SENDS`, further sends and receives will be disallowed. This function raises the `SysErr` exception if the socket is not connected or has been closed.

type `sock_desc`

This type is an abstract name for a socket, which is used to support polling on collections of sockets.

val `sockDesc : ('af, 'sock_type) sock -> sock_desc`

`sockDesc sock` returns a socket descriptor that names the socket `sock`.

val `sameDesc : sock_desc * sock_desc -> bool`

`sameDesc (sd1, sd2)` returns `true` if the two socket descriptors `sd1` and `sd2` describe the same underlying socket. Thus, the expression `sameDesc(sockDesc sock, sockDesc sock)` will always return `true` for any socket `sock`.

```
val select : {
                rds : sock_desc list,
                wrs : sock_desc list,
                exs : sock_desc list,
                timeout : Time.time option
            }
          -> {
                rds : sock_desc list,
                wrs : sock_desc list,
                exs : sock_desc list
            }
```

select {*rds*, *wrs*, *exs*, *timeout*} examines the sockets in *rds*, *wrs*, and *exs* to see if they are ready for reading, writing, or have an exceptional condition pending, respectively. The calling program is blocked until either one or more of the named sockets is "ready" or the specified timeout expires (where a timeout of NONE never expires). The result of select is a record of three lists of socket descriptors containing the ready sockets from the corresponding argument lists. The order in which socket descriptors appear in the argument lists is preserved in the result lists. A timeout is signified by a result of three empty lists.

This function raises SysErr if any of the argument sockets have been closed or if the timeout value is negative.

Note that one can test if a call to accept will block by using select to see if the socket is ready to read. Similarly, one can use select to test if a call to connect will block by seeing if the socket is ready to write.

```
val ioDesc : ('af, 'sock_type) sock -> OS.IO.iodesc
```

ioDesc *sock* returns the I/O descriptor corresponding to socket *sock*. This descriptor can be used to poll the socket via pollDesc and poll in the OS.IO structure. Using the polling mechanism from OS.IO has the advantage that different kinds of I/O objects can be mixed, but not all systems support polling on sockets this way. If an application is only polling sockets, then it is more portable to use the select function defined above.

```
type out_flags = {don't_route : bool, oob : bool}
```

Flags used in the general form of socket output operations.

```
type in_flags = {peek : bool, oob : bool}
```

Flags used in the general form of socket input operations.

```
val sendVec : ('af, active stream) sock
                * Word8VectorSlice.slice -> int
val sendArr : ('af, active stream) sock
                * Word8ArraySlice.slice -> int
```

```
     sendVec (sock, slice)
     sendArr (sock, slice)
```
These functions send the bytes in the slice `slice` on the active stream socket `sock`. They return the number of bytes actually sent.

These functions raise `SysErr` if `sock` has been closed.

```
val sendVec' : ('af, active stream) sock
                    * Word8VectorSlice.slice
                    * out_flags -> int
val sendArr' : ('af, active stream) sock
                    * Word8ArraySlice.slice
                    * out_flags -> int
```

```
     sendVec' (sock, slice, {don't_route, oob})
     sendArr' (sock, slice, {don't_route, oob})
```
These functions send the bytes in the slice `slice` on the active stream socket `sock`. They return the number of bytes actually sent. If the `don't_route` flag is true, the data are sent by bypassing the normal routing mechanism of the protocol. If `oob` is true, the data are sent out-of-band, that is, before any other data that may have been buffered.

These functions raise `SysErr` if `sock` has been closed.

```
val sendVecNB : ('af, active stream) sock
                    * Word8VectorSlice.slice -> int option
val sendVecNB' : ('af, active stream) sock
                    * Word8VectorSlice.slice
                    * out_flags -> int option
val sendArrNB : ('af, active stream) sock
                    * Word8ArraySlice.slice -> int option
val sendArrNB' : ('af, active stream) sock
                    * Word8ArraySlice.slice
                    * out_flags -> int option
```

These functions are the non-blocking versions of `sendVec`, `sendVec'`, `sendArr`, and `sendArr'` (resp.). They have the same semantics as their blocking forms, with the exception that when the operation can complete without blocking, then the result is wrapped in `SOME` and if the operation has to wait to send the data, then `NONE` is returned instead.

```
val recvVec : ('af, active stream) sock * int
                    -> Word8Vector.vector
val recvVec' : ('af, active stream) sock * int * in_flags
                    -> Word8Vector.vector
```

```
     recvVec (sock, n)
     recvVec'(sock, n, {peek, oob})
```
These functions receive up to n bytes from the active stream socket `sock`. The size of the resulting vector is the number of bytes that were successfully received, which may be less than n. If the connection has been closed at the other end (or if n is 0), then the empty vector will be returned.

In the second version, if `peek` is true, the data are received but not discarded from the connection. If *oob* is `true`, the data are received out-of-band, that is, before any other incoming data that may have been buffered.

These functions raise `SysErr` if the socket *sock* has been closed and they raise `Size` if $n<0$ or $n>$`Word8Vector.maxLen`.

```
val recvArr : ('af, active stream) sock
                  * Word8ArraySlice.slice -> int
val recvArr' : ('af, active stream) sock
                  * Word8ArraySlice.slice
                  * in_flags -> int
```

recvArr (*sock*, *slice*)
recvArr' (*sock*, *slice*, {*peek*, *oob*})
These functions read data from the socket *sock* into the array slice *slice*. They return the number of bytes actually received. If the connection has been closed at the other end or the slice is empty, then 0 is returned.

For `recvArr'`, if *peek* is `true`, the data are received but not discarded from the connection. If *oob* is `true`, the data are received out-of-band, that is, before any other incoming data that may have been buffered.

These functions raise `SysErr` if *sock* has been closed.

```
val recvVecNB : ('af, active stream) sock * int
                  -> Word8Vector.vector option
val recvVecNB' : ('af, active stream) sock * int * in_flags
                  -> Word8Vector.vector option
val recvArrNB : ('af, active stream) sock
                  * Word8ArraySlice.slice -> int option
val recvArrNB' : ('af, active stream) sock
                  * Word8ArraySlice.slice
                  * in_flags -> int option
```

These functions are the non-blocking versions of `recvVec`, `recvVec'`, `recvArr`, and `recvArr'` (resp.). They have the same semantics as their blocking forms, with the exception that when the operation can complete without blocking, then the result is wrapped in `SOME` and if the operation has to wait for input, then `NONE` is returned instead.

```
val sendVecTo : ('af, dgram) sock
                  * 'af sock_addr
                  * Word8VectorSlice.slice -> unit
val sendArrTo : ('af, dgram) sock
                  * 'af sock_addr
                  * Word8ArraySlice.slice -> unit
```

sendVecTo (*sock*, *sa*, *slice*)
sendArrTo (*sock*, *sa*, *slice*)
These functions send the message specified by the slice *slice* on the datagram socket *sock* to the address *sa*.

These functions raise `SysErr` if *sock* has been closed or if the socket has been connected to a different address than *sa*.

```
val sendVecTo' : ('af, dgram) sock
                     * 'af sock_addr
                     * Word8VectorSlice.slice
                     * out_flags -> unit
val sendArrTo' : ('af, dgram) sock
                     * 'af sock_addr
                     * Word8ArraySlice.slice
                     * out_flags -> unit
```

sendVecTo' (*sock*, *sa*, *slice*, {*don't_route*, *oob*})
sendArrTo' (*sock*, *sa*, *slice*, {*don't_route*, *oob*})
These functions send the message specified by the slice *slice* on the datagram socket *sock* to the address

If the *don't_route* flag is true, the data are sent by bypassing the normal routing mechanism of the protocol. If *oob* is true, the data are sent out-of-band, that is, before any other data that may have been buffered.

These functions raise SysErr if *sock* has been closed or if the socket has been connected to a different address than *sa*.

```
val sendVecToNB : ('af, dgram) sock
                     * 'af sock_addr
                     * Word8VectorSlice.slice -> bool
val sendVecToNB' : ('af, dgram) sock
                     * 'af sock_addr
                     * Word8VectorSlice.slice
                     * out_flags -> bool
val sendArrToNB : ('af, dgram) sock
                     * 'af sock_addr
                     * Word8ArraySlice.slice -> bool
val sendArrToNB' : ('af, dgram) sock
                     * 'af sock_addr
                     * Word8ArraySlice.slice
                     * out_flags -> bool
```

These functions are the non-blocking versions of sendVecTo, sendVecTo', send-ArrTo, and sendArrTo' (resp.). They have the same semantics as their blocking forms, with the exception that if the operation can complete without blocking, then the operation is performed and true is returned. Otherwise, false is returned and the message is not sent.

```
val recvVecFrom  : ('af, dgram) sock * int
                        -> Word8Vector.vector
                        * 'sock_type sock_addr
val recvVecFrom' : ('af, dgram) sock * int * in_flags
                        -> Word8Vector.vector
                        * 'sock_type sock_addr
```

recvVecFrom (*sock, n*)
recvVecFrom' (*sock, n, {peek, oob}*)
These functions receive up to n bytes on the datagram socket *sock* and return a pair
(*vec, sa*), where the vector *vec* is the received message and *sa* is the socket address
from the which the data originated. If the message is larger than n, then data may be lost.

In the second form, if *peek* is true, the data are received but not discarded from the
connection. If *oob* is true, the data are received out-of-band, that is, before any other
incoming data that may have been buffered.

These functions raise SysErr if *sock* has been closed; they raise Size if $n<0$ or
$n>$Word8Vector.maxLen.

```
val recvArrFrom  : ('af, dgram) sock * Word8ArraySlice.slice
                        -> int * 'af sock_addr
val recvArrFrom' : ('af, dgram) sock
                        * Word8ArraySlice.slice
                        * in_flags -> int * 'af sock_addr
```

recvArrFrom (*sock, slice*)
recvArrFrom' (*sock, slice*)
These functions read a message from the datagram socket *sock* into the array slice *slice*.
If the message is larger than the size of the slice, then data may be lost. They return the
number of bytes actually received. If the connection has been closed at the other end or the
slice is empty, then 0 is returned.

For recvArrFrom', if *peek* is true, the data is received but not discarded from
the connection. If *oob* is true, the data is received out-of-band, that is, before any other
incoming data that may have been buffered.

These functions raise SysErr if *sock* has been closed.

```
val recvVecFromNB : ('af, dgram) sock * int
                         -> (Word8Vector.vector
                       * 'sock_type sock_addr) option
val recvVecFromNB' : ('af, dgram) sock * int * in_flags
                          -> (Word8Vector.vector
                       * 'sock_type sock_addr) option
val recvArrFromNB : ('af, dgram) sock
                       * Word8ArraySlice.slice
                       -> (int * 'af sock_addr) option
val recvArrFromNB' : ('af, dgram) sock
                        * Word8ArraySlice.slice
                        * in_flags
                       -> (int * 'af sock_addr) option
```

These functions are the non-blocking versions of recvVecFrom, recvVecFrom', recv-ArrFrom, and recvArrFrom' (resp.). They have the same semantics as their blocking forms, with the exception that when the operation can complete without blocking, then the result is wrapped in SOME and if the operation has to wait for input, then NONE is returned instead.

Discussion

Implementation note: On Unix systems, the non-blocking mode of socket operations is controlled by changing the socket's state using the setsockopt() system call. Thus, implementing the non-blocking operations in the Socket structure may require tracking the socket's blocking/non-blocking state in the representation of the sock type.

See also

GenericSock (§11.12; p. 153), INetSock (§11.16; p. 166),
NetHostDB (§11.28; p. 220), NetServDB (§11.30; p. 225),
UnixSock (§11.63; p. 398)

11.52   The `STREAM_IO` signature

The `STREAM_IO` signature defines the interface of the *stream I/O* layer in the I/O stack. This layer provides buffering over the readers and writers of the primitive I/O layer.

Input streams are treated in the lazy functional style; that is, input from a stream f yields a finite vector of elements, plus a new stream f'. Input from f again will yield the same elements; to advance within the stream in the usual way, it is necessary to do further input from f'. This interface allows arbitrary lookahead to be done very cleanly, which should be useful both for *ad hoc* lexical analysis and for table-driven, regular-expression-based lexing.

Output streams are handled more conventionally, since the lazy functional style does not seem to make sense for output.

Stream I/O functions may raise the `Size` exception if a resulting vector of elements exceeds the maximum vector size or the `IO.Io` exception. In general, when `IO.Io` is raised as a result of a failure in a lower-level module, the underlying exception is caught and propagated up as the `cause` component of the `IO.Io` exception value. This exception will usually be a `Subscript`, `IO.ClosedStream`, `OS.SysErr`, or `Fail` exception (the last possible because of user-supplied readers or writers), but the stream I/O module will rarely (perhaps never) need to inspect it.

Synopsis
```
signature STREAM_IO
```

Interface
```
type elem
type vector

type instream
type outstream
type out_pos

type reader
type writer
type pos

val input : instream -> vector * instream
val input1 : instream -> (elem * instream) option
val inputN : instream * int -> vector * instream
val inputAll : instream -> vector * instream
val canInput : instream * int -> int option
val closeIn : instream -> unit
val endOfStream : instream -> bool
```

```
val output : outstream * vector -> unit
val output1 : outstream * elem -> unit
val flushOut : outstream -> unit
val closeOut : outstream -> unit

val mkInstream : reader * vector -> instream
val getReader : instream -> reader * vector
val filePosIn : instream -> pos

val setBufferMode : outstream * IO.buffer_mode -> unit
val getBufferMode : outstream -> IO.buffer_mode

val mkOutstream : writer * IO.buffer_mode -> outstream
val getWriter : outstream -> writer * IO.buffer_mode
val getPosOut : outstream -> out_pos
val setPosOut : out_pos -> outstream
val filePosOut : out_pos -> pos
```

Description

type elem
type vector

> The abstract types of stream elements and vectors of elements. For text streams these types are Char.char and String.string, while for binary streams they are Word8.word and Word8Vector.vector.

type instream

> The type of buffered functional input streams.
>
> Input streams are in one of three states: active, truncated, or closed. When initially created, the stream is active. When disconnected from its underlying primitive reader (e.g., by getReader), the stream is truncated. When closeIn is applied to the stream, the stream enters the closed state. A closed stream is also truncated. The only real difference between a truncated stream and a closed one is that, in the latter case, the stream's primitive I/O reader is closed.
>
> Reading from a truncated input stream will never block; after all buffered elements are read, input operations always return empty vectors.

type outstream

> The type of buffered output streams. Unlike input streams, these are imperative objects.
>
> Output streams are in one of three states: active, terminated, or closed. When initially created, the stream is active. When disconnected from its underlying primitive writer (e.g., by getWriter), the stream is terminated. When closeOut is applied to the stream, the stream enters the closed state. A closed stream is also terminated. The only real difference between a terminated stream and a closed one is that, in the latter case, the stream's primitive I/O writer is closed.

In a terminated output stream, there is no mechanism for performing more output, so any output operations will raise the `IO.Io` exception.

type `out_pos`

The type of positions in output streams. These values can be used to reconstruct an output stream at the position recorded in the `out_pos` value. Thus, the canonical representation for the type is `(outstream * pos)`.

type `reader`
type `writer`

The readers and writers types that underlie the input and output streams.

type `pos`

The type of positions in the underlying readers and writers. In some instantiations of this signature (e.g., `TextIO.StreamIO`), `pos` is abstract; in others, it may be concrete (e.g., `Position.int` in `BinIO.StreamIO`).

val `input : instream -> vector * instream`

`input` `f` returns a vector of one or more elements from `f` and the remainder of the stream, if any elements are available. If an end-of-stream has been reached, then the empty vector is returned. The function may block until one of these conditions is satisfied. This function raises the `Io` exception if there is an error in the underlying reader.

val `input1 : instream -> (elem * instream) option`

`input1` `f` returns the next element in the stream `f` and the remainder of the stream. If the stream is at the end, then `NONE` is returned. It may block until one of these conditions is satisfied. This function raises the `Io` exception if there is an error in the underlying reader.

val `inputN : instream * int -> vector * instream`

`inputN` `(f, n)` returns a vector of the next `n` elements from `f` and the rest of the stream. If fewer than `n` elements are available before the next end-of-stream, it returns all of the elements up to that end-of-stream. It may block until it can determine if additional characters are available or an end-of-stream condition holds. This function raises the `Io` exception if there is an error in the underlying reader. It raises `Size` if `n < 0` or the number of elements to be returned is greater than `maxLen`. Note that `inputN(f,0)` returns immediately with an empty vector and `f`.

Using `instreams`, one can synthesize a non-blocking version of `inputN` from input-N and `canInput`, as `inputN` is guaranteed not to block if a previous call to `canInput` returned `SOME(_)`.

val inputAll : instream -> vector * instream

> inputAll *f* returns the vector of the rest of the elements in the stream *f* (i.e., up to an end-of-stream) and a new stream *f'*. Care should be taken when using this function, since it can block indefinitely on interactive streams. This function raises the Io exception if there is an error in the underlying reader. The stream *f'* is immediately past the next end-of-stream of *f*. For ordinary files in which only one end-of stream is expected, *f'* can be ignored. If a file has multiple end-of-stream conditions (which can happen under some operating systems), inputAll returns all the elements up to the next end-of-stream. It raises Size if the number of elements to be returned is greater than maxLen for the relevant vector type.

val canInput : instream * int -> int option

> canInput (*f*, *n*) returns NONE if any attempt at input would block. It returns SOME(*k*), where $0 \leq k \leq n$, if a call to input would return immediately with at least *k* characters. Note that $k = 0$ corresponds to the stream being at the end-of-stream.
>
> Some streams may not support this operation, in which case the Io exception will be raised. This function also raises the Io exception if there is an error in the underlying reader. It raises the Size exception if n < 0.

> **Implementation note:** It is suggested that implementations of canInput should attempt to return as large a *k* as possible. For example, if the buffer contains 10 characters and the user calls canInput (*f*, 15), canInput should call readVecNB(5) to see if an additional 5 characters are available.
>
> Such a lookahead commits the stream to the characters read by readVecNB, but it does not commit the stream to return those characters on the next call to input. Indeed, a typical implementation will simply return the remainder of the current buffer, in this case consisting of 10 characters, if input is called. On the other hand, an implementation can decide to always respond to input with all the elements currently available, provided an earlier call to input has not committed the stream to a particular response. The only requirement is that any future call of input on the same input stream must return the same vector of elements.

val closeIn : instream -> unit

> closeIn *f* marks the stream closed and closes the underlying reader. Applying close-In on a closed stream has no effect. This function raises the Io exception if there is an error in the underlying reader.

val endOfStream : instream -> bool

> endOfStream *f* tests if *f* satisfies the end-of-stream condition. If there is no further input in the stream, then this call returns true; otherwise, it returns false. This function raises the Io exception if there is an error in the underlying reader.
>
> This function may block when checking for more input. It is equivalent to
>
> $$(\text{length}(\#1(\text{input } f)) = 0)$$

where `length` is the vector length operation

Note that, even if `endOfStream` returns `true`, subsequent input operations may succeed if more data become available. A stream can have multiple end-of-streams interspersed with normal elements. For example, on Unix if a user types control-D (`#"\^D"`) on a terminal device and then keeps typing characters; it may also occur on file descriptors connected to sockets.

Multiple end-of-streams is a property of the underlying reader. Thus, `readVec` on a `reader` may return an empty string, then another call to `readVec` on the same `reader` may return a non-empty string, and then a third call may return an empty string. It is always true, however, that

$$\text{endOfStream } f = \text{endOfStream } f$$

In addition, if `endOfStream` f returns `true`, then `input` f returns (`""`, f') and `endOfStream` f' may or may not be true.

val `output : outstream * vector -> unit`

`output` (`f`, `vec`) writes the vector of elements *vec* to the stream `f`. This function raises the exception `Io` if `f` is terminated. This function also raises the `Io` exception if there is an error in the underlying writer.

val `output1 : outstream * elem -> unit`

`output1` (`f`, `el`) writes the element `el` to the stream `f`. This function raises the exception `Io` if `f` is terminated. This function also raises the `Io` exception if there is an error in the underlying writer.

val `flushOut : outstream -> unit`

`flushOut` `f` flushes any output in `f`'s buffer to the underlying writer; it is a no-op on terminated streams. This function raises the `Io` exception if there is an error in the underlying writer.

val `closeOut : outstream -> unit`

`closeOut` `f` flushes `f`'s buffers, marks the stream closed, and closes the underlying writer. This operation has no effect if `f` is already closed. Note that if `f` is terminated, no flushing will occur. This function raises the `Io` exception if there is an error in the underlying writer or if flushing fails. In the latter case, the stream is left open.

val `mkInstream : reader * vector -> instream`

`mkInstream` (`rd`, `v`) returns a new `instream` built on top of the reader `rd` with the initial buffer contents `v`.

If the reader does not implement all of its fields (for example, if random access operations are missing), then certain operations will raise exceptions when applied to the resulting `instream`. The following table describes the minimal relationship between `instream` operations and a reader:

instream supports:	if reader implements:
input, inputN, etc.	readVec
canInput	readVecNB
endOfStream	readVec
filePosIn	getPos and setPos

If the reader provides more operations, the resulting stream may use them.

mkInstream should construct the input stream using the reader provided. If the user wishes to employ synthesized functions in the reader, the user may call mkInstream with an augmented reader augmentReader(rd). See PRIM_IO for a description of the functions generated by augmentReader.

Building more than one input stream on top of a single reader has unpredictable effects, since readers are imperative objects. In general, there should be a one-to-one correspondence between a reader and a sequence of input streams. Also note that creating an input stream this way means that the stream could be unaware that the reader has been closed until the stream actually attempts to read from it.

val getReader : instream -> reader * vector

getReader f marks the input stream f as truncated and returns the underlying reader along with any unconsumed data from its buffer. The data returned will have the value (closeIn f; inputAll f). The function raises the exception Io if f is closed or truncated.

val filePosIn : instream -> pos

filePosIn f returns the primitive-level reader position that corresponds to the next element to be read from the buffered stream f. This function raises the exception Io if the stream does not support the operation or if f has been truncated.

It should be true that, if #1(inputAll f) returns vector v, then

        (setPos (filePosIn f); readVec (length v))

should also return v, assuming all operations are defined and terminate.

Implementation note: If the pos type is a concrete integer corresponding to a byte offset, and the translation function (between bytes and elements) is known, the value can be computed directly. If not, the value is given by

```
fun pos (bufp, n, r as RD rdr) = let
        val readVec = valOf (#readVec rdr)
        val getPos = valOf (#getPos rdr)
        val setPos = valOf (#setPos rdr)
        val savep = getPos ()
    in
      setPos bufp;
      readVec n;
      getPos () before setPos savep
    end
```

where bufp is the file position corresponding to the beginning of the current buffer, n is the number of elements already read from the current buffer, and r is the stream's underlying reader.

```
val setBufferMode : outstream * IO.buffer_mode -> unit
val getBufferMode : outstream -> IO.buffer_mode
```

setBufferMode (*f, mode*)
getBufferMode *f*
These functions set and get the buffering mode of the output stream *f*. Setting the buffer
mode to IO.NO_BUF causes any buffered output to be flushed. If the flushing fails, the Io
exception is raised. Switching the mode between IO.LINE_BUF and IO.BLOCK_BUF
should not cause flushing. If, in going from IO.BLOCK_BUF to IO.LINE_BUF, the
user desires that the buffer contain no newline characters, the user should call flushOut
explicitly.

```
val mkOutstream : writer * IO.buffer_mode -> outstream
```

mkOutstream (*wr, mode*)   returns a new output stream built on top of the writer
wr with the indicated buffer mode.
    If the writer does not implement all of its fields (for example, if random access op-
erations are missing), then certain operations will raise exceptions when applied to the
resulting outstream. The following table describes the minimal relationship between
outstream operations and a writer:

outstream supports:	if augmented writer implements:
output, output1, etc.	writeArr
flushOut	writeArr
setBufferMode	writeArr
getPosOut	writeArr and getPos
setPosOut	writeArr and setPos

If the writer provides more operations, the resulting stream may use them.
    mkOutstream should construct the output stream using the writer provided. If the user
wishes to employ synthesized functions in the writer, the user may call mkOutstream
with an augmented writer augmentWriter(*wr*). See PRIM_IO for a description of
the functions generated by augmentWriter.
    Building more than one outstream on top of a single writer has unpredictable effects,
since buffering may change the order of output. In general, there should be a one-to-one
correspondence between a writer and an output stream. Also note that creating an output
stream this way means that the stream could be unaware that the writer has been closed
until the stream actually attempts to write to it.

```
val getWriter : outstream -> writer * IO.buffer_mode
```

getWriter *f*   flushes the stream *f*, marks it as being terminated, and returns the underlying writer and the stream's buffer mode. This function raises the exception Io if *f* is
closed or if the flushing fails.

```
val getPosOut : outstream -> out_pos
```

getPosOut *f*   returns the current position of the stream *f*. This function raises the
exception Io if the stream does not support the operation, if any implicit flushing fails, or
if *f* is terminated.

Implementation note: A typical implementation of this function will require calculating a value of type pos, capturing where the next element written to f will be written in the underlying file. If the pos type is a concrete integer corresponding to a byte offset, and the translation function (between bytes and elements) is known, the value can be computed directly using getPos. If not, the value is given by

```
fun pos (f, w as WR wtr) = let
        val getPos = valOf (#getPos wtr)
        in
            flushOut f;
            getPos ()
        end
```

where f is the output stream and w is the stream's underlying writer.

```
val setPosOut : out_pos -> outstream
```

setPosOut *opos* flushes the output buffer of the stream underlying *opos*, sets the current position of the stream to the position recorded in *opos*, and returns the stream. This function raises an Io exception if the flushing fails, if the stream does not support the operation, or if the stream underlying *opos* is terminated.

```
val filePosOut : out_pos -> pos
```

filePosOut *opos* returns the primitive-level writer position that corresponds to the abstract output stream position *opos*.

Suppose we are given an output stream f and a vector of elements v, and let opos equal getPosOut(f). Then the code

```
(setPos opos; writeVec{buf=v,i=0,sz=NONE})
```

should have the same effect as the last line of the function

```
fun put (outs, x) = (flushOut outs;
                     output(outs,x); flushOut outs)
```

when called with (f,v), assuming all operations are defined and terminate and that the call to writeVec returns length v.

Discussion

Note that the type of input1 makes it a (char, instream) StringCvt.reader and thus a source of characters for the various scan functions.

Another point to notice about input1 is that it cannot be used to read beyond an end-of-stream. When an end-of-stream is encountered. the programmer will need to use one of the other input functions to obtain the stream after the end-of-stream. For example, if input1(f) returns NONE, a call to inputN(f,1) will return immediately with (fromList [], f'), and f' can be used to continue input.

It is possible that a stream's underlying reader/writer, or its operating system file descriptor, could be closed while the stream is still active. When this condition is detected, typically by an exception being raised by the lower level, the stream should raise the IO.- Io exception with cause set to IO.ClosedStream. On a related point, one can close a truncated or terminated string. This behavior is intended as a convenience, with the inactive stream providing a handle to the underlying file, but it also provides an opportunity to close a reader or writer being actively used by another stream.

Output flushing can occur by calls to any output operation or by calls to `flushOut`, `closeOut`, `getWriter`, `setPosOut`, `getPosOut`, or if `setBufferMode` is called with mode `IO.NO_BUF`. If flushing finds that it can do only a partial write (i.e., `write-Vec` or a similar function returns a number of elements written less than its *sz* argument), then the stream function must adjust the stream's buffer for the items written and then try again. If the first or any successive write attempt raises an exception, then the stream function must raise the `IO.Io` exception.

For the remainder of this chapter, we shall assume the following binding:

structure TS = TextIO.StreamIO

and that `elem` = `char`. Also, the predicates used to illustrate a point should all evaluate to true, assuming they complete without exception.

Input is semi-deterministic: `input` may read any number of elements from *f* the "first" time, but then it is committed to its choice and must return the same number of elements on subsequent reads from the same point:

```
fun chkInput f= let
        val (a, _) = TS.input f
        val (b, _) = TS.input f
    in a=b end
```

always returns true. In general, any expression involving input streams and functions defined in the `STREAM_IO` signature should always evaluate to the same value, barring exceptions.

Closing or truncating a stream just causes the not-yet-determined part of the stream to be empty:

```
fun chkClose f = let
        val (a, f') = TS.input f
        val _ = TS.closeIn f
        val (b, _) = TS.input f
    in
        a=b andalso TS.endOfStream f'
    end
```

Closing a closed stream is legal and harmless:

```
fun closeTwice f = (TS.closeIn f; TS.closeIn f; true)
```

If a stream has already been at least partly determined, then `input` cannot possibly block:

```
fun noBlock f = let
        val (s, _) = TS.input f
    in
      case TS.canInput (f, 1)
        of SOME 0 => (size s = 0)
         | SOME _ => (size s > 0)
         | NONE => false
    end
```

Note that a successful `canInput` does not imply that more characters remain before the end-of-stream, just that reading will not block.

A freshly opened stream is still undetermined (i.e., no "read" has yet been done on the underlying reader):

```
fun newStr rdr = let
      val a = TS.mkInstream (rdr, "")
      in
         TS.closeIn a;
         size(#1(TS.input a)) = 0
      end
```

This property has the useful consequence that if one opens a stream and then extracts the underlying reader, the reader has not yet been advanced in its file.

A generalization of this property says that the first time any stream value is produced, it is up-to-date with respect to its reader:

```
fun nreads(f,0) = f
  | nreads(f,n) = let
      val (_,f') = TS.input f
      in
         nreads(f',n-1)
      end
fun reads (rdr, n) = let (* for any n>=0 *)
      val f = nreads(TS.mkInstream (rdr, ""),n)
      in
         TS.closeIn f;
         size(#1(TS.input f)) = 0
      end
```

The sequence of strings returned from a fresh stream by `input` is exactly the sequence returned by the underlying reader including end-of-stream conditions, which the reader indicates by returning a zero-element vector and `input` indicates in the same way.

The `endOfStream` test is equivalent to `input` returning an empty sequence:

```
fun isEOS f = let
      val (a,_) = TS.input f
      in
         ((size a)=0) = (TS.endOfStream f)
      end
```

The semantics of `inputAll` can be defined in terms of `input`:

```
fun inputAll f  =
      case TS.input f of
         ("",f') => ("",f')
       | (s,f') => let
            val (rest,f'') = inputAll f'
            in
               (s ^ rest, f'')
            end
```

An actual implementation, however, is likely to be much more efficient; for example, on a large file, `inputAll` might read the whole file in a single system call or use memory mapping. Note that if a stream f contains data `"abc"` followed by an end-of-stream followed by `"defg"` and another end-of-stream, then `inputAll f` returns (`"abc"`,f'), and `inputAll f'` returns (`"defg"`,f'').

The semantics of `inputN` can be related to `inputAll` by the following predicate:

```
fun allAndN (f,n) = let
     val (s,f1) = TS.inputN(f,n)
     val (t,f2)= TS.inputAll f
     in
        size s < n andalso s=t andalso equiv(f1,f2)
        orelse let
          val (r,f3) = TS.inputAll f1
          in
             size s = n andalso t = s ^ r andalso equiv(f2,f3)
          end
     end
```

where the `equiv` predicate represents that the two argument streams behave identically under `input`:

```
           fun equiv (f,g) = let
                 val (s,f') = TS.input f
                 val (t,g') = TS.input g
                 in
                    s=t andalso equiv(f',g')
                 end
```

ignoring termination conditions. If `f` contained exactly `n` characters before the end-of-stream, then `r` in `allAndN` will be the empty string. Another way of stating this property is that `inputN` returns fewer than `n` characters if and only if those elements are followed by an end-of-stream.

The semantics of `input1` can be defined in terms of `inputN`:

```
           fun input1 f = (case TS.inputN (f,1)
                 of ("",_) => NONE
                  | (s,f')=> SOME(String.sub(s,0),f')
                 (* end case *))
```

If `chunkSize = 1` in the underlying `reader`, then input operations should be unbuffered. Thus, the following function always returns true:

```
fun isTrue (rdr : TextPrimIO.reader) = let
     val f = TS.mkInstream(rdr, "")
     val (_,f') = TS.input f
     val (TextPrimIO.RD{chunkSize,...},s) = TS.getReader f'
     in
        (chunkSize > 1) orelse (size s = 0)
     end
```

where `rdr` denotes a `reader` created from a newly opened file. Although `input` may perform a primitive I/O read operation on the reader for $k \geq 1$ elements, it must immediately return all the elements it receives. This property does not hold, however, for partly determined input streams. For example, the function

```
fun maybeTrue (rdr : TextPrimIO.reader) = let
     val f = TS.mkInstream(rdr, "")
     val _ = TS.input (#2 (TS.input f))
     val (_,f') = TS.input f
     val (TextPrimIO.RD{chunkSize,...},s) = TS.getReader f'
     in
        (chunkSize > 1) orelse (size s = 0)
     end
```

might return false. In this case, the stream `f` has accumulated a history of more input, which will not be emptied by a single call to `input`.

Similarly, if a writer sets `chunkSize = 1`, it suggests that output operations should be unbuffered. An application can specify that a stream should be unbuffered using the `setBufferMode` function.

Implementation note: A general rule for implementing stream input is "do not bother the reader." Whenever it is possible to do so, input must be done by using elements from the buffer, without any operation on the underlying reader. This behavior is necessary so that repeated calls to `endOfStream` will not make repeated system calls.

Implementations may require a device such as an extra boolean to mark multiple end-of-streams, in order that `input` applied to the same stream always returns the same vector.

The manual page of the `StreamIO` functor lists a variety of implementation suggestions, many of which are applicable to any implementation of the `STREAM_IO` signature.

In general, if an exception occurs during any stream I/O operation, then the stream must leave itself in a consistent state, without losing or duplicating data. In some SML systems, a user interrupt aborts execution and returns control to a top-level prompt without raising any exception that the current execution can handle. It may be the case that some information must be lost or duplicated. Data (input or output) must *never* be duplicated but may be lost. This behavior can be implemented without stream I/O doing any explicit masking of interrupts or locking. On output, the internal state (saying how much has been written) should be updated *before* doing the *write* operation; on input, the *read* should be done before updating the count of valid characters in the buffer.

See also

IMPERATIVE_IO (§11.14; p. 158), PRIM_IO (§11.48; p. 308),
StreamIO (§11.53; p. 358), TEXT_STREAM_IO (§11.59; p. 386)

11.53   The `StreamIO` functor

The optional `StreamIO` functor provides a way to build a stream I/O layer on top of
an arbitrary primitive I/O implementation. For example, given an implementation of
readers and writers for pairs of integers, one can define streams of pairs of integers.

Synopsis

```
signature STREAM_IO
functor StreamIO (...): STREAM_IO
  where type elem = PrimIO.elem
  where type vector = PrimIO.vector
  where type reader = PrimIO.reader
  where type writer = PrimIO.writer
  where type pos = PrimIO.pos
```

Functor Argument Interface

```
structure PrimIO : PRIM_IO
structure Vector : MONO_VECTOR
structure Array : MONO_ARRAY
sharing type PrimIO.elem = Vector.elem = Array.elem
sharing type PrimIO.vector = Vector.vector = Array.vector
sharing type PrimIO.array = Array.array

val someElem : PrimIO.elem
```

Description

```
structure PrimIO : PRIM_IO
```

    The underlying primitive I/O structure.

```
val someElem : PrimIO.elem
```

    Some arbitrary element used to initialize buffer arrays.

Discussion

    The `Vector` and `Array` structures provide vector and array operations for manipulating
the vectors and arrays used in `PrimIO` and `StreamIO`. The element *someElem* is used
to initialize buffer arrays; any element will do.

    The types `instream` and `outstream` in the result of the `StreamIO` functor must
be abstract.

    Implementation note: Here are some suggestions for efficient performance:

- Operations on the underlying readers and writers (`readVec`, etc.) are expected to
  be expensive (involving a system call, with context switch).

- Small input operations can be done from a buffer; the `readVec` or `readVecNB` operation of the underlying reader can replenish the buffer when necessary.

- Each reader may provide only a subset of `readVec`, `readVecNB`, `block`, `canInput`, etc. An augmented reader that provides more operations can be constructed using `PrimIO.augmentReader`, but it may be more efficient to use the functions directly provided by the reader, instead of relying on the constructed ones. The same applies to augmented writers.

- Keep the position of the beginning of the buffer on a multiple-of-`chunkSize` boundary and do **read** or **write** operations with a multiple-of-`chunkSize` number of elements.

- For very large `inputAll` or `inputN` operations, it is (somewhat) inefficient to read one `chunkSize` at a time and then concatenate all the results together. Instead, it is good to try to do the read all in one large system call, that is, `readVec(n)`. In a typical implementation of `readVec`, this operation requires pre-allocating a vector of size n. In `inputAll`, however, the size of the vector is not known *a priori*, and if the argument to `inputN` is large, the allocation of a much-too-large buffer is wasteful. Therefore, for large input operations, query the remaining size of the reader using `avail` and try to read that much. But one should also keep things rounded to the nearest `chunkSize`.

- The use of `avail` to try to do (large) read operations of just the right size will be inaccurate on translated readers. But this inaccuracy can be tolerated: if the translation is anything close to one-to-one, `avail` will still provide a very good hint about the order-of-magnitude size of what remains to be read.

- Similar suggestions apply to very large output operations. Small outputs go through a buffer; the buffer is written with `writeArr`. Very large outputs can be written directly from the argument string using `writeVec`.

- A lazy functional input stream can (should) be implemented as a sequence of immutable (vector) buffers, each with a mutable **ref** to the next "thing," which is either another buffer, the underlying reader, or an indication that the stream has been truncated.

- The `input` function should return the largest sequence that is most convenient. Usually this requirement means "the remaining contents of the current buffer."

- To support non-blocking input, use `readVecNB` if it exists; otherwise, do `canInput` followed (if appropriate) by `readVec`.

- To support blocking input, use `readVec` if it exists; otherwise, do `readVecNB` followed (if it would block) by `block`. and then another `readVecNB`.

- To support lazy functional streams, `readArr` and `readArrNB` are not useful. If necessary, `readVec` should be synthesized from `readArr` and `readVecNB` from `readArrNB`.

- `writeArr` should, if necessary, be synthesized from `writeVec`, and vice versa. Similarly for `writeArrNB` and `writeVecNB`.

See also

ImperativeIO (§11.15; p. 165), MONO_ARRAY (§11.23; p. 193),
MONO_VECTOR (§11.26; p. 211), PrimIO (§11.49; p. 317), PRIM_IO (§11.48; p. 308),
STREAM_IO (§11.52; p. 346)

11.54   The STRING signature

The STRING signature specifies the basic operations on a string type, which is a vector of the underlying character type char as defined in the structure.

The STRING signature is matched by two structures, the required String and the optional WideString. The former implements strings based on the extended ASCII 8-bit character set and is a companion structure to the Char structure. The latter provides strings of characters of some size greater than or equal to 8 bits and is related to the structure WideChar. In particular, the type String.char is identical to the type Char.char, and, when WideString is defined, the type WideString.char is identical to the type WideChar.char. These connections are made explicit in the Text and WideText structures, which match the TEXT signature.

Synopsis

```
signature STRING
structure String :> STRING
  where type string = string
  where type string = CharVector.vector
  where type char = Char.char
structure WideString :> STRING
  where type string = WideCharVector.vector
  where type char = WideChar.char
```

Interface

```
eqtype string
eqtype char

val maxSize : int
val size : string -> int

val sub : string * int -> char

val str : char -> string
val extract   : string * int * int option -> string
val substring : string * int * int -> string

val ^ : string * string -> string
val concat : string list -> string
val concatWith : string -> string list -> string

val implode : char list -> string
val explode : string -> char list
val map : (char -> char) -> string -> string
val translate : (char -> string) -> string -> string
val tokens : (char -> bool) -> string -> string list
val fields : (char -> bool) -> string -> string list
```

```
val isPrefix    : string -> string -> bool
val isSubstring : string -> string -> bool
val isSuffix    : string -> string -> bool

val compare : string * string -> order
val collate : (char * char -> order)
                    -> string * string -> order
val <  : string * string -> bool
val <= : string * string -> bool
val >  : string * string -> bool
val >= : string * string -> bool

val toString : string -> String.string
val scan          : (char, 'a) StringCvt.reader
                      -> (string, 'a) StringCvt.reader
val fromString : String.string -> string option
val toCString : string -> String.string
val fromCString : String.string -> string option
```

Description

```
val maxSize : int
```

The longest allowed size of a string.

```
val size : string -> int
```

size s returns $|s|$, the number of characters in string s.

```
val sub : string * int -> char
```

sub (s, i) returns the ith character of s, counting from zero. This function raises Subscript if $i < 0$ or $|s| \leq i$.

```
val str : char -> string
```

str c is the string of size one containing the character c.

```
val extract : string * int * int option -> string
val substring : string * int * int -> string
```

extract (s, i, NONE)
extract $(s, i, \text{SOME } j)$
substring (s, i, j)
These functions return substrings of s. The first returns the substring of s from the ith character to the end of the string, i.e., the string $s[i..|s| - 1]$. This function raises

Subscript if $i < 0$ or $|s| < i$. The second form returns the substring of size j starting at index i, i.e., the string $s[i..i+j-1]$. It raises Subscript if $i < 0$ or $j < 0$ or $|s| < i + j$. Note that, if defined, extract returns the empty string when $i = |s|$.

The third form returns the substring $s[i..i+j-1]$, i.e., the substring of size j starting at index i. It equivalent to extract(s, i, SOME j).

Implementation note: Implementations of these functions must perform bounds checking in such a way that the Overflow exception is not raised.

val `^ : string * string -> string`

s `^` t is the concatenation of the strings s and t. This function raises Size if $|s| + |t| >$ maxSize.

val `concat : string list -> string`

concat l is the concatenation of all the strings in l. This function raises Size if the sum of all the sizes is greater than maxSize.

val `concatWith : string -> string list -> string`

concatWith s l returns the concatenation of the strings in the list l using the string s as a separator. This function raises Size if the size of the resulting string is greater than maxSize.

val `implode : char list -> string`

implode l generates the string containing the characters in the list l. This expression is equivalent to concat (List.map str l). This function raises Size if the resulting string has size greater than maxSize.

val `explode : string -> char list`

explode s is the list of characters in the string s.

val `map : (char -> char) -> string -> string`

map f s applies f to each element of s from left to right, returning the resulting string. It is equivalent to implode(List.map f (explode s)).

val `translate : (char -> string) -> string -> string`

translate f s returns the string generated from s by mapping each character in s by f. It is equivalent to concat(List.map f (explode s)).

```
val tokens : (char -> bool) -> string -> string list
val fields : (char -> bool) -> string -> string list
```

> tokens *f s*
> fields *f s*

These functions return a list of tokens or fields, respectively, derived from *s* from left to right. A token is a non-empty maximal substring of *s* not containing any delimiter. A field is a (possibly empty) maximal substring of *s* not containing any delimiter. In both cases, a delimiter is a character satisfying the predicate *f*.

Two tokens may be separated by more than one delimiter, whereas two fields are separated by exactly one delimiter. For example, if the delimiter is the character #"|", then the string "|abc||def" contains two tokens "abc" and "def", whereas it contains four fields "", "abc", "" and "def".

```
val isPrefix : string -> string -> bool
val isSubstring : string -> string -> bool
val isSuffix : string -> string -> bool
```

> isPrefix *s1 s2*
> isSubstring *s1 s2*
> isSuffix *s1 s2*

These functions return true if the string *s1* is a prefix, substring, or suffix (respectively) of the string *s2*. Note that the empty string is a prefix, substring, and suffix of any string, and that a string is a prefix, substring, and suffix of itself.

```
val compare : string * string -> order
```

> compare (*s*, *t*) does a lexicographic comparison of the two strings using the ordering Char.compare on the characters. It returns LESS, EQUAL, or GREATER if *s* is less than, equal to, or greater than *t*, respectively.

```
val collate : (char * char -> order)
                 -> string * string -> order
```

> collate *cmp* (*s*, *t*) performs a lexicographic comparison of the two strings using the given ordering *cmp* on characters.

```
val < : string * string -> bool
val <= : string * string -> bool
val > : string * string -> bool
val >= : string * string -> bool
```

> These functions compare two strings lexicographically, using the underlying ordering on the char type.

val toString : string -> String.string

> toString *s* returns a string corresponding to *s*, with non-printable characters replaced by SML escape sequences. This expression is equivalent to
>
>   translate Char.toString *s*

val scan : (char, 'a) StringCvt.reader
            -> (string, 'a) StringCvt.reader
val fromString : String.string -> string option

> scan *getc strm*
> fromString *s*
> These functions scan their character source as a sequence of printable characters, converting SML escape sequences into the appropriate characters. They do not skip leading whitespace. They return as many characters as can successfully be scanned, stopping when they reach the end of the source or a non-printing character (i.e., one not satisfying isPrint) or if they encounter an improper escape sequence. fromString ignores the remaining characters, while scan returns the remaining characters as the rest of the stream.
>
> The function fromString is equivalent to the StringCvt.scanString scan.
>
> If no conversion is possible, e.g., if the first character is non-printable or begins an illegal escape sequence, NONE is returned. Note, however, that fromString "" returns SOME("").
>
> For more information on the allowed escape sequences, see the entry for CHAR.fromString. SML source also allows escaped formatting sequences, which are ignored during conversion. The rule is that if any prefix of the input is successfully scanned, including an escaped formatting sequence, the functions returns some string. They only return NONE in the case where the prefix of the input cannot be scanned at all. Here are some sample conversions:

Input string *s*	fromString *s*
"\\q"	NONE
"a\^D"	SOME "a"
"a\\ \\\\q"	SOME "a"
"\\ \\"	SOME ""
""	SOME ""
"\\ \\\^D"	SOME ""
"\\ a"	NONE

Implementation note: Because of the special cases, such as fromString "" = SOME "", fromString "\\ \\\^D" = SOME "", and fromString "\^D" = NONE, the functions cannot be implemented as a simple iterative application of CHAR.scan.

val toCString : string -> String.string

> toCString *s* returns a string corresponding to *s*, with non-printable characters replaced by C escape sequences. This expression is equivalent to
>
>   translate Char.toCString *s*

val fromCString : String.string -> string option

> fromCString *s* scans the string *s* as a string in the C language, converting C escape sequences into the appropriate characters. The semantics are identical to fromString above, except that C escape sequences are used (see ISO Cstandard [ISO90]).
>
> For more information on the allowed escape sequences, see the entry for CHAR.from-CString. Note that fromCString accepts an unescaped single quote character but does not accept an unescaped double quote character.

See also

> CHAR (§11.8; p. 135), CharArray (§11.23; p. 193), CharVector (§11.26; p. 211), StringCvt (§11.55; p. 366), SUBSTRING (§11.56; p. 372), TEXT (§11.57; p. 380), WideCharArray (§11.23; p. 193), WideCharVector (§11.26; p. 211)

11.55   The `StringCvt` structure

The `StringCvt` structure provides types and functions for handling the conversion
between strings and values of various basic types.

Synopsis

```
signature STRING_CVT
structure StringCvt :> STRING_CVT
```

Interface

```
datatype radix = BIN | OCT | DEC | HEX
datatype realfmt
   = SCI of int option
   | FIX of int option
   | GEN of int option
   | EXACT

type ('a,'b) reader = 'b -> ('a * 'b) option

val padLeft  : char -> int -> string -> string
val padRight : char -> int -> string -> string

val splitl : (char -> bool)
                  -> (char, 'a) reader -> 'a -> string * 'a
val takel : (char -> bool)
                  -> (char, 'a) reader -> 'a -> string
val dropl : (char -> bool) -> (char, 'a) reader -> 'a -> 'a
val skipWS : (char, 'a) reader -> 'a -> 'a
type cs
val scanString : ((char, cs) reader -> ('a, cs) reader)
                     -> string -> 'a option
```

Description

```
datatype radix = BIN | OCT | DEC | HEX
```

> The values of type `radix` are used to specify the radix of a representation of an integer,
> corresponding to the bases 2, 8, 10, and 16, respectively.

```
datatype realfmt
   = SCI of int option
   | FIX of int option
   | GEN of int option
   | EXACT
```

> Values of type `realfmt` are used to specify the format of a string representation for a real
> or floating-point number.
>
> The first corresponds to scientific representation:

$$[\tilde{}]^{?}[0-9](.[0-9]^{+})^{?}E[0-9]^{+}$$

where there is always one digit before the decimal point, which is non-zero if the number is non-zero. The optional integer value specifies the number of decimal digits to appear after the decimal point, with six being the default. In particular, if zero is specified, there should be no fractional part. The exponent is zero if the value is zero.

The second corresponds to a fixed-point representation:

$$[\tilde{}]^{?}[0-9]^{+}(.[0-9]^{+})^{?}$$

where there is always at least one digit before the decimal point. The optional integer value specifies the number of decimal digits to appear after the decimal point, with six being the default. In particular, if zero is specified, there should be no fractional part.

The third constructor, GEN, allows a formatting function to use either the scientific or fixed-point notation, whichever is shorter, breaking ties in favor of fixed-point notation. The optional integer value specifies the maximum number of significant digits used, with 12 the default. The string should display as many significant digits as possible, subject to this maximum. There should not be any trailing zeros after the decimal point. There should not be a decimal point unless a fractional part is included.

The fourth constructor, EXACT, specifies that the string should represent the real using an exact decimal representation. The string contains enough information in order to reconstruct a semantically equivalent real value using REAL.fromDecimal o valOf o IEEEReal.fromString. Refer to the description of IEEEReal.toString for more precise information concerning this format.

In all cases, positive and negative infinities are converted to "inf" and "~inf", respectively, and NaN values are converted to the string "nan".

```
type ('a,'b) reader = 'b -> ('a * 'b) option
```

The type of a reader producing values of type $'a$ from a stream of type $'b$. A return value of SOME(a, b) corresponds to a value a scanned from the stream, plus the remainder b of the stream. A return value of NONE indicates that no value of the correct type could be scanned from the prefix of the stream.

The reader type is designed for use with a stream or functional view of I/O. Scanning functions using the reader type, such as skipWS, splitl, and Int.scan, will often use lookahead characters to determine when to stop scanning. If the character source ($'b$ in an ($'a$, $'b$) reader) is imperative, the lookahead characters will be lost to any subsequent scanning of the source. One mechanism for combining imperative I/O with the standard scanning functions is provided by the TextIO.scanStream function.

```
val padLeft  : char -> int -> string -> string
val padRight : char -> int -> string -> string
```

```
padLeft c i s
padRight c i s
```
These functions return s padded, on the left or right, respectively, with $i - |s|$ copies of the character c. If $|s| \geq i$, they just return the string s. In other words, these functions right- and left-justify s in a field i characters wide, never trimming off any part of s. Note

that if $i \leq 0$, s is returned. These functions raise `Size` if the size of the resulting string is greater than `String.maxSize`.

val `splitl : (char -> bool)`
`                -> (char, 'a) reader -> 'a -> string * 'a`

`splitl f rdr src` returns (*pref, src'*), where *pref* is the longest prefix (left substring) of *src*, as produced by the character reader *rdr*, all of whose characters satisfy *f*, and *src'* is the remainder of *src*. Thus, the first character retrievable from *src'* is the leftmost character not satisfying *f*.

   This function can be used with scanning functions such as `scanString` by composing it with SOME, e.g., `scanString (fn rdr => SOME o (splitl f rdr))`.

val `takel : (char -> bool)`
`                -> (char, 'a) reader -> 'a -> string`
val `dropl : (char -> bool) -> (char, 'a) reader -> 'a -> 'a`

`takel f rdr src`
`dropl f rdr src`
These routines scan the source *src* for the first character not satisfying the predicate *f*. The function `dropl` drops the maximal prefix consisting of characters satisfying the predicate, returning the rest of the source, while `takel` returns the maximal prefix consisting of characters satisfying the predicate. These can be defined in terms of `splitl`:

$$\text{takel } f \text{ } rdr \text{ } s \text{ = \#1(splitl } f \text{ } rdr \text{ } s)$$
$$\text{dropl } f \text{ } rdr \text{ } s \text{ = \#2(splitl } f \text{ } rdr \text{ } s)$$

val `skipWS : (char, 'a) reader -> 'a -> 'a`

`skipWS rdr src` strips whitespace characters from a stream *src* using the reader *rdr*. It returns the remaining stream. A whitespace character is one that satisfies the predicate `Char.isSpace`. It is equivalent to `dropl Char.isSpace`.

type `cs`

The abstract type of the character stream used by `scanString`. A value of this type represents the state of a character stream. The concrete type is left unspecified to allow implementations a choice of representations. Typically, `cs` will be an integer index into a string.

val `scanString : ((char, cs) reader -> ('a, cs) reader)`
`                -> string -> 'a option`

The function `scanString` provides a general framework for converting a string into some value. The user supplies a scanning function and a string. `scanString` converts the string into a character source (type `cs`) and applies the scanning function. A scanning function converts a reader of characters into a reader of values of the desired type. Typical scanning functions are `Bool.scan` and `Date.scan`.

Discussion

Implementation note: The SML Basis Library emphasizes a functional view for scanning values from text. This view provides a natural and elegant way to write simple scanners and parsers, especially as these typically involve some form of reading ahead and backtracking. The model involves two types of components: ways to produce character readers and functions to convert character readers into value readers. For the latter, most types `ty` have a corresponding scanning function of type

```
(char, 'a) reader -> (ty, 'a) reader
```

Character readers are provided for the common sources of characters, either explicitly, such as the `SUBSTRING.getc` and `STREAM_IO.input1` functions, or implicitly, such as the `TEXT_IO.scanStream`. As an example, suppose we expect to read a decimal integer followed by a date from `TextIO.stdIn`. This task could be handled by the following code:

```
local
  structure TIO = TextIO
  structure SIO = TextIO.StreamIO
  val scanInt = Int.scan StringCvt.DEC SIO.input1
  val scanDate = Date.scan SIO.input1
in
  fun scanID () = (case scanInt (TIO.getInstream TIO.stdIn)
       of NONE => raise Fail "No integer"
        | SOME(intVal, ins') => (case scanDate ins'
            of NONE => raise Fail "No date"
             | SOME (dateVal, _) => (intVal, dateVal)
          (* end case *))
        (* end case *))
end
```

In this example, we used the underlying stream I/O component of `TextIO.stdIn`, which is cleaner and more efficient. If, at some later point, we wish to return to the imperative model and do input directly using `TextIO.stdIn`, we need to reset it with the current stream I/O value using `TextIO.setInstream`. Alternatively, we could rewrite the code using imperative I/O:

```
local
  structure TIO = TextIO
  val scanInt = TIO.scanStream (Int.scan StringCvt.DEC)
  val scanDate = TIO.scanStream Date.scan
in
  fun scanID () = (case scanInt TIO.stdIn
       of NONE => raise Fail "No integer"
        | SOME intVal => (case scanDate TIO.stdIn
            of NONE => raise Fail "No date"
             | SOME dateVal => (intVal,dateVal)
          (* end case *))
        (* end case *))
end
```

The scanString function was designed specifically to be combined with the scan function of some type T, producing a function

val fromString : string -> T option

for the type. For this reason, scanString only returns a scanned value, and not some indication of where scanning stopped in the string. For the user who wants to receive a scanned value and the unscanned portion of a string, the recommended technique is to convert the string into a substring and combine scanning functions with Substring.getc, e.g., Bool.scan Substring.getc. Or, the user can create an input stream with TextIO.openString using the string as the source.

When the input source is a list of characters, scanning values can be accomplished by applying the appropriate scan function to the function List.getItem. Thus, Bool.scan List.getItem has the type

(bool, char list) reader

which will scan a boolean value and return that value and the remainder of the list.

Listing 11.1 provides a reference implementation for then StringCvt.GEN conversion.

See also

String (§11.54; p. 360), Char (§11.8; p. 135)

```
local
  structure S = String
  structure SS = Substring
  structure SC = StringCvt

  fun cvt (x,n) = let
        val (prefix, x) =
            if x < 0.0 then ("~", ~ x) else ("", x)
        val ss = SS.full (Real.fmt (SC.SCI (SOME (n - 1)))) x
        fun notE #"E" = false | notE _ = true
        fun isZero #"0" = true | isZero _ = false
        val expS = SS.string (SS.taker notE ss)
        val exp = valOf (Int.fromString expS)
        val manS =
            SS.string (SS.dropr isZero (SS.takel notE ss))
        fun transf #"." = ""
          | transf c = str c
        val man = S.translate transf manS
        val manSize = S.size man
        fun zeros i = CharVector.tabulate (i, fn _ => #"0")
        fun dotAt i = [S.substring (man, 0, i),
              ".", S.extract (man, i, NONE)]
        fun sci () = if manSize = 1
              then [prefix, man, "E", expS]
              else prefix :: (dotAt 1 @ ["E", expS])
      in
        if exp >= (if manSize = 1 then 3 else manSize + 3)
          then sci ()
        else if exp >= manSize - 1
          then [prefix, man, zeros (exp - (manSize - 1))]
        else if exp >= 0
          then prefix :: dotAt (exp + 1)
        else if exp >= (if manSize = 1 then ~2 else ~3)
          then [prefix, "0.", zeros(~exp - 1), man]
        else sci ()
      end
in
  fun gcvt (x: real, n: int): string = (case Real.class x
        of IEEEReal.INF => if x > 0.0 then "inf" else "~inf"
         | IEEEReal.NAN _ => "nan"
         | _ => concat (cvt (x, n))
      (* end case *))
end
```

Listing 11.1: Implementing StringCvt.GEN.

11.56   The SUBSTRING signature

The SUBSTRING signature specifies manipulations on an abstract representation of a sequence of contiguous characters embedded in a string. A substring value can be modeled as a triple $(s,\ i,\ n)$, where s is the underlying string, i is the starting index, and n is the size of the substring, with the constraint that $0 \le i \le i + n \le |s|$.

The substring type and its attendant functions provide a convenient abstraction for performing a variety of common analyses of strings, such as finding the leftmost occurrence, if any, of a character in a string. In addition, using the substring functions avoids much of the copying and bounds checking that occur if similar operations are implemented solely in terms of strings.

The SUBSTRING signature is matched by two structures, the required Substring and the optional WideSubstring. The former is a companion structure to the Char and String structures, which are based on the extended ASCII 8-bit character set. The structure WideSubstring is related in the same way to the structures Wide-Char and WideString, which are based on characters of some size greater than or equal to 8 bits. In particular, the types Substring.string and Substring.char are identical to those types in the structure String, and, when WideSubstring is defined, the types WideSubstring.string and WideSubstring.char are identical to those types in the structure WideString.

All of these connections are made explicit in the Text and WideText structures, which match the TEXT signature. In the exposition below, references to a String structure refer to the substructure of that name defined in either the Text or the Wide-Text structure, whichever is appropriate.

The design of the SUBSTRING interface was influenced by the paper "Subsequence References: First-Class Values for Substrings," by Wilfred J. Hansen [Han92].

Synopsis
```
signature SUBSTRING
structure Substring :> SUBSTRING
  where type substring = CharVectorSlice.slice
  where type string = String.string
  where type char = Char.char
structure WideSubstring :> SUBSTRING
  where type substring = WideCharVectorSlice.slice
  where type string = WideString.string
  where type char = WideChar.char
```

Interface
```
type substring
eqtype char
eqtype string

val size : substring -> int
```

```
val base : substring -> string * int * int
val isEmpty : substring -> bool

val sub : substring * int -> char
val getc : substring -> (char * substring) option
val first : substring -> char option

val extract    : string * int * int option -> substring
val substring : string * int * int -> substring
val slice : substring * int * int option -> substring
val full : string -> substring
val string : substring -> string

val concat : substring list -> string
val concatWith : string -> substring list -> string

val explode : substring -> char list
val translate : (char -> string) -> substring -> string
val app : (char -> unit) -> substring -> unit
val foldl : (char * 'a -> 'a) -> 'a -> substring -> 'a
val foldr : (char * 'a -> 'a) -> 'a -> substring -> 'a
val tokens : (char -> bool) -> substring -> substring list
val fields : (char -> bool) -> substring -> substring list
val isPrefix    : string -> substring -> bool
val isSubstring : string -> substring -> bool
val isSuffix    : string -> substring -> bool

val compare : substring * substring -> order
val collate : (char * char -> order)
                    -> substring * substring -> order

val triml : int -> substring -> substring
val trimr : int -> substring -> substring
val splitl : (char -> bool)
                -> substring -> substring * substring
val splitr : (char -> bool)
                -> substring -> substring * substring
val splitAt : substring * int -> substring * substring
val dropl : (char -> bool) -> substring -> substring
val dropr : (char -> bool) -> substring -> substring
val takel : (char -> bool) -> substring -> substring
val taker : (char -> bool) -> substring -> substring
val position : string -> substring -> substring * substring

val span : substring * substring -> substring
```

Description

val size : substring -> int

>size *s* returns the size of *s*. This function is equivalent to both #3 o base and String.size o string.

val base : substring -> string * int * int

>base *ss* returns a triple (*s*, *i*, *n*) giving a concrete representation of the substring. *s* is the underlying string, *i* is the starting index, and *n* is the size of the substring. It will always be the case that $0 \leq i \leq i + n \leq |s|$.

val isEmpty : substring -> bool

>isEmpty *s* returns true if *s* has size 0.

val sub : substring * int -> char

>sub (*s*, *i*) returns the ith character in the substring, counting from the beginning of *s*. It is equivalent to String.sub(string *s*, *i*). The exception Subscript is raised unless $0 \leq i < |s|$.

val getc : substring -> (char * substring) option

>getc *s* returns the first character in *s* and the rest of the substring, or NONE if *s* is empty.

val first : substring -> char option

>first *s* returns the first character in *s*, or NONE if *s* is empty.

val extract : string * int * int option -> substring
val substring : string * int * int -> substring

>extract (*s*, *i*, NONE)
>extract (*s*, *i*, SOME *j*)
>substring (*s*, *i*, *j*)
>The first returns the substring of *s* from the ith character to the end of the string, i.e., the string $s[i..|s| - 1]$. This function raises Subscript unless $0 \leq i \leq |s|$. The second form returns the substring of size *j* starting at index *i*, i.e., the string $s[i..i+j-1]$. It raises Subscript if $i < 0$ or $j < 0$ or $|s| < i + j$. Note that, if defined, extract returns the empty substring when $i = |s|$.
>
>The third form returns the substring $s[i..i+j-1]$, i.e., the substring of size *j* starting at index *i*. This form is equivalent to extract(*s*, *i*, SOME *j*).
>
>We require that base o substring be the identity function on valid arguments.

Implementation note: Implementations of these functions must perform bounds checking in such a way that the `Overflow` exception is not raised.

val `slice : substring * int * int option -> substring`

> `slice (s, i, SOME m)`
> `slice (s, i, NONE)`
> These functions return a substring of s starting at the ith character. In the former case, the size of the resulting substring is m. Otherwise, the size is $|s| - i$. To be valid, the arguments in the first case must satisfy $0 \leq i$, $0 \leq m$, and $i + m \leq |s|$. In the second case, the arguments must satisfy $0 \leq i \leq |s|$. If the arguments are not valid, the exception `Subscript` is raised.

val `full : string -> substring`

> `full s` creates a substring representing the entire string s. It is equivalent to the expression `substring(s, 0, String.size s)`.

val `string : substring -> string`

> `string s` creates a string value corresponding to the substring. It is equivalent to `String.substring o base` for the corresponding `String` structure.

val `concat : substring list -> string`

> `concat l` generates a string that is the concatenation of the substrings in l. This function is equivalent to `String.concat o (List.map string)`. This function raises `Size` if the sum of all the sizes is greater than the corresponding `maxSize` for the `string` type.

val `concatWith : string -> substring list -> string`

> `concatWith s l` returns the concatenation of the substrings in the list l using the string s as a separator. This function raises `Size` if the size of the resulting string is greater than `maxSize` for the `string` type.

val `explode : substring -> char list`

> `explode s` returns the list of characters composing the substring. This expression is equivalent to `String.explode (string s)`.

val `translate : (char -> string) -> substring -> string`

> `translate f s` applies f to every character of s, from left to right, and returns the concatenation of the results. This expression is equivalent to `String.concat(List.-map f (explode s))`.

val app : (char -> unit) -> substring -> unit

> app *f* *s* applies *f* to each character of *s* from left to right. It is equivalent to List.-app *f* (explode *s*).

val foldl : (char * 'a -> 'a) -> 'a -> substring -> 'a
val foldr : (char * 'a -> 'a) -> 'a -> substring -> 'a

> foldl *f* *a* *s*
> foldr *f* *a* *s*
> These fold the function *f* over the substring *s*, starting with the value *a*, from left to right and from right to left, respectively. They are the analogues of the identically named functions in the List structure. In particular, they are respectively equivalent to:

$$\text{List.foldl } f\ a\ (\text{explode } s)$$
$$\text{List.foldr } f\ a\ (\text{explode } s)$$

val tokens : (char -> bool) -> substring -> substring list
val fields : (char -> bool) -> substring -> substring list

> tokens *f* *s*
> fields *f* *s*
> These functions decompose a substring into a list of tokens or fields from left to right. A token is a non-empty maximal substring not containing any delimiter. A field is a (possibly empty) maximal substring of *s* not containing any delimiter. In both cases, a delimiter is a character satisfying predicate *f*.
>
> Two tokens may be separated by more than one delimiter, whereas two fields are separated by exactly one delimiter. For example, if the delimiter is the character #"|", then the string "|abc||def" contains two tokens "abc" and "def", whereas it contains four fields "", "abc", "" and "def".

val isPrefix : string -> substring -> bool
val isSubstring : string -> substring -> bool
val isSuffix : string -> substring -> bool

> isPrefix *s* *ss*
> isSubstring *s* *ss*
> isSuffix *s* *ss*
> These functions return true if the string *s* is a prefix, substring, or suffix (respectively) of the substring *ss*. The functions are equivalent to their versions from STRING. For example, isPrefix *s* *ss* is the same as String.isPrefix *s* (string *ss*).

val compare : substring * substring -> order

> compare (*s*, *t*) compares the two substrings lexicographically using the default character comparison function. This expression is equivalent to

$$\text{String.compare (string } s, \text{ string } t)$$

```
val collate : (char * char -> order)
                 -> substring * substring -> order
```

collate *cmp* (*s*, *t*) compares the two substrings lexicographically using the character comparison function *cmp*. This expression is equivalent to

```
       String.collate f (string s, string t)
```

```
val triml : int -> substring -> substring
val trimr : int -> substring -> substring
```

 triml *k s*
 trimr *k s*
These functions remove *k* characters from the left (respectively, right) of the substring *s*. If *k* is greater than the size of the substring, an empty substring is returned. Specifically, for substring *ss* = substring(*s*, *i*, *j*) and *k* ≤ *j*, we have:

```
            triml k ss = substring(s, i+k, j-k)
            trimr k ss = substring(s, i, j-k)
```

The exception Subscript is raised if *k* < 0. This exception is raised when triml *k* or trimr *k* is evaluated.

```
val splitl : (char -> bool)
                 -> substring -> substring * substring
val splitr : (char -> bool)
                 -> substring -> substring * substring
```

 splitl *f s*
 splitr *f s*
These functions scan *s* from left to right (respectively, right to left) looking for the first character that does not satisfy the predicate *f*. They return the pair (*ls*, *rs*) giving the split of the substring into the span up to that character and the rest. *ls* is the left side of the split, and *rs* is the right side. For example, if the characters a and c satisfy the predicate, but character X does not, then these functions work as follows on the substring aaaXbbbbXccc:

```
            splitl    :            aaa         XbbbbXccc
            splitr    :            aaaXbbbbX   ccc
```

```
val splitAt : substring * int -> substring * substring
```

splitAt (*s*, *i*) returns the pair of substrings (*ss*, *ss′*), where *ss* contains the first *i* characters of *s* and *ss′* contains the rest, assuming 0 ≤ *i* ≤ size *s*. Otherwise, it raises Subscript.

```
val dropl : (char -> bool) -> substring -> substring
val dropr : (char -> bool) -> substring -> substring
val takel : (char -> bool) -> substring -> substring
val taker : (char -> bool) -> substring -> substring
```

> dropl *f s*
> dropr *f s*
> takel *f s*
> taker *f s*

These routines scan the substring *s* for the first character not satisfying the predicate *p*. The functions dropl and takel scan left to right (i.e., increasing character indices), while dropr and taker scan from the right. The drop functions drop the maximal substring consisting of characters satisfying the predicate, while the take functions return the maximal such substring. These can be defined in terms of the split operations:

$$\begin{array}{rcl} \texttt{takel } p\ s & = & \texttt{\#1(splitl } p\ s\texttt{)} \\ \texttt{dropl } p\ s & = & \texttt{\#2(splitl } p\ s\texttt{)} \\ \texttt{taker } p\ s & = & \texttt{\#2(splitr } p\ s\texttt{)} \\ \texttt{dropr } p\ s & = & \texttt{\#1(splitr } p\ s\texttt{)} \end{array}$$

```
val position : string -> substring -> substring * substring
```

position *s ss* splits the substring *ss* into a pair (*pref*, *suff*) of substrings, where *suff* is the longest suffix of *ss* that has *s* as a prefix and *pref* is the prefix of *ss* preceding *suff*. More precisely, let *m* be the size of *s* and let *ss* correspond to the substring (*s'*, *i*, *n*). If there is a least index *k* ≥ *i* such that *s* = *s'*[*k*..*k*+*m*-1], then *suff* corresponds to (*s'*, *k*, *n*+*i*-*k*) and *pref* corresponds to (*s'*, *i*, *k*-*i*). If there is no such *k*, then *suff* is the empty substring corresponding to (*s'*, *i*+*n*, 0) and *pref* corresponds to (*s'*, *i*, *n*), i.e., all of *ss*.

```
val span : substring * substring -> substring
```

span (*ss*, *ss'*) produces a substring composed of a prefix *ss*, a suffix *ss'*, plus all intermediate characters in the underlying string. It raises Span if *ss* and *ss'* are not substrings of the same underlying string or if the start of *ss* is to the right of the end of *ss'*. More precisely, if we have

> **val** (s, i, n) = base *ss*
> **val** (s', i', n') = base *ss'*

then span returns substring(s, i, (i'+n')-i) unless s <> s' or i'+n' < i, in which case it raises Span. Note that this condition does not preclude *ss'* from beginning to the left of *ss* or *ss* from ending to the right of *ss'*.

This function allows one to scan for a substring using multiple pieces and then coalescing the pieces. For example, given a URL string such as

> "http://www.standardml.org/Basis/overview.html"

to scan the protocol and host ("http://www.standardml.org"), one could write:

```
local
  open Substring
in
  fun protoAndHost url = let
        fun notc (c : char) = fn c' => c <> c'
        val (proto,rest) = splitl (notc #":") (full url)
        val host = takel (notc #"/") (triml 3 rest)
      in
        span (proto, host)
      end
end
```

Implementation note: When applied to substrings derived from the identical base string, the string equality test should be constant-time, which can be achieved by first doing a pointer test and, only if that fails, then checking the strings character by character.

Discussion

Implementation note: Functions that extract pieces of a substring, such as splitl or tokens, must return substrings with the same base string. This requirement is particularly important if span is to be used to put the pieces back together again.

See also

CHAR (§11.8; p. 135), List (§11.20; p. 180), STRING (§11.54; p. 360), StringCvt (§11.55; p. 366), TEXT (§11.57; p. 380)

11.57   The TEXT signature

The TEXT signature collects together various text-related structures based on the representation of the shared character type.

The TEXT signature is matched by two structures, the required Text and the optional WideText. The former implements strings based on the extended ASCII 8-bit characters and the latter provides strings of characters of some size greater than or equal to 8 bits.

Synopsis

```
signature TEXT
structure Text :> TEXT
  where type Char.char = Char.char
  where type String.string = String.string
  where type Substring.substring = Substring.substring
  where type CharVector.vector = CharVector.vector
  where type CharArray.array = CharArray.array
  where type CharVectorSlice.slice = CharVectorSlice.slice
  where type CharArraySlice.slice = CharArraySlice.slice
structure WideText :> TEXT
  where type Char.char = WideChar.char
  where type String.string = WideString.string
  where type Substring.substring = WideSubstring.substring
  where type CharVector.vector = WideCharVector.vector
  where type CharArray.array = WideCharArray.array
  where type CharVectorSlice.slice = WideCharVectorSlice.slice
  where type CharArraySlice.slice = WideCharArraySlice.slice
```

Interface

```
structure Char : CHAR
structure String : STRING
structure Substring : SUBSTRING
structure CharVector : MONO_VECTOR
structure CharArray : MONO_ARRAY
structure CharVectorSlice : MONO_VECTOR_SLICE
structure CharArraySlice : MONO_ARRAY_SLICE
sharing type Char.char = String.char = Substring.char
  = CharVector.elem = CharArray.elem = CharVectorSlice.elem
  = CharArraySlice.elem
sharing type Char.string = String.string = Substring.string
  = CharVector.vector = CharArray.vector
  = CharVectorSlice.vector = CharArraySlice.vector
sharing type CharArray.array = CharArraySlice.array
sharing type CharVectorSlice.slice
  = CharArraySlice.vector_slice
```

See also

CHAR (§11.8; p. 135), MONO_ARRAY (§11.23; p. 193), MONO_VECTOR (§11.26; p. 211), STRING (§11.54; p. 360), SUBSTRING (§11.56; p. 372)

11.58   The TEXT_IO signature

The TEXT_IO interface provides input/output of characters and strings. Most of the operations themselves are defined in the IMPERATIVE_IO signature.

The TEXT_IO signature is matched by two structures, the required TextIO and the optional WideTextIO. The former implements strings based on the extended ASCII 8-bit characters and the latter provides strings of characters of some size greater than or equal to 8 bits.

The signature given below for TEXT_IO is not valid SML, in that the substructure StreamIO is respecified. (It is initially specified as a substructure having the signature STREAM_IO in the included signature IMPERATIVE_IO.) This abuse of notation seems acceptable in that the intended meaning is clear (a structure matching TEXT_IO also matches IMPERATIVE_IO and has a substructure StreamIO that matches TEXT_STREAM_IO) while avoiding a textual inclusion of the whole signature of IMPERATIVE_IO except its StreamIO substructure.

Synopsis

```
signature TEXT_IO
structure TextIO :> TEXT_IO
structure WideTextIO :> TEXT_IO
```

Interface

```
include IMPERATIVE_IO

structure StreamIO : TEXT_STREAM_IO
  where type reader = TextPrimIO.reader
  where type writer = TextPrimIO.writer
  where type pos = TextPrimIO.pos

val inputLine : instream -> string option

val outputSubstr : outstream * substring -> unit

val openIn  : string -> instream
val openOut : string -> outstream
val openAppend : string -> outstream
val openString : string -> instream

val stdIn  : instream
val stdOut : outstream
val stdErr : outstream

val print : string -> unit
```

```
val scanStream : ((Char.char, StreamIO.instream)
                       StringCvt.reader
                   -> ('a, StreamIO.instream)
                       StringCvt.reader)
                -> instream -> 'a option
```

Description

```
val inputLine : instream -> string option
```

> inputLine *strm* returns SOME(*ln*), where *ln* is the next line of input in the stream *strm*. Specifically, *ln* returns all characters from the current position up to and including the next newline (`#"\n"`) character. If it detects an end-of-stream before the next newline, it returns the characters read appended with a newline. Thus, *ln* is guaranteed to always be new-line terminated (and thus non-empty). If the current stream position is the end-of-stream, then it returns NONE. It raises `Size` if the length of the line exceeds the length of the longest string.

```
val outputSubstr : outstream * substring -> unit
```

> outputSubstr (*strm*, *ss*) outputs the substring *ss* to the text stream *strm*. This expression is equivalent to:
> $$\text{output } (strm, \text{ Substring.string } ss)$$

```
val openIn : string -> instream
val openOut : string -> outstream
```

> openIn *name*
> openOut *name*
> These functions open the file named *name* for input and output, respectively. If *name* is a relative pathname, the file opened depends on the current working directory. For the function openOut, the file is created if it does not already exist and is truncated to length zero otherwise. It raises `Io` if a stream cannot be opened on the given file or, in the case of openIn, the file *name* does not exist.

```
val openAppend : string -> outstream
```

> openAppend *name* opens the file named *name* for output in append mode, creating it if it does not already exist. If the file already exists, the file pointer is positioned at the end of the file. It raises `Io` if a stream cannot be opened on the given file.
>
> Beyond having the initial file position be at the end of the file, any additional properties are system and implementation dependent. On operating systems (e.g., Unix) that support an "atomic append mode," each (flushed) output operation to the file will be appended to the end, even if there are other processes writing to the file simultaneously. Due to buffering, however, these writes need not be atomic, i.e., output from a different process may interleave the output of a single write using the stream library. On certain other operating systems, having the file open for writing prevents any other process from opening the file for writing.

val openString : string -> instream

openString *s* creates an input stream whose content is *s*.

val stdIn : instream
val stdOut : outstream
val stdErr : outstream

These correspond to the standard input, output, and error streams, respectively.

val print : string -> unit

print *s* prints the string *s* to the standard output stream and flushes the stream. No newline character is appended. It is equivalent to the expression:
```
(output (stdOut, s); flushOut stdOut)
```
This function is available in the top-level environment as print.

val scanStream : ((Char.char, StreamIO.instream)
                        StringCvt.reader
                  -> ('a, StreamIO.instream)
                        StringCvt.reader)
               -> instream -> 'a option

scanStream *scanFn* converts a stream-based scan function into one that works on imperative I/O streams. For example, to attempt to scan a decimal integer from stdIn, one could use the expression
```
scanStream (Int.scan StringCvt.DEC) stdIn
```
The function can be implemented as:
```
fun scanStream scanFn strm = let
      val instrm = getInstream strm
    in
      case (scanFn StreamIO.input1 instrm)
       of NONE => NONE
        | SOME(v, instrm') => (
            setInstream (strm, instrm');
            SOME v)
    end
```
In addition to providing a convenient way to use stream I/O scanning functions with imperative I/O, the scanStream assures that input is not inadvertently lost due to lookahead during scanning.

Discussion

All streams created by mkInstream, mkOutstream, and the open functions in Text-IO will be closed (and the output streams among them flushed) when the SML program exits. The output streams TextIO.stdOut and TextIO.stdErr will be flushed, but not closed, on program exit.

When opening a stream for writing, the stream will be block buffered by default, unless the underlying file is associated with an interactive or terminal device (i.e., the kind of the underlying `iodesc` is `OS.IO.Kind.tty`), in which case the stream will be line buffered. Similarly, `stdOut` will be line buffered in the interactive case but may be block buffered otherwise. The `stdErr` stream is initially unbuffered.

The `openIn`, `openOut`, and `openAppend` functions allow the creation of text streams. Certain implementations may provide other ways to open files in structures specific to an operating system. In such cases, there should be related functions for converting the open file into a value compatible with the Basis I/O subsystem. For example, the `Posix.IO` defines the function `mkTextWriter`, which generates a `TextPrimIO.writer` value from a POSIX file descriptor. The `TextIO.StreamIO.mkOutstream` function can use that value to produce an output stream.

See also

`IMPERATIVE_IO` (§11.14; p. 158), `OS.Path` (§11.35; p. 241),
`STREAM_IO` (§11.52; p. 346), `TEXT` (§11.57; p. 380),
`TEXT_STREAM_IO` (§11.59; p. 386), `TextPrimIO` (§11.48; p. 308)

11.59   The `TEXT_STREAM_IO` signature

The signature `TEXT_STREAM_IO` extends the `STREAM_IO` signature to accommodate text I/O. In particular, it binds the I/O element to `Char.char` and provides several text-based I/O operations.

Synopsis
```
signature TEXT_STREAM_IO
```

Interface
```
include STREAM_IO
  where type vector = CharVector.vector
  where type elem = Char.char

val inputLine : instream -> (string * instream) option

val outputSubstr : outstream * substring -> unit
```

Description

```
val inputLine : instream -> (string * instream) option
```

> `inputLine` *strm* returns `SOME(`*ln, strm′*`)`, where *ln* is the next line of input in the stream *strm* and *strm′* is the residual stream. Specifically, *ln* returns all characters from the current position up to and including the next newline (`#"\n"`) character. If it detects an end-of-stream before the next newline, it returns the characters read appended with a newline. Thus, *ln* is guaranteed to always be new-line terminated (and thus non-empty). If the current stream position is the end-of-stream, then it returns `NONE`. It raises `Size` if the length of the line exceeds the length of the longest string.

```
val outputSubstr : outstream * substring -> unit
```

> `outputSubstr (`*strm, ss*`)` outputs the substring *ss* to the text stream *strm*. This expression is equivalent to:
>
> ```
>           output (strm, Substring.string ss)
> ```

See also

> `BinIO` (§11.4; p. 127), `IMPERATIVE_IO` (§11.14; p. 158), `OS.Path` (§11.35; p. 241)

11.60   The `Time` structure

The structure `Time` provides an abstract type for representing times and time intervals and functions for manipulating, converting, writing, and reading them.

Synopsis

```
signature TIME
structure Time :> TIME
```

Interface

```
eqtype time
exception Time
val zeroTime : time
val fromReal : LargeReal.real -> time
val toReal : time -> LargeReal.real
val toSeconds        : time -> LargeInt.int
val toMilliseconds : time -> LargeInt.int
val toMicroseconds : time -> LargeInt.int
val toNanoseconds    : time -> LargeInt.int
val fromSeconds        : LargeInt.int -> time
val fromMilliseconds : LargeInt.int -> time
val fromMicroseconds : LargeInt.int -> time
val fromNanoseconds    : LargeInt.int -> time

val + : time * time -> time
val - : time * time -> time

val compare : time * time -> order
val <  : time * time -> bool
val <= : time * time -> bool
val >  : time * time -> bool
val >= : time * time -> bool

val now : unit -> time

val fmt       : int -> time -> string
val toString : time -> string
val scan        : (char, 'a) StringCvt.reader
                    -> (time, 'a) StringCvt.reader
val fromString : string -> time option
```

Description

`eqtype time`

> The type used to represent both absolute times and durations of time intervals, including negative values moving to the past. Absolute times are represented in the same way as time intervals and can be thought of as time intervals starting at some fixed reference

point. Their discrimination is only conceptual. Consequently, operations can be applied to all meaningful combinations (but also meaningless ones) of absolute times and intervals.

Implementation note: The precision and range of time values is implementation dependent, but they are required to have fixed-point semantics. When converting a number to a time value, rounding toward zero may occur because of precision limits. Furthermore, if the number is outside the range of representable time values, then the `Time` exception is raised.

exception `Time`

The exception raised when the result of conversions to `time` or of operations over `time` is not representable or when an illegal operation has been attempted.

val `zeroTime : time`

This value denotes both the empty time interval and a common reference point for specifying absolute time values. It is equivalent to `fromReal(0.0)`.

Absolute points on the time scale can be thought of as being represented as intervals starting at `zeroTime`. The function `Date.fromTimeLocal` can be used to see what time `zeroTime` actually represents in the local time zone.

val `fromReal : LargeReal.real -> time`

`fromReal` r converts the real number r to the time value denoting r seconds. Depending on the resolution of `time`, fractions of a microsecond may be lost. It raises `Time` when the result is not representable.

val `toReal : time -> LargeReal.real`

`toReal` t converts the time value t to a real number denoting the value of t in seconds. When the type `real` has less precision than `Time.time` (for example, when it is implemented as a single-precision float), information about microseconds or, for very large values, even seconds, may be lost.

val `toSeconds : time -> LargeInt.int`
val `toMilliseconds : time -> LargeInt.int`
val `toMicroseconds : time -> LargeInt.int`
val `toNanoseconds : time -> LargeInt.int`

```
toSeconds t
toMilliseconds t
toMicroseconds t
toNanoseconds t
```
These functions return the number of full seconds (respectively, milliseconds, microseconds, or nanoseconds) in t; fractions of the time unit are dropped, i.e., the values are rounded towards zero. Thus, if t denotes 2.01 seconds, the functions return 2, 2010, 2010000, and 2010000000, respectively. When the result is not representable by `LargeInt.int`, the exception `Overflow` is raised.

```
val fromSeconds : LargeInt.int -> time
val fromMilliseconds : LargeInt.int -> time
val fromMicroseconds : LargeInt.int -> time
val fromNanoseconds : LargeInt.int -> time
```

> fromSeconds *n*
> fromMilliseconds *n*
> fromMicroseconds *n*
> fromNanoseconds *n*

These convert the number n to a time value denoting n seconds (respectively, milliseconds, microseconds, or nanoseconds). If the result is not representable by the time type, then the exception Time is raised.

```
val + : time * time -> time
```

> $t1$ + $t2$ returns a time interval denoting the duration of $t1$ plus that of $t2$, when both $t1$ and $t2$ are interpreted as intervals. Equivalently, when $t1$ is interpreted as an absolute time and $t2$ as an interval, the absolute time that is $t2$ later than $t1$ is returned. (Both views are equivalent as absolute times are represented as intervals from zeroTime). When the result is not representable as a time value, the exception Time is raised. This operation is commutative.

```
val - : time * time -> time
```

> $t1$ - $t2$ returns a time interval denoting the duration of $t1$ minus that of $t2$, when both $t1$ and $t2$ are interpreted as intervals. Equivalently, when $t1$ is interpreted as an absolute time and $t2$ as an interval, the absolute time that is $t2$ earlier than $t1$ is returned; when both $t1$ and $t2$ are interpreted as absolute times, the interval between $t1$ and $t2$ is returned. (All views are equivalent as absolute times are represented as intervals from zeroTime). When the result is not representable as a time value, the exception Time is raised.

```
val compare : time * time -> order
```

> compare ($t1$, $t2$) returns LESS, EQUAL, or GREATER when the time interval $t1$ is shorter than, of the same length as, or longer than $t2$, respectively, or the absolute time $t1$ is earlier than, coincides with, or is later than the absolute time $t2$.

```
val < : time * time -> bool
val <= : time * time -> bool
val > : time * time -> bool
val >= : time * time -> bool
```

These functions return true if the corresponding relation holds between the two times.

val now : unit -> time

The current time, which is interpreted as an absolute time, the time at which the function call was made. Although now does not normally raise an exception, some implementations may raise Time if the time is not representable.

val fmt : int -> time -> string
val toString : time -> string

    fmt *n t*
    toString *t*
These functions return a string containing a decimal number representing *t* in seconds. Using fmt, the fractional part is rounded to *n* decimal digits. If $n = 0$, there should be no fractional part. Having $n < 0$ causes the Size exception to be raised. The toString function rounds its argument to three decimal digits. It is equivalent to fmt 3.

Example:
                    fmt 3 (fromReal 1.8) = "1.800"
                    fmt 0 (fromReal 1.8) = "2"
                    fmt 0 zeroTime = "0"

val scan : (char, 'a) StringCvt.reader
                 -> (time, 'a) StringCvt.reader
val fromString : string -> time option

    scan *getc src*
    fromString *s*
These functions scan a time value from a character stream or a string. They recognize a number of seconds specified as a string that matches the regular expression:

$$[+\tilde{}-]^?([0-9]^+(.[0-9]^+)^? \mid .[0-9]^+)$$

Initial whitespace is ignored. Both functions raise Time when the value is syntactically correct but not representable.

The function scan takes a character source *src* and a reader *getc* and tries to parse a time value from *src*. It returns SOME(*t*, *r*), where *t* is the time value denoted by a prefix of *src* and *r* is the rest of *src*; or it returns NONE when no prefix of *src* is a representation of a time value.

The function fromString parses a time value from the string *s*, returning SOME(*t*), where *t* is the time value denoted by a prefix of *s* or NONE when no prefix of *s* is a representation of a time value. Note that this function is equivalent to StringCvt.-scanString scan.

See also
Date (§11.10; p. 144), StringCvt (§11.55; p. 366), Timer (§11.61; p. 391)

11.61   The `Timer` structure

The `Timer` structure provides facilities for measuring the passing of real or wall clock time. The module also tracks the CPU time used by a process, noting especially the amount of time spent in garbage collection (GC time) and the time used for system calls in the operating system kernel (system time).

Synopsis

```
signature TIMER
structure Timer :> TIMER
```

Interface

```
type real_timer
type cpu_timer

val startRealTimer : unit -> real_timer
val checkRealTimer : real_timer -> Time.time
val totalRealTimer : unit -> real_timer

val startCPUTimer : unit -> cpu_timer
val checkCPUTimes : cpu_timer
                         -> {
                             nongc : {
                                 usr : Time.time,
                                 sys : Time.time
                             },
                             gc : {
                                 usr : Time.time,
                                 sys : Time.time
                             }
                         }
val checkCPUTimer : cpu_timer
                         -> {usr : Time.time, sys : Time.time}
val checkGCTime : cpu_timer -> Time.time
val totalCPUTimer : unit -> cpu_timer
```

Description

```
type real_timer
```

> This type is the representation of a timer that measures real or wall clock time.

```
type cpu_timer
```

> This type is the representation of a timer that measures CPU time, in particular, keeping track of system and GC time.

val `startRealTimer : unit -> real_timer`

This function returns a timer that measures how much real or wall clock time has passed, starting from the time of this call.

val `checkRealTimer : real_timer -> Time.time`

`checkRealTimer` *rt* returns the amount of (real) time that has passed since the timer *rt* was started.

val `totalRealTimer : unit -> real_timer`

This function returns a timer that measures how much real or wall clock time has passed, starting from some system-dependent initialization time.

val `startCPUTimer : unit -> cpu_timer`

This function returns a CPU timer that measures the time the process is computing (has control of the CPU) starting at this call.

val `checkCPUTimes : cpu_timer`
```
                  -> {
                      nongc : {
                          usr : Time.time,
                          sys : Time.time
                      },
                      gc : {
                          usr : Time.time,
                          sys : Time.time
                      }
                  }
```

`checkCPUTimes` *timer* returns the CPU time used by the program since the *timer* was started. The time is split into time spent in the program (`nongc`) and time spent in the garbage collector (`gc`). For each of these categories, the time is further split into time spent in the operating system kernel on behalf of the program (`sys`), and time spent by code in *user space* (`usr`), i.e., not in the kernel. The total CPU time used by the program will be the sum of these four values.

val `checkCPUTimer : cpu_timer`
```
                      -> {usr : Time.time, sys : Time.time}
```

`checkCPUTimer` *timer* returns the user time (`usr`) and system time (`sys`) that have accumulated since the timer *timer* was started. This function is equivalent to

```
fun checkCPUTimer ct = let
        val {nongc, gc} = checkCPUTimes ct
        in {
          usr = Time.+(#usr nongc, #usr gc),
          sys = Time.+(#sys nongc, #sys gc)
        } end
```

val checkGCTime : cpu_timer -> Time.time

checkGCTime *timer* returns the user time spent in garbage collection since the timer *timer* was started. This function is equivalent to

```
fun checkGCTime ct = #usr(#gc(checkCPUTimes ct))
```

val totalCPUTimer : unit -> cpu_timer

This function returns a CPU timer that measures the time the process is computing (has control of the CPU) starting at some system-dependent initialization time.

Discussion

The accuracy of the user, system, and GC times depends on the resolution of the system timer and the function call overhead in the OS interface. In particular, very small intervals might not be reported accurately.

On a Unix system, the user and system times reported by a CPU timer do not include the time spent in child processes.

Implementation note: Some operating systems may lack the ability to measure CPU time consumption, in which case the real time should be returned instead.

See also

Time (§11.60; p. 387)

11.62   The Unix structure

The Unix structure provides several high-level functions for creating and communicating with separate processes, in analogy with the popen interface provided in the Unix operating system. This module provides a more flexible interface than that provided by the OS.Process.system function. Using this module, a program can invoke a separate process and obtain input and output streams connected to the standard output and input streams, respectively, of the other process.

Synopsis

```
signature UNIX
structure Unix :> UNIX
```

Interface

```
type ('a,'b) proc
type signal

datatype exit_status
  = W_EXITED
  | W_EXITSTATUS of Word8.word
  | W_SIGNALED of signal
  | W_STOPPED of signal

val fromStatus : OS.Process.status -> exit_status

val executeInEnv : string * string list * string list
                       -> ('a, 'b) proc
val execute : string * string list -> ('a, 'b) proc

val textInstreamOf : (TextIO.instream, 'a) proc
                         -> TextIO.instream
val binInstreamOf  : (BinIO.instream, 'a) proc
                         -> BinIO.instream
val textOutstreamOf : ('a, TextIO.outstream) proc
                         -> TextIO.outstream
val binOutstreamOf  : ('a, BinIO.outstream) proc
                         -> BinIO.outstream
val streamsOf : (TextIO.instream, TextIO.outstream) proc
                   -> TextIO.instream * TextIO.outstream

val reap : ('a, 'b) proc -> OS.Process.status
val kill : ('a, 'b) proc * signal -> unit

val exit : Word8.word -> 'a
```

Description

type ('a,'b) proc

A type representing a handle for an operating system process.

type signal

A Unix-like signal that can be sent to another process. Note that signal values must be obtained from some other structure. For example, an implementation providing the Posix module should equate the signal and Posix.Signal.signal types.

datatype exit_status
```
= W_EXITED
| W_EXITSTATUS of Word8.word
| W_SIGNALED of signal
| W_STOPPED of signal
```

These values represent the ways in which a Unix process might stop. They correspond to, respectively, successful termination, termination with the given exit value, termination upon receipt of the given signal, and stopping upon receipt of the given signal. The value carried by W_EXITSTATUS will be non-zero.

If an implementation provides both the Posix and Unix structures, then Posix.-Process.exit_status and exit_status must be the same type.

val fromStatus : OS.Process.status -> exit_status

fromStatus *sts* returns a concrete view of the given status.

val executeInEnv : string * string list * string list
                    -> ('a, 'b) proc

executeInEnv (*cmd*, *args*, *env*) asks the operating system to execute the program named by the string *cmd* with the argument list *args* and the environment *env*. The program is run as a child process of the calling program; the return value of this function is an abstract proc value naming the child process. Strings in the *env* list typically have the form "name=value" (see OS.Process.getEnv).

The executeInEnv function raises the OS.SysErr exception if it fails. Reasons for failure include insufficient memory, too many processes, and the case where *cmd* does not name an executable file. If the child process fails to execute the command (i.e., the execve call fails), then it should exit with a status code of 126.

val execute : string * string list -> ('a, 'b) proc

execute (*cmd*, *args*) asks the operating system to execute the program named by the string *cmd* with the argument list *args*. The program is run as a child process of the calling program, and it inherits the calling process's environment; the return value of this function is an abstract `proc` value naming the child process. The failure semantics of this function are the same as for `executeInEnv`.

For implementations providing the `Posix` modules, this function is equivalent to

```
fun execute (cmd, args) =
        executeInEnv (cmd, args, Posix.ProcEnv.environ ())
```

```
val textInstreamOf : (TextIO.instream, 'a) proc
                        -> TextIO.instream
val binInstreamOf : (BinIO.instream, 'a) proc
                        -> BinIO.instream
```

`textInstreamOf` *pr*
`binInstreamOf` *pr*
These functions return a text or binary `instream` connected to the standard output stream of the process *pr*.

Note that multiple calls to these functions on the same `proc` value will result in multiple streams that all share the same underlying open file descriptor, which can lead to unpredictable effects because of the state inherent in file descriptors.

```
val textOutstreamOf : ('a, TextIO.outstream) proc
                        -> TextIO.outstream
val binOutstreamOf : ('a, BinIO.outstream) proc
                        -> BinIO.outstream
```

`textOutstreamOf` *pr*
`binOutstreamOf` *pr*
These functions return a text or binary `outstream` connected to the standard input stream of the process *pr*.

Note that multiple calls to these functions on the same `proc` value will result in multiple streams that all share the same underlying open file descriptor, which can lead to unpredictable effects due to buffering.

```
val streamsOf : (TextIO.instream, TextIO.outstream) proc
                    -> TextIO.instream * TextIO.outstream
```

`streamsOf` *pr* returns a pair of input and output text streams associated with *pr*. This function is equivalent to (`textInstream` *pr*, `textOutstream` *pr*) and is provided for backward compatibility.

```
val reap : ('a, 'b) proc -> OS.Process.status
```

`reap` *pr* closes the input and output streams associated with *pr* and then suspends the current process until the system process corresponding to *pr* terminates. It returns the exit status given by the process *pr* when it terminated. If `reap` is applied again to *pr*, it should immediately return the previous exit status.

Implementation note: Typically, one cannot rely on the underlying operating system to provide the exit status of a terminated process after it has done so once. Thus, the exit status probably needs to be cached. Also note that `reap` should not return until the process being monitored has terminated. In particular, implementations should be careful not to return if the process has only been suspended.

val `kill : ('a, 'b) proc * signal -> unit`

    `kill (pr,s)` sends the signal `s` to the process `pr`.

val `exit : Word8.word -> 'a`

    `exit st` executes all actions registered with `OS.Process.atExit`, flushes and closes all I/O streams opened using the Library, and then terminates the SML process with the termination status `st`.

Discussion

Note that the interpretation of the string `cmd` in the `execute` and `executeInEnv` functions depends very much on the underlying operating system. Typically, the `cmd` argument will be a full pathname.

The semantics of Unix necessitates that processes that have terminated must be reaped. If not, information concerning the dead process continues to reside in system tables. Thus, a program using `execute` or `executeInEnv` should invoke `reap` on any subprocess it creates.

Implementation note: Although the flavor of this module is heavily influenced by Unix, and the module is simple to implement given the `Posix` subsystem, the functions are specified at a sufficiently high level that implementations, including non-Unix ones, could provide this module without having to supply all of the `Posix` modules.

See also

`BinIO` (§11.4; p. 127), `OS.Process` (§11.36; p. 250), `Posix` (§11.39; p. 257), `Posix.ProcEnv` (§11.43; p. 284), `Posix.Process` (§11.44; p. 289), `Posix.Signal` (§11.45; p. 294), `TextIO` (§11.58; p. 382), `Windows` (§11.66; p. 409)

11.63   The `UnixSock` structure

This structure is used to create sockets in the Unix address family. This structure is only present when the underlying operating system supports Unix-domain sockets.

Binding a name to a Unix-domain socket with `bind` causes a socket file to be created in the file system. This file is not removed when the socket is closed; `OS.FileSys.-remove` can be used to remove the file. The usual file system permission mechanisms are applied when referencing Unix-domain sockets; e.g., the file representing the destination of a `connect` or `sendVec` must be writable.

Synopsis
```
signature UNIX_SOCK
structure UnixSock :> UNIX_SOCK
```

Interface
```
type unix
type 'sock_type sock = (unix, 'sock_type) Socket.sock
type 'mode stream_sock = 'mode Socket.stream sock
type dgram_sock = Socket.dgram sock
type sock_addr = unix Socket.sock_addr
val unixAF : Socket.AF.addr_family
val toAddr : string -> sock_addr
val fromAddr : sock_addr -> string
structure Strm : sig
    val socket : unit -> 'mode stream_sock
    val socketPair : unit
                        -> 'mode stream_sock
                        * 'mode stream_sock
  end
structure DGrm : sig
    val socket : unit -> dgram_sock
    val socketPair : unit -> dgram_sock * dgram_sock
  end
```

Description

`type unix`

> The witness type of the Unix address family.

`type 'sock_type sock = (unix, 'sock_type) Socket.sock`

> The type-scheme for all Unix-domain sockets.

`type 'mode stream_sock = 'mode Socket.stream sock`

> The type-scheme of Unix-domain (passive or active) stream sockets.

```
type dgram_sock = Socket.dgram sock
```

The type of Unix-domain datagram sockets.

```
type sock_addr = unix Socket.sock_addr
```

The type of a Unix-domain socket address.

```
val unixAF : Socket.AF.addr_family
```

The Unix address family value.

```
val toAddr : string -> sock_addr
```

toAddr *s* converts a pathname *s* into a socket address (in the Unix address family); it does not check the validity of the path *s*.

```
val fromAddr : sock_addr -> string
```

fromAddr *addr* returns the Unix file system path corresponding to the Unix-domain socket address *addr*.

structure Strm : **sig ... end**

```
    val socket : unit -> 'mode stream_sock
```

This function creates a stream socket in the Unix address family. It raises SysErr if there are too many sockets in use.

```
    val socketPair : unit
                        -> 'mode stream_sock * 'mode stream_sock
```

This function creates an unnamed pair of connected stream sockets in the Unix address family. It is similar to the Posix.IO.pipe function in that the returned sockets are connected, but, unlike pipe, the sockets are bidirectional. It raises SysErr if there are too many sockets in use.

structure DGrm : **sig ... end**

```
    val socket : unit -> dgram_sock
```

This function creates a datagram socket in the Unix address family. It raises SysErr if there are too many sockets in use.

val socketPair : unit **->** dgram_sock ***** dgram_sock

This function creates an unnamed pair of connected datagram sockets in the Unix address family. It raises SysErr if there are too many sockets in use.

See also

GenericSock (§11.12; p. 153), INetSock (§11.16; p. 166), Socket (§11.51; p. 330)

11.64 The `Vector` structure

The `Vector` structure defines polymorphic vectors, which are immutable sequences with constant-time access.

Synopsis

```
signature VECTOR
structure Vector :> VECTOR
```

Interface

```
eqtype 'a vector = 'a vector

val maxLen : int
val fromList : 'a list -> 'a vector
val tabulate : int * (int -> 'a) -> 'a vector
val length : 'a vector -> int
val sub : 'a vector * int -> 'a
val update : 'a vector * int * 'a -> 'a vector
val concat : 'a vector list -> 'a vector
val appi : (int * 'a -> unit) -> 'a vector -> unit
val app  : ('a -> unit) -> 'a vector -> unit
val mapi : (int * 'a -> 'b) -> 'a vector -> 'b vector
val map  : ('a -> 'b) -> 'a vector -> 'b vector
val foldli : (int * 'a * 'b -> 'b) -> 'b -> 'a vector -> 'b
val foldri : (int * 'a * 'b -> 'b) -> 'b -> 'a vector -> 'b
val foldl  : ('a * 'b -> 'b) -> 'b -> 'a vector -> 'b
val foldr  : ('a * 'b -> 'b) -> 'b -> 'a vector -> 'b
val findi : (int * 'a -> bool)
                 -> 'a vector -> (int * 'a) option
val find  : ('a -> bool) -> 'a vector -> 'a option
val exists : ('a -> bool) -> 'a vector -> bool
val all : ('a -> bool) -> 'a vector -> bool
val collate : ('a * 'a -> order)
                 -> 'a vector * 'a vector -> order
```

Description

```
val maxLen : int
```

The maximum length of vectors supported by this implementation. Attempts to create larger vectors will result in the `Size` exception being raised.

```
val fromList : 'a list -> 'a vector
```

`fromList` l creates a new vector from the list l whose length is `length` l and with the ith element of l used as the ith element of the vector. If the length of the list is greater than `maxLen`, then the `Size` exception is raised.

val `tabulate : int * (int -> 'a) -> 'a vector`

> `tabulate` (n, f) creates a vector of n elements, where the elements are defined in order of increasing index by applying f to the element's index. This expression is equivalent to the following:
>
> $$\texttt{fromList (List.tabulate } (n, f))$$
>
> If $n < 0$ or `maxLen` $< n$, then the `Size` exception is raised.

val `length : 'a vector -> int`

> `length` vec returns $|vec|$, the length of the vector vec.

val `sub : 'a vector * int -> 'a`

> `sub` (vec, i) returns the ith element of the vector vec. If $i < 0$ or $|vec| \leq i$, then the `Subscript` exception is raised.

val `update : 'a vector * int * 'a -> 'a vector`

> `update` (vec, i, x) returns a new vector, identical to vec, except the ith element of vec is set to x. If $i < 0$ or $|vec| \leq i$, then the `Subscript` exception is raised.

val `concat : 'a vector list -> 'a vector`

> `concat` l returns the vector that is the concatenation of the vectors in the list l. If the total length of these vectors exceeds `maxLen`, then the `Size` exception is raised.

val `appi : (int * 'a -> unit) -> 'a vector -> unit`
val `app : ('a -> unit) -> 'a vector -> unit`

> `appi` f vec
> `app` f vec
> These functions apply the function f to the elements of a vector in left-to-right order (i.e., in order of increasing indices). The more general `appi` function supplies both the element and the element's index to the function f. These functions are respectively equivalent to:
> ```
> List.app f (foldri (fn (i,a,l) => (i,a)::l) [] vec)
> List.app f (foldr (fn (a,l) => a::l) [] vec)
> ```

val `mapi : (int * 'a -> 'b) -> 'a vector -> 'b vector`
val `map : ('a -> 'b) -> 'a vector -> 'b vector`

> `mapi` f vec
> `map` f vec
> These functions produce new vectors by mapping the function f from left to right over the argument vector. The more general form `mapi` supplies f with the vector index of an element along with the element. These functions are respectively equivalent to:
>
> ```
> fromList (List.map f (foldri (fn (i,a,l) => (i,a)::l) [] vec))
> fromList (List.map f (foldr (fn (a,l) => a::l) [] vec))
> ```

```
val foldli : (int * 'a * 'b -> 'b) -> 'b -> 'a vector -> 'b
val foldri : (int * 'a * 'b -> 'b) -> 'b -> 'a vector -> 'b
val foldl : ('a * 'b -> 'b) -> 'b -> 'a vector -> 'b
val foldr : ('a * 'b -> 'b) -> 'b -> 'a vector -> 'b
```

> foldli *f init vec*
> foldri *f init vec*
> foldl *f init vec*
> foldr *f init vec*

These fold the function *f* over all the elements of a vector, using the value *init* as the initial value. The functions foldli and foldl apply the function *f* from left to right (increasing indices), while the functions foldri and foldr work from right to left (decreasing indices). The more general functions foldli and foldri supply both the element and the element's index to the function *f*.

Refer to the MONO_ARRAY manual pages for reference implementations of the indexed versions.

The last two expressions are respectively equivalent to:

> foldli (**fn** (_, *a*, *x*) **=>** *f*(*a*, *x*)) *init vec*
> foldri (**fn** (_, *a*, *x*) **=>** *f*(*a*, *x*)) *init vec*

```
val findi : (int * 'a -> bool)
                -> 'a vector -> (int * 'a) option
val find : ('a -> bool) -> 'a vector -> 'a option
```

> findi *pred vec*
> find *pred vec*

These functions apply *pred* to each element of the vector *vec*, from left to right (i.e., increasing indices), until a true value is returned. These functions return the first such element, if it exists; otherwise, they return NONE. The more general version findi also supplies *pred* with the vector index of the element and, upon finding an entry satisfying the predicate, returns that index with the element.

```
val exists : ('a -> bool) -> 'a vector -> bool
```

exists *pred vec* applies *pred* to each element *x* of the vector *vec*, from left to right (i.e., increasing indices), until *pred*(*x*) evaluates to true; it returns true if such an *x* exists and false otherwise.

```
val all : ('a -> bool) -> 'a vector -> bool
```

all *pred vec* applies *pred* to each element *x* of the vector *vec*, from left to right (i.e., increasing indices), until *pred*(*x*) evaluates to false; it returns false if such an *x* exists and true otherwise. It is equivalent to not(exists (not o *pred*) *vec*)).

```
val collate : ('a * 'a -> order)
                -> 'a vector * 'a vector -> order
```

collate *cmp* (*v1*, *v2*) performs a lexicographic comparison of the two vectors using the given ordering *cmp* on elements.

See also

Array (§11.1; p. 112), MONO_VECTOR (§11.26; p. 211),
VectorSlice (§11.65; p. 405)

11.65   The VectorSlice structure

The VectorSlice structure provides an abstraction of subvectors for polymorphic vectors. A slice value can be viewed as a triple (v, i, n), where v is the underlying vector, i is the starting index, and n is the length of the subvector, with the constraint that $0 \leq i \leq i + n \leq |v|$, where $|v|$ is the length of v. Slices provide a convenient notation for specifying and operating on a contiguous subset of elements in a vector.

Synopsis

```
signature VECTOR_SLICE
structure VectorSlice :> VECTOR_SLICE
```

Interface

```
type 'a slice

val length : 'a slice -> int
val sub : 'a slice * int -> 'a
val full : 'a Vector.vector -> 'a slice
val slice : 'a Vector.vector * int * int option -> 'a slice
val subslice : 'a slice * int * int option -> 'a slice
val base : 'a slice -> 'a Vector.vector * int * int
val vector : 'a slice -> 'a Vector.vector
val concat : 'a slice list -> 'a Vector.vector
val isEmpty : 'a slice -> bool
val getItem : 'a slice -> ('a * 'a slice) option
val appi : (int * 'a -> unit) -> 'a slice -> unit
val app  : ('a -> unit) -> 'a slice -> unit
val mapi : (int * 'a -> 'b) -> 'a slice -> 'b Vector.vector
val map  : ('a -> 'b) -> 'a slice -> 'b Vector.vector
val foldli : (int * 'a * 'b -> 'b) -> 'b -> 'a slice -> 'b
val foldri : (int * 'a * 'b -> 'b) -> 'b -> 'a slice -> 'b
val foldl  : ('a * 'b -> 'b) -> 'b -> 'a slice -> 'b
val foldr  : ('a * 'b -> 'b) -> 'b -> 'a slice -> 'b
val findi : (int * 'a -> bool)
                  -> 'a slice -> (int * 'a) option
val find  : ('a -> bool) -> 'a slice -> 'a option
val exists : ('a -> bool) -> 'a slice -> bool
val all : ('a -> bool) -> 'a slice -> bool
val collate : ('a * 'a -> order)
                  -> 'a slice * 'a slice -> order
```

Description

```
val length : 'a slice -> int
```

> length *sl* returns |*sl*|, the length (i.e., number of elements) of the slice.

val sub : 'a slice * int -> 'a

sub (*sl*, *i*) returns the ith element of the slice *sl*. If $i < 0$ or $|sl| \leq i$, then the Subscript exception is raised.

val full : 'a Vector.vector -> 'a slice

full *vec* creates a slice representing the entire vector *vec*. It is equivalent to
$$\text{slice}(vec, \ 0, \ \text{NONE})$$

val slice : 'a Vector.vector * int * int option -> 'a slice

slice (*vec*, *i*, *sz*) creates a slice based on the vector *vec* starting at index *i* of the vector *vec*. If *sz* is NONE, the slice includes all of the elements to the end of the vector, i.e., $vec[i..|vec|-1]$. This function raises Subscript if $i < 0$ or $|vec| < i$. If *sz* is SOME(*j*), the slice has length *j*, that is, it corresponds to $vec[i..i+j-1]$. It raises Subscript if $i < 0$ or $j < 0$ or $|arr| < i + j$. Note that, if defined, slice returns an empty slice when $i = |vec|$.

val subslice : 'a slice * int * int option -> 'a slice

subslice (*sl*, *i*, *sz*) creates a slice based on the given slice *sl* starting at index *i* of *sl*. If *sz* is NONE, the slice includes all of the elements to the end of the slice, i.e., $sl[i..|sl| - 1]$. This function raises Subscript if $i < 0$ or $|sl| < i$. If *sz* is SOME(*j*), the slice has length *j*, that is, it corresponds to $sl[i..i+j-1]$. It raises Subscript if $i < 0$ or $j < 0$ or $|sl| < i + j$. Note that, if defined, slice returns an empty slice when $i = |sl|$.

val base : 'a slice -> 'a Vector.vector * int * int

base *sl* returns a triple (*vec*, *i*, *n*) representing the concrete representation of the slice. *vec* is the underlying vector, *i* is the starting index, and *n* is the length of the slice.

val vector : 'a slice -> 'a Vector.vector

vector *sl* generates a vector from the slice *sl*. Specifically, the result is equivalent to
$$\text{Vector.tabulate (length } sl, \ \textbf{fn } i \Rightarrow \text{sub } (sl, \ i))$$

val concat : 'a slice list -> 'a Vector.vector

concat *l* is the concatenation of all the slices in *l*. This function raises Size if the sum of all the lengths is greater than Vector.maxLen.

val isEmpty : 'a slice -> bool

isEmpty *sl* returns true if *sl* has length 0.

```
val getItem : 'a slice -> ('a * 'a slice) option
```

getItem *sl* returns the first item in *sl* and the rest of the slice or NONE if *sl* is empty.

```
val appi : (int * 'a -> unit) -> 'a slice -> unit
val app : ('a -> unit) -> 'a slice -> unit
```

appi *f sl*
app *f sl*

These functions apply the function *f* to the elements of a slice in left-to-right order (i.e., increasing indices). The more general appi function supplies *f* with the index of the corresponding element in the slice. The expression app *f sl* is equivalent to appi (*f* o #2) *sl*.

```
val mapi : (int * 'a -> 'b) -> 'a slice -> 'b Vector.vector
val map : ('a -> 'b) -> 'a slice -> 'b Vector.vector
```

mapi *f sl*
map *f sl*

These functions generate new vectors by mapping the function *f* from left to right over the argument slice. The more general mapi function supplies both the element and the element's index in the slice to the function *f*. The first expression is equivalent to:

```
let
    fun ff (i,a,l) = f(i,a)::l
in
    Vector.fromList (rev (foldli ff [] sl))
end
```

The latter expression is equivalent to:

```
mapi (f o #2) sl
```

```
val foldli : (int * 'a * 'b -> 'b) -> 'b -> 'a slice -> 'b
val foldri : (int * 'a * 'b -> 'b) -> 'b -> 'a slice -> 'b
val foldl : ('a * 'b -> 'b) -> 'b -> 'a slice -> 'b
val foldr : ('a * 'b -> 'b) -> 'b -> 'a slice -> 'b
```

foldli *f init sl*
foldri *f init sl*
foldl *f init sl*
foldr *f init sl*

These fold the function *f* over all the elements of a vector slice, using the value *init* as the initial value. The functions foldli and foldl apply the function *f* from left to right (increasing indices), while the functions foldri and foldr work from right to left (decreasing indices). The more general functions foldli and foldri supply *f* with the index of the corresponding element in the slice.

Refer to the MONO_ARRAY manual pages for reference implementations of the indexed versions.

The expression foldl *f init sl* is equivalent to:

```
foldli (fn (_, a, x) => f(a, x)) init sl
```

The analogous equivalence holds for foldri and foldr.

```
val findi : (int * 'a -> bool)
                -> 'a slice -> (int * 'a) option
val find : ('a -> bool) -> 'a slice -> 'a option
```

findi *pred sl*
find *pred sl*
These functions apply *pred* to each element of the slice *sl*, from left to right (i.e., increasing indices), until a true value is returned. These functions return the first such element, if it exists; otherwise, they return NONE. The more general version findi also supplies *pred* with the index of the element in the slice and, upon finding an entry satisfying the predicate, returns that index with the element.

```
val exists : ('a -> bool) -> 'a slice -> bool
```

exists *pred sl* applies *pred* to each element x of the slice *sl*, from left to right (i.e., increasing indices), until *pred*(x) evaluates to true; it returns true if such an x exists and false otherwise.

```
val all : ('a -> bool) -> 'a slice -> bool
```

all *pred sl* applies *pred* to each element x of the slice *sl*, from left to right (i.e., increasing indices), until *pred*(x) evaluates to false; it returns false if such an x exists and true otherwise. It is equivalent to not(exists (not o *pred*) *sl*)).

```
val collate : ('a * 'a -> order)
                -> 'a slice * 'a slice -> order
```

collate *cmp* (*sl*, *sl2*)   performs a lexicographic comparison of the two slices using the given ordering *cmp* on elements.

See also

Array (§11.1; p. 112), ArraySlice (§11.3; p. 122), MONO_VECTOR (§11.26; p. 211)

11.66 The Windows structure

The Windows structure provides a high-level interface to various system features based on the Microsoft Windows operating system model. These functions include the ability to create and communicate with separate processes, as well as to interact with the registry and file subsystems. In particular, using this module, a program can invoke a separate process and obtain input and output streams connected to the standard output and input streams, respectively, of the other process. The functions provide a richer and more detailed interface than the comparable functions provided by the substructures in OS.

Synopsis

```
signature WINDOWS
structure Windows :> WINDOWS
```

Interface

```
structure Key : sig
    include BIT_FLAGS

    val allAccess : flags
    val createLink : flags
    val createSubKey : flags
    val enumerateSubKeys : flags
    val execute : flags
    val notify : flags
    val queryValue : flags
    val read : flags
    val setValue : flags
    val write : flags
  end

structure Reg : sig
    eqtype hkey

    val classesRoot      : hkey
    val currentUser      : hkey
    val localMachine     : hkey
    val users            : hkey
    val performanceData  : hkey
    val currentConfig    : hkey
    val dynData          : hkey

    datatype create_result
      = CREATED_NEW_KEY of hkey
      | OPENED_EXISTING_KEY of hkey
```

```sml
    val createKeyEx : hkey * string * Key.flags
                            -> create_result
    val openKeyEx : hkey * string * Key.flags -> hkey
    val closeKey : hkey -> unit
    val deleteKey : hkey * string -> unit
    val deleteValue : hkey * string -> unit
    val enumKeyEx : hkey * int -> string option
    val enumValueEx : hkey * int -> string option

    datatype value
       = SZ of string
       | DWORD of SysWord.word
       | BINARY of Word8Vector.vector
       | MULTI_SZ of string list
       | EXPAND_SZ of string

    val queryValueEx : hkey * string -> value option
    val setValueEx : hkey * string * value -> unit
  end

structure Config : sig
    val platformWin32s       : SysWord.word
    val platformWin32Windows : SysWord.word
    val platformWin32NT      : SysWord.word
    val platformWin32CE      : SysWord.word
    val getVersionEx : unit
                         -> {
                             majorVersion : SysWord.word,
                             minorVersion : SysWord.word,
                             buildNumber : SysWord.word,
                             platformId : SysWord.word,
                             csdVersion : string
                            }
    val getWindowsDirectory : unit -> string
    val getSystemDirectory : unit -> string
    val getComputerName : unit -> string
    val getUserName : unit -> string
  end

structure DDE : sig
    type info
    val startDialog : string * string -> info
    val executeString : info * string * int * Time.time
                          -> unit
    val stopDialog : info -> unit
  end
```

```
val getVolumeInformation : string
                            -> {
                                volumeName : string,
                                systemName : string,
                                serialNumber : SysWord.word,
                                maximumComponentLength : int
                            }

val findExecutable : string -> string option
val launchApplication : string * string -> unit
val openDocument : string -> unit
val simpleExecute : string * string -> OS.Process.status

type ('a,'b) proc

val execute : string * string -> ('a, 'b) proc
val textInstreamOf : (TextIO.instream, 'a) proc
                        -> TextIO.instream
val binInstreamOf  : (BinIO.instream, 'a) proc
                        -> BinIO.instream
val textOutstreamOf : ('a, TextIO.outstream) proc
                         -> TextIO.outstream
val binOutstreamOf  : ('a, BinIO.outstream) proc
                         -> BinIO.outstream
val reap : ('a, 'b) proc -> OS.Process.status

structure Status : sig
    type status = SysWord.word
    val accessViolation      : status
    val arrayBoundsExceeded  : status
    val breakpoint           : status
    val controlCExit         : status
    val datatypeMisalignment : status
    val floatDenormalOperand : status
    val floatDivideByZero    : status
    val floatInexactResult   : status
    val floatInvalidOperation : status
    val floatOverflow        : status
    val floatStackCheck      : status
    val floatUnderflow       : status
    val guardPageViolation   : status
    val integerDivideByZero  : status
    val integerOverflow      : status
    val illegalInstruction   : status
    val invalidDisposition   : status
    val invalidHandle        : status
```

```
      val inPageError                   : status
      val noncontinuableException : status
      val pending                       : status
      val privilegedInstruction   : status
      val singleStep                    : status
      val stackOverflow                 : status
      val timeout                       : status
      val userAPC                       : status
   end

val fromStatus : OS.Process.status -> Status.status

val exit : Status.status -> 'a
```

Description

structure Key : **sig** ... **end**

The Key substructure contains flags for specifying security settings when opening and creating keys in the registry.

val allAccess : flags

The union of the queryValue, enumerateSubKeys, notify, createSub-Key, createLink, and setValue flags.

val createLink : flags

Permission to create a symbolic link. This value is included for completeness, as the rest of the structure does not support links.

val createSubKey : flags

Permission to create subkeys.

val enumerateSubKeys : flags

Permission to enumerate subkeys.

val execute : flags

Permission for read access.

val notify : flags

Permission for change notification. This value is included for completeness, as the rest of the structure does not support notification.

val queryValue : flags

Permission to query subkey data.

val read : flags

> The union of the queryValue, enumerateSubKeys, and notify flags.

val setValue : flags

> Permission to set subkey data.

val write : flags

> The union of the setValue and createSubKey flags.

structure Reg : **sig** ... **end**

> This substructure provides Microsoft Windows registry functions.

eqtype hkey

> Type of registry key values.

val classesRoot : hkey
val currentUser : hkey
val localMachine : hkey
val users : hkey
val performanceData : hkey
val currentConfig : hkey
val dynData : hkey

> These are identifiers for top-level registry keys.

val createKeyEx : hkey ***** string ***** Key.flags
            -> create_result

> createKeyEx (*hkey*, *skey*, *regsam*) opens or creates a subkey of *hkey*, with the name *skey* and security access specified by *regsam*.
>
> **Implementation note:** This function passes the REG_OPTION_NON_VOLATILE option, NULL Class, and SECURITY_ATTRIBUTE arguments to the underlying Windows call.

val openKeyEx : hkey ***** string ***** Key.flags **->** hkey

> openKeyEx (*hkey*, *skey*, *regsam*) opens a subkey of *hkey* with the name *skey* and security access specified by *regsam*.

val closeKey : hkey **->** unit

> closeKey *hkey* closes the key *hkey*.

val deleteKey : hkey ***** string **->** unit

> deleteKey (*hkey*, *skey*) deletes the subkey *skey* of *hkey*.

val deleteValue : hkey * string -> unit

    deleteValue (*hkey*, *valname*) deletes the value *valname* of *hkey*.

val enumKeyEx : hkey * int -> string option

    enumKeyEx (*hkey*, *ind*) returns the subkey of index *ind* of the key *hkey*, where indices start from zero. The function returns SOME of a string for each defined subkey. To enumerate all the subkeys, start with the index at zero and increment it until the function returns NONE. The function raises the Subscript exception if *ind* is invalid.

val enumValueEx : hkey * int -> string option

    enumValueEx (*hkey*, *ind*) returns the value of index *ind* of the key *hkey*, where indices start from zero. The function returns SOME of a string for each defined value. To enumerate all the values, start with the index at zero and increment it until the function returns NONE. The function raises the Subscript exception if *ind* is invalid.

datatype value
    = SZ **of** string
    | DWORD **of** SysWord.word
    | BINARY **of** Word8Vector.vector
    | MULTI_SZ **of** string list
    | EXPAND_SZ **of** string

    This type describes the kinds of values that can be saved to the registry or extracted from it. The constructor SZ corresponds to strings, DWORD to 32-bit numbers, BINARY to arbitrary binary values, MULTI_SZ to lists of strings, and EXPAND_SZ to strings containing environment variables.

val queryValueEx : hkey * string -> value option

    queryValueEx (*hkey*, *name*) returns the data associated with *name* in the open registry key *hkey*. A value whose type does not correspond to a more specific instance of the value datatype is returned as a BINARY value. If the value does not exist in the key, the function returns NONE. Any other error, such as having insufficient access rights to the registry key, results in the OS.SysErr exception being raised.

    A common use of a registry value is to override the default behavior of a program. The normal case is when the registry value is unset. Using an option type allows for the result of queryValueEx to indicate the presence or absence of the key.

val setValueEx : hkey * string * value -> unit

    setValueEx (*hkey*, *name*, *v*) associates the value *v* with *name* in the open key *hkey*.

structure Config : **sig** ... **end**

This substructure contains functions to obtain information about the operating system.

```
val platformWin32s : SysWord.word
val platformWin32Windows : SysWord.word
val platformWin32NT : SysWord.word
val platformWin32CE : SysWord.word
```

These are values corresponding to the indicated Microsoft Windows platforms.

```
val getVersionEx : unit
                      -> {
                         majorVersion : SysWord.word,
                         minorVersion : SysWord.word,
                         buildNumber : SysWord.word,
                         platformId : SysWord.word,
                         csdVersion : string
                      }
```

This function returns the major and minor versions of the operating system, the build number, platform identifier, and a supplementary version string. The platform identifier `platformId` can be compared with values `platformWin32s`, `platformWin32Windows`, `platformWin32NT`, and `platformWin32CE` to determine the type of platform. Note that additional values for other platforms may be returned.

The major and minor version numbers allow additional distinctions. In the case where `platformId` is `platformWin32Windows`, we have:

minorVersion	**System**
0	Windows 95
> 0	Windows 98

In the case where `platformId` is `platformWin32NT`, we have:

majorVersion	minorVersion	**System**
4	0	Windows NT
5	0	Windows 2000
5	> 0	Windows XP

```
val getWindowsDirectory : unit -> string
```

The Windows directory, typically `"C:\Windows"` on Windows 95 or `"C:\Winnt"` on Windows NT.

```
val getSystemDirectory : unit -> string
```

The Windows system directory, typically `"C:\Windows\System"` or `"C:\Winnt\System"`.

```
val getComputerName : unit -> string
```

The name of the computer.

```
val getUserName : unit -> string
```

The name of the current user.

structure DDE : **sig** ... **end**

> This substructure provides a high-level, client-side interface for simple dynamic data exchange (DDE) interactions. All transactions are synchronous. Advise loops and poke transactions are not supported by this interface.

val startDialog : string * string -> info

> startDialog (*service*, *topic*) initiates DDE and connects to the given service and topic. It returns the info value created by these operations.

val executeString : info * string * int * Time.time -> unit

> executeString (*info*, *cmd*, *retry*, *delay*) attempts to execute the command *cmd* on the service and topic specified by the *info* value. The *retry* argument specifies the number of times to attempt the transaction if the server is busy, pausing for *delay* between each attempt.

val stopDialog : info -> unit

> stopDialog *info* disconnects the service and topic specified by the *info* argument and frees the associated resources.

val getVolumeInformation : string

```
                          -> {
                              volumeName : string,
                              systemName : string,
                              serialNumber : SysWord.word,
                              maximumComponentLength : int
                          }
```

> getVolumeInformation *root* returns information about the file system and volume specified by the root pathname *root*. The volumeName field contains the name of the volume; the systemName field contains its type (e.g., "FAT" or "NTFS"), the serialNumber field contains the serial number, and the maximumComponentLength field specifies the maximum length of any component of a pathname on this system.

val findExecutable : string -> string option

> findExecutable *name* returns the full executable name associated with *name* or NONE if no such file exists.

val launchApplication : string * string -> unit

> launchApplication (*file*, *arg*) runs the specified executable *file* passing it the argument *arg*. It raises OS.SysErr if *file* is not executable or if it cannot be run.

> **Implementation note:** This function should be implemented using ShellExecute, passing SW_SHOWNORMAL to the underlying API call.

val openDocument : string -> unit

> openDocument *file* opens *file* using its associated application.

> **Implementation note:** This function should pass SW_SHOWNORMAL to the underlying ShellExecute API call.

val simpleExecute : string * string -> OS.Process.status

> simpleExecute (*cmd*, *arg*) creates the process specified by *cmd* with command-line arguments represented by the string *arg*, redirecting standard input and standard output to the null device. It then waits for the subprocess to terminate and returns its exit status. This function is similar to the OS.Process.system, but it can be used in cases where the latter does not work, and its return value provides more information about the exit status of the child process.

> **Implementation note:** This function corresponds to the use of CreateProcess.

type ('a,'b) proc

> The type of a process created by execute. The type parameters are witness types for the types of streams that can be returned.

val execute : string * string -> ('a, 'b) proc

> execute (*cmd*, *arg*) creates a process specified by *cmd* with command-line arguments represented by the string *arg* and returns a handle for the resulting process.

> **Implementation note:** This also corresponds to the use of CreateProcess. Redirection of the standard streams can be handled using the hStdInput and hStdOutput fields in the STARTUPINFO parameter.

val textInstreamOf : (TextIO.instream, 'a) proc
                          -> TextIO.instream
val binInstreamOf : (BinIO.instream, 'a) proc
                          -> BinIO.instream

textInstreamOf *pr*
binInstreamOf *pr*
These functions return a text or binary instream connected to the standard output stream of the process *pr*.

   Note that multiple calls to these functions on the same proc value will result in multiple streams that all share the same underlying open file descriptor, which can lead to unpredictable effects because of the state inherent in file descriptors.

```
val textOutstreamOf : ('a, TextIO.outstream) proc
                          -> TextIO.outstream
val binOutstreamOf : ('a, BinIO.outstream) proc
                          -> BinIO.outstream
```

textOutstreamOf *pr*
binOutstreamOf *pr*
These functions return a text or binary outstream connected to the standard input stream
of the process *pr*.

Note that multiple calls to these functions on the same proc value will result in multiple streams that all share the same underlying open file descriptor, which can lead to unpredictable effects due to buffering.

```
val reap : ('a, 'b) proc -> OS.Process.status
```

reap *pr* closes the standard streams associated with *pr* and then suspends the current process until the system process corresponding to *pr* terminates. It returns the exit status given by the process *pr* when it terminated. If reap is applied again to *pr*, it should immediately return the previous exit status.

Implementation note: Typically, one cannot rely on the underlying operating system to provide the exit status of a terminated process after it has done so once. Thus, the exit status probably needs to be cached. Also note that reap should not return until the process being monitored has terminated. In particular, implementations should be careful not to return if the process has only been suspended.

```
structure Status : sig ... end
```

The Status substructure defines the possible system-specific interpretations of OS.-Process.status values.

```
val fromStatus : OS.Process.status -> Status.status
```

fromStatus *s* decodes the abstract exit status *s* into system-specific information.

```
val exit : Status.status -> 'a
```

exit *st* executes all actions registered with OS.Process.atExit, flushes and closes all I/O streams, and then terminates the SML process with termination status *st*.

Discussion

This structure provides a minimal view of the system calls available across the various Microsoft Windows operating systems. It focuses on managing the registry and executing programs. The function Windows.findExecutable and the facilities in the Config substructure allow the programmer to determine if and where a program can be found on a given machine.

Future extensions of the Basis Library might give access to more features, either by including additional substructures or as a separate top-level module.

Rationale: As usual, platform identification and exit status values are not handled by datatypes to allow for future extensions.

See also

BIT_FLAGS (§11.5; p. 129), OS.FileSys (§11.33; p. 231),
OS.Process (§11.36; p. 250), TextIO (§11.58; p. 382), Time (§11.60; p. 387),
Unix (§11.62; p. 394)

11.67   The WORD signature

Instances of the signature WORD provide a type of unsigned integer with modular arithmetic and logical operations and conversion operations. They are also meant to give efficient access to the primitive machine word types of the underlying hardware and support bit-level operations on integers.

In order to provide a more intuitive description of the shift operators below, we assume a bit ordering in which the most significant bit is leftmost and the least significant bit is rightmost.

Synopsis

```
signature WORD
structure Word :> WORD
  where type word = word
structure Word8 :> WORD
structure LargeWord :> WORD
structure WordN :> WORD
structure SysWord :> WORD
```

Interface

```
eqtype word

val wordSize : int

val toLarge      : word -> LargeWord.word
val toLargeX     : word -> LargeWord.word
val toLargeWord  : word -> LargeWord.word
val toLargeWordX : word -> LargeWord.word
val fromLarge     : LargeWord.word -> word
val fromLargeWord : LargeWord.word -> word
val toLargeInt  : word -> LargeInt.int
val toLargeIntX : word -> LargeInt.int
val fromLargeInt : LargeInt.int -> word
val toInt  : word -> int
val toIntX : word -> int
val fromInt : int -> word

val andb : word * word -> word
val orb  : word * word -> word
val xorb : word * word -> word
val notb : word -> word
val << : word * Word.word -> word
val >> : word * Word.word -> word
val ~>> : word * Word.word -> word

val + : word * word -> word
val - : word * word -> word
```

```
val * : word * word -> word
val div : word * word -> word
val mod : word * word -> word

val compare : word * word -> order
val < : word * word -> bool
val <= : word * word -> bool
val > : word * word -> bool
val >= : word * word -> bool

val ~ : word -> word
val min : word * word -> word
val max : word * word -> word

val fmt : StringCvt.radix -> word -> string
val toString : word -> string
val scan : StringCvt.radix
                -> (char, 'a) StringCvt.reader
                -> (word, 'a) StringCvt.reader
val fromString : string -> word option
```

Description

```
val wordSize : int
```

> The number of bits in type `word`. `wordSize` need not be a power of 2. Note that `word` has a fixed, finite precision.

```
val toLarge : word -> LargeWord.word
val toLargeX : word -> LargeWord.word
val toLargeWord : word -> LargeWord.word
val toLargeWordX : word -> LargeWord.word
```

> `toLarge` w
> `toLargeX` w
> These convert w to a value of type `LargeWord.word`. In the first case, w is converted to its equivalent `LargeWord.word` value in the range $[0, 2^{\text{wordSize}} - 1]$. In the second case, w is "sign-extended," i.e., the `wordSize` low-order bits of w and `toLargeX` w are the same, and the remaining bits of `toLargeX` w are all equal to the most significant bit of w.
>
> Note that `toLargeWord` and `toLargeWordX` are respective synonyms of the first two and are deprecated.

```
val fromLarge : LargeWord.word -> word
val fromLargeWord : LargeWord.word -> word
```

> fromLarge *w*
> fromLargeWord *w*
> These functions convert *w* to the value *w* (mod 2^{wordSize}) of type word. This operation
> has the effect of taking the low-order wordSize bits of the 2's complement representation
> of *w*.
>
> > fromLargeWord is a deprecated synonym for fromLarge.

```
val toLargeInt : word -> LargeInt.int
val toLargeIntX : word -> LargeInt.int
```

> toLargeInt *w*
> toLargeIntX *w*
> These functions convert *w* to a value of type LargeInt.int. In the former case, *w* is
> viewed as an integer value in the range $[0, 2^{\text{wordSize}} - 1]$. In the latter case, *w* is treated
> as a 2's-complement signed integer with wordSize precision, thereby having a value in
> the range $[-2^{\text{wordSize}-1}, 2^{\text{wordSize}-1} - 1]$. toLargeInt raises Overflow if the target
> integer value cannot be represented as a LargeInt.int. Since the precision of Large-
> Int.int is always at least wordSize (see the discussion below), toLargeIntX will
> never raise an exception.

```
val fromLargeInt : LargeInt.int -> word
```

> fromLargeInt *i* converts *i* of type LargeInt.int to a value of type word. This
> operation has the effect of taking the low-order wordSize bits of the 2's complement
> representation of *i*.

```
val toInt : word -> int
val toIntX : word -> int
```

> toInt *w*
> toIntX *w*
> These functions convert *w* to a value of the default integer type. In the former case, *w* is
> viewed as an integer value in the range $[0, 2^{\text{wordSize}} - 1]$. In the latter case, *w* is treated as
> a 2's-complement signed integer with wordSize precision, thereby having a value in the
> range $[-2^{\text{wordSize}-1}, 2^{\text{wordSize}-1} - 1]$. They raise Overflow if the target integer value
> cannot be represented as an Int.int.

```
val fromInt : int -> word
```

> fromInt *i* converts *i* of the default integer type to a value of type word. This opera-
> tion has the effect of taking the low-order wordSize bits of the 2's complement represen-
> tation of *i*. If the precision of Int.int is less than wordSize, then *i* is sign-extended
> to wordSize bits.

```
val andb : word * word -> word
val orb : word * word -> word
val xorb : word * word -> word
```

These functions return the bit-wise AND, OR, and exclusive OR, respectively, of their arguments.

```
val notb : word -> word
```

`notb` i returns the bit-wise complement (NOT) of i.

```
val << : word * Word.word -> word
```

`<< (i, n)` shifts i to the left by n bit positions, filling in zeros from the right. When i and n are interpreted as unsigned binary numbers, this function returns $(i*2^n) \pmod{2^{\texttt{wordSize}}}$. In particular, shifting by greater than or equal to `wordSize` results in 0. This operation is similar to the "(logical) shift left" instruction in many processors.

```
val >> : word * Word.word -> word
```

`>> (i, n)` shifts i to the right by n bit positions, filling in zeros from the left. When i and n are interpreted as unsigned binary numbers, it returns $\lfloor i/2^n \rfloor$. In particular, shifting by greater than or equal to `wordSize` results in 0. This operation is similar to the "logical shift right" instruction in many processors.

```
val ~>> : word * Word.word -> word
```

`~>> (i, n)` shifts i to the right by n bit positions. The value of the leftmost bit of i remains the same; in a 2's-complement interpretation, this operation corresponds to sign extension. When i is interpreted as a `wordSize`-bit 2's-complement integer and n is interpreted as an unsigned binary number, it returns $\lfloor i/2^n \rfloor$. In particular, shifting by greater than or equal to `wordSize` results in either 0 or all 1's. This operation is similar to the "arithmetic shift right" instruction in many processors.

```
val + : word * word -> word
```

i `+` j returns $(i+j) \pmod{2^{\texttt{wordSize}}}$ when i and j are interpreted as unsigned binary numbers. It does *not* raise `Overflow`.

```
val - : word * word -> word
```

i `-` j returns the difference of i and j modulo $(2^{\texttt{wordSize}})$:

$$(2^{\texttt{wordSize}} + i - j) \pmod{2^{\texttt{wordSize}}}$$

when i and j are interpreted as unsigned binary numbers. It does *not* raise `Overflow`.

val `* : word * word -> word`

$i * j$ returns the product $(i * j)$ (mod 2^{wordSize}) when i and j are interpreted as unsigned binary numbers. It does *not* raise `Overflow`.

val `div : word * word -> word`

i `div` j returns the truncated quotient of i and j, $\lfloor i/j \rfloor$, when i and j are interpreted as unsigned binary numbers. It raises `Div` when $j = 0$.

val `mod : word * word -> word`

i `mod` j returns the remainder of the division of i by j:

$$i - j * \lfloor i/j \rfloor$$

when i and j are interpreted as unsigned binary numbers. It raises `Div` when $j = 0$.

val `compare : word * word -> order`

`compare` (i, j) returns `LESS`, `EQUAL`, or `GREATER` if and only if i is less than, equal to, or greater than j, respectively, considered as unsigned binary numbers.

val `< : word * word -> bool`
val `<= : word * word -> bool`
val `> : word * word -> bool`
val `>= : word * word -> bool`

These functions return `true` if and only if the input arguments satisfy the given relation when interpreted as unsigned binary numbers.

val `~ : word -> word`

`~` i returns the 2's-complement of i.

val `min : word * word -> word`
val `max : word * word -> word`

These functions return the smaller (respectively, larger) of the arguments.

val `fmt : StringCvt.radix -> word -> string`
val `toString : word -> string`

`fmt` *radix i*
`toString` *i*
These functions return a string containing a numeric representation of i. No prefix (i.e., `"0w"`, `"0wX"`, etc.) is generated. The version using `fmt` creates a representation specified

by the given *radix*. The hexadecimal digits in the range [10,15] are represented by the characters #"A" through #"F". The version using toString is equivalent to fmt StringCvt.HEX *i*.

val scan : StringCvt.radix
                  -> (char, 'a) StringCvt.reader
                   -> (word, 'a) StringCvt.reader
val fromString : string -> word option

scan *radix getc strm*
fromString *s*

These functions scan a word from a character source. In the first version, if an unsigned number in the format denoted by *radix* can be parsed from a prefix of the character strm *strm* using the character input function *getc*, the expression evaluates to SOME(w,rest), where w is the value of the number parsed and rest is the remainder of the character stream. Initial whitespace is ignored. NONE is returned otherwise. It raises Overflow when a number can be parsed but is too large to fit in type word.

The format that scan accepts depends on the *radix* argument. Regular expressions defining these formats are as follows:

Radix	Format
StringCvt.BIN	$(0w)^?[0-1]^+$
StringCvt.OCT	$(0w)^?[0-7]^+$
StringCvt.DEC	$(0w)^?[0-9]^+$
StringCvt.HEX	$(0wx \mid 0wX \mid 0x \mid 0X)^?[0-9a-fA-F]^+$

The fromString version returns SOME(w) if an unsigned hexadecimal number in the format $(0wx \mid 0wX \mid 0x \mid 0X)^?[0-9a-fA-F]^+$ can be parsed from a prefix of string *s*, ignoring initial whitespace, where w is the value of the number parsed. NONE is returned otherwise. This function raises Overflow when a hexadecimal numeral can be parsed but is too large to be represented by type word. It is equivalent to

        StringCvt.scanString (scan StringCvt.HEX)

Discussion

A structure WordN implements N-bit words. The type LargeWord.word represents the largest word supported. We require that

$$LargeWord.wordSize \leq LargeInt.precision$$

If LargeWord is not the same as Word, then there must be a structure WordN equal to LargeWord.

The structure SysWord is used with the optional Posix and Windows modules. The type SysWord.word is guaranteed to be large enough to hold any unsigned integral value used by the underlying system.

For words and integers of the same precision/word size, the operations fromInt and toIntX act as bit-wise identity functions. Even in this case, however, toInt will raise Overflow if the high-order bit of the word is set.

Note that operations on words, and conversions of integral types into words, never cause exceptions to arise due to lost precision.

Conversion between words and integers of any size can be handled by intermediate conversion into `LargeWord.word` and `LargeInt.int`. For example, the functions `fromInt`, `toInt` and `toIntX` are respectively equivalent to:

```
fromLargeWord o LargeWord.fromLargeInt o Int.toLarge
Int.fromLarge o LargeWord.toLargeInt   o toLargeWord
Int.fromLarge o LargeWord.toLargeIntX  o toLargeWordX
```

Typically, implementations will provide very efficient word operations by expanding them inline to a few machine instructions. It also is assumed that implementations will catch the idiom of converting between words and integers of differing precisions using an intermediate representation (e.g., `Word32.fromLargeWord o Word8.toLargeWord`) and optimize these conversions.

See also

`Byte` (§11.7; p. 133), `Int` (§11.17; p. 169), `LargeInt` (§11.17; p. 169), `StringCvt` (§11.55; p. 366)

Bibliography

[FPC95] Floating-point C extensions. *Technical Report ANSI X3J11*, March 1995.

[Gay90] Gay, D. M. Correctly rounded binary-decimal and decimal-binary conversions. *Technical Report 90-10*, AT&T Bell Laboratories, Murray Hill, NJ, USA, 1990.

[Han92] Hansen, W. J. Subsequence references: First-class values for substrings. *ACM Transactions on Programming Languages and Systems*, **14**(4), October 1992, pp. 471–489.

[IEE85] IEEE standard for binary floating-point arithmetic. *Technical Report IEEE Std 754-1985*, 1985.

[IEE87] IEEE standard for radix-independent floating-point arithmetic. *Technical Report ANSI/IEEE Std 854-1987*, 1987.

[ISO90] Programming Languages — C. *Technical Report ISO/IEC 9899:1990(E)*, 1990.

[Jon03] Jones, S. P. (ed.). *Haskell 98 Language and Libraries*. Cambridge University Press, 2003.

[Kah96] Kahan, W. Lecture notes on the status of IEEE Standard 754 for binary floating-point arithmetic. *Technical report*, University of California — Berkeley, May 1996.

[LM99] Leijen, D. and E. Meijer. Domain specific embedded compilers. In *Proceedings of the Second Conference on Domain-Specific Languages*, October 1999, pp. 109–122.

[MTH90] Milner, R., M. Tofte, and R. Harper. *The Definition of Standard ML*. The MIT Press, Cambridge, MA, 1990.

[MTHM97] Milner, R., M. Tofte, R. Harper, and D. MacQueen. *The Definition of Standard ML — Revised 1997*. The MIT Press, Cambridge, MA, 1997.

[POS96] Portable operating system interface — Part 1: System application program interface (API) [C Language]. *Technical Report ISO/IEC 9945-1: 1996 (E) IEEE Std 1003.1*, 1996.

[Pos03] Poskanzer, J. pbmplus — image file format conversion package. `http://www.acme.com/software/pbmplus/`, 2003.

[Rep99] Reppy, J. H. *Concurrent Programming in ML*. Cambridge University Press, 1999.

[SG97] Scheifler, R. W. and J. Gettys. *X Window System*. Digital Press, Newton, MA, 1997.

[Ste98] Stevens, W. R. *UNIX Network Programming*. Prentice Hall, 2nd edition, 1998.

[Uni03] Unicode Consortium. *The Unicode Standard, Version 4.0*. Addison-Wesley, Reading, MA, 2003.

[Wad90] Wadler, P. L. Comprehending monads. In *Proceedings of the 1990 ACM Conference on LISP and Functional Programming*, New York, NY, 1990. ACM, pp. 61–78.

General index

SML identifier index

Raised exception index